The Humanities
Culture, Continuity & Change

SECOND EDITION

Henry M. Sayre

OREGON STATE UNIVERSITY

BOOK 2
THE MEDIEVAL WORLD AND THE SHAPING OF CULTURE: 200 CE TO 1400

Prentice Hall

Boston   Columbus   Indianapolis   New York   San Francisco   Upper Saddle River
Amsterdam   Cape Town   Dubai   London   Madrid   Milan   Munich   Paris   Montréal   Toronto
Delhi   Mexico City   São Paulo   Sydney   Hong Kong   Seoul   Singapore   Taipei   Tokyo

For Bud Therien, art publisher and editor par excellence, and a good friend.

Editorial Director: Craig Campanella
Editor in Chief: Sarah Touborg
Acquisitions Editor: Billy Grieco
Assistant Editor: David Nitti
Editor-in-Chief, Development: Rochelle Diogenes
Development Editor: Margaret Manos
Media Director: Brian Hyland
Senior Media Editor: David Alick
Media Project Manager: Rich Barnes
Vice President of Marketing: Brandy Dawson
Executive Marketing Manager: Kate Stewart Mitchell
Senior Managing Editor: Ann Marie McCarthy
Associate Managing Editor: Melissa Feimer
Senior Project Manager: Barbara Marttine Cappuccio
Project Manager: Marlene Gassler

Senior Manufacturing Manager: Mary Fisher
Senior Operations Specialist: Brian Mackey
Senior Art Director: Pat Smythe
Interior Design: PreMedia Global
Cover Designer: Pat Smythe
Manager, Visual Research: Beth Brenzel
Photo Research: Francelle Carapetyan / Image Research Editorial Services
Pearson Imaging Center: Corin Skidds, Robert Uibelhoer
Full-Service Project Management: PreMediaGlobal
Composition: PreMediaGlobal
Printer/Binder: Courier / Kendallville
Cover Printer: Phoenix Color, Corp.
Cover Image: Canali Photobank, Milan Italy

Credits and acknowledgments borrowed from other sources and reproduced, with permission, in this textbook appear on appropriate page within text and beginning on page Credits-1.

Library of Congress Cataloging-in-Publication Data
Sayre, Henry M.
  The humanities : culture, continuity & change / Henry M. Sayre. -- 2nd ed.
    p. cm.
  Includes bibliographical references and index.
  ISBN-13: 978-0-205-78215-4 (alk. paper)
  ISBN-10: 0-205-78215-9 (alk. paper)
  1. Civilization--History--Textbooks. 2. Humanities--History--Textbooks. I. Title.
CB69.S29 2010
909--dc22
                        2010043097

10 9 8 7 6 5 4 3 2 1

Prentice Hall
is an imprint of

PEARSON

www.pearsonhighered.com

ISBN 10: 0-205-02003-8
ISBN 13: 978-0-205-02003-4

SERIES CONTENTS

CONTENTS

DEAR READER,

You might be asking yourself, why should I be interested in the Humanities? Why do I care about ancient Egypt, medieval France, or the Qing Dynasty of China?

I asked myself the same question when I was a sophomore in college. I was required to take a year long survey of the Humanities, and I soon realized that I was beginning an extraordinary journey. That course taught me where it was that I stood in the world, and why and how I had come to find myself there. My goal in this book is to help you take the same journey of discovery. Exploring the humanities will help you develop your abilities to look, listen, and read closely; and to analyze, connect, and question. In the end, this will help you navigate your world and come to a better understanding of your place in it.

What we see reflected in different cultures is something of ourselves, the objects of beauty and delight, the weapons and wars, the melodies and harmonies, the sometimes troubling but always penetrating thought from which we spring. To explore the humanities is to explore ourselves, to understand how and why we have changed over time, even as we have, in so many ways, remained the same.

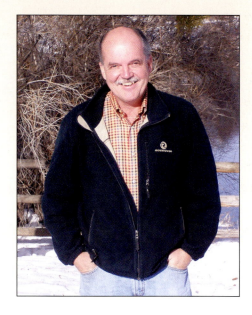

I've come to think of this second edition in something of the same terms. What I've tried to do is explore new paths of inquiry even as I've tried to keep the book recognizably the same. My model, I think, has been Bob Dylan. Over the years, I've heard the man perform more times than I can really recall, and I just saw him again in concert this past summer. He has been performing "Highway 61" and "Just Like a Woman" for nearly fifty years, but here they were again, in new arrangements that were totally fresh—recognizably the same, but reenergized and new. That should be the goal of any new edition of a book, I think, and I hope I've succeeded in that here.

ABOUT THE AUTHOR

Henry M. Sayre is Distinguished Professor of Art History at Oregon State University–Cascades Campus in Bend, Oregon. He earned his Ph.D. in American Literature from the University of Washington. He is producer and creator of the 10-part television series, *A World of Art: Works in Progress*, aired on PBS in the Fall of 1997; and author of seven books, including *A World of Art*, *The Visual Text of William Carlos Williams*, *The Object of Performance: The American Avant-Garde since 1970*; and an art history book for children, *Cave Paintings to Picasso*.

The Humanities: Culture, Continuity & Change helps students see context and make connections across the humanities by tying together the entire cultural experience through a narrative storytelling approach. Written around Henry Sayre's belief that students learn best by remembering stories rather than memorizing facts, it captures the voices that have shaped and influenced human thinking and creativity throughout our history.

With a stronger focus on engaging students in the critical thinking process, this new edition encourages students to deepen their understanding of how cultures influence one another, how ideas are exchanged and evolve over time, and how this collective process has led us to where we stand today. With several new features, this second edition helps students to understand context and make connections across time, place, and culture.

To prepare the second edition, we partnered with our current users to hear what was successful and what needed to be improved. The feedback we received through focus groups, online surveys, and reviews helped shape and inform this new edition. For instance, to help students make stronger global connections, the organization of the text and the Table of Contents have been modified. As an example, reflections of this key goal can be seen in Chapters 6 and 7, which are now aligned to show parallels more easily in the developments of urban culture and imperial authority between Rome, China, and India.

Through this dialogue, we also learned how humanities courses are constantly evolving. We learned that more courses are being taught online and that instructors are exploring new ways to help their students engage with course material. We developed MyArtsLab with these needs in mind. With powerful online learning tools integrated into the book, the online and textbook experience is more seamless than ever before. In addition, there are wonderful interactive resources that you, as the instructor, can bring directly into your classroom.

All of these changes can be seen through the new, expanded, or improved features shown here.

NEW
THINKING AHEAD

These questions open each chapter and represent its major sections, leading students to think critically and focus on important issues.

NEW
THINKING BACK

These end-of-chapter reviews follow up on the **Thinking Ahead** questions, helping students further engage with the material they've just read and stimulate thought and discussion.

NEW
CLOSER LOOK

Previously called "Focus" in the first edition, these highly visual features offer an in-depth look at a particular work from one of the disciplines of the humanities. The annotated discussions give students a personal tour of the work—with informative captions and labels—to help students understand its meaning. A new critical thinking question, *Something to Think About*, prompts students to make connections and further apply this detailed knowledge of the work.

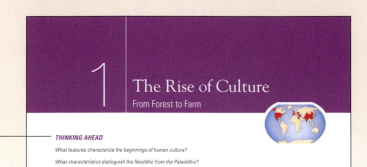

1 The Rise of Culture
From Forest to Farm

THINKING AHEAD

What features characterize the beginnings of human culture?

What characteristics distinguish the Neolithic from the Paleolithic?

What is a megalith?

How can we understand the role of myth in prehistoric culture?

THINKING BACK

What features characterize the beginnings of human culture?

The widespread use of stone tools and weapons by Homo sapiens, the hominid species that evolved around 120,000 to 100,000 years ago, gives rise to the name of the earliest era of human development, the Paleolithic era. Carvers fashioned stone figures, both in the round and in relief. In cave paintings, such as those discovered at Chauvet Cave, the artists' great skill in rendering animals helps us to understand that the ability to represent the world with naturalistic fidelity is an inherent human skill, unrelated to cultural sophistication. Culture can be defined as a way of living—religious, social, and/or political—formed by a group of people and passed on from one generation to the next. What can the earliest art tell us about the first human cultures? What questions remain a mystery?

What characteristics distinguish the Neolithic from the Paleolithic?

As the ice that covered the Northern Hemisphere slowly melted, people began cultivating edible grasses and domesticating animals. Gradually, farming supplanted hunting as the primary means of sustaining life, especially in the great river valleys where water was abundant. The rise of agriculture is the chief characteristic of the Neolithic age. Along with agriculture, permanent villages such as Skara Brae begin to appear. What does the appearance of fire-baked pottery tell us about life in Neolithic culture?

What is a megalith?

During the fifth millennium BCE, Neolithic peoples began constructing monumental stone architecture, or megaliths, in France and England. Upright, single stone posts called menhirs were placed in the ground, either individually or in groups, as at Carnac in Brittany. Elementary post-and-lintel construction was employed to create dolmens, two posts roofed with a capstone. The most famous of the third type of monumental construction, the circular cromlech, is Stonehenge, in England. What does the enormous amount of human labor required for the construction of these megaliths suggest about the societies that built them?

How can we understand the role of myth in prehistoric culture?

Neolithic culture in the Americas lasted well into the second millennium CE. Much of our understanding of the role of myth in prehistoric cultures derives from the traditions of contemporary Native American tribes that still survive in tribes such as the Hopi and Zuni, who are the direct descendents of the Anasazi. Their legends, such as the Zuni emergence tale, encapsulate the fundamental religious principles of the culture. Such stories, and the ritual practices that accompany them, reflect the general beliefs of most Neolithic peoples. Can you describe some of these beliefs? What role do sacred sites, such as those at Ise in Japan, or Cahokia in the Mississippi Valley, play?

PRACTICE MORE Get flashcards for images and terms and review chapter material with quizzes at **www.myartslab.com**

CLOSER LOOK
The Design and Making of Stonehenge

How the Neolithic peoples of Britain constructed Stonehenge is uncertain. Scholars believe that the giant stones of the Sarsen Circle, which weigh up to 50 tons, were transported from the Marlborough Downs, roughly 20 miles to the north, by rolling them on logs. Most of the way, the going is relatively easy, but at the steepest part of the route, at Redhorn Hill, modern work studies estimate that it would have taken at least 600 men to push the stones up the hill. A relatively sophisticated understanding of basic physics—the operation of levers and pulleys—was needed to lift the stones, and their lintels, into place.

Recently, archeologists at Stonehenge have uncovered a second cromlech-like circle at Durrington Wells, about 2 miles north of the stone megalith, consisting of a circular ditch surrounding a ring of postholes out of which very large timber posts would have risen. The circle was the center of a village consisting of as many as 300 houses. The site is comparable in scale to Stonehenge itself. These discoveries—together with the ability to carbon-date human remains found at Stonehenge with increased accuracy—suggest that Stonehenge was itself a burial grounds. Archeologist Mike Parker-Pearson of the University of Sheffield speculates that villagers would have transported their dead down an avenue leading to the River Avon, then journeyed downstream, in a ritual symbolizing the passage to the afterlife, finally arriving at an avenue leading up to Stonehenge from the river. "Stonehenge wasn't set in isolation," Parker-Pearson says, "but was actually one half of this monument complex. We are looking at a pairing—one in timber to represent the transience of life, the other in stone marking the eternity of the ancestral dead."

Something to Think About . . .
The circle is a geometric form that appears in the earliest manifestations of art and architecture. Can you speculate on its appeal?

The Heel Stone On Midsummer's Eve, it casts a shadow directly into the circle. The stone stands 16 feet high and weighs 35 tons. It was brought from a quarry 23 miles away.

The Avenue The shadow cast by the Heel Stone on Midsummer's Eve would extend directly down this ceremonial approach.

The Slaughter Stone It was once believed that humans were sacrificed on this stone, which now lies flat on the ground, but it was originally part of a great portal.

The Sarsen Circle Erected about 1500 BCE, the circle is capped by lintel stones held in place by mortise-and-tenon joints, similar to those used by woodworkers. The end of the post is narrowed and slotted into a hole in the lintel.

The sarsen stone is raised with a long lever. Logs are placed under the stone, and then it is rolled into place.

One by one, layers of timber are placed under the lever, both raising the stone and dropping it into the prepared pit.

As many as 200 men pull the stone upright on ropes as timbers support it from behind.

The pit around the stone is filled with stones and chalks to pack it into place.

The lintel is raised on successive layers of a timber platform.

Once the platform reaches the top of the posts, the lintel is levered onto the posts.

Finally, the platform is removed, and the trilithon is complete.

The Outer Bank This ditch, 330 feet in diameter, is the oldest construction at the site, originally exposing the white limestone beneath the surface soil to form a giant circle.

Five Massive Trilithons Inside the outer circle stood a horseshoe of trilithons, two on each side and the largest at the closed end at the southwest. Only one of the largest trilithons still stands. It rises 22 feet above ground, with 8 feet more below ground level. The stone weighs about 50 tons.

The Altar Stone One of the most distinct stones in Stonehenge, the so-called altar stone is a 16-foot block of smoothed green sandstone located near the center of the complex.

The Bluestone Circle This circle of 80 smallish slabs was built in about 2000 BCE from stone quarried in South Wales.

SEE MORE For a Closer Look at Stonehenge, go to **www.myartslab.com**

CONTINUITY & CHANGE ESSAYS

These full-page essays at the end of each chapter illustrate the influence of one cultural period upon another and show cultural changes over time.

CONTINUITY & CHANGE ICONS

These in-text references provide a window into the past. The eye-catching icons enable students to refer to material in other chapters that is relevant to the topic at hand.

CONTINUITY & CHANGE

The Pyramids of Menkaure, p. 74

CONTEXT

These boxes summarize important background information in an easy-to-read format.

MATERIALS AND TECHNIQUES

These features explain and illustrate the methods artists and architects use to produce their work.

CONTINUITY & CHANGE

Representing the Power of the Animal World

The two images shown here in some sense bracket the six volumes of *The Humanities*. The first (Fig. 1.24), from the Chauvet Cave, is one of the earliest known drawings of a horse. The second (Fig. 1.25), a drawing by contemporary American painter Susan Rothenberg (b. 1945), also represents a horse, though in many ways less realistically than the cave drawing. The body of Rothenberg's horse seems to have disappeared and, eyeless, as if blinded, it leans forward, its mouth open, choking or gagging or gasping for air.

In his catalog essay for a 1993 retrospective exhibition of Rothenberg's painting, Michael Auping, chief curator at

the Albright-Knox Museum in Buffalo, New York, described Rothenberg's kind of drawing: "Relatively spontaneous, the drawings are Rothenberg's psychic energy made imminent . . . . [They] uncover realms of the psyche that are perhaps not yet fully explicable." The same could be said of the cave drawing executed by a nameless hunter-gatherer more than 20,000 years ago. That artist's work must have seemed just as strange as Rothenberg's, lit by flickering firelight in the dark recesses of the cave, its body disappearing, too, into the darkness that surrounded it.

It seems certain that in some measure both drawings were the expression of a psychic need on the part of the artist—whether derived from the energy of the hunt or the vulnerability of the animal world. That drive, which we will see in the art of the Bronze Age of the Middle East in the next chapter—for instance, in the haunting image of a dying lion in the palace complex of an Assyrian king at Nineveh—remains constant from the beginnings of art to the present day. It is the compulsion to express the inexpressible, to visualize the mind as well as the world. ■

Fig. 1.24 Horse. Detail from Chauvet Cave, Vallon-Pont-d'Arc, Ardèche gorge, France, ca. 30,000 BCE. Note the realistic shading that defines the volume of the horse's head. It is a realism that artists throughout history have sometimes sought to achieve, and sometimes ignored, in their efforts to express for the forces that drive them.

Fig. 1.25 Susan Rothenberg, Untitled, 1978. Acrylic, flashe, and pencil on paper. 20" × 20". Collection Walker Art Center, Minneapolis. Art Center Acquisition Fund, 1979. © 2008 Susan Rothenberg/Artist's Rights Society (ARS), NY. Part of the eeriness of this image comes from Rothenberg's use of flashe, a French vinyl-based color that is clear and so creates a misty, ghostlike surface.

Materials & Techniques

Methods of Carving

Carving is the act of cutting or incising stone, bone, wood, or another material into a desired form. Surviving artifacts of the Paleolithic era were carved from stone or bone. The artist probably held a sharp instrument, such as a stone knife or a chisel, in one hand and drove it into the stone or bone with another stone held in the other hand to remove excess material and realize the figure. Finer details could be scratched into the material with a pointed stone instrument. Artists can carve into any material softer than the instrument they are using. Harder varieties of stone can cut into softer stone as well as bone. The work was probably painstakingly slow.

There are basically two types of sculpture: sculpture in the round and relief sculpture. **Sculpture in the round** is fully three-dimensional; it occupies 360 degrees of space. The Willendorf statuette (see Fig. 1.3) was carved from stone and is an example of sculpture in the round. **Relief sculpture** is carved out of a flat background surface; it has a distinct front and no back. Not all relief sculptures are

alike. In *high relief* sculpture, the figure extends more than 180 degrees from the background surface. *Woman Holding an Animal Horn*, found at Laussel, in the Dordogne region of France, is carved in high relief and is one of the earliest relief sculptures known. This sculpture was originally part of a great stone block that stood in front of a Paleolithic rock shelter. In *low* or *bas relief*, the figure extends less than 180 degrees from the surface. In *sunken relief*, the image is carved, or incised, into the surface, so that the image recedes below it. When a light falls on relief sculptures at an angle, the relief casts a shadow. The higher the relief, the larger the shadows and the greater the sense of the figure's three-dimensionality.

Woman Holding an Animal Horn, Laussel (Dordogne), France. ca. 30,000–15,000 BCE. Limestone, height 17-³/₈". Musée des Antiquités Nationales, St. Germain-en-Laye, France.

EXPLORE MORE To see a studio video about carving, go to **www.myartslab.com**

PRIMARY SOURCES

Each chapter of *The Humanities* includes Primary Source Readings in two formats. Brief readings from important works are included within the body of the text. Longer readings located at the end of each chapter allow for a more in-depth study of particular works. The organization offers great flexibility in teaching the course.

READINGS

READING 2.3

from the *Epic of Gilgamesh*, Tablet I (ca. 1200 BCE) (translated by Maureen Gallery Kovacs)

The Epic of Gilgamesh describes the exploits of the Sumerian ruler Gilgamesh and his friend Enkidu. The following passage, from the first of the epic's 12 tablets, recounts how Enkidu, the primal man raised beyond the reach of civilization and fully at home with wild animals, loses his animal powers, and with them his innocence, when a trapper, tired of Enkidu freeing animals from his traps, arranges for a harlot from Uruk to seduce him. The story resonates in interesting ways with the biblical tale of Adam and Eve and their loss of innocence in the Garden of Eden.

TABLET I
THE HARLOT
The trapper went, bringing the harlot, Shamhat, with him,
they set off on the journey, making direct way.
On the third day they arrived at the appointed place,
and the trapper and the harlot sat down at their posts(?).
A first day and a second they sat opposite the watering hole.
The animals arrived and drank at the watering hole,
the wild beasts arrived and slaked their thirst with water.
Then he, Enkidu, offspring of the mountains,
who eats grasses with the gazelles,
came to drink at the watering hole with the animals,
with the wild beasts he slaked his thirst with water.
Then Shamhat saw him—a primitive,
a savage fellow from the depths of the wilderness!
"That is he, Shamhat! Release your clenched arms,
expose your sex so he can take in your voluptuousness.

Shamhat unclutched her bosom, exposed her sex, and he took in her voluptuousness.
She was not restrained, but took his energy.
She spread out her robe and he lay upon her,
she performed for the primitive the task of womankind.
His lust groaned over her;
for six days and seven nights Enkidu stayed aroused,
and had intercourse with the harlot
until he was sated with her charms.
But when he turned his attention to his animals,
the gazelles saw Enkidu and darted off,
the wild animals distanced themselves from his body.
Enkidu . . . his utterly depleted (?) body,
his knees that wanted to go off with his animals went rigid;
Enkidu was diminished, his running was not as before.
But then he drew himself up, for his understanding had broadened.

(for example, "findings shattered like a pot").

Perhaps most important, the epic illuminates the development of a nation or race. It is a national poem, describing a people's common heritage and celebrating its cultural identity. It is hardly surprising, then, that Ashurbanipal preserved the Epic of *Gilgamesh*. Just as Sargon II depicted himself at the gates of Khorsabad in the traditional horned crown of Akkad and the beard of Sumer, containing within himself all Mesopotamian history, the Epic of *Gilgamesh* preserves the historical lineage of all Mesopotamian kings—Sumerian, Akkadian, Assyrian, and Babylonian. The tale embodies their own heroic grandeur, and thus the grandeur of their peoples.

The poem opens with a narrator guiding a visitor (the reader) around Uruk. The narrator explains that the epic was written by Gilgamesh himself and was deposited in the city's walls, where visitors can read it for themselves. Then the narrator introduces Gilgamesh as an epic hero, two parts god and one part human. The style of the following list of his deeds is the same as in hymns to the gods (**Reading 2.3a**):

READING 2.3a
from the *Epic of Gilgamesh*, Tablet I
(ca. 1200 BCE)

Supreme over other kings, lordly in appearance,
he is the hero, born of Uruk, the goring wild bull.
He walks out in front, the leader,
and walks at the rear, trusted by his companions.
Mighty net, protector of his people,
raging flood-wave who destroys even walls of stone! . . .
It was he who opened the mountain passes,
who dug wells on the flank of the mountain.

Enkidu,
born . . .
His w . . .
he ha . . .
He kn . . .
He at . . .
and je . . .

Enkidu . . .
frontatia . . .
ture, rep . . .
Seduced . . .
loses his . . .
ally lose . . .
gamesh, . . .
friends. . . .

Gilg . . .
great ad . . .
present- . . .
its guard . . .
cut dow . . .
journey . . .
which Enkidu manages to interpret in a positive light. As the friends approach the forest, the god Shamash informs Gilgamesh that Humbaba is wearing only one of his seven coats of armor and is thus extremely vulnerable. When Gilgamesh and Enkidu enter the forest and begin cutting down trees, Humbaba comes roaring up to warn them off. An epic battle ensues, and Shamash intervenes to help the two heroes defeat the great guardian. Just before Gilgamesh cuts off Humbaba's head, Humbaba curses Enkidu, promising that he will find no peace in the world and will die before his friend Gilgamesh. In a gesture that clearly evokes the triumph of civilization over nature, Gilgamesh and Enkidu

SEE CONTEXT AND MAKE CONNECTIONS . . .

MORE CONNECTIONS TO MyArtsLab

The text is keyed to the dynamic resources on MyArtsLab, allowing instructors and students online access to additional information, music, videos, and interactive features.

The **'SEE MORE'** icon correlates to the Closer Look features in the text, directing students to MyArtsLab to view interactive **Closer Look** tours online. These features enable students to zoom in to see detail they could not otherwise see on the printed page or even in person. **'SEE MORE'** icons also indicate when students can view works of architecture in full 360-degree panoramas.

No trace of the city's famous Hanging Gardens survives, once considered among the Seven Wonders of the World, and only the base and parts of the lower stairs of the Marduk ziggurat still remain. But in the fifth century BCE, the Greek historian Herodotus [he-ROD-uh-tus] (ca. 484–430/420 BCE) described the ziggurat as follows:

There was a tower of solid masonry, a furlong in length and breadth, on which was raised a second tower, and on that a third, and so on up to eight. The ascent to the top is on the outside, by a path which winds round all the towers. . . . On the topmost tower, there is a spacious temple, and inside the temple stands a couch of unusual size, richly adorned with a golden table by its side. . . . They also declare that the god comes down in person into this chamber, and sleeps on the couch, but I do not believe it.

Although the ziggurat has disappeared, we can glean some sense of the city's magnificence from the Ishtar Gate (Fig. 2.18), named after the Babylonian goddess of fertility.

Fig. 2.18 Ishtar Gate (restored), from Babylon. ca. 575 BCE. Glazed brick. Staatliche Museen, Berlin. The dark blue bricks are glazed—that is, covered with a film of glass—and they would have shown brilliantly in the sun.

SEE MORE To view a Closer Look feature about the Ishtar Gate, go to **www.myartslab.com**

CHAPTER 2 *Mesopotamia* **55**

Fig. 9.13 Great Mosque of Córdoba. Begun 785, extensions 852, 950, 961–76, and 987. The caliphs of Spain intended their mosque to rival those in Jerusalem, Damascus, and Iraq. The forestlike expanse of the interior is a result of these aspirations. Even though only 80 of the original 1,200 columns survive, the space appears infinite, like some giant hall of mirrors.

LEARN MORE View an architectural simulation of Islamic arches at **www.myartslab.com**

by the Umayyads in Toledo [toh-LEH-doh] soon was responsible for spreading the nearly forgotten texts throughout the West. Muslim mathematicians in Spain invented algebra and introduced the concept of zero to the West, and soon their Arabic numerals replaced the unwieldy Roman system. By the time of Abd ar-Rahman III (r. 912–61), Córdoba was renowned for its medicine, science, literature, and commercial wealth, and it became the most important center of learning in Europe. The elegance of Abd ar-Rahman III's court was unmatched, and his tolerance and benevolence extended to all, as Muslim students from across the Mediterranean soon found their way to the mosque-affiliated madrasa that he founded—the

earliest example of an institution of higher learning in the Western world.

Outside of Córdoba, Abd ar-Rahman III built a huge palace complex, Madinat al-Zahra, to honor his wife. (Its extensive remains are still being excavated.) Its staff included 13,750 male servants along with another 3,500 pages, slaves, and eunuchs. Its roof required the support of 4,300 columns, and elaborate gardens surrounded the site. As many as 1,200 loaves of bread were required daily just to feed the fish in the garden ponds.

The decorative arts of the era are equally impressive. A famous example is a pyxis, a small, cylindrical box with a lid, made for Prince al-Mughira, Abd ar-Rahman III's

CHAPTER 9 *The Rise and Spread of Islam* **301**

The **'HEAR MORE'** icons indicate where musical performances can be listened to in streaming audio on www.myartslab.com. Online audio also includes **'Voices'**—vivid first-person accounts of the experiences of ordinary people during the period covered in the chapter.

The **'LEARN MORE'** icons lead students online for additional primary source readings or to watch architectural simulations.

The **'EXPLORE MORE'** icons direct students to videos of artists at work in their studios, allowing them to see and understand a wide variety of materials and techniques used by artists throughout time.

Designed to save instructors time and to improve students' results, MyArtsLab, is keyed specifically to the chapters of Sayre's *The Humanities*, second edition. In addition, MyArtsLab's many features will encourage students to experience and interact with works of art. Here are some of those key features:

• A complete **Pearson eText** of the book, enriched with multimedia, including: a unique human-scale figure by all works of fine art, an audio version of the text, primary source documents, video demonstrations, and much more. Students can highlight, make notes, and bookmark pages.

• 360-degree **Architectural Panoramas** for major monuments in the book help students understand buildings from the inside and out.

• **Closer Look Tours** These interactive walk-throughs offer an in-depth look at key works of art, enabling students to zoom in to see detail they could not otherwise see on the printed page or even in person. Enhanced with expert audio, they help students understand the meaning and message behind the work of art.

• Robust **Quizzing** and **Grading Functionality** is included in MyArtsLab. Students receive immediate feedback from the assessment questions that populate the instructor's gradebook. The gradebook reports give an in-depth look at the progress of individual students or the class as a whole.

• MyArtsLab is your one stop for instructor material. Instructors can access the Instructor's Manual, Test Item File, PowerPoint images, and the Pearson MyTest assessment-generation program.

MyArtsLab with eText is available for no additional cost when packaged with *The Humanities*, second edition. The program may also be used as a stand-alone item, which costs less than a used text.

To register for your MyArtsLab account, contact your local Pearson representative or visit the instructor registration page located on the homepage of www.myartslab.com.

FLEXIBLE FORMATS

CourseSmart eTextbooks offer the same content as the printed text in a convenient online format—with highlighting, online search, and printing capabilities. With a CourseSmart eText, student can search the text, make notes online, print out reading assignments that incorporate lecture notes, and bookmark important passages for later review. *Students save 60% over the list price of the traditional book. www.coursesmart.com.*

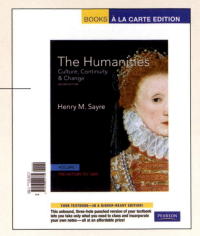

Books à la Carte editions feature the exact same text in a convenient, three-hole-punched, loose-leaf version at a discounted price—allowing students to take only what they need to class. Books à la Carte editions are available both with and without access to MyArtsLab. *Students save 35% over the net price of the traditional book.*

Custom Publishing Opportunities

The Humanities is available in a custom version specifically tailored to meet your needs. You may select the content that you would like to include or add your own original material. See you local publisher's representative for further information. **www.pearsoncustom.com**

INSTRUCTOR RESOURCES

Classroom Response System (CRS) In-Class Questions

Get instant, class-wide responses to beautifully illustrated chapter-specific questions during a lecture to gauge students' comprehension—and keep them engaged. Available for download under the "For Instructors" tab within your MyArtsLab account–**www.myartslab.com.**

Instructor's Manual and Test Item File

This is an invaluable professional resource and reference for new and experienced faculty. Each chapter contains the following sections: Chapter Overview, Chapter Objectives, Key Terms, Lecture and Discussion Topics, Resources, and Writing Assignments and Projects. The test bank includes multiple-choice, true/false, short-answer, and essay questions. Available for download from the instructor support section at **www.myartslab.com.**

ClassPrep

Instructors who adopt Sayre's *The Humanities* will receive access to ClassPrep, an online site designed to make lecture preparation simpler and less time-consuming. The site includes the images from the text in both high-resolution JPGs, and ready-made PowerPoint slides for your lectures. ClassPrep can be accessed through your MyArtsLab instructor account.

WITH THESE ADDITIONAL RESOURCES

MyTest

This flexible, online test-generating software includes all questions found in the printed Test Item File. Instructors can quickly and easily create customized tests with MyTest. **www.pearsonmytest.com**

ADDITIONAL PACKAGING OPTIONS

Penguin Custom Editions: The Western World lets you choose from an archive of more than 1,800 readings excerpted from the Penguin Classics™, the most comprehensive paperback library of Western history, literature, culture, and philosophy available. You'll have the freedom to craft a reader for your humanities course that matches your teaching approach exactly! Using our online book-building system, you get to select the readings you need, in the sequence you want, at the price you want your students to pay. **www.pearsoncustom.com** keyword: penguin

 Titles from the renowned Penguin Classics series can be bundles with *The Humanities* for a nominal charge. Please contact your Pearson Arts and Sciences sales representative for details.

 The Prentice Hall Atlas of World History, second edition includes over 100 full-color maps in world history, drawn by Dorling Kindersley, one of the world's most respected cartographic publishers. Copies of the Atlas can be bundled with *The Humanities* for a nominal charge. Please contact your Pearson Arts and Sciences sales representative for details.

 Connections: Key Themes in World History. Series Editor Alfred J. Andrea. Concise and tightly focused, the titles in the popular Connections Series are designed to place the latest research on selected topics of global significance, such as disease, trade, slavery, exploration, and modernization, into an accessible format for students. Available for a 50% discount when bundled with *The Humanities*. For more information, please visit **www.pearsonhighered.com.**

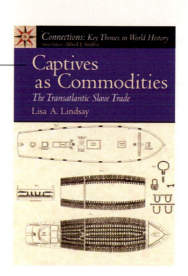

THE HUMANITIES: *CULTURE, CONTINUITY & CHANGE*

is the result of an extensive development process involving the contributions of over one hundred instructors and their students. We are grateful to all who participated in shaping the content, clarity, and design of this text. Manuscript reviewers and focus group participants include:

ALABAMA
Cynthia Kristan-Graham, Auburn University

CALIFORNIA
Collette Chattopadhyay, Saddleback College
Laurel Corona, San Diego City College
Cynthia D. Gobatie, Riverside Community College
John Hoskins, San Diego Mesa College
Gwenyth Mapes, Grossmont College
Bradley Nystrom, California State University-Sacramento
Joseph Pak, Saddleback College
John Provost, Monterey Peninsula College
Chad Redwing, Modesto Junior College
Stephanie Robinson, San Diego City College
Alice Taylor, West Los Angeles College
Denise Waszkowski, San Diego Mesa College

COLORADO
Renee Bragg, Arapahoe Community College
Marilyn Smith, Red Rocks Community College

CONNECTICUT
Abdellatif Hissouf, Central Connecticut State University

FLORIDA
Wesley Borucki, Palm Beach Atlantic University
Amber Brock, Tallahassee Community College
Connie Dearmin, Brevard Community College
Kimberly Felos, St. Petersburg College
Katherine Harrell, South Florida Community College
Ira Holmes, College of Central Florida
Dale Hoover, Edison State College
Theresa James, South Florida Community College
Jane Jones, State College of Florida, Manatee-Sarasota
Jennifer Keefe, Valencia Community College
Mansoor Khan, Brevard Community College
Connie LaMarca-Frankel, Pasco-Hernando Community College
Sandi Landis, St. Johns River Community College-Orange Park
Joe Loccisano, State College of Florida
David Luther, Edison College
James Meier, Central Florida Community College
Brandon Montgomery, State College of Florida
Pamela Wood Payne, Palm Beach Atlantic University
Gary Poe, Palm Beach Atlantic University
Frederick Smith, Florida Gateway College
Kate Myers de Vega, Palm Beach Atlantic University
Bill Waters, Pensacola State College

GEORGIA
Leslie Harrelson, Dalton State College
Lawrence Hetrick, Georgia Perimeter College
Priscilla Hollingsworth, Augusta State University
Kelley Mahoney, Dalton State College
Andrea Scott Morgan, Georgia Perimeter College

IDAHO
Jennifer Black, Boise State University
Rick Davis, Brigham Young University-Idaho
Derek Jensen, Brigham Young University-Idaho

ILLINOIS
Thomas Christensen, University of Chicago
Timothy J. Clifford, College of DuPage
Leslie Huntress Hopkins, College of Lake County
Judy Kaplow, Harper College
Terry McIntyre, Harper College
Victoria Neubeck O'Connor, Moraine Valley Community College
Sharon Quarcini, Moraine Valley Community College
Paul Van Heuklom, Lincoln Land Community College

INDIANA
Josephina Kiteou, University of Southern Indiana

KENTUCKY
Jonathan Austad, Eastern Kentucky University
Beth Cahaney, Elizabethtown Community and Technical College
Jeremy Killian, University of Louisville
Lynda Mercer, University of Louisville
Sara Northerner, University of Louisville
Elijah Pritchett, University of Louisville

MASSACHUSETTS
Peter R. Kalb, Brandeis University

MICHIGAN
Martha Petry, Jackson Community College
Robert Quist, Ferris State University

MINNESOTA
Mary Johnston, Minnesota State University

NEBRASKA
Michael Hoff, University of Nebraska

NEVADA
Chris Bauer, Sierra College

NEW JERSEY
Jay Braverman, Montclair State University
Sara E. Gil-Ramos, New Jersey City University

NEW MEXICO
Sarah Egelman, Central New Mexico Community College

NEW YORK
Eva Diaz, Pratt Institute
Mary Guzzy, Corning Community College
Thelma Ithier Sterling, Hostos Community College
Elizabeth C. Mansfield, New York University
Clemente Marconi, New York University

NORTH CAROLINA
Melodie Galloway, University of North Carolina at Asheville
Jeanne McGlinn, University of North Carolina at Asheville

Sophie Mills, University of North Carolina at Asheville
Constance Schrader, University of North Carolina at Asheville
Ronald Sousa, University of North Carolina at Asheville
Samer Traboulsi, University of North Carolina at Asheville

NORTH DAKOTA
Robert Kibler, Minot State University

OHIO
Darlene Alberts, Columbus State Community College
Tim Davis, Columbus State Community College
Michael Mangus, The Ohio State University at Newark
Keith Pepperell, Columbus State Community College
Patrice Ross, Columbus State Community College

OKLAHOMA
Amanda H. Blackman, Tulsa Community College-Northeast Campus
Diane Boze, Northeastern State University
Jacklan J. Renee Cox, Rogers State University
Jim Ford, Rogers State University
Diana Lurz, Rogers State University
James W. Mock, University of Central Oklahoma
Gregory Thompson, Rogers State University

PENNSYLVANIA
Elizabeth Pilliod, Rutgers University-Camden
Douglas B. Rosentrater, Bucks County Community College
Debra Thomas, Harrisburg Area Community College

RHODE ISLAND
Mallica Kumbera Landrus, Rhode Island School of Design

TEXAS
Mindi Bailey, Collin County Community College
Peggy Brown, Collin County Community College
Marsha Lindsay, Lone Star College-North Harris
Aditi Samarth, Richland College
Lee Ann Westman, University of Texas at El Paso

UTAH
Matthew Ancell, Brigham Young University
Terre Burton, Dixie College
Nate Kramer, Brigham Young University
Joseph D. Parry, Brigham Young University

VIRGINIA
Margaret Browning, Hampton University
Carey Freeman, Hampton University
John Long, Roanoke College
Anne Pierce, Hampton University
Jennifer Rosti, Roanoke College

ACKNOWLEDGMENTS

No project of this scope could ever come into being without the hard work and perseverance of many more people than its author. In fact, this author has been humbled by a team at Pearson Prentice Hall that never wavered in their confidence in my ability to finish this enormous undertaking (or if they did, they had the good sense not to let me know); never hesitated to cajole, prod, and massage me to complete the project in something close to on time; and always gave me the freedom to explore new approaches to the materials at hand. At the down-and-dirty level, I am especially grateful to fact-checker, Julia Moore; to Mary Ellen Wilson for the pronunciation guides; for the more specialized pronunciations offered by David Atwill (Chinese and Japanese), Jonathan Reynolds (African), Nayla Muntasser (Greek and Latin), and Mark Watson (Native American); to Margaret Gorenstein for tracking down the readings; to Laurel Corona for her extraordinary help with Africa; to Arnold Bradford for help with critical thinking questions; and to Francelle Carapetyan for her remarkable photo research. The maps and some of the line art are the work of cartographer and artist, Peter Bull, with Precision Graphic drafting a large portion of the line art for the book. I find both in every way extraordinary.

In fact, I couldn't be more pleased with the look of the book, which is the work of Pat Smythe, senior art director. Cory Skidds, senior imaging specialist, worked on image compositing and color accuracy of the artwork. The production of the book was coordinated by Melissa Feimer, associate managing editor, Barbara Cappuccio, senior production project manager, and Marlene Gassler, production project manager, who oversaw with good humor and patience the day-to-day, hour-to-hour crises that arose. Brian Mackey, production-planning and operations specialist, ensured that this project progressed smoothly through its production route. And I want to thank Lindsay Bethoney and the staff at PreMedia Global for working so hard to make the book turn out the way I envisioned it.

The marketing and editorial teams at Prentice Hall are beyond compare. On the marketing side, Brandy Dawson, vice president of marketing, and Kate Mitchell, executive marketing manager, helped us all to understand just what students want and need. On the editorial side, my thanks to Yolanda de Rooy, president of the Social Sciences and the Arts division; to Sarah Touborg, editor-in-chief; Billy Grieco, editor; Bud Therien, special projects manager; David Nitti, assistant editor; and Theresa Graziano, editorial assistant. The combined human hours that this group has put into this project are staggering. This book was Bud's idea in the first place; Billy and Sarah have supported me every step of the way in making it as good, or even better, than I envisioned; and Yolanda's over-arching vision is responsible for helping to make Pearson such an extraordinarily good publisher to write for.

Deserving of special mention is my development team, Rochelle Diogenes, editor-in-chief of development; and Margaret Manos, development editor. Margaret has been an especially valuable partner, helping me literally to "re-vision" this revision and bringing clarity and common sense to those moments where they were lost.

Finally, I want to thank, with all my love, my beautiful wife, Sandy Brooke, who has supported this project in every way. She has continued to teach, paint, and write, while urging me on, listening to my struggles, humoring me when I didn't deserve it, and being a far better wife than I was a husband. In some ways, enduring what she did in the first edition must have been tougher in the second, since she knew what was coming from the outset. She was, is, and will continue to be, I trust, the source of my strength.

The Medieval World and the Shaping of Culture

200 CE TO 1400

Simone Martini, *Maestà*, Council Chamber, Palazzo Pubblico, Siena. ca. 1311–17, repaired 1321 (see Fig 13.6).

Following the last 300 years of the Roman Empire, from 200 to about 500 CE, the Middle Ages span a period of about a thousand years of European history, from the collapse of the Empire to the beginning of the fifteenth century. Its opening centuries, until about 800 CE, were once commonly referred to as the "Dark Ages." During this time, the great cultural achievements of the Greeks and Romans were forgotten, so-called barbarian tribes from the North overran the continent, and ignorance reigned. But this era was followed by an age of remarkable innovation and achievement, marked by

the ascendancy of three great religions—Christianity, Buddhism, and newborn Islam. Because of the way these three religions dominated their respective cultures, the centuries covered in Book Two might be best thought of as the Age of Faith.

This was the age of the monastery, the religious pilgrimage, the cathedral, the mosque, and the spread of Buddhism across Asia. By the sixth century, a new Christian mode of representation, reflecting a new ideal of beauty, had asserted itself in Byzantium, the Eastern Roman Empire. Unlike the Romans and Greeks, Byzantine artists showed little interest in depicting the visual appearance of the material world. They abandoned perspectival depth and rendered figures as highly stylized, almost geometric configurations. In other words, they depicted a spiritual rather than physical ideal.

In the first half of the seventh century, after the death of the prophet Muhammad, Islam began its rapid spread from Arabia across the Middle East to North Africa and into Spain. At the same time, in the rest of Europe, Christian and feudal traditions gradually merged. By the time Charlemagne was crowned emperor by Pope Leo III in the year 800, fidelity to one's chief could be understood as analogous to fidelity to one's God. By the late twelfth century, this brand of loyalty had found its way into the social habits of court life, where it took the form known as courtly love. In the love songs of the troubadour poets, the loyalty that a knight or nobleman had once conferred upon his lord was now transferred to a lady.

Charlemagne's passionate interest in education and the arts was broadcast across Europe through the development first of monastic schools and later of universities, which were themselves made possible by a resurgence of economic activity and trade. The Christian Crusades to recapture the Holy Land, principally Jerusalem, from Muslim control contributed to this economic revitalization, as did the practice of pilgrimage journeys to the Holy Land and to churches that housed sacred relics. The art of creating monumental stone sculpture was revived to decorate these churches, which grew ever larger to accommodate the throngs that visited them. The culmination of this trend was the Gothic cathedral, adorned with stained glass and rising to formerly unachieved heights. The sacred music of the liturgy became more complex and ornate as well, reflecting the architecture of the buildings in which it was played. To appeal to the masses of worshippers, the sculpture and painting that decorated these churches became increasingly naturalistic. Similarly, poetry and prose were more frequently written in the vernacular—the everyday language of the people—and less often in Latin. In both literature and art, the depiction of universal types, or generalized characters, gave way to the depiction of real characters and actual personalities.

We can begin to account for this shift by recognizing that, by the late Middle Ages, the center of intellectual life had shifted from the monastery to the town. From the great metropolis of Hangzhou, China that Marco Polo visited in 1271, to the cities of Teotihuacán and Palenque in Mesoamerica, daily life was an increasingly urban experience. In Asia and the Americas, these centers reflected the aspirations and power of the ruling nobility. But in Europe, towns like Florence and Siena flourished as a result of ever-enlarging trade networks. Now, suddenly, merchants and bankers began to assert themselves with as much or more power than either pope or king, ruling local governments and commissioning civic and religious works of architecture and art.

4 BCE–30 CE
Lifetime of Jesus

300 CE
Buddha carvings at Bamiyan, Silk Road

313
Pyramid of the Sun at Teotihuacán, Mesoamerica

313
Emperor Constantine grants religious freedom to all

410
Visigoths sack Rome

610–632
Prophet Muhammad transcribes the *Qur'an*

752
Todaiji Temple, Nara, Japan

768–814
Reign of Charlemagne

700–1000
Epic English poem *Beowulf* composed from Anglo-Saxon myths

937–1014
Lifetime of Murasaki Shikibu, author of *Tale of Genji*, world's first novel, Japan

1066
Bayeux Tapestry depicts Norman invasion of England at Hastings

1100
Ife culture, Africa, develops brass casting

1150
Chartres cathedral, first phase

1187
Muslim Saladin conquers Jerusalem

1279
Kublai Khan conquers China

1300–1450
Inca granite construction at Machu Picchu

1304–1374
Lifetime of Petrarch, author of *Canzoniere* (1349)

1338
Allegory of Good Government, Ambrogio Lorenzetti, Palazzo Publico, Siena

1338–1390
Alhambra palace at Granada, Spain

1364–1430
Lifetime of Christine de Pizan, author of *The Book of the City of Ladies* and *Tale of Joan of Arc*

LEARN MORE Explore an interactive timeline on **www.myartslab.com**

8

The Flowering of Christianity

Faith and the Power of Belief in the Early First Millennium

THINKING AHEAD

How did Christianity arise?

What was Rome's reaction to the early Christians?

How did Augustine of Hippo shape the development of Christianity?

How did the Byzantine Empire originate?

Where is Ravenna?

What is iconoclasm?

High above the Dead Sea, atop a giant citadel, lie the ruins of the ancient fortress of Masada [muh-SAHD-uh] (Fig. **8.1**). It is, in many ways, the final symbol of the Jewish Diaspora, the "dispersion" of the Jewish people that had begun with their scattering across the Mediterranean after the Assyrian attack on the northern kingdom of Israel in 722 BCE, the Babylonian invasion of the southern kingdom of Judah in 587 BCE, and the 60-year Babylonian Captivity that ensued (see Fig. 2.16). Nearly 800 years after the Assyrian onslaught, in 66 CE, now oppressed by Roman rule, the Jews revolted, but unsuccessfully. In 70 CE, the Romans sacked the Third Temple of Jerusalem, as depicted on the Arch of Titus in Rome (see Fig. 6.21). Meanwhile, at Masada, originally built as a fortress for himself in case of Jewish revolt by the Roman-installed client king, Herod (r. 37–4 BCE), a band of Jewish rebels took control of the mountaintop and held out against Roman authority until in 74 CE, when the Roman general Flavius Silva surrounded the mountain with a wall and eight encampments, then built a huge earthen rampway up the mountainside. Rather than submit to the Romans, the Jews inside committed mass suicide. Each man was responsible for killing his own family and then, because suicide is strongly discouraged by the Jewish faith, the rebels drew lots and killed each other in turn,

down to the last man standing, who would be the only one who would actually have to take his own life. Masada today is one of the most symbolic sites in all of Israel. There Israeli soldiers swear an oath: "Masada shall not fall again."

After the fall of Jerusalem and Masada, the Romans changed the name of the land from Judea, "land of the Jews," to Palestine, "land of the Philistines" [FIL-ih-steenz]—in other words, the land of a people lacking in culture. Finally, in 135 CE, after yet another Jewish revolt, the Emperor Hadrian rebuilt Jerusalem as a Roman city named Aelia Capitolina, which Jews were forbidden to enter. Many Jews were sold into slavery; others fled throughout the Mediterranean and Middle East. But the Diaspora that had begun with the Assyrian invasion of Israel 900 years earlier was now complete. Not until 1948, when the state of Israel was established by the United Nations, would Jews see their original homeland again.

DEVELOPMENTS IN JUDAIC CULTURE

From the time of the Babylonian Captivity to the rise of rabbinic Judaism (the Judaism of the rabbis, the scholars and teachers of the Jewish faith), at about the time of the Roman destruction of the Third Temple, the Jewish religion

◄ **Fig. 8.1 Masada, the fortress of King Herod on the Dead Sea. Late first century CE.** Herod built a magnificent palace here, on three terraces at the point of the promontory. A steep ramp built by the Roman army commander Flavius Silva in 73 CE, as part of the Roman effort to take the palace back from Jewish rebels, is visible on the left.

HEAR MORE Listen to an audio file of your chapter at **www.myartslab.com**

had become increasingly **messianic**—that is, it prophesied that the world would end in **apocalypse**, the coming of God on the day of judgment, and that the postapocalyptic world would be led by a **Messiah**, or Anointed One, in everlasting peace. These feelings were first fueled in 168 BCE, when the Seleucid [suh-LOO-sid] king Antiochus [an-TY-uh-kus] IV tried to impose worship of the Greek gods on the Jews, placing a statue of Zeus in the Second Temple of Jerusalem and allowing pigs to be sacrificed there. The Jews were outraged. From their point of view, the Greek conquerors had not merely transformed the sacred temple into a pagan shrine, but had replaced the Ark with a "graven image." The slaughter of pigs rendered the Temple impure. Still worse, Antiochus made observance of the Hebrew law punishable by death. Led by Judas Maccabeus [JOO-dus mak-uh-BEE-us], a priest of the Maccabean family, the Jews revolted, defeating Antiochus, purifying the temple, and reestablishing Jewish control of the region for the period 142–63 BCE. In 63 BCE, the Romans, led by their great general Pompey, conquered Judea (modern Israel).

Sectarianism and Revolt

It was a deeply unsettled time and place. In the early first century CE, large numbers of people claiming to be the Messiah and larger numbers of apocalyptic preachers roamed Judea. This situation was complicated by the growing sectarianism of Judaism itself. Much of what we know about this time comes from the writings of Josephus [joe-SEE-fus], a Jewish historian (ca. 37–ca. 100 CE). Josephus's *Jewish War*, completed in the early 80s CE, outlines Jewish history from the rise of the Maccabees to the destruction of the temple in 70 CE and the subsequent fall of Masada. "There are three philosophical sects among the Jews," Josephus writes, "The followers of the first of which are the Pharisees [FAIR-uh-sees], a scribal group associated with the masses; of the second, the Sadducees [SAD-juh-seez] priests and high priests associated with the aristocracy; and the third sect, which pretends to a severer discipline, are called Essenes [ESS-eenz]." (For Josephus's extended description of these sects, see **Reading 8.1**, pages 280–281.)

A **sect** is a small, organized group that separates itself from the larger religious movement because it asserts that it alone understands God's will and therefore it alone embodies the ideals of the religion. As a result, a sect generally creates strongly enforced social boundaries between its members and all others. Finally, members of a sect view themselves as good and all others as evil. Of the three sects Josephus described, the Essenes were the most conservative, going so far as to ban women from their community so that they might live in celibacy and purity. The Essenes are generally identified with the group of Jews who lived at Qumran [kum-RAHN], on the Dead Sea southeast of Jerusalem, where in 1947 a Bedouin [BED-uh-wun] shepherd discovered the oldest extant version of the Hebrew Scriptures, dating from around the time of Jesus—the so-called Dead Sea Scrolls. These documents are the richest source of our knowledge of Jewish sectarianism, for they include the Hebrew Scriptures—the Torah [TOH-ruh] (the five books of Moses), *Nevi'im* [neh-fee-EEM] (the Prophets), and *Ketubim* [kuh-tuh-BEEM] (the Writings), what Christians call the "Old Testament"—as well as other works originating in sectarian circles within and outside the Qumran community.

The Jews of Qumran abandoned their coreligionists to seek salvation on their own. Unlike the Pharisees and Sadducees, they never engaged in the Jewish political struggle with the Romans or with the other sects. The Pharisees and Sadducees argued, sometimes violently, over questions of philosophy, the temple, and purity. Philosophically, the Sadducees denied the resurrection of the dead, while the Pharisees affirmed it.

The purity laws were a point of special contention with far-reaching implications for the temple. According to Leviticus and Numbers (two books of the Hebrew Bible), the house of God (the temple) must be pure, and that which is impure must be expelled. In practice, the laws of purity prevented normal social relations between those who observed them and those who did not, to the point that even routine physical contact (a handshake, for instance) with a nonobserver was forbidden. Since all the sects developed their own purity laws, they were in essence forbidding contact with one another. The Qumran Essenes withdrew completely from Jewish society. Furthermore, the sectarian communities, especially the Pharisees, considered the Jerusalem Temple, the traditional center of Jewish worship, to be polluted, its priests—particularly the Sadducees—corrupt, and its rituals debased. The Pharisees, and perhaps the Sadducees as well, considered the house of God to be the larger state of Judea rather than just the temple in Jerusalem, and they felt compelled to expel the "impure" Romans from their midst.

The Romans had been careful not to make the same mistake as Antiochus IV. They installed the same Herod who built the fortress at Masada as their client king. Herod claimed to be Jewish but was not according to Jewish law. He tried, nevertheless, to reconcile Jews and Romans, primarily through religious tolerance and a massive building program. During his reign (37–4 BCE), he rebuilt the city of Jerusalem, constructing a large palace and enlarging the Second Temple (Fig. **8.2**). We can see the Hellenistic influence in its tall, engaged Corinthian columns and its decorative frieze, and its Roman roots in its triple-arched gateway. Herod also engaged in other massive building programs, including a port at Caesarea and the fortress at Masada. Though Herod's three sons ruled briefly after their father's death, Rome became less and less tolerant of the Jewish faith—the laws of Rome often coming into conflict with the Law of the Book—and direct Roman rule was soon imposed.

The Rabbis and the Mishnah

With the destruction of the temple in 70 CE and the subsequent Diaspora, the center and focal point of Jewish faith evaporated. From then on, Judaism developed as a religion in a sectarian manner. The sects, after all, had viewed the temple and temple rituals with deep skepticism and had practiced their religion outside the temple, in localized **synagogues,** or "houses of assembly," engaging in daily prayer, studying the Torah, and observing the laws of purity more or less independently of priests. Yet despite growing sectarianism, a community of scholars known as Sanhedrin, who had met for centuries to discuss and interpret the Torah, continued to provide a strong intellectual center for the Jews. In the town of Yavneh, where the group had moved after the destruction of the Second Temple by the Babylonians, ongoing study of the Torah and other traditional teachings known as the Oral Torah had been sufficient to maintain continuity about what it meant to live and think properly as Jews. After the Diaspora of the second century CE, however, it seemed likely that the Jews would be living for generations in many different places under widely varying circumstances, and without an institution such as the Sanhedrin, maintaining a strong, collective Jewish identity was unlikely.

The solution to this problem came from the rabbis, to whom, in the second to the sixth centuries CE, Jewish communities throughout the Mediterranean world turned for guidance and instruction. The rabbis, who were scholars functioning as both teachers and scribes, realized the importance of writing down the Oral Torah, a massive body of explanations and interpretations of the covenant, as well as traditional stories told to each new generation. In the early

years of the third century CE, under the leadership of Rabbi Judah haNasi (ca. 165–220 CE), the Oral Torah was recorded in a work called the Mishnah [MISH-nuh].

Almost immediately, the work was viewed as inadequate. The Oral Torah was part of a dynamic intellectual tradition of applying what was perceived as the perfect and unchanging word of God to the circumstances and demands of the changing times. The Mishnah seemed too permanent, too dry, too incomplete. To capture some of the stimulating discussion characteristic of the Sanhedrin, as well as its traditional respect for well-reasoned but differing points of view, a commentary known as the Gemara began to surround the text of each passage of the Mishnah. The Gemara was a record of what had been debated, preserving disagreements as well as consensus. Commentaries on the commentaries continued to be added by successive generations of rabbis, and the Gemara did not take its final shape until around 700 CE. The combined Mishnah and Gemara came to be known as the Talmud.

THE RISE OF CHRISTIANITY

The development of Christianity, the religion that would have such a profound effect upon the history of the Western world, can only be understood in the context of Jewish history. It developed as one among many other minor sects of Judaism, at first so inconsequential that Josephus only briefly mentions it. Later theological writings, as opposed to actual historical accounts written at the time, tell us that in Judea's sectarian climate, Jesus of Nazareth was born to Mary and Joseph of Judea in about 4 BCE. At about the age of 30, Jesus began to lead the life of an itinerant rabbi. He preached repentance, compassion for the poor and meek, love of God and neighbor, and the imminence of the apocalypse, which he called the coming of the kingdom of God.

Although his teachings were steeped in the wisdom of the Jewish tradition, they antagonized both Jewish and Roman leaders. Jesus, in the spirit of reform, had challenged the commercialization of the Jewish Temple in Jerusalem, especially the practice of money-changing within its sacred precincts, alienating the Sadducee sect that managed it. After his followers identified him as the Messiah, or Savior—he did not make the claim for himself—both conservative Jewish leaders and Roman rulers were threatened. The proclamation by his followers that he was the son of God amounted to a crime against the Roman state, since the emperor was considered to be the only divine human on earth. In fact, since Jews were monotheistic and refused to worship other gods, including the emperor, their beliefs were a political threat to the Romans. The Christian sect's belief in the divinity of Jesus posed a special problem.

An enemy of the state, denounced by the other Jews that he had antagonized, betrayed by his disciple Judas (a betrayal now called into question with the publication of the Gospel of Judas), Jesus was crucified in about 30 CE, a degrading fate reserved for criminals and non-Roman citizens. Christian tradition has it—we possess no actual historical account—that the crucifixion occurred outside the city walls on a hillside known as Golgotha, now the site of the Church of the Holy Sepulchre (Fig. **8.3**), and that Jesus was buried in a rock tomb just behind the site. Three days later, his followers reported that he rose from the dead and reappeared among them. The promise of resurrection, already a fundamental tenet of the Pharisee and Essene sects, became the foundation of Christian faith.

The Evangelists

Upon his death, Jesus' reputation grew as his **evangelists** spread the word of his life and resurrection (the word *evangelist* comes from the Greek *evangelos* [eh-van-GEH-los], meaning "bearer of good"—and note the root *angel* in the word as well). Preeminent among these was Paul, who had persecuted Jews in Judea before converting to the new faith in Damascus (in modern Syria) in 35 CE. Paul's epistles, or letters, are the earliest writings of the new Christian faith. In letters written to churches he founded or visited in Asia Minor, Greece, Macedonia, and Rome, which comprise 14 books of the Christian Scriptures, he argues the nature of religious truth and interprets the life of Christ—his preferred name for Jesus, one that he coined. *Christ* means, literally, "the Anointed One." It refers to the Jewish tradition of anointing priests, kings, and prophets with oil, and the fact that by Jesus' time Jews had come to expect a savior who embodied all the qualities of priest, king, and prophet. In true sectarian tradition, for Paul, the only correct expression of Judaism included faith in Christ. Paul conflated Jewish tradition, then, with his belief that Jesus' crucifixion was the act of his salvation of humankind. He argued that Christ was blameless and suffered on the cross to pay for the sins of humanity. Resurrection, he believed, was at the heart of the Christian faith, but redemption was by no means automatic—sinners had to show their faith in Christ and his salvation. Faith, he argues in his Epistle to the Church in Rome, ensures salvation (**Reading 8.2**):

the hillside dug away in the 4th century to allow the church to be built around the Tomb

burial chambers that had existed here since the 1st century BCE

Christ's Tomb

present church

Rock of Golgotha

Fig. 8.3 Cutaway drawing of the Church of the Holy Sepulchre, Jerusalem, showing site of Christ's Tomb. This site was originally a small rocky hill, Golgotha, upon which Jesus was crucified, and an unused stone quarry in which tombs had been cut. The first basilica on the site was built by the Emperor Constantine between 326 and 335 CE.

READING 8.2

from the Bible, Romans 5:1–11

[1]Therefore, since we are justified by faith, we have peace with God through our Lord Jesus Christ, [2]through whom we have obtained access to this grace in which we stand; and we boast in our hope of sharing the glory of God. [3]And not only that, but we also boast in our sufferings, knowing that suffering produces endurance, [4]and endurance produces character, and character produces hope, [5]and hope does not disappoint us, because God's love has been poured into our hearts through the Holy Spirit that has been given to us.

[6]For while we were still weak, at the right time Christ died for the ungodly. . . . [8]But God proves his love for us in that while we still were sinners Christ died for us. [9]Much more surely then, now that we have been justified by his blood, will we be saved through him from the wrath of God. [10]For if while we were enemies, we were reconciled to God through the death of his Son, much more surely, having been reconciled, will we be saved by his life. [11]But more than that, we even boast in God through our Lord Jesus Christ, through whom we have now received reconciliation.

Fifteen centuries after Paul wrote these words, the Church would find itself divided between those who believed that salvation was determined by faith alone, as Paul argues, and those who believed in the necessity of good works to gain entry to Heaven, a tradition that survives in the Epistle of James—"What use is it, my brethren, if a man says he has faith, but he has no works?" (2:14). Other aspects of Paul's writings would also have lasting significance, particularly his emphasis, like that of the Essene sect, on sexual chastity. Although it was better to marry than engage in sexual activity out of marriage, it was better still to live chastely. In later years, the celibate lives of priests, monks, and nuns, as well as the Church's teaching that sexuality was sinful except for the purposes of procreation, were directly inspired by Paul's position.

Not long after Paul's death, as the religion spread rapidly through Asia Minor and Greece, other evangelists began to write gospels, or "good news," specifically narrating the story of Jesus' life. What would become the first three books of the Christian New Testament, the gospels of Matthew, Mark, and Luke, are believed by scholars to have been written between 70 and 90 CE. Each emphasizes slightly different aspects of Jesus' life, though all focus particularly on his last days. It is important to recognize that many early Christian documents do not describe a virgin birth or a resurrection, a difference from Paul that reflects sectarian differences already present in the Jewish community. Evidence suggests that both the virgin birth and the resurrection were Matthew and Luke's additions to Mark's gospel. Luke also wrote the Acts of the Apostles, narrating the activities of Jesus' apostles, literally "those who have been sent" by God as his witness, immediately after the resurrection. The apostles were originally those who had seen or lived with Jesus, and the book contains descriptions of miraculous events, signs from God that validate the apostles' teachings.

The Gnostic Gospels Many New Testament scholars say that the actions and sayings attributed to Jesus in the Gospels cannot be factually traced to him, and that since they were written many decades after his death, they are composites of hearsay, legends, and theological interpolations, reflecting the hopes and beliefs of the early Christian community. There are, furthermore, other versions of Jesus' life than those contained in the Bible, especially among the 52 texts dating from the fourth century buried in a jar discovered by an Arab peasant in 1945 in Naj Hammadi [nazh ham-MAH-dee], Upper Egypt. These texts are **Gnostic** [NOS-tik] (from the Greek *gnosis*, "knowledge" in the sense of "insight"), written by Christians who claimed special, even secret, knowledge of Jesus' life.

The Gospel of Thomas claims that Jesus had a twin. Other relationships are suggested in these books as well; among the most controversial was the implication in the Gospel of Philip that Christ had a sexual relationship with Mary Magdalene [MAG-duh-lun]. At other points in the

Gnostic texts, common Christian beliefs, such as the virgin birth and the bodily resurrection, are criticized as naïve misunderstandings. In the late 1970s, another batch of Gnostic gospels was discovered near El Minya in Egypt. These contained the Gospel of Judas, in which, unlike the accounts in the canonical Gospels of Matthew, Mark, Luke, and John, where Judas is portrayed as a reviled traitor, Judas is described as acting at Jesus' request in handing him over to the authorities.

As the Church developed, it banned the Gnostic books (and other texts like them) as **heresy**, opinion or doctrine at odds with what would become normative belief. Although extremely diverse in their beliefs, with opinions at least as various as the Jewish sects, Gnostics tended to believe that a transcendent and impersonal God rules the heavens, while Christianity, as it developed, came to believe that God resided in Jesus, in the human realm. John's insistence that "Jesus Christ has come in the flesh" (1 John 4:2) suggests that his gospel is aimed directly at refuting Gnostic gospels. Gnostics believed that the material world in which humankind finds itself is evil and ruled by darkness, while the heavenly world is good and ruled by light.

In contrast, Christianity as it developed would come to argue that humankind is inherently good, and although fallen in sin, is capable of repentance. Normative Christians would argue that salvation is acquired through faith, not knowledge, but Gnostics would cite the example of Jesus himself, who, they believed, was sent to earth to open humanity's eyes, offering them enlightenment or *gnosis* [NO-sis]. Finally, the Gnostics believed that only those with great intellectual strength might, through the acquisition of *gnosis*, regain the spiritual condition lost in the material world. The normative Christian position was that salvation was available to all believers.

It seems possible, perhaps even likely, that the Gnostics were influenced by Indian philosophy. Gnostic doctrine is decidedly Eastern in spirit (see Chapter 7). Alexander the Great had introduced the teachings of the Brahmins [BRAH-mins], and the Christian bishop Hippolytus [hih-POL-ih-tus], writing in approximately 225 CE in Rome, directly attributed Gnostic belief to Indian thought:

> There is . . . among the Indians a heresy of those who philosophize among the Brahmins, who live a self-sufficient life, abstaining from (eating) living creatures and all cooked food. . . . They say that God is light, not like the light one sees, nor like the sun nor fire, but to them God is discourse, not that which finds expression in articulate sounds, but that of knowledge (*gnosis*) through which the secret mysteries of nature are perceived by the wise.

Brahmins and Gnostics share one important trait—their common belief that spiritual ascendancy is acquired through knowledge, not mere faith. Gnosticism was eventually rejected as sectarian and nonauthoritative as the Church developed.

The Gospels of Matthew, Mark, and Luke Particularly important to the normative view of Jesus' life is the recording in the Gospel of Matthew of the so-called Sermon on the Mount. The Gospel was probably written in the last decades of the first century CE. So many of the principles of Jesus' message are included in this sermon that some scholars believe it is more an anthology of many sermons than a single address. In fact, it incorporates many traditional Jewish teachings, and Jesus' primary source is his Judaism. The sermon contains Jesus' most famous sayings, and his most famous metaphors. It includes the famous Lord's Prayer—itself a kind of collage of passages from the Hebrew Scriptures—and it differentiates, particularly, between accepted wisdom ("You have heard that it was said, 'You shall love your neighbor and hate your enemy . . .' ") and the compassionate wisdom of the new faith ("But I say to you, Love your enemies and pray for those who persecute you, so that you may be children of your Father in heaven"). It is, furthermore, a masterpiece of rhetorical persuasion.

Consider the famous "lilies of the field" section (6:25–34) (**Reading 8.3**):

READING 8.3

from the Bible, Matthew 6:25–33

^{25}Therefore I tell you, do not worry about your life, what you will eat or what you will drink, or about your body, what you will wear. Is not life more than food, and the body more than clothing? ^{26}Look at the birds of the air; they neither sow nor reap nor gather into barns, and yet your heavenly Father feeds them. Are you not of more value than they? ^{27}And can any of you by worrying add a single hour to your span of life? ^{28}And why do you worry about clothing? Consider the lilies of the field, how they grow; they neither toil nor spin, ^{29}yet I tell you, even Solomon in all his glory was not clothed like one of these. ^{30}But if God so clothes the grass of the field, which is alive today and tomorrow is thrown into the oven, will he not much more clothe you—you of little faith? ^{31}Therefore do not worry, saying, "What will we eat?" or "What will we drink?" or "What will we wear?" ^{32}For it is the Gentiles who strive for all these things; and indeed your heavenly Father knows that you need all these things. ^{33}But strive first for the kingdom of God and his righteousness, and all these things will be given to you as well.

Jesus employs the natural metaphor of lilies clothing the landscape more richly than even Solomon in all his glory to convince his listeners that God will provide for them, thus creating an analogy between what they cannot know for sure and what they can see for themselves with certainty. This is one of 36 times in his gospel that Matthew refers to the "kingdom of God," which, it is important to

understand, is not "heaven" but a spiritual kingdom on earth that people willingly enter through belief, spiritual rebirth, and carrying out the will of God. Thus, Matthew argues that God's promise is available to all through the agency of faith.

The gospels of Matthew, Mark, and Luke are known as the **synoptic gospels** [sih-NOP-tik]—literally, "seeing together." That is, they tell the same stories, in the same sequence, often using the same words, although they differ in their details. Sometime between 90 and 100 CE, the apostle John gave a different picture of Jesus. John's gospel omits materials found in the first three books, including the temptation of Jesus and the story of the Last Supper, and provides new material, including Jesus' early ministry in Galilee, his several visits to Jerusalem prior to the final one (the only one mentioned in the first three books), and the raising of Lazarus [LAZ-uh-rus].

One of its most notable features is its prologue, which consciously echoes the opening motif of the Hebrew Scriptures in Genesis: "In the beginning," John begins, "was the Word, and the Word was with God, and the Word was God" (John 1:1). Where Genesis 1 focuses on God's creation, John 1 focuses on the Word of God (*logos* in Greek) and its significance in the already created world. The term *logos* was widely used by the Greek Stoics, who in turn had adopted it from the sixth-century BCE writings of Heraclitus. They believed that the universe is pervaded by *logos*, or ultimate rationality, which permeates and directs all things. Thus, John begins his gospel by appealing directly to a Greek audience in terms that would be familiar to them.

Symbols and Iconography in Christian Thinking and Art

The new Christian faith did not immediately abandon its traditions as a Jewish sect. Jesus, for instance, never thought of himself as anything other than a Jew. All of his associates and disciples were Jews. He regularly worshipped in Jewish communal worship and he preached from the Torah, the authority of which he never denied. The major distinction was that Christian Jews believed in Jesus' resurrection and status as Messiah, while non-Christian Jews did not. Christian Jews regarded the failure of the larger Jewish community to recognize the importance of Jesus as reason to separate themselves from that community to pursue what they believed to be the true will of God. Not until sometime in the early second century CE did Christianity cease to be a Jewish sect. By then, Christians had abandoned Jewish rituals, including circumcision, but even as it slowly distinguished itself from its Jewish roots, Christianity had to come to terms with those roots. In doing so, it found a distinctive way to accept the Hebrew Scriptures.

Christians believed the stories in the Hebrew Scriptures prefigured the life of Jesus. For example, Adam and Eve's fall from grace in the Garden of Eden—the original sin that was believed to doom all of humanity—was seen as anticipating the necessity of God's sacrifice of his son, Jesus, to atone for the sins of humankind. Similarly, Christians interpreted Abraham's willingness to sacrifice his son, Isaac, as prefiguring God's sacrifice of his son. This view of history is called **typology**, from the Greek *tupos* [TOO-pus], meaning "example" or "figure." Thus Solomon, in his wisdom, is a *type* for Christ.

Very little early Christian art survives, and most of what we have dates from the third and fourth centuries. In paintings decorating catacombs, underground cemeteries, and a few sculptures, certain themes and elements are so prevalent that we can assume they reflect relatively long-standing representational traditions. In almost all of these works, it is not so much the literal meaning of the image that matters, but rather its symbolic significance. Likewise, the aesthetic dimension of the work is clearly less important than its message. A very common image is that of Christ as the Good Shepherd, which derives from Jesus' promise, "I am the good shepherd. A good shepherd lays down his life for the sheep" (John 10:11). The overwhelming message of this symbolism involves the desire of the departed to join Jesus' flock in heaven, to be miraculously reborn like Jonah. As the Lamb of God, a reference to the age-old role of the lamb in sacrificial offerings, Jesus is, of course, both shepherd and sheep—guardian of his flock and God the Father's sacrificial lamb. In fact, it is unclear whether images such as the free-standing representation of *The Good Shepherd* (Fig. **8.4**) represent Christ or symbolize a more general concept of God caring for his flock, perhaps even capturing a sheep for sacrifice. The naturalism of the sculpture echoes Classical and Hellenistic traditions.

CONTINUITY & CHANGE

Doryphoros, p. 125

We see this too in monumental funerary sculpture, such as the *Sarcophagus of Junius Bassus* (see *Closer Look*, pages 252–253). The shepherd adopts a *contrapposto* pose, reminiscent of Polyclitus's *Doryphoros* (see Fig. 5.4). His body is confidently modeled beneath the drapery of his clothing. He turns as if engaged with some other person or object outside the scope of the sculpture itself, animating the space around him. And the sheep he carries on his back seems to struggle to set itself free.

These examples make clear the importance of symbolism to Christian thinking. Over the course of the first 200 years of Christianity, before freedom of worship was legalized, Christians developed many symbols that served to identify them to each other and to mark the articles of their faith. Their symbols allowed them to represent their faith in full view of a general populace that largely rejected it. They adopted the symbol of the fish, for instance, because the Greek word for fish, *ichthys* [IK-tis], is a form of acronym, a combination of the first letters of the Greek words for "Jesus Christ, Son of

Fig. 8.4 *The Good Shepherd.* **ca. 300 CE.** Marble, height 39′. Vatican Museums, Rome. The legs of this figure have been restored. Free-standing sculptures such as this one are rare in the early Christian period. Much more common are wall paintings.

The stone coffin known as the *Sarcophagus of Junius Bassus* is one of the most extraordinary pieces of sculpture of the late Roman Empire. It consists of ten individual scenes on two tiers, each separated from the next by a column (in fact, the two top right-hand scenes are one, representing Christ's confrontation with Pontius Pilate). The columns framing the central two scenes are decorated with *putti* [POO-tee], plump, naked boys who in Classical art are usually cupids and in Christian art are called *cherubs*. They can be seen here harvesting grapes, symbolic of the blood of Christ and his sacrifice. This element underscores the importance of these two central panels, which depict Christ in his glory. The bottom panel represents Christ's triumphal entry into Jerusalem on Palm Sunday, the top his presentation of the Christian law to Peter and Paul after his resurrection. In the top panel, Christ's feet rest on what is generally taken to be a symbolic personification of the sky, the figure of Aeolus, suggesting Christ's position in heaven.

Across the top of the sarcophagus these words are written: "Junius Bassus, a man of highest rank, who lived 42 years, 2 months, in his own prefecture of the city, went to God, the 8th day from the Kalends of September, Eusebius [yoo-SEE-bee-us] and Hypatius [hie-PAY-shus] being consuls [25 August 359]." Thus, the sarcophagus collapses the "present" time of Junius Bassus's death into historical time. Four scenes from the Old Testament prophesy the story of Christ, itself represented in four panels, as well as the arrest and persecution of two Roman martyrs, Paul and Peter, who represent the fate of all Roman Christians up until the Edict of Milan, which Constantine endorsed just four years before Junius Bassus's birth. In his sarcophagus, Bassus assumes his place in Christian history.

Something to Think About. . .

Although the drapery, poses, and deep relief of this sculpture demonstrate the continued influence of classical tradition, the heads of the figures appear disproportionately large. How does this relate to the colossal portrait sculpture of Constantine the Great in Rome (see Fig. 8.9)?

Sarcophagus of Junius Bassus. 359 CE. Marble, Museo Storico del Tesoro della Basilica di San Pietro, Vatican City.

SEE MORE For a Closer Look at the *Sarcophagus of Junius Bassus,* go to **www.myartslab.com**

The arrest of **St. Peter**, who would be crucified in Rome in imitation of Christ. At his own insistence, Peter was crucified upside down, to emphasize his status as lesser than his Savior's.

Abraham ready to sacrifice his son Isaac, prefiguring God's sacrifice of Christ.

Job in his distress, evidence of humankind's testing by God.

Adam and Eve in the Garden of Eden, at the moment when they succumbed to the Temptation of Satan, who is shown wrapped around the Tree of the Knowledge of Good and Evil in his guise as a serpent.

The *Sarcophagus of Junius Bassus*

Christ presenting the law to Peter and Paul after the Resurrection, an act prefigured in God's presenting the Ten Commandments to Moses.

Christ's arrest, just after Judas has kissed him at Gethsemane, a prearranged signal to Roman soldiers.

Christ's triumphant entry into Jerusalem on Palm Sunday, a week before the Crucifixion.

Daniel in the lion's den where, because of his faithfulness to God, he was spared.

The arrest of **St. Paul**, who was later martyred for his beliefs in Rome.

Christ's trial before Pontius Pilate, charged with treason for calling himself King of the Jews. Pilate is shown here about to wash his hands, symbolizing his denial of responsibility for Jesus' death.

alpha   omega

alpha and omega
I and X

chi rho

Fig. 8.5 Traditional Christian symbols.

God, Savior." The first and last letters of the Greek alphabet, *alpha* and *omega* [oh-MEG-uh], symbolize Christ's presence from the beginning to the end of time. The *alpha* and *omega* often flank the initials *I* and *X*, the first letters of Jesus and Christ in Greek, and the initials *XP* were the first two letters of the word *Christos* [KRIH-stohs] (Fig. **8.5**).

Over the years, Christians developed a consistent **iconography**—the subject matter of a work, both literal (factual) and figurative (symbolic)—in their art and literature. A story or person might be a type for some other story or person. A figure might symbolize something else, as particular figures symbolized each of the four evangelists—an man with wings for Matthew, symbolizing his humanity; a lion for Mark; an ox for Luke; an eagle for John. And the stories surrounding Jesus' life coalesced into distinct story "cycles," each part in some sense signifying the whole, and all of them becoming standard themes in the arts throughout the history of the West.

CHRISTIAN ROME

Christianity spread rapidly across the Roman Empire (Map **8.1**). As the map indicates, Christian areas of the empire increased dramatically from 200 to 400 CE, and as Christian authority increased, Roman authority naturally waned. The emperor Constantine's predecessor, Diocletian (see Chapter 6, *Continuity & Change*), had unleashed a furious persecution of Christians that lasted for eight years beginning in 303, but he also moved to cement Roman authority by implementing a scheme of government known as the **tetrarchy**, a four-part monarchy. Diocletian ruled from Solana, a city on the Adriatic near modern-day Split, Croatia, and controlled the East, with the other regions of the Empire governed by monarchs in Milan, the Balkans, and Gaul. In the sculpture representing the four (Fig. **8.6**), they are almost indistinguishable from one another, except that the two senior tetrarchs are bearded and their juniors clean-shaven. They hold identical bird-headed swords and wear flat caps from Pannonia. This Roman province was bordered on the north and east by the Danube River in present-day Central Europe, which is the meeting place of the Eastern and Western empires. Their sameness symbolizes their equality, just as their embrace symbolizes their solidarity. Even the sculpture's material is symbolic: Porphyry is a

Map 8.1 The spread of Christianity by 600 CE.

Fig. 8.6 Portrait group of the Tetrarchs. ca. 305 CE. Porphyry, height 51″. Basilica of San Marco, Venice. Originally decorating a crossroads square in Constantinople known as the Philadelphion, this sculpture was probably the base of a porphyry column. It was removed to Venice after 1204.

deep-purple Egyptian stone traditionally reserved for imperial portraits.

This shift of the Empire's administration from Rome to its provincial capitals had dramatic implications for Rome itself. Perhaps most important was Diocletian's removal to Asia Minor (modern Turkey). There, he almost completely deified the role of the emperor, presenting himself more as the divine manifestation of the gods than as a leader of a citizen-state. He dressed in robes of blue- and gold-threaded silk, glittering with jewels, to symbolize sky and sun. He had his fingernails gilded and gold dust sprinkled in his hair to create the sense of a halo or nimbus encircling his head. When he entered the throne room, servants sprinkled perfume behind him and fan-bearers spread the scent through the room. All kneeled in his presence. He was addressed as *dominus* [DOM-ih-nus], "lord," and his right to rule, he claimed, was derived not from the people but from God.

The Nicene Creed Constantine recognized that Diocletian's scheme for controlling the Empire was, in most respects,

sound. Particularly important was an imperial presence near the eastern and Danubian frontiers of the Empire. To provide this imperial presence in the East, in 324 CE, Constantine founded the city of Constantinople, modern Istanbul, on the site of the Greek city of Byzantium [bih-ZAN-tee-um]. The city was dedicated with both pagan rites and Christian ceremonies on May 11, 330. Constantine's own Christianity became more and more pronounced in his new eastern capital. Though he did not persecute pagans, he officially rejected pagan practices, openly favored Christians as officials, and admitted Church clergy to his court. Perhaps his most important act was to convene the first **ecumenical**, or worldwide, **council** of Church leaders in 325 CE at Nicea [nye-SEE-uh] (modern Iznik), a site just southeast of Constantinople. The council produced a document, the Nicene [NYE-seen] Creed, that unified the Church behind a prescribed doctrine, or **dogma**, creating, in effect, an orthodox faith. Church leaders believed that by memorizing the Creed, laypeople would be able to easily identify deviations from orthodox Christianity.

The Creed was revised and extended in 381 by a Second Ecumenical Council in Constantinople, quoted here (**Reading 8.4**):

READING 8.4

The Nicene Creed

We believe in one God the Father All-Sovereign, maker of heaven and earth, and of all things visible and invisible;

And in one Lord Jesus Christ, the only-begotten Son of God, Begotten of the Father before all the ages, Light of Light, true God of true God, begotten not made, of one essence with the Father, through whom all things were made; who for us men and for our salvation came down from the heavens, and was made flesh of the Holy Spirit and the Virgin Mary, and became man, and was crucified for us under Pontius Pilate [PON-chus PYE-lut], and suffered and was buried, and rose again on the third day according to the Scriptures, and ascended into the heavens, and sitteth on the right hand of the Father, and cometh again with glory to judge living and dead, of whose kingdom there shall be no end;

And [we believe] in the Holy Spirit, the Lord and the Life-giver, that proceedeth from the Father, who with Father and Son is worshiped together and glorified together, who spake through the prophets;

In one holy catholic and apostolic Church: We acknowledge one baptism unto remission of sins. We look for a resurrection of the dead, and the life of the age to come.

The Creed is an article of mystical faith, not a doctrine of rational or empirical observation. In its very first line, it states its belief in the invisible. It argues for the virgin birth of Jesus, for a holy "spirit," for the resurrection of the dead. It imagines what cannot be rationally known: Jesus in heaven at the right hand of God (perhaps not coincidentally an image evocative of Diocletian modeling himself as *dominus*, "lord," ruling at the will of and beside God). Nothing could be further from the Aristotelian drive to describe the knowable world and to represent it in naturalistic terms. (See Chapter 5.)

But perhaps most important, the Nicene Creed establishes "the one holy catholic and apostolic Church," that is, a united church that is universal ("catholic") and based on the teachings of the apostles ("apostolic"). The Church was organized around the administrative divisions of the Roman state—archbishops oversaw the provinces, bishops the dioceses, and priests the parishes—an organization that provided Constantine with the means to impose the Creed throughout the Empire, eliminate rivalries within the Empire, and rule over both church and state. Finally, the Church's **liturgy**, the rites prescribed for public worship, was established. In Rome, Saint Jerome (ca. 342–420) translated the Hebrew Bible and the Greek books of the New Testament into Latin. The resulting **Vulgate**, meaning "common" or "popular," became the official Bible of the Roman Catholic Church. As the version of the Bible known by the faithful for over a thousand years, from about 400 CE to 1530, it would exert an influence over Western culture, which came to consider it virtually infallible.

The Abandonment of Classicism in Art Roman art was transformed in this period as well. For instance, one of

Fig. 8.7 Arch of Constantine (south side), Rome. 312–315 CE.
Constantine built the arch to celebrate his victory over Maximian.

Constantine's first projects after his victory at the Milvian Bridge in Rome was to construct an impressive triple arch in celebration (Fig. **8.7**), for which he raided the artworks of other Roman monuments. Comparing the reliefs made for Constantine's arch, particularly the horizontal panel that shows *Constantine Speaking to the People*, with the circular **roundels** (round reliefs) above it, provides insight into the changes in the art and culture of this period that the Christian faith inspired. The roundels come from a monument to Hadrian made almost 200 years earlier (Fig. **8.8**). In the roundel on the

Fig. 8.9 *Constantine Addressing the People*, **Arch of Constantine. ca. 130–138 CE.** Marble, height of panel approx. 40". Compared to Fig. 8.11, the lack of spatial complexity in this relief is striking.

Fig. 8.8 *Hadrian Sacrificing to Apollo,* **roundel imported from a monument to Hadrian (ca. 130–138 CE) and reused over the left arch on the Arch of Constantine.** Diameter of roundel 40″. Constantine recycled many works from other monuments as well, including reliefs taken from a monument celebrating Marcus Aurelius's victory over the Germans in 174 CE.

right, Hadrian and two companions stand before the statue of Apollo. The space is illusionistic, rendered realistically so that the figures seem to stand well in front of the sculpture. The horse on the right emerges from behind its master on a diagonal that emphasizes a logical progression from background to foreground. The draperies in the figures fall naturalistically.

The relief depicting *Constantine Addressing the People* is quite different (Fig. **8.9**). No real sense of illusionistic space exists. Constantine stands in the middle (his head has not survived), surrounded by a linear arrangement of mostly frontally posed attendants whose clothing is rendered merely by lines cut into the flat surface of the stone—they are not really sculpted at all. All of the figures are the same height, their heads abutting on a line dividing the upper piece of marble from the bottom. But the real difference between the two pieces becomes apparent when we realize that the two seated figures on either side of the podium are themselves sculptures—statues of Hadrian and Marcus Aurelius. These statues signal Constantine's dedication to them and his identification with their imperial majesty. Unlike the statue of the deity in the Hadrian roundel, they are undistinguishable from the other figures. This comparison indicates that by the fourth century CE, naturalism is no longer an important aim of art, and the classical heritage of the Greek and Roman tradition has been abandoned. How large a role Christianity played in this transition is difficult to say, but the symbolic function of art has supplanted its illusionistic purposes; the spiritual has replaced the physical. Additionally, the standards of beauty that defined Classical art, specifically those defining the beauty of the human body, have been replaced by a more abstract standard of beauty. The new standard still depends on visual balance and order, but it has little or no interest in the body, since it is in the symbolism of an image that true beauty is believed to lie.

A giant portrait of Constantine erected at the Basilica Nova in Rome offers a different example of the increasing tendency of Roman-Christian art to capture the spiritual rather than physical beauty of its subject (Fig. **8.10**). The head alone is 8 ½ feet high, composed entirely of marble, and the entire seated figure was approximately 30 feet in height. The emperor's hair is composed of repeated geometric arcs. His eyes are disproportionately large, symbolizing contact with the divine. He looks both serene and imposing, appearing to gaze into the far distance, as if symbolically contemplating spiritual things beyond the material world itself. Even if the jutting chin and hawklike nose reflect his actual appearance, the totality has been transformed into a godlike presence, more an abstract image of imperial majesty and power than a realistic representation of the human emperor.

ROMAN AND GREEK INFLUENCES ON CHRISTIAN CHURCHES AND RITUALS

The community that developed around the new Christian liturgy embodied in the Nicene Creed required a physical church, and Constantine obliged with a building that became a model for many subsequent churches: Saint Peter's Basilica, begun in 320 on the site of Peter's tomb in Rome (Figs. **8.11** and **8.12**). Its original dimensions are difficult to fathom, but an eighteenth-century print of a nearly contemporary church in Rome, Saint Paul's Outside the Walls, gives us a fair idea (Fig. **8.13**). The church was as long, as high, and as wide as the Roman **basilicas** upon which it was modeled (see Figs. 6.31 and 6.32). It was approached by a set of stairs to a podium, reminiscent of the Roman Temple of Fortuna Virilis (see Figs. 6.7 and 6.8). Entering through a triple-arched gateway (again reminiscent of Roman triumphal arches), visitors found themselves in a colonnaded atrium with a fountain in the center (reminiscent of the Roman *domus*, Fig. 6.27—perhaps suggesting the "House of God").

CONTINUITY & CHANGE

Temple of
Fortuna Virilis, *p. 179*

The church proper consisted of a **narthex**, or entrance hall, and a **nave**, with two aisles on each side. At the eastern end was an **apse**, housing the altar framed by a giant triumphal arch, where the sacrament of Holy Communion was performed. A transverse aisle, or **transept**, crossed between the nave and the apse; in other church plans, it could be extended north and south to form a **Latin cross** (a long arm, the nave, with three shorter arms—the apse and the arms of the transept). The nave was two stories high, the aisles one story, allowing for a **clerestory**, a zone with windows that lit the length of the church. Open timberwork tresses supported the roof (making the structure particularly susceptible to fire).

All in all, the basilica church was far more than an assembly hall. It was a richly decorated spiritual performance

Fig. 8.10 Fragment of *Constantine the Great*, from the Basilica of Maxentius and Constantine, Rome. ca. 315–330 CE. Marble, height of bust approx. 8 ½'. Palazzo dei Conservatori, Rome. The flesh of Constantine's body, wherever revealed beneath its bronze armor, was sculpted in marble. Fragments of the right hand, the upper right arm, the lower left leg, and both feet survive.

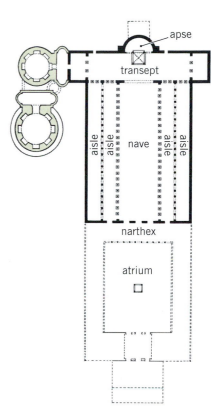

apse

transept

aisle aisle nave aisle aisle

narthex

atrium

Figs. 8.11 and 8.12 Reconstruction drawing and plan of Old St. Peter's, Rome. ca. 320–327, atrium added in the later fourth century. Vatican Museums, Rome. What we know of Old St. Peter's (a "new" St. Peter's replaced it in the sixteenth century) comes from modern archeological finds from written descriptions, drawings made both before and during its destruction, and the surviving churches it inspired.

Fig. 8.13 Interior of Saint Paul's Outside the Walls, Rome. Begun 386 CE. Etching by Gianbattista Piranesi, 1749. Note the wooden tresses of the ceiling and the spaciousness of the interior, reminiscent of the Roman baths.

ambulatory

columns

narthex

Figs. 8.14 and 8.15 Interior view and plan of the Church of Santa Costanza, Rome. ca. 350 CE. The view above is from the ambulatory into the central space. This is the earliest surviving central plan building in the world. Originally, the central plan was used for mausoleums or shrines. Another central-plan church very much like this one originally covered Christ's tomb in Jerusalem, but it was later incorporated into the basilica. The Church of Santa Costanza was originally attached to the now destroyed basilica of Saint Agnes Outside the Walls.

space, designed to elicit awe and wonder in worshippers. As the liturgy was performed, as the congregation—consisting of literally thousands—raised their voices together in song and then fell silent in prayer, the effect would have been stunning. No one, it was hoped, could leave without their faith reenergized.

A second type of Christian church also first developed in Rome, although it was initially conceived as a mausoleum for the daughter of Constantine, Constantia, a devout Christian who died in 354. Santa Costanza [koh-STAN-zuh] is a **central-plan church**, so called because of its circular structure, topped by a dome (Figs. **8.14** and **8.15**). This type of church has an architectural legacy that includes the high domed space of the Pantheon (see Fig. 6.26).

A double ring of paired columns separates the circular central space from the barrel-vaulted **ambulatory**, the walkway or passage encircling the domed interior. (Later Christian churches would adapt this ambulatory to encircle the apse.) This ambulatory is elaborately decorated with mosaics (Fig. **8.16**), consisting of an overall vine pattern interspersed with small scenes, such as laborers picking grapes and putting them into carts, transporting them to a press, and then crushing them underfoot.

One of the Christian references here is to the use of wine in the Eucharist, symbolizing the blood of Christ. But the Dionysian implications of the scene, with its unruly swirls of undulating line—the very opposite of the Roman (and Classical) sense of order and proportion—are unmistakable. Used to decorate a church, these lines imply the very nature of

faith—that is, the abandonment by faith of reason and logic, the very principles of Classical balance and proportion.

Greek and Roman Myths in Christianity

The design makes clear, in fact, the ways in which Christianity incorporated into itself many Greek and Roman mythic traditions—a practice known as **syncretism** [SIN-kruh-tiz-um], the reconciliation of different rites and practices into a single philosophy or religion. This occurred not only in the design of Christian churches but also in the symbolism of its art and literature—and it makes perfect sense. How better to convert pagan peoples than to present your religious program in their own terms? After all, the Greek wine god Dionysus had, like Christ, promised human immortality in the manner of the grapevine itself, which appears to die each autumn only to be reborn in the spring. Just as Christians had found prefigurings of Christ in the Hebrew Bible, it was possible to argue that Dionysus was a pagan type of Christ.

The cult of Bacchus, as the Romans referred to Dionysus, was extremely popular in Rome. So high-spirited were the drunken orgies engaged in by the cult of Dionysus that the Roman Senate had restricted its activities in 186 BCE. Other cults, known as **mystery cults** because their initiation rites were secret, were also popular among the Romans, and Christianity borrowed freely from these as well. In fact, the evidence suggests a remarkable process of cross-fertilization, each cult adapting elements from the

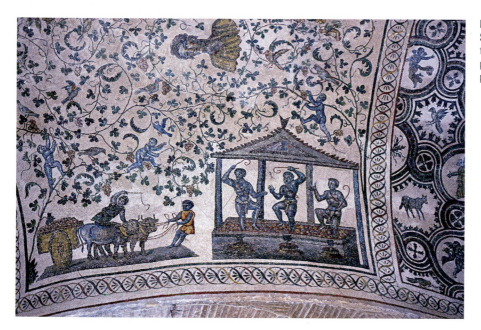

Fig. 8.16 Ambulatory vault mosaic, Church of Santa Costanza, Rome. ca. 350 CE. The figure at the top of this reproduction (which is actually positioned in the center of the volute motif) is probably Constantine's daughter Constantia herself.

others that were attractive or popular as they competed for followers. By the second century CE, in Rome, the *taurobolium* [toh-roh-BOH-lee-um], or sacrifice of a bull, usually associated with the Great Mother of the Gods, was performed annually on March 24. The bull's blood would run over a person beneath the sacrificial altar, who received the blood on his face, tongue, and palate, and who was said to be "reborn for eternity," as a consequence of the ceremony. Note that the *taurobolium's* date is near the beginning of the Christian Easter season, which celebrates rebirth and resurrection. And it resonates as well with the practice of the Eucharist, or Communion, the part of the liturgy when Christians, in taking bread and wine, are believed to partake of the body and blood of Christ.

The cult of Isis in Rome had originated in Egypt and was based on the ebb and flow of the Nile. Each summer, Isis would see Egypt's arid desert landscape and she would be moved to tears of compassion for the Egyptian people. Her tears, in turn, would cause the Nile to flood, bringing the land back to life—regarded by the Isis cult as an act of resurrection, not unlike the return of the vines in the Dionysian cult. In Egypt, in the late fourth and early fifth centuries, a new representation of Isis suckling the baby Horus began to appear (Fig. 8.17). (Remember, too, Horus is the son of Osiris, just as, in Christian

Fig. 8.17 *Isis Lactans*, Isis giving the breast to the infant Horus, from Antinoe, Egypt, late fourth or early fifth century. Limestone, height 35″. Staatliche Museen, Berlin. This is one example of a Greco-Egyptian motif that was popular in the first four or five centuries CE.

tradition, Jesus is the son of God.) In a Christian context, an image of a mother with a child at her breast could easily be mistaken for Mary and Jesus, and it is entirely possible that the Isis cult was the inspiration for the Virgin and Child theme in Christian art.

Finally, the secret cult of Mithras [MITH-rus], which originated in Persia perhaps as far back as Neolithic times, became very popular among the Roman troops stationed in Palestine at the time of Christ. In the second through fourth centuries, it spread across the Empire, and examples of its iconography can be found in Mithraic temples from Syria to Britain. Almost no texts explaining the cult survive; its rites and traditions were likely passed down orally among initiates. What we know of it comes from wall paintings and relief sculptures in its sanctuaries. It appears to have derived from a Persian religion, based on the teachings of Zoroaster [zor-oh-AS-ter] (born between 1000 BCE and the early seventh century BCE). The Avesta, the Zoroastrian sacred book, teaches that life is a battlefield between the forces of good and evil, truth and deceit. Free to choose between these forces, humans await a Last Judgment consigning those who choose evil to eternal darkness, and those who choose good to a place of eternal luxury and light—the Persian *pairidaeza* [pie-ree-DEE-zah], the origin of the English word "paradise." In Zoroastrian tradition, Mithras appears as a judge at the Last Judgment.

In the most widespread of his representations, Mithras is depicted killing a bull by stabbing him in the neck, as a snake and dog lap up the bull's blood and a scorpion clutches the bull's testicles (Fig. **8.18**). The end of the bull's tail is metamorphosed into an ear of wheat. At the top left and right are busts of the sun and moon. Zoroastrian sources suggest that Mithras was sent to earth by a divine bull, and all living things sprang from the bull's blood. The story can be read as a reverse version of God's sacrifice of Jesus. Mithras sacrifices his "father"—or, at least, his divine ruler, the bull—in order to create life itself. The cult had seven stages of initiation, one of which was baptism. We also know that the birthday of Mithras was celebrated each year on December 25. When this date was adopted in about 350 CE as the traditional birth date of Jesus, the choice was most likely an attempt to appropriate the rites of Mithraic cults, then still active throughout the Roman Empire, to Christianity.

Mithraism shares many ritual practices with Christianity—baptism, periods of fasting, a communal meal of bread and wine representing the flesh and blood of the bull, reminiscent of the Christian Eucharist (in which bread and wine are believed to be transformed into the flesh and blood of Christ)—as well as many themes, especially sacrifice for the good of humanity. And it was Christianity's chief rival among the Roman people through the first four centuries CE. Christianity's ability to supplant the various mystery cults probably had several related causes. The new religion's advocates labeled the cults "pagan" and "heretical," at the same time they codified and promoted their own rituals, beliefs, and sacred texts.

Fig. 8.18 Mithraic relief. Early third century CE. The Metropolitan Museum of Art, Gift of Mr. and Mrs. Klaus G. Peris, 1997 (1997.145.3). Image copyright © The Metropolitan Museum of Art/Art Resource, NY. Similar versions of this image have been found throughout the Roman Empire.

AUGUSTINE AND EARLY CHRISTIAN PHILOSOPHY

There is one other aspect of Mithras's cult that we also know—he was the god of truth and light. How much the Mithras cult influenced the Church Fathers is unclear, but light played an important role in their writing, and images of light appear often in the writings of early Christians. For instance, the Roman prelate Ambrose (339–397), bishop of Milan, refers to God as the "Light of light, light's living spring" in his "Ancient Morning Hymn." Perhaps the most important of the early Church Fathers, Augustine of Hippo (modern Annaba, Algeria), describes the moment of his conversion to Christianity as one in which he was infused with "the light of full certainty."

Confessions and *The City of God*

Augustine, who lived from 354 to 430 CE, was in his forties and had recently been made bishop of Hippo when he felt the need to come to terms with his past. He did this in the form of a prose work, the *Confessions*, the first Western autobiography. Though addressed to God, it was intended to be read by fellow Christians. Augustine had enjoyed an apparently wild adolescence. He describes it as a kind of "overcast" and "shadowy" atmosphere in which he gave up the "bright path" of friendship for carnal pleasure (**Reading 8.5a**):

> ### READING 8.5a
>
> #### from Augustine, *Confessions*
>
> As I became a youth, I longed to be satisfied with worldly things, and I dared to grow wild in a succession of various and shadowy loves. . . . But what was it that delighted me save to love and to be loved? Still I did not keep the moderate way of the love of mind to mind—the bright path of friendship. Instead, the mists of passion steamed up out of the puddly concupiscence of the flesh, and the hot imagination of puberty, and they so obscured and overcast my heart that I was unable to distinguish pure affection from unholy desire. Both boiled confusedly within me, and dragged my unstable youth down over the cliffs of unchaste desires and plunged me into a gulf of infamy.

Such thinking about the dangers of sexuality has exercised enormous influence over Western thought. For Augustine, sexuality is not so much an act, but an inferior state of mind, and all sensual pleasure represents a triumph of the carnal will over the spiritual. Sex is the means of transmission of original sin, and sexual desire is evidence of humanity's inability to resist it. The exercise of the carnal will inevitably lead, in his mind, to the famous episode of "The Pear Tree" in Book 2, where he describes his darkest moment: his theft of a neighbor's pears when he was 16. Later, in Book 8, still leading a dissolute life as a student, but despairing of his lifestyle, he describes his conversion to Christianity in a garden near Carthage (see **Reading 8.5**, page 281, for both episodes).

Augustine's storytelling is so compelling that the *Confessions* became one of the most influential books of the Middle Ages. The frankness of Augustine's autobiographical self-assessment—for instance, he is not proud of the follies of his youth though he is clearly still fascinated by them—would also make it influential later, in the context of the general rediscovery of the self that defines the great awakening to awareness of the human body known as the Renaissance.

But the *Confessions* is also a profoundly religious treatise that became influential on the merits of its religious arguments as well as its narrative power. For Augustine, humankind is capable of understanding true ideas only when they are illuminated by the soul of God. He adds to the Platonic emphasis on pure ideas a Christian belief in the sacred word of God, in which God's "light" is understood to shine. In the *Confessions*, too, Augustine codified the idea of typological readings of the Bible, proposing, for example, Eve, the biological mother of humanity, as a type for Mary, the spiritual mother. Similarly, he saw the deliverance of the Israelites from Egypt as a prefiguration of the redemption of Jesus.

Augustine was a prolific writer and thinker and a renowned teacher. One of his most important works is *The City of God*, written between 413 and 425. It is a reinterpretation of history from a theological point of view. In many ways, the book was a response to the sack of Rome by the Visigoths in 410. What had happened to the once powerful empire that had controlled the world, in a common phrase, "to its very edge"? How had such a disaster come to pass? Augustine attempts to answer these questions.

Many Romans blamed the Christians for the city's downfall, but Augustine argued, to the contrary, that pagan religion and philosophy, and particularly the hubris, or arrogance, of the emperors in assuming to be divine had doomed Rome from the beginning. Even more to the point, Augustine argued that the fall of Rome was inevitable, since the city was a product of humankind, and thus corrupt and mortal. Even a Christian Rome was inevitably doomed. As described in *The City of God*, history is a forward movement—at least in a spiritual sense—to the Day of Judgment, a movement from the earthly city, with its secular ways, to the heavenly city, untouched by worldly concerns (**Reading 8.6a**):

READING 8.6a

from Augustine, *The City of God*

The two cities were created by two kinds of love: the earthly city by a love of self even to the point of contempt for God, the heavenly city by a love of God carried even to the point of contempt for self. Consequently, the earthly city glories in itself while the heavenly city glories in the Lord. . . . In the one, the lust for dominion has dominion over its princes as well as over the nations it subdues; in the other, both those put in charge and those placed under them serve one another in love, the former by their counsel, the latter by their obedience. . . .

Thus, in the earthly city . . . if any of [its wise men] were able to know God, "they did not honor him as God, or give thanks to him, but they became futile in their thinking and their senseless minds were darkened . . . [and] they became fools, and exchanged the glory of the immortal God for images resembling mortal man or birds or beasts or reptiles," for in adoration of idols of this sort they were either leaders or followers of the populace, "and worshiped and served the creature rather than the creator, who is blessed forever."

The quotations at the end of this excerpt from *The City of God* are from Romans 1:21–25, Paul's first epistle to the Romans. The Romans are portrayed here as Stoics, "futile in their thinking," and worshippers of pagan images, but they are not necessarily lost souls. Paul, after all, is preaching to them. For Augustine, as for Paul, evil is a deficiency of good, the result of incorrect choices, as prefigured by Adam and Eve's choice to eat the forbidden fruit in the Garden of Eden, not something that exists in its own right. The Romans can be saved, then, but only if they give up the earthly city and accept the City of God. And if history was the progress of humankind from the earthly city to the heavenly one, then the church was "the mediator between God and men," between one city and the other.

Augustine's worldview is essentially dualistic, composed of two parts. In his writings, the movement of history (and of life itself) follows a linear progression from darkness to light, from body to soul, from evil to goodness, from doubt to faith, and from blindness to understanding. His own life story, as described in *Confessions*, revealed him as the sinner saved. He saw himself, in fact, as a type for all Christians, whose ultimate place, he believed, would one day be the City of God.

He reads the Bible in much the same terms, seeing its characters and stories as symbolic of larger abstract and universal qualities—that is, he reads the Bible as a kind of **allegory**, the representation of abstract or spiritual meanings through concrete or material forms. In this way, not only does Noah become a type for all men on the path toward salvation, but his ark is symbolic, at once, of the body of Christ, the Church itself, and the City of God (see **Reading 8.6**, page 282, for Augustine's allegorical interpretation of the story of Noah's ark). Augustine's symbolic readings of the scripture provide the foundation of biblical interpretation down to the present day.

Augustine, Ambrose, and Music in the Liturgy

In his *Confessions*, St. Augustine declared that "the practice and singing of hymns and psalms . . . was established so that the people [of Milan] would not become weak as a result of boredom or sorrow. It has been retained from that day to this; many, in fact, nearly all of God's flocks now do likewise throughout the rest of the world." These hymns and songs, Augustine says, represented a "kind of consolation and exhortation, in which the voice and the hearts of the brethren joined in zealous harmony." The bishop of Milan, Ambrose, wrote hymns to be sung by the congregation, recognizing them, like Augustine, to be an important part of the new liturgy. Recognizing that common people, with no musical training, were to sing along with the clergy, Ambrose composed simple, melodic songs or psalms, generally characterized by one syllable for each note of the hymn. His description of them, as evidenced in the most famous of them, the "Ancient Morning Hymn" (**Reading 8.7**, pages 282–283), again reflects the importance of the image of light in the early Christian liturgy. "The psalm is our armor by night," he wrote, "our instructor by day. The dawn of the day resounds with the psalm, and with the psalm re-echoes at sunset."

Ambrose's authorship is certain for only four hymns, all attributed to him by Augustine. The melodies survive only in tenth- and eleventh-century versions, and their authenticity is disputed. Each hymn is composed of eight four-line stanzas, each written in a strict **iambic tetrameter** (short-long, short-long, short-long, short-long). Ambrose also seems to have introduced an **antiphonal** method of chanting,

where one side of the choir responds to the other. What is certain, however, is that music was now employed to bring the community of worshippers together in common practice.

THE BYZANTINE EMPIRE AND ITS CHURCH

Constantine had built his new capital at Constantinople in 325 CE in no small part because Rome was too vulnerable to attack from Germanic tribes. Located on a highly defensible peninsula, Constantinople was far less susceptible to threat, and indeed, while Rome finally collapsed after successive Germanic invasions in 476, Constantinople would serve as the center of Christian culture throughout the early Middle Ages, surviving until 1453 when Ottoman Turks finally succeeded in overrunning it.

In Constantine's Constantinople, Christian basilicas stood next to Roman baths, across from a Roman palace and senate, the former connected to a Roman hippodrome, all but the basilicas elaborately decorated with pagan art and sculpture gathered from across the Empire (Map **8.2**). Christians soon developed an important new understanding of these pagan works: They could ignore their pagan

Map 8.2 Early Byzantine and medieval Constantinople.

Fig. 8.19 Hagia Sophia, Istanbul (formerly Constantinople). 532–37. Originally dedicated to Christ as the personification of Holy (*hagia*) Wisdom (*sophia*), Muslim conquerors transformed the cathedral into a mosque in 1453. Today, it serves as a museum, although it remains one of the oldest religious sanctuaries in the world.

elements and think of them simply as *art*. This was the argument of Basil the Great (ca. 329–79), the major theologian of the day. In his twenties, he had studied the classics of Greek literature in Athens and had fallen in love with them. He believed it was possible to understand them as literature, not theology, as great works of art, not as arguments for the existence of pagan gods.

Nonetheless, Roman pagan ways soon gave way to Christian doctrine. Constantine himself outlawed pagan sacrifices, and though the emperor Julian the Apostate (r. 361–63) briefly attempted to reinstate paganism, by the time of Theodosius [the-uh-DOE-she-us] I's rule (379–95), all pagan temples were closed throughout the Empire, and Christianity was the official religion. However, Roman law, not Biblical law, remained the norm in Byzantine culture, schools taught classical Greek texts, especially Homer's *Iliad*, and important writers still modeled their work on classical precedents. Nevertheless, by the middle of the sixth century, the emperor Justinian had closed the Academy of Athens, the last pagan school of philosophy in the Empire, and over 100 churches and monasteries stood in Constantinople alone.

Justinian's Empire

After Rome collapsed in 476, Odoacer, a Germanic leader, named himself king of Italy (r. 476–93), which he governed from the northern Italian city of Ravenna. Finally, the Ostrogothic ("Eastern Gothic") king Theodoric the Great overthrew Odoacer in 493 and ruled Italy until 526. The Byzantine emperors tolerated Theodoric's rule in Italy largely because he was Christian and had been raised in the imperial palace in Constantinople. But after a new, young emperor, Justinian (r. 527–65), assumed the Byzantine throne, things quickly changed. Justinian launched a massive campaign to rebuild Constantinople, including the construction of a giant new Hagia Sophia (Fig. **8.19**) at the site of the old one when the latter was burned to the ground in 532 by rioting civic "clubs"—that probably were more like modern "gangs." The riots briefly caused Justinian to consider abandoning Constantinople, but his queen, Theodora [the-oh-DOR-uh], persuaded him to stay: "If you wish to save yourself, O Emperor," she is reported to have counseled, "that is easy. For we have much money, there is the sea, here are the boats. But think

LEARN MORE Gain insight from a primary source document from Procopius of Caesarea on Justinian at **www.myartslab.com**

Map 8.3 The Byzantine Empire at the death of Justinian in 565 and in 1025. The insert shows the Empire nearly 500 years after Justinian's reign, in 1025. Although it had shrunk in size, the Byzantine Empire remained a powerful force in the Eastern Mediterranean throughout the Middle Ages.

whether after you have been saved you may not come to feel that you would have preferred to die." Justinian may well have begun construction of the new Hagia Sophia to divert attention from the domestic turmoil stirred up by the warring gangs. And he may have conceived his imperial adventuring to serve the same end (Map **8.3**). In 535, he retook North Africa from the Visigoths, and a year later, he launched a campaign, headed by his general Belisarius, to retake Italy from the successors of Theodoric. But through his massive building program, especially, Justinian aimed to assert not only his political leadership but his spiritual authority as well. His rule was divine, as his divine works underscored.

Hagia Sophia At the emperor's request, Procopius [pruh-KOH-pee-us] of Caesarea (ca. 490–ca. 560), Justinian's official court historian, wrote a treatise, *On Justinian's Buildings*, celebrating the emperor's building campaign. Book 1 is dedicated to the new Hagia Sophia (Figs. **8.19** and **8.20**) that Justinian erected on the site of the one that had burned down. As a result of Procopius's writings, we know a great deal about the building itself, including the identity of its architects, two mathematicians named Isidorus of Miletus and Anthemius of Tralles. Isidorus had edited the works of Archimedes, the third-century BCE geometrician who established the theory of the lever in mechanics, and both he and Anthemius had made studies

of parabolas and curved surfaces. Their deep understanding of mathematics and physics is evident in their plan for Hagia Sophia.

Their completely original design (Fig. **8.21**) consisted of a giant dome on a square base, the thrust of the dome carried on four giant arches that make up each side of the square. Between these arches are triangular curving vault sections, called **pendentives**, that spring from the corners of the base. The dome that rises from these pendentives has around its base 40 windows, creating a circle of light that makes the dome appear to float above the *naos*, underscoring its symbolic function as the dome of heaven. The sheer height of the dome adds to this effect—it is 184 feet high (41 feet higher than the Pantheon), and 112 feet in diameter. In his treatise *Justinian's Buildings*, Procopius describes the central domed section of the church (**Reading 8.8**):

READING 8.8

from Procopius, *On Justinian's Buildings* (ca. 537)

So the church has been made a spectacle of great beauty, stupendous to those who see it and altogether incredible to those who hear of it. . . . It abounds exceedingly in gleaming sunlight.

You might say that the [interior] space is not illuminated by the sun from the outside, but that the radiance is generated within, so great an abundance of light bathes this shrine all round. In the middle of the church there rise four man-made eminences which are called piers, two on the north and two on the south, each pair having between them exactly four columns. The eminences are built to a great height. As you see them, you could suppose them to be precipitous mountain peaks. Upon these are placed four arches so as to form a square, their ends coming together in pairs and made fast at the summit of those piers, while the rest of them rise to an immense height. Two of the arches, namely those facing the rising and setting sun, are suspended over empty air, while the others have beneath them some kind of structure and rather tall columns. Above the arches the construction rises in a circle. Rising above this circle is an enormous spherical dome which makes the building exceptionally beautiful. It seems not to be founded on solid masonry, but to be suspended from heaven by that golden chain and so covers the space.

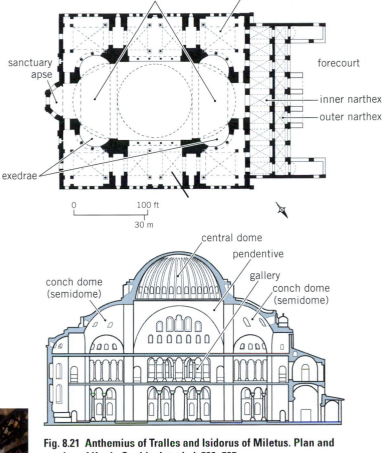

Fig. 8.21 **Anthemius of Tralles and Isidorus of Miletus. Plan and section of Hagia Sophia, Istanbul. 532–537.**

Fig. 8.20 **Interior of Hagia Sophia, Istanbul. 532–537.** So vast is the central dome of the church that it was likened, in its own time, to the dome of heaven. It was said that to look up at the dome from below was akin to experiencing the divine order of the cosmos.

Procopius does not mention that to the east and west, beneath the arches, are conch domes, or half domes, semicircular structures that spread out from a central dome, extending the space, and that these in turn are punctuated by yet smaller conch domes. Thus, a succession of curving spaces draw the visitor's eyes both upward to the symbolically heavenly space of the dome and forward to the sanctuary apse, seat of the altar and the liturgy. The intricate and lacy carving on the lower levels lends the stonework an almost immaterial lightness. The domes above are believed to have been covered with mosaics, probably consisting in the sixth century of plain gold grounds ornamented with crosses. Light from the windows around the base of the dome and conch domes would have ricocheted around the gold-covered interior, creating the magical, even celestial light that Procopius describes.

St. Catherine's Monastery Justinian was not content merely to rebuild Constantinople. Bridges, roads, aqueducts, monuments, churches, and monasteries sprang up around the Empire. Not the least important of these sixth-century works was the fortress and monastery known as St. Catherine's

LEARN MORE View an architectural simulation of pendentives at **www.myartslab.com**

Byzantine Mural Mosaics

Byzantine mural mosaics were made by embedding into a soft cement or plaster more or less regular squares of naturally colored stone, together with squares of opaque glass, which offered an even greater variety of color. These squares are called *tesserae* (singular *tessera*), from the Greek word meaning "squares" or "groupings of four." Gold tesserae could be made by sandwiching gold leaf between two layers of glass, a practice widely used in Byzantine mosaics. Artists first outlined the image on the wall, then covered successive areas with cement or plaster, filling in the tesserae as they went. Each tessera was set at a slight angle to the one adjacent to it, so that as light struck the squares, the changing angle of refraction would create a shimmering, almost heavenly radiance, both mystical and spiritual. In contrast, Greek, Roman, and earlier floor mosaics were usually laid with flat tesserae in a perfectly even surface so as not to impede walking. And the tesserae were usually limited to pebble, stone, and shell.

(Fig. 8.22), at the foot of Mount Sinai [SY-nye], in the desert near the tip of the Sinai peninsula, in modern Egypt. It was at Mount Sinai that, according to the Old Testament, God gave Moses the Ten Commandments. The monastery was sited on the spot of the burning bush, where tradition held that God had first addressed Moses and instructed him to go to Egypt and lead the Jews to the Promised Land. Thus, the monastery had great symbolic significance.

Justinian decorated the monastery church with marble imported from quarries on an island in the Sea of Marmara, approximately 112 miles southwest of Constantinople. On the east end of the monastery, above these marble panels, in the conch dome of the apse, artisans created an extraordinary mosaic of the *Transfiguration of Christ* (Fig. 8.23). The scene depicts the moment described in Matthew 17:1–6 when Jesus becomes a dazzling vision on Mount Tabor and a heavenly voice proclaims him to be God's son. In the center of the mosaic, Jesus appears within a **mandorla** [MAN-dor-luh], the light encircling or emanating from the entire figure of a sacred person, here an almond-shaped halo that signifies his glory. At his sides are the Old Testament prophets Elijah and Moses, and the disciples John, Peter, and James cower beneath his feet in amazement. Mount Tabor seems to be represented by the layered bands of greens and yellows at the bottom of the image—each of the figures except Christ seems to stand, kneel, or lie on it—but there is no real sense of space here. Rather, the entire scene is bathed in the celestial gold light that emanates in rays from Christ's white tunic. This effect is heightened by the way light reflects off the irregular surface of the *tesserae*, the small pieces of stone or glass, that make up the mosaic (see *Materials & Techniques*, above).

The Abandonment of Naturalism The naturalism that dominates Greek and Roman classical art is not apparent in the St. Catherine mosaics. The artists evidently had no interest in depicting the visual appearance of the material world; instead, they turned their attention to the supernatural event of the Transfiguration. There is no perspectival depth—as if the vision of Christ's transformation obliterates the possibility of even thinking in terms of real space.

Although the event depicted is highly dramatic, the participants' gestures are stiff, lacking the natural drama of Hellenistic sculpture (compare with Fig. 5.23, the *Dying Gaul*). The figures are highly stylized and realized in a uniform geometric configuration. Notice the

CONTINUITY & CHANGE

Dying Gaul, **p. 162**

repeated use of a lozenge shape to depict the thighs of the disciples. And despite being bathed in light, these figures cast no shadows. The robes of both John, on the left, and James, on the right, blow backward in identical but improbable folds. The feet of the two prophets and Christ not only look alike but are similarly positioned. The sandaled feet of the three disciples could be transferred one to the other without a problem.

The artists, in other words, employed a standardized shorthand to depict the events. It is as if their artistic vocabulary consisted of a limited repertoire of feet, hands, robes, and faces, all of which could be used over and over again in any context, the most important figure being the largest. We call this style,

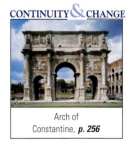

CONTINUITY & CHANGE

Arch of
Constantine, **p. 256**

which is at once formally abstract and priestly, **hieratic**. In retrospect, we can see the abstraction developing in earlier Christian art, in the reliefs, for instance, on Constantine's triumphal arch in Rome (see Fig. 8.7). But whereas the figures on Constantine's relief are squat and blocky, now, 300 years later, they are tall, thin, and elegant. These priestly figures float weightlessly in an ethereal space, as if, in witnessing the supernatural mystery of the Transfiguration, they have been transfigured themselves. But the differences between these figures and earlier ones are not just stylistic—they extend to meaning as well. Constantine had built and decorated his triumphant arch to celebrate his temporal power, but the mosaic at St. Catherine's celebrates a power that is otherworldly, just as Christ stands wholly disconnected from the ground.

Fig. 8.22 St. Catherine's Monastery, Sinai. ca. 548–65. The fortress around the monastery was built to protect pilgrims and monks from marauding "Saracens" (i.e., Arabs).

Fig. 8.23 *Transfiguration of Christ*, Church of the Virgin, St. Catherine's Monastery, Sinai. ca. 548–65. Mosaic. The marble panels, below the mosaic, must have been brought to the relatively remote site at great expense. The creators of the mosaic were probably also from elsewhere, though an inscription attributes the work to "the zeal" of Theodoros the Priest. He may have cultivated Justinian's patronage of the monastery.

RAVENNA AND THE WESTERN EMPIRE

The most extensive examples of Byzantine art survive in Ravenna [ruh-VEN-uh], a relatively small city in northern Italy near the Adriatic [ay-dree-AT-ik] Sea. (In the Eastern Empire, conquering Muslims were not nearly so interested in preserving Christian art and architecture as their Christian counterparts in the West.) Ravenna's art was the result of over 250 years of Byzantine rule, beginning in 402 when Honorius, son of Theodosius I, made it the capital of the Western Empire. Surrounded by marshes and easily defended from the waves of Germanic invasion that struck at Rome, by the fifth and sixth centuries, Ravenna was the most prosperous city in the West, the economic, political, and religious center of Western culture. Its art reflected its stature.

Honorius was succeeded by the first of several women to rise to positions of power in the Byzantine world, the empress Galla Placidia [GAL-uh pluh-SID-ee-uh], whose name means "the gentle, or mild, woman of Gaul." Galla Placidia was Honorius's half-sister. The Goths captured her in Rome in 410, where she became the wife of the Goth ruler. By 416, her Goth husband dead, she returned to Ravenna and married the consul Constantius, who apparently tried to usurp the throne. Ultimately, she ruled as Galla Placidia Augusta until 450.

In Ravenna, Galla Placidia built a large basilica dedicated to Saint John the Evangelist. (Only the columns, capitals, and bases of the original church survive in the present San Giovanni Evangelista.) The story goes that on her return to Ravenna, while caught in a severe storm at sea, she prayed to Saint John for deliverance, promising to build him a church if she survived. She also built a second large, cross-shaped church, Santa Croce [KROH-chay], which reputedly contained a relic of the True Cross, the one upon which Christ had been sacrificed.

Church Building under Theodoric

A period of turmoil followed Galla Placidia's death and the murder of her son and successor. It culminated in the capture of Ravenna by the Germanic leader Odoacer in 476 and Theodoric's defeat of Odoacer in 493. Like Galla Placidia, Theodoric soon constructed his own basilica, now called Sant'Apollinare Nuovo [sant uh-POL-ih-NAHR-eh noo-OH-voh] (Fig. 8.24), one of the best-preserved sixth-century Byzantine churches. On both sides of the nave, there are three tiers of mosaic decoration. At the top, in the clerestory, 26 scenes depict the life of Christ, 13 on each side (Fig. 8.25). Below these rather small scenes, between the clerestory windows, are 16 figures on each side, possibly representing the prophets of the Hebrew Bible on one side and the apostles and evangelists of the New Testament on the other. The bottom tier of mosaics was radically altered under Justinian, whose general Belisarius conquered Ravenna in 540. Ostrogothian Ravenna had followed the theological position of Bishop Arius of Alexandria. The Arians denied that Christ and God could be of the same essence, nature, or substance. Christ is therefore not like God, not equal in dignity with God, nor even coeternal with God. In contrast, Orthodox Christians, like Justinian, argued that God and his Son were one and the same. Justinian could thus justify his military campaign on the grounds that he was overthrowing a heretical Christian state.

Fig. 8.24 Nave of Sant'Apollinare Nuovo, looking east, Ravenna. ca. 500 and later. The rising water table in Ravenna has caused the floor of the church to be raised four feet since the sixth century. In the process, a fourth tier of mosaics has been lost, cut out of the wall to accommodate the higher floor. It is not clear what was represented in this tier of mosaic, nor do we know what originally decorated the apse, which was also destroyed.

SEE MORE For a Closer Look at Sant'Apollinare Nuovo, go to **www.myartslab.com**

Fig. 8.25 *The Healing of the Blind*, wall mosaic, Sant'Apollinare Nuovo, Ravenna. ca. 500. This is one of the 26 scenes that depict the life of Christ at the top of the nave mosaics above the clerestory windows. The series as a whole is the earliest surviving example of such a complete iconography. It has survived unaltered from Theodoric's time. The Crucifixion, which is not included, may have decorated at least part of the original apse, which has been destroyed.

But Justinian had other motives as well. Theodoric's Ravenna was not only the center of both civic and Church authority in the West, it was also a thriving trade center, connected to the nearby port of Classis, on the Adriatic, by canal. The luxurious decoration of the port's many churches—as many as 60 churches may have been built in the city between 400 and 750—is the result of its trade with the Eastern Empire and the importance the Eastern emperors attached to the city as their seat of power in the West. The emperor Justinian's decision to send Belisarius to seize Ravenna in 540 is at least partly attributable to the city's wealth and reputation.

San Vitale

In Ravenna, Justinian's new Orthodox clergy oversaw the construction of the church of San Vitale [ve-TAHL-eh], a unique central-plan building, similar to Santa Costanza [koh-STAHN-zuh] in Rome (see Figs. 8.14 and 8.15), but octagonal in design rather than circular (Figs. 8.26 and 8.27). On seven of its eight sides, the central space opens out into

Figs. 8.26 and 8.27 Exterior and plan of San Vitale, Ravenna. Dedicated 547. Like most Byzantine churches, San Vitale is a study in contrasts. The exterior is exceedingly plain. (The decorated doorway is a later addition.) But inside, the elaborate decoration symbolizes the richness of the spiritual world.

semicircular bays or niches called **exedrae** [EK-suh-dree], which themselves open, through a triple arcade, to the ambulatory. On the eighth side, the bay extends into a rectangular sanctuary and apse. The narthex (entrance hall), which has long since disappeared, was a lozenge-shaped space set at an angle to the church itself. Entering from the double doors, the visitor has two options. One is to look either directly across into the exedrae spaces, seeing a complex pattern of curves, niches, columns, and mosaics. The other is to glance directly across the central space to the sanctuary and apse, which rose two stories to a gorgeously decorated conch dome, decorated with intricately interwoven vines and animals in a predominantly gold and green mosaic.

On the side walls of the apse, level with the windows, are two mosaics, one featuring the emperor Justinian (Fig. **8.28**) and the other the empress Theodora (Fig. **8.29**). Perhaps inspired by the as yet unaltered processions in Sant'Apollinare Nuovo, which, as we have seen, probably featured Theodoric and his court, the artist has the emperor and empress lead retinues of courtiers toward the back of the apse. Possibly they proceeded toward reunion with Christ in paradise, as depicted in the conch-dome mosaic of the apse. A haloed Justinian carries a paten, the plate on which the bread is placed in the celebration of the Eucharist [YOO-kuh-rist]. On the other side of the apse, the empress holds a chalice of wine for the Eucharist, and on the bottom of her robe are the Three Magi, who, like her, come bearing gifts to the Virgin and Child. These mosaics possess a distinct political agenda, serving as propaganda to remind the faithful of the emperor's divine authority—the union of the political and spiritual spheres.

The most intriguing aspect of the two mosaics, however, is their composition. Even though Theodora, for instance, stands before a scalloped half-dome niche and the attendant to her right pulls back a curtain as if to reveal the space beyond, these mosaics do not represent a view into a natural world extending back toward a distant horizon (compare Fig. 6.29). Rather, Byzantine artists conceived of space as extending forward from the picture plane, with parallel lines converging on the eye of the beholder. This technique, known as **reverse perspective**, makes objects appear to tip upward—note the top of the fountain to Theodora's right—and elongates and heightens figures. Human eyesight, Byzantine artists believed, is imperfect and untrustworthy, a fact demonstrated by the apparent decrease in the size of objects as they recede in

Figs. 8.28 and 8.29 (top) *Emperor Justinian with Maximian, Clergy, Courtiers, and Soldiers;* and **(bottom)** *Empress Theodora with Courtiers and Ladies of Her Court,* **wall mosaics, San Vitale, Ravenna. ca. 547.** Standing between and behind Justinian and Maximian is Julianus Argentarius, the benefactor of the church.

the distance. By depicting objects in reverse perspective and in shallow space, Byzantine artists rejected earthly illusion, privileging the sacred space of the image over the mundane space of the viewer.

Music in Ravenna

We know about the music of the Church in Ravenna almost exclusively at a theoretical level. Music was considered a branch of mathematics and studied as such, and no medieval manuscripts of musical notation have survived from before the late ninth century. Yet as early as the fifth century, in Augustine of Hippo's *Confessions*, the role of music in the Church liturgy was a topic of much discussion. Augustine was himself ambivalent about it:

> I realize that when they are sung . . . sacred words stir my mind to greater religious fervor and kindle in me a more ardent flame of piety than they would if they were not sung. . . . But I ought not to allow my mind to be paralyzed by the gratification of my senses, which often leads it astray. . . . Sometimes, too, from over-anxiety to avoid this particular trap I make the mistake of being too strict. When this happens, I have no wish but to exclude from my ears, and from the ears of the Church as well, all the melody of those lovely chants to which the Psalms of David are habitually sung. . . . But I remember the tears that I shed on hearing the songs of the Church in the early days, soon after I had recovered my faith . . . so I waver between the danger that lies in gratifying the senses and the benefits which, as I know from experience, can accrue from singing.

Thus, we know that as early as the late fourth century, not long after Augustine's revelation in the garden (see Reading 8.5), "lovely chants" based on the Psalms of David were habitually sung in Christian churches. Just what they sounded like is another question entirely, although Ambrose's surviving hymns give us some clue.

Among the ministers who served Theodoric in Ravenna was Boethius [boh-EE-the-us], author of *De institutione musica* (*The Fundamentals of Music*), which would remain in obscurity until the late ninth century. There are, Boethius argues, three classes of music: *musica mundana*, *musica humana*, and *musica instrumentalis*. These are illustrated in the twelfth-century frontispiece to one of the earliest compilations of medieval music for the liturgy, the *Magnus liber organi*, or *Great Book of Polyphony* (Fig. 8.30), showing Boethius's continuing influence throughout the medieval period. In the top register of the frontispiece, the allegorical figure of Musica points her baton at a sphere containing the four elements—earth, water, air, and fire (represented by the stars). This is *musica mundana*, the highest form of music, created by planetary motion, the classical "harmony of the spheres." Below, in the second register, she lifts her baton for *musica humana*, the music humans create through the harmonious attunement of mind and body, reason and spirit. Finally, at the bottom,

Fig. 8.30 ***The Three Varieties of Music*, frontispiece to *Magnus liber organi* F. ca. 1245–55, probably in Paris.** Firenze, Biblioteca Medicea Laurenziana Ms. Laur. Plut. 29.1, c. 1v. Su Concessione del Ministero per i Beni e le Attività Culturali. È vietata ogni ulteriore riproduzione con qualsiasi mezzo. Photo: Donato Pineider. There are four surviving manuscripts of the *Magnus liber organi*. This one is referred to as "F" because it is housed in Florence, Italy. It is the largest and the oldest of the four.

she shakes her finger, somewhat disapprovingly, at *musica instrumentalis*, the music of sound, the only one of the three that can be heard by mortals. Likewise, for Boethius, there were three classes of musician—those who play instruments, those who sing, and those who judge performance and song. These last, persons grounded in reason and thought, are the most musical, he argues, once again demonstrating the medieval emphasis on music as a form of philosophical thought.

THE LATER BYZANTINE EMPIRE

Strange as it may seem, Justinian and Theodora never actually set foot in Ravenna, let alone San Vitale, and their depiction on its walls is probably best understood as a symbol of the relations between Church and State in the Byzantine Empire. Intimately interrelated and mutually dependent, the two balanced one another. Thus, while Maximian, the bishop of Ravenna, stands a little forward of Justinian in the San Vitale mosaic, Justinian's arm and the paten it holds lie (somewhat improbably) in front of Maximian. It is easy to understand, then, how the century and a half of military and political setbacks that followed Justinian's rule were interpreted in Byzantium as church related. Germanic tribes overran Italy and the Balkans. Persian forces sacked Jerusalem in 614. But even more important was the rise of Islam after the death of Muhammad [moh-HAM-ud] in 632 (see Chapter 9). Although the Byzantine emperor Heraclius [her-uh-KLY-us] (r. 610–41) recaptured Jerusalem in 620, the Muslim Arabs took it in 638. Within two years, the Muslim Arabs had conquered Syria, Palestine, and Iraq. In 642, the Byzantine army abandoned Alexandria, and Islam in effect controlled all of what once had been Byzantine Asia Minor. Constantinople itself did not fall, but it was besieged twice, from 674 to 678 and from 717 to 718. Only its invincible walls held the Muslim invaders at bay.

The Iconoclast Controversy

The sudden rise of Islam as a powerful military force had a chilling effect on Byzantine art. The Byzantine emperor Leo III (r. 717–41), who came to power during the second Muslim siege of Constantinople, began to formulate a position opposing the use of holy images. He understood that the Muslims, who were still regarded as Christian heretics, had barred images from their mosques and, so the logic went, their military successes against the Byzantine Empire were a sign both of God's approval of their religious practice and disapproval of Byzantium's. Like the Muslims, Leo argued that God had prohibited religious images in the Ten Commandments—"Thou shalt not make any graven image, or any likeness of any thing that is in heaven above, or that is in the earth beneath, or that is in the water under the earth: Thou shalt not bow down thyself to them nor serve them" (Exodus 20:4–5). Therefore, anyone worshiping such images was an idolater and was offending God. The solution was to ban images.

Thus was inaugurated a program of **iconoclasm**, from the Greek *eikon* ("icon" or "image") and *klao* (to "break" or "destroy"), the practice of destroying religious images. By the eighth century, the icon had a rich history in Byzantium. Mosaic icons decorated all churches, and most homes had an icon stand at the front door which visitors greeted even before greeting their host. Among the earliest examples of icons are a set of paintings on wooden panels from St. Catherine's Monastery, Mount Sinai, among them a *Theotokos* [the-OT-uh-kus] *and Child* (Fig. **8.31**). *Theotokos* means "God-bearing," an epithet defining Mary as the Mother of God, an official Byzantine Church view after 431. If Mary is the mother of Jesus, the Church argued, and if Jesus is God, then Mary is the Mother of God. Such images, and the doctrine associated with them, were expected to stir the viewer to prayer. Mary's eyes are averted from the viewer's, but the Christ Child, like the two military saints, Theodore (left) and George, who flank the central pair, looks straight out. The two angels behind raise their eyes to the sky, down from which God's hand descends in blessing.

Fig. 8.31 *Theotokos and Child with Saint Theodore and Saint George.* **Sixth century.** Encaustic on board, 27″ × 19³/₄″. Monastery of St. Catherine, Mount Sinai. Byzantine culture rarely, if ever, referred to Mary as "the Virgin." Instead she was rather the *Theotokos*, the "Mother of God."

The words of the sixth-century Byzantine poet Agathias (ca. 536–82) are useful here: "The mortal man who beholds the image directs his mind to a higher contemplation. . . . The eyes encourage deep thoughts, and art is able by means of colors to ferry over the prayer of the mind." Thus, the icon was in some sense a vessel of prayer directed to the saint, and, given her military escort, must have offered the viewer her protection.

Leo would have none of this. In 726, he removed the image of Christ above the Chalke (Bronze) Gate of the Imperial Palace, resulting in a pitched battle between his soldiers and iconophiles ("lovers of icons") in which several soldiers died. In 730, he issued an edict requiring the removal of all religious images from all churches. The righteousness of his position was established, Leo believed, by a quick succession of military victories over the Muslims and cemented by the length of his reign—25 years, longer than the reigns of his five predecessors combined.

As the incident at the Chalke Gate suggests, not everyone was happy with the iconoclast position. John of Damascus (ca. 675–749) led the Orthodox defense of icons. He argued that the Incarnation itself justified the icon: "When he who is bodiless and without form, immeasurable

Fig. 8.32 *The Crucifixion and Iconoclasts*, folio **67r**, *Chludov Psalter*. **ca. 850–75.** 7 3/4″ × 6″. State Historical Museum, Moscow. The psalter gets its name from its nineteenth-century Russian owner.

in the boundlessness of his own nature, existing in the form of God, empties himself and is found in a body of flesh, then you may draw his image and show it to anyone willing to gaze upon it." The iconophiles furthermore argued that the honor that worshippers bestow upon an image passes on to whomever the image represents.

A page from a Russian Psalter (Book of Psalms) showing *The Crucifixion and Iconoclasts* sums up the iconophile position toward iconoclasts (Fig. **8.32**). The passage quoted on this page is from Psalm 21, which is interpreted as a prophecy of the Crucifixion: "They gave me also gall for my meat; and in my thirst they gave me vinegar to drink." On the right, a soldier offers Jesus a drink from a vinegar-soaked sponge, stuck on the end of a long stick. At the bottom of the page, two iconoclasts raise a sponge, just dipped in a vase of lime whitewash, to an icon of Christ and begin to paint it over. The image suggests that to destroy an image of Christ is tantamount to crucifying Jesus.

The importance of the iconoclast controversy to the history of Western art cannot be overstated. Iconoclasm would reappear several hundred years later during the Renaissance, but more important, the controversy affirmed the centrality of visual imagery to Western culture. In the debate over the function of the image—ranging from the artist's motives for creating it to the viewer's understanding of it to the patron's support of it—attention focused on the role of the visual not only in religion but also in communication, learning, and understanding. The iconoclast controversy could be said to have instigated the very notion of "visual literacy"—the idea that understanding certain images is central to cultural literacy. It also contributed to the radical division, or schism, between the Roman Catholic and Eastern Orthodox churches that developed especially in the last half of the first millennium. The two churches disputed papal authority—from the Eastern point of view the pope's rule of the Eastern Church was merely nominal. There were huge cultural differences as well, for few in the West spoke Greek, few in the East Latin. Doctrinal issues having to do with the Catholic position that the Holy Spirit proceeded from both the Father *and* the Son, an idea wholly unknown in the East, also played a part.

In terms of iconography, most Roman Catholics believed that images of God the Father, Christ, and the Virgin served to inspire reverence and piety, while, as we have seen, a very large segment of the Eastern Church did not. Once the iconoclast controversy in the East was settled in favor of imagery, the theological conservatism of the Eastern Orthodox Church discouraged innovation to the point that its art remained remarkably consistent right down to modern times. In contrast, the Church in the West was consistently open to artistic innovation, especially after the twelfth and thirteenth centuries. Any visitor to a Greek or Russian Orthodox church today would be struck by the similarity of its art to that of early medieval Constantinople. When Russia accepted Christianity in 988, Byzantine artists were dispatched to Kiev and other artistic centers in order to pass on the traditions of icon painting to Russian monks. While an individual painter might interpret tradition in an individual way—in the manner, for instance, that a musician might interpret a score—tradition dominates the art of Eastern Orthodoxy.

Tradition and Innovation: The Icon in the Second Golden Age

When the Macedonian [mas-uh-DOE-nee-un] dynasty (867–1056) initiated by Basil I came to power, the Empire enjoyed a cultural rebirth of art and architecture, often referred to as the Second Golden Age. Although the Empire's reach was somewhat reduced, its wealthy autocracy could claim control of present-day Turkey and other areas around the Black Sea, the Balkan peninsula including Greece, and southern Italy, including Sicily. It also exerted influence over Russia, Ukraine, and Venice, its major trading partner in the Adriatic.

The artists of the Macedonian era turned to both classical and Justinian models for their church decoration, lending the traditional icon a more naturalistic air and an almost Hellenistic emotional appeal. While images of Christ on the cross had occasionally appeared in earlier centuries, after the iconoclast controversy, they appeared with greater frequency. A particularly fine example survives at Daphni [DAF-nee], near Athens, Greece, in the Church of the Dormition [dor-MISH-un] (from the Latin

Fig. 8.33 *Crucifixion*, mosaic in the north arm of the east wall, Church of the Dormition, Daphni, Greece. **Late eleventh century.** The skull at the foot of the cross symbolizes Golgotha, the "place of the skull," a hill outside Jerusalem. Many believed it was the site of Adam's burial and of the Crucifixion.

word for "sleep" and referring to the assumption into heaven of the Virgin Mary at the moment of her death) (Fig. **8.33**). The image remains completely traditional in its reverse perspective (noticeable particularly on the platform at Christ's feet) and in its refusal to create a realistic spatial setting, opting instead for the spiritual space of its golden background. But the nudity of Christ and the graceful gestures of the Virgin and Saint John, the draperies of their clothing falling almost softly in comparison to the stiff folds of the Justinian and Theodora mosaics at San Vitale, are clearly inspired by classical antecedents. Even more classical is the pure human emotion that the figures convey. Where early Christian art had emphasized the Savior's power, wisdom, and personal strength, this image hints at his vulnerability, the human pathos of his sacrifice. The arc of blood and water springing from his side, referring to both the Eucharist and the Baptism, connects his "passion" to our own.

No single image underscores the role of the Theotokos as protectress more than the tenth-century mosaic *Theotokos and Child with Justinian and Constantine* that decorates the vestibule to Hagia Sophia (Fig. **8.34**). To the right of the Theotokos and Child at the center stands "Justinian the Glorious King," as his inscription calls him, holding an architectural model of Hagia Sophia. To their left is "Constantine the Great, numbered among the saints," holding a model of the walled city of Constantinople. The city, the mosaic suggests, has been under the protection of the Mother of God since its inception. The implication is that such protection will continue, as indeed it would, until the year 1453, when Constantinople would finally fall to the Turks.

Fig. 8.34 *Theotokos and Child with Justinian and Constantine*, vestibule mosaic, Hagia Sophia, **Istanbul. Early tenth century.** Constantine and Justinian are beardless, which distinguished them from contemporary emperors, all of whom wore beards and had long hair. Note the reverse perspective, so typical of Byzantine art, of the throne upon which the Theotokos Mary sits.

Byzantine Influences

Located at the crossroads of Europe and Asia and serving as the focal point of a vast trade network that stretched as far east as China, Constantinople was the economic center of first the Roman Empire and then the entire Mediterranean for nearly a thousand years. Only Venice would ever rival it as a center of trade, and Venice would finally conquer Constantinople during the Fourth Crusade in 1204 in order to draw the city into its own sphere of influence. Venetian mercenaries looted the city in the process, taking back to Italy art and artifacts representing over 900 years of accumulated wealth and artistic tradition. In the early years of the twelfth century, Venetian artists copied more than 110 scenes for the atrium of St. Mark's Cathedral from Byzantine originals. And St. Mark's itself was directly inspired by Byzantine architecture and decoration (Fig. 8.35).

The wealth of Constantinople in artifacts would spread to the north as well. In 1238, Venetian merchants purchased from Byzantine officials one of the most precious relics of Western Christendom [KRIS-en-dum], the Crown of Thorns, supposedly worn by Jesus during the Crucifixion. The same year, King Louis [LOO-ee] IX of France paid the Venetians 13,304 gold coins to take the crown to Paris and place it in his newly dedicated Gothic church, Sainte-Chappelle [SANT-sha-PELL].

Throughout its history, Byzantine Constantinople was constantly under attack, not only by the rest of Christendom but also by Islam, the new religion that had originated to the south, which is the subject of Chapter 9. Many in Constantinople attributed the Muslims' success to their refusal to allow images in their mosques, and this belief fed the iconoclast controversy in Byzantine political and religious life, as we have seen. The Christian West, in turn, would come to see the Muslim world not merely as barbarian, but as a direct threat to Christian dominance—political, economic, and religious—of the Mediterranean world. Increasingly, the region's two competing empires, east and west, would cease to be Byzantine and Catholic, but instead would become Muslim and Christian. The traditions of Byzantine art lived on, however, especially in Greece and Russia, where in the thirteenth through sixteenth centuries especially, Byzantine art continued to flourish. ■

Fig. 8.35 St. Mark's Cathedral, Venice, west facade. 1063–1094, with decorations added for centuries after. The original brick front of the cathedral is inlaid with marble slabs and carvings, much of it looted from Constantinople in 1204.

Why did Christianity arise?

By the first century CE, Judaism had become increasingly sectarian in nature, each sect believing that it possessed the one true understanding of God's will. It had also become increasingly messianic and apocalyptic. Christianity developed out of this situation, and spread across the Roman Empire. Both orthodox and Gnostic versions of Christ's life developed. How do they differ?

To incorporate its Jewish heritage, early Christianity viewed its history as a typology. How does typology work? Early Christian art is clearly indebted to Classical and Hellenistic precedents, but it includes many symbols designed to indicate the Christian content of the image. What are some of the iconographic features of these symbols?

What was Rome's reaction to the early Christians?

Christians were consistently blamed for the troubles that beset Rome. Diocletian unleashed a furious persecution in 303 and divided the Empire into four areas of rule—the tetrarchy. Diocletian ruled in Asia Minor, where he presented himself as the divine manifestation of the Roman gods on Earth. Thus Christians, who were monotheistic and worshipped their own god, were a direct threat to his own authority. In 312, Constantine I ("Constantine the Great") assumed total authority. Constantine became increasingly supportive of Christianity, convening the first ecumenical council of Church leaders in 325 at Nicea, near his new capital at Constantinople. What are the basic tenets of the resulting Nicene Creed? How does it serve to define the nature of Christian belief?

Like so many Roman emperors before him, the victorious Constantine celebrated with a campaign of public works. How does the traditional style of Roman art compare to the relief *Constantine Addressing the People*? What new standards of beauty began to define Christian art? Constantine erected the last great imperial building in Rome, the Basilica Nuova. Its architectural features anticipate the first great Christian church, St. Peter's Basilica. A second type of Christian church was built as a mausoleum for Constantine's daughter, Constantia. How would you describe the principal features of this church? It was decorated with mosaics of a vine pattern. How do these mosaics suggest the ways that Christianity incorporated Greek and Roman mythic traditions? What features of the mystery cults of Isis and Mithras can be seen to surface in Christian practice?

Who was Augustine of Hippo? How did he shape Christianity's development?

Augustine's *Confessions* are the first Western autobiography, describing his conversion to Christianity. What temptations does he find most difficult to overcome and how do you think these difficulties have impacted

Western theology? His *City of God* argues that the demise of the Roman Empire was caused by the arrogance of its emperors and the worldly concerns of the citizens of the earthly city. Romans, he argues, might be saved if they turn their attention to the heavenly City of God. Much of the argument is based on an allegorical reading of the Bible. How do you see allegory developing out of the tradition of typological reading in Christian thought? Augustine began to realize that music might play a meaningful role in the liturgy, and he was drawn, particularly, to the hymns of the bishop of Milan, Ambrose. What value do they see in music? How does the imagery of Ambrose's "Ancient Morning Hymn" recall the Mithraic mystery cult?

When did the Byzantine Empire originate?

When in 325 the emperor Constantine began to build his new capital at Byzantium (in modern-day Turkey), he modeled it on Rome, but instead of temples dedicated to the Roman gods, he erected Christian basilicas. By the sixth century, when the emperor Justinian closed the last pagan school of philosophy in the Empire, there were over 100 churches and monasteries in the city. Justinian ordered the mammoth new church Hagia Sophia to be built and oversaw construction of bridges, roads, aqueducts, monuments, churches, and monasteries all around the Empire, including St. Catherine's monastery on the Sinai Peninsula with its extraordinary mosaic of *The Transfiguration of Christ*. The naturalism that marks Classical art disappears here. What replaces it? Why?

Where is Ravenna?

A small city in northern Italy near the Adriatic Sea, Ravenna contains the most extensive survivals of Byzantine Christian art and architecture. What motivated Justinian to conquer Ravenna? The clergy installed in Ravenna by Justinian constructed a new central plan church, San Vitale, decorated with two mosaics featuring Justinian and Theodora. How do these compare to the mosaic *Transfiguration of Christ* at St. Catherine's monastery in the Sinai? Music played a role in the liturgy, and, although we have little surviving music from the period, we do have an important treatise on the topic, Boethius's *The Fundamentals of Music*. What are the three forms of music as outlined by Boethius? What is their relationship to Byzantine beliefs about art?

What is iconoclasm?

The rise of Islam motivated the emperor Leo III to inaugurate a program of iconoclasm in 726 requiring the removal of all religious images from all churches. Muslims barred images from their mosques, and like them

Leo suspected that religious images fostered idolatry. What were the arguments against iconoclasm? Later Macedonian emperors brought about a cultural revival, a Second Golden Age of Byzantine art, reinvigorating the traditional icon. Along with differences in language and doctrine, however, the iconoclast controversy contributed to the radical division, or schism, between the Roman Catholic and Eastern Orthodox churches.

PRACTICE MORE Get flashcards for images and terms and review chapter material with quizzes at **www.myartslab.com**

GLOSSARY

allegory The representation of abstract or spiritual meanings through concrete or material forms.

ambulatory A processional aisle around the outside of an apse in a basilica or, in a central-plan church, encircling the central space.

antiphonal Musical form of chanting in which one side of the choir responds to the other.

apocalypse The coming of God on the day of judgment.

apse The semicircular niche at the end of the *nave* of a Christian *basilica* containing the altar.

basilica An early Christian church having a central *nave*, side aisles, and an *apse* at one or both ends.

central-plan church A circular structure topped by a dome with an *ambulatory* around the central space.

clerestory The topmost zone of the wall of a *basilica* containing windows.

dogma Prescribed Church doctrine.

ecumenical council Worldwide council of Church leaders.

evangelist One who spreads the word of Jesus' life and resurrection.

exedrae A semicircular bay or niche.

Gnostic gospels Gospels written by those who profess secret knowledge of Jesus' life.

heresy Opinion or doctrine at odds with orthodox belief.

hieratic style A style in which the importance of figures is indicated by size, so that the most important figure is largest.

iambic tetrameter The three-beat rhythm of Ambrose's hymns, consisting of three iambs (short-long).

iconoclasm The idea, practice, or doctrine of an iconoclast to destroy or ban religious images and their veneration.

iconography The literal (factual) and figurative (symbolic) significance of an image.

Latin cross The design of a Christian *basilica* with a long arm (the *nave*) and three shorter arms—the *apse* and the arms of the *transept*.

liturgy The rites prescribed for public worship.

mandorla The light encircling or emanating from the figure of a sacred person.

Messiah Anointed One.

messianic Prophesied that the world will end in apocalypse.

mystery cult Religious group with secret initiation rituals.

narthex The entrance hall of a Christian *basilica*.

nave The central space of a Christian *basilica*, usually flanked by aisles.

pendentive A triangular curving vault section that supports a dome over a square space.

reverse perspective A technique for conceiving of space as extending forward from the picture plane, with parallel lines converging on the eye of the beholder.

roundel A round field for relief sculpture or painting.

sect A small, organized group that separates itself from the larger religious movement.

synagogue Jewish house of worship.

syncretism The reconciliation of different rites and practices into a single philosophy or religion.

synoptic gospels Gospels that tell the same stories, in the same sequence, often using the same words.

tetrarchy The four-part monarchy begun by Diocletian that divided the Empire into two areas ruled by an Eastern and Western emperor, each with a designated successor.

transept The arm of the Latin cross church perpendicular to the *nave*.

type A prefigurative symbol.

typology The doctrine of prefigurative symbols, or *types*, in scriptural literature.

Vulgate The Latin Bible.

READINGS

Josephus, *The Jewish War*, Book 2, "The Three Sects"

At the beginning of The Jewish War, *its author introduces himself as "Joseph, son of Matthias, an ethnic Hebrew, a priest from Jerusalem." He had fought the Romans in the First Jewish-Roman War beginning in 66 CE, as a commander in Galilee [GAL-uh-lee], but after the destruction of the temple in 70 CE, he apparently joined Titus's entourage when it returned to Rome with all its spoils. Despite living rather comfortably under the patronage of the Flavian emperors, he remained, in his own eyes at least, a loyal and observant Jew, intent on advocating for the Jewish people in the hostile atmosphere of the Roman Empire.*

Josephus wrote all his works, including The Jewish War, *in Rome. His is the most thorough account we have of Roman-Jewish relations in the first century CE. It also provides much information about Jewish sectarian thought, since he blamed the Jewish War on "unrepresentative and over-zealous fanatics" among the Jews—sects, that is, other than the aristocratic Pharisees to which he belonged. The passage from* The Jewish War *excerpted here concentrates on one of the "overzealous" sects, the Essenes.*

2 For there are three philosophical sects among the Jews. The followers of the first of which are the Pharisees; of the second, the Sadducees; and the third sect, which pretends to a severer discipline, are called Essenes. These last are Jews by birth, and seem to have a greater affection for one another than the other sects have. These Essenes reject pleasures as an evil, but esteem continence, and the conquest over our passions, to be virtue. They neglect wedlock, but choose out other persons' children, while they are pliable, and fit for learning, and esteem them to be of their kindred, and form them according to their own manners. They do not absolutely deny the fitness of marriage, and the succession of mankind thereby continued; but they guard against the lascivious behavior of women, and are persuaded that none of them preserve their fidelity to one man.

3 These men are despisers of riches, and so very communicative as raises our admiration. Nor is there any one to be found among them who hath more than another; for it is a law among them, that those who come to them must let what they have be common to the whole order—insomuch that among them all there is no appearance of poverty, or excess of riches, but every one's possessions are intermingled with every other's possessions; and so there is, as it were, one patrimony among all the brethren. They think that oil is a defilement; and if any one of them be anointed without his own approbation, it is wiped off his body; for they think to be sweaty is a good thing, as they do also to be clothed in white garments. They also have stewards appointed to take care of their common affairs, who every one of them have no separate business for any, but what is for the uses of them all. . . .

5 And as for their piety towards God, it is very extraordinary; for before sun-rising they speak not a word about profane matters, but put up certain prayers which they have received from their forefathers, as if they made a supplication for its rising. After this every one of them are sent away by their curators, to exercise some of those arts wherein they are skilled, in which they labor with great diligence till the fifth hour. After which they assemble themselves together again into one place; and when they have clothed themselves in white veils, they then bathe their bodies in cold water. And after this purification is over, they every one meet together in an apartment of their own, into which it is not permitted to any of another sect to enter; while they go, after a pure manner, into the dining-room, as into a certain holy temple, and quietly set themselves down; upon which the baker lays them loaves in order; the cook also brings a single plate of one sort of food, and sets it before every one of them; but a priest says grace before meat; and it is unlawful for any one to taste of the food before grace be said. The same priest, when he hath dined, says grace again after meat; and when they begin, and when they end, they praise God, as he that bestows their food upon them; after which they lay aside their [white] garments, and betake themselves to their labors again till the evening; then they return home to supper, after the same manner; and if there be any strangers there, they sit down with them. Nor is there ever any clamor or disturbance to pollute their house, but they give every one leave to speak in their turn; which silence thus kept in their house appears to foreigners like some tremendous mystery; the cause of which is that perpetual sobriety they exercise, and the same settled measure of meat and drink that is allotted them, and that such as is abundantly sufficient for them. . . .

11 For their doctrine is this: That bodies are corruptible, and that the matter they are made of is not permanent; but that the souls are immortal, and continue for ever; and that they come out of the most subtile air, and are united to their bodies as to prisons, into which they are drawn by a certain natural enticement; but that when they are set free from the bonds of the flesh, they then, as released from a long bondage, rejoice and mount upward. And this is like the opinions of the Greeks, that good souls have their habitations beyond the ocean, in a region that is neither oppressed with storms of rain or snow, or with intense heat, but that this place is such as is refreshed by the gentle breathing of a west wind, that is perpetually blowing from the ocean; while they allot to bad souls a dark and tempestuous den, full of neverceasing punishments. . . .

14 But then as to the two other orders at first mentioned, the Pharisees are those who are esteemed most skillful in the exact explication of their laws, and introduce the first sect. These ascribe all to fate [or providence], and to God, and yet allow, that to act what is right, or the contrary, is principally in the power of men, although fate does co-operate in every action. They say that all souls are incorruptible, but that the souls of good men only are removed into other bodies—but that the souls of bad men are subject to eternal punishment. But the Sadducees are those that compose the second order, and take away fate entirely, and suppose that God is not concerned in our doing or not doing what is evil; and they say, that to act what is good, or what is evil, is at men's own choice, and that the one or the other belongs so to every one, that they may act as they please. They also take away the belief of the immortal duration of the soul, and the punishments and rewards in Hades. Moreover, the Pharisees are friendly to one another, and are for the exercise of concord, and regard for the public; but the behavior of the Sadducees one towards another is in some degree wild, and their conversation with those that are of their own party is as barbarous as if they were strangers to them. And this is what I had to say concerning the philosophic sects among the Jews.

READING CRITICALLY

Is there any correspondence between the doctrines of the Essene sect and Christianity, which was also developing as a sect of Judaism in Josephus's time? In terms of their relations with others, both Jewish and non-Jewish, Essenes and Christians differed dramatically. How do they differ, and what do you think are the consequences of those differences?

READING 8.5

from Augustine's *Confessions*

Of all the Latin Church fathers, Augustine of Hippo was the most influential. His Confessions *are unique in the history of early Christianity because they represent the personal struggle of an individual to overcome his love of worldly pleasures and come, instead, to love God. The distinction he draws between the rewards of the physical appetites as opposed to those of spiritual knowledge, between the demands of the body and those of the soul, are fundamental to the development of Christian doctrine. In the first of the two passages excerpted below, the famous episode of "The Pear Tree" in Book 2, he describes what can only be called his darkest moment, when, in his sixteenth year, his stole a neighbor's pears. Later, in Book 8, still leading a dissolute life as a student but despairing of his lifestyle, he describes his conversion to Christianity in a garden near Carthage at the age of 33.*

from Book II:

There was a pear tree close to our own vineyard, heavily laden with fruit, which was not tempting either for its color or for its flavor. Late one night—having prolonged our games in the streets until then, as our bad habit was—a group of young scoundrels, and I among them, went to shake and rob this tree. We carried off a huge load of pears, not to eat ourselves, but to dump out to the hogs, after barely tasting some of them ourselves. Doing this pleased us all the more because it was forbidden. Such was my heart, O God, such was my heart—which thou didst pity even in that bottomless pit. Behold, now let my heart confess to thee what it was seeking there, when I was being gratuitously wanton, having no inducement to evil but the evil itself. It was foul, and I loved it. I loved my own undoing. I loved my error—not that for which I erred but the error itself. A depraved soul, falling away from security in thee to destruction in itself, seeking nothing from the shameful deed but shame itself.

from Book VIII:

The streams of my eyes gushed out. . . . And, not indeed in these words, but to this effect, I cried to thee: "And thou, O Lord, how long? How long, O Lord? Wilt thou be angry forever? . . . How long, how long? Tomorrow and tomorrow? Why not now? Why not this very hour make an end to my uncleanness?"

I was saying these things and weeping in the most bitter contrition of my heart, when suddenly I heard the voice of a boy or a girl I know not which—coming from the neighboring house, chanting over and over again, "Pick it up, read it; pick it up, read it." Immediately I ceased weeping and began most earnestly to think whether it was usual for children in some kind of game to sing such a song, but I could not remember ever having heard the like. So, damming the torrent of my tears, I got to my feet, for I could not but think that this was a divine command to open the Bible and read the first passage I should light upon. So I quickly returned to the bench where . . . I had put down the apostle's book when I had left there. I snatched it up, opened it, and in silence read the paragraph on which my eyes first fell: "Not in rioting and drunkenness, not in chambering and wantonness, not in strife and envying, but put on the Lord Jesus Christ, and make no provision for the flesh to fulfill the lusts thereof" [Romans 13:13]. I wanted to read no further, nor did I need to. For instantly, as the sentence ended, there was infused in my heart something like the light of full certainty and all the gloom of doubt vanished away.

READING CRITICALLY

What do you believe motivated Augustine to write his *Confessions*?

from Augustine's *The City of God*

The following passage is representative of Augustine's use of allegory in The City of God. *In allegory, meanings of an abstract or spiritual nature are revealed in material and concrete forms. Thus, here, Augustine sees Noah's ark as an allegorical figure for, first, the wooden cross upon which Christ was crucified, then the lives of the saints, and then the Church itself.*

Now God, as we know, enjoined the building of an ark upon Noah, a man who was righteous and according to the true testimony of Scripture, perfect in his generation [see Genesis 6:9], that is, perfect, not as the citizens of the City of God are to become in that immortal state where they will be made equal with the angels of God, but as they can be during their sojourn here on earth. In this ark he was to be rescued from the devastation of the flood with his family, that is, his wife, sons and daughters-in-law, as well as with the animals that came to him in the 10 ark at God's direction. We doubtless have here a symbolic representation of the City of God sojourning as an alien in this world, that is, of the church which wins salvation by virtue of the wood on which the mediator between God and men, the man Christ Jesus, was suspended.

The very measurements of the ark's length, height and breadth symbolize the human body, in the reality of which it was prophesied that Christ would come to mankind, as, in fact, he did come. For the length of the human body from top to toe is six times its breadth from one side to the other 20 and ten times its thickness measured on a side from back to belly. Thus if you measure a man lying on his back or face down, his length from head to foot is six times his breadth from right to left or from left to right and ten times his elevation from the ground. This is why the ark was made three hundred cubits in length, fifty in breadth and thirty in height. And as for the door that it received on its side, that surely is the wound that was made when the side of the crucified one was pierced by the spear. This is the way by which those who come to him enter, because from this opening 30 flowed the sacraments with which believers are initiated. Moreover, that order that it should be made of squared beams contains an allusion to the foursquare stability of saints' lives, for in whatever direction you turn a squared object, it will stand firm. In similar fashion, everything else mentioned in the construction of this ark symbolizes some aspect of the church. . . .

READING CRITICALLY

Augustine's allegory is based on the fact that both the ark and the cross were made of wood. How does he extend and expand on this analogy?

Ambrose's "Ancient Morning Hymn"

Ambrose was a Roman aristocrat, a generation older than Augustine, who became the bishop of Milan in 374, about 13 years before Augustine's conversion to Christianity in a garden near Carthage. A great mediator between different factions of the Church, he was also the first to compose hymns to be sung by the entire congregation. The simplicity of his diction and direct optimism embodied in his imagery go a long way toward accounting for the popularity of his hymns—to say nothing of their survival in the liturgy. In short, the crowds could both enjoy singing his verses and iden-tify with his vision.

O Splendor of God's glory bright,
O Thou who bringest light from light,
O Light of light, light's living spring,
O Day, all days illumining!

O Thou true Sun, on us Thy glance
Let fall in royal radiance;
The Spirit's sanctifying beam
Upon our earthly senses stream.

The Father, too, our prayers implore,
Father of glory evermore.   10
The Father of all grace and might,
To banish sin from our delight.

To guide whate'er we nobly do,
With love all envy to subdue,
To make ill-fortune turn to fair,
And give us grace our wrongs to bear.

Rejoicing may this day go hence,
Like virgin dawn our innocence,
Like fiery noon our faith appear,
Nor know the gloom of twilight clear.   20

Morn in her rosy car is borne;
Let him come forth, our perfect morn,
The Word in God the Father one,
The Father perfect in the Son.

All laud to God the Father be;
All praise, eternal Son, to Thee;
All glory, as is ever meet,
To God the holy Paraclete.[1]

READING CRITICALLY

Both Ambrose's hymn and the Egyptian *Akhenaten's Hymn to the Sun* (see Reading 3.3) are addressed to the sun. How do they otherwise compare?

[1] Holy Spirit; the Comforter

9 The Rise and Spread of Islam

A New Religion

THINKING AHEAD

What was the message of the Prophet Muhammad?

Why did Islam spread so rapidly?

How did Islam come to Africa and Spain?

What place do the arts hold in the Islamic world?

The Dome of the Rock (Fig. **9.1**) stands atop the Temple Mount in Jerusalem, on the site where, in Jewish tradition, Abraham prepared to sacrifice his son Isaac. The Jewish Temple of Solomon originally stood here, and the site is further associated—by Jews, Christians, and Muslims alike—with God's creation of Adam. The Second Temple of Jerusalem also stood on this spot until it was destroyed by Roman soldiers when they sacked the city in 70 CE to put down a Jewish revolt (see Fig. 6.21). Only the Wailing Wall remains, part of the original retaining wall for the platform supporting the Temple Mount and for Jews the most sacred site in Jerusalem. To this day, the plaza in front of the wall functions as an open-air synagogue where daily prayers are recited and other Jewish rituals are performed. On Tisha B'Av, the ninth day of the month of Av, which occurs either in July or August, a fast is held commemorating the destruction of the successive temples on this site, and people sit on the ground before the wall reciting the Book of Lamentations.

One of the earliest examples of Muslim architecture, built in the 680s, the Dome's ambulatory—its circular, colonnaded walkway—encloses a projecting rock that lies directly beneath its golden dome. By the sixteenth century, Islamic faithful claimed that the Prophet Muhammad ascended to heaven from this spot, on a winged horse named Buraq, but there is no evidence that this story was in circulation when the Dome was originally built. Others thought that it represents the ascendancy of Islam over Christianity in the Holy Land. Still others believed the rock is the center of the world, or that it could refer to the Temple of Solomon, the importance of which is fully acknowledged by Muslims, who consider Solomon a founding father of their own faith. All of this suggests that the Dome was meant to proselytize, or convert, both Jews and Christians to the Muslim faith.

The sanctity of this spot, then, at the heart of Jerusalem, is recognized equally by the three great faiths of the Western world—Judaism, Christianity, and Islam—but it is the rise of Islam that is the subject of this chapter, and if the Dome of the Rock is one of Islam's most venerated sites, its holiest city is Mecca, located 760 miles to the south, about 50 miles inland from the Red Sea in modern Saudi Arabia (Map **9.1**). Its natural spring originally made it an important stopping point for nomadic Arabs, known as Bedouins, who traded along caravan routes across the arid peninsula.

◀ **Fig. 9.1 The Dome of the Rock, Jerusalem. Late 680s–691.** The golden dome of the building, one of the earliest Muslim constructions, rises above a projecting rock that is surrounded by an ambulatory. The building's function remains unclear. It is not a mosque, although it is certainly some kind of religious memorial. Inscriptions from the Qur'an decorate its interior. These are the oldest excerpts from the text to have survived.

HEAR MORE Listen to an audio file of your chapter at **www.myartslab.com**

Until the seventh century CE, they worshiped more than one god. They stored images of those gods in a square structure in the center of the city that came to be known as the *Kaaba* [KAAH-buh], literally "cube" (Fig. 9.2). Scholars believe that the original Kaaba was linked to the astronomical year, containing an array of 360 idols, each associated with seasonal rituals and the passing of the days and months. Built with a bluish-gray stone from the hills surrounding Mecca, it is now usually covered with a black curtain. The Kaaba also held a sacred Black Stone, probably a meteorite, which reportedly "fell from heaven." Legend has it that when workers who had been rebuilding the Kaaba were ready to place the sacred stone inside, a quarrel broke out among the principal Arab tribes regarding who would have the privilege of laying the stone. Everyone agreed that the first passerby would do the honor. That passerby turned out to be the Muslim prophet Muhammad (ca. 570–632), who placed the stone on his cloak and then gave a corner of the cloak to the head of each tribe to carry into the building (Fig. 9.3). The story establishes Muhammad as a political as well as spiritual leader, and, perhaps more important, as a prophet capable of uniting the diverse elements of Arab culture.

Today, practitioners of the Muslim faith from all over the world face toward the Kaaba when they pray. They believe it is their place of origin, the site of the first "house of God," built at God's command by the biblical Abraham and his son Ismael, the ancestors of all Muslims, on the spot where, in Muslim tradition, Abraham prepared to sacrifice Ismael (not Isaac, as in the Jewish tradition, at the Dome of the Rock). Thus, walking around the Kaaba is a key ritual in the Muslim pilgrimage to Mecca, for the cube represents the physical center of the planet and the universe. It is the physical center of Muslim life, around which all things turn and to which all things in the universe are connected, symbolic of the cosmos itself. The Islamic transformation of Middle Eastern and Western culture, which began in Mecca in the seventh century and spread outward from that city, is the subject of this chapter.

Map 9.1 The Muslim world. ca. 700 CE.

Fig. 9.2 The Kaaba, center of the Haram Mosque, Mecca, Saudi Arabia. Traditionally, all Muslims must make a pilgrimage to Mecca, in Syria, at least once in their lives. Once there, they must walk around the Kaaba seven times. The Kaaba has been rebuilt many times over the years, the last time in 1631.

آرامگاه دجل ثم وضع والاساس علی اساس ابراهیم واسمعیل الی اساس ابرهیم وهم علیهم السلم وقل انهم ماوصلوا علیها السلم

Fig. 9.3 *Muhammad Placing the Black Stone on His Cloak,* from Rashid al-Din's *Jami al-Tawarikh (Universal History),* copied and illustrated at Tabriz, Iran. 1315. 5¹⁄₈″ × 10¹⁄₄″. University Library, Edinburgh. Notice that the figures in back of the central section are lifting a veil that covers the Kaaba. Today, the veil, the meaning of which is obscure, is black, with quotations from the Qur'an woven across it in gold thread.

Just as Muslims physically turn toward Mecca when they pray, they turn their thoughts toward the teachings of their prophet Muhammad. Wherever Muslims found themselves—and Islam rapidly spread across the Middle East, North Africa, and even into Spain—they built places of worship modeled on Muhammad's home in Medina, the city on the Arabian peninsula where Muhammad moved when he was driven from Mecca (see Map 9.1). And, as individuals, they submitted themselves to the authority of their faith, so much so that the Muslim religion quickly became synonymous with the Islamic state itself. Because Arabic, as the language of divine revelation, was believed to have a sacred nature, writing too was revered, and **calligraphy** developed into the preeminent form of visual art in Islam, creating an almost wholly abstract standard of beauty devoid of figurative elements. As a faith that considered sensory satisfaction, love, luxury, sensuality, and enjoyment to be manifestations of divine grace, the Muslim religion enveloped Islamic culture, its art, music, and literature, in the pursuit of beauty.

THE PROPHET MUHAMMAD

Born in Mecca in about 570 to a prominent family that traced its ancestry back to Ismael, son of Abraham, Muhammad was orphaned at age six and received little formal education. He worked in the desert caravan trade, first as a camel driver for his uncle, and then, after marry-ing a wealthy widow 15 years his senior, as head of his wife's flourishing caravan firm. At the age of 40, in 610, he heard a voice in Arabic—the Archangel Gabriel's, as the story goes—urging him, "Recite!" He responded, "What shall I recite?" And for the next 22 years, he claimed to receive messages, or "recitations," from God through the agency of Gabriel. These he memorized and dictated to scribes, who collected them to form the scriptures of Islam, the **Qur'an** [kuh-RAN] (or Koran), which means "recitations." Muhammad also claimed that Gabriel commanded him to declare himself the "Seal of the Prophets," that is, the messenger of the one and only Allah (the Arab word for God) and the final prophet in a series of prophets extending from Abraham and Moses to Jesus.

At the core of Muhammad's revelations is the concept of submission to God—the word *Islam,* in fact, means "submission" or "surrender." God, or Allah, is all—all-powerful, all-seeing, all-merciful. Because the universe is his creation, it is necessarily good and beautiful, and the natural world reflects Allah's own goodness and beauty. To immerse oneself in nature is thus to be at one with God. But the most beautiful creation of Allah is humankind, which God made in his own image. Like Christians, Muslims believe that human beings possess immortal souls and that they can live eternally in heaven if they surrender to Allah and accept him as the one and only God.

Muslims, or practitioners of Islam, dedicate themselves to the "five pillars" of the religion:

1. **Witness (Shahadah):** The repetition of the *shahadah* [sha-HAH-dah], or "witness," which consists of a single sentence, "There is no God but Allah; Muhammad is the messenger of Allah."
2. **Prayer (Salat):** The practice of daily prayer, recited facing Mecca, five times each day, at dawn, midday, mid-afternoon, sunset, and nightfall, and the additional requirement for all men to gather for a noon prayer and sermon on Fridays.
3. **Alms (Zakat):** The habit of giving alms to the poor and needy, consisting of at least one-fortieth of a Muslim's assets and income.
4. **Fasting (Sawm):** During the lunar month of Ramadan (which, over a 33-year period, will occur in every season of the year), the ritual obligation to fast by abstaining from food, drink, medicine, tobacco, and sexual intercourse from sunrise to sundown each day.
5. **Pilgrimage (Hajj):** At least once in every Muslim's life, in the twelfth month of the Muslim calendar, the undertaking of a pilgrimage to Mecca.

The five pillars are supported by the teachings of the Qur'an, which, slightly shorter than the New Testament, consists of 114 *surahs* [SOO-rahs], or chapters, each numbered but more commonly referred to by their titles. Each begins, as do most Muslim texts, with the **bismillah** [bees-mee-LAH], a sacred invocation that can be translated "In the name of Allah, the Beneficent, Ever-Merciful" (see *Closer Look*, pages 290–291). When, after Muhammad's death in 632, the Qur'an's text was established in its definitive form, the 114 *surahs* were arranged from the longest to the shortest. Thus, the first *surah* contains 287 *ayas* [ay-YAS], or verses, while the last consists of only 3. The mandatory ritual prayer (*salat*) [sah-LAAT] that is performed five times a day consists of verses from *Surahs* 2, 4, and 17.

The Qur'an

The Qur'an is a work of poetry, and in pre-Islamic Arabia, poetry was the highest form of art. Poets recited their own works, or professional reciters performed the works of others. The beauty of the poetry inspired the creation of many beautiful editions of the work (Fig. **9.4**) and, as we shall see, the art of calligraphy. But unfortunately, the beautiful, melodic qualities of the Arabic language are completely lost in translation, a fact that has helped to inspire generations of non-Arabic-speaking Muslims to learn the language. Almost all Muslims regularly read the Qur'an in Arabic, and many have memorized it completely. Translations of the Qur'an are problematic on another, more important level. Since the Qur'an is believed to be the direct word of God, it cannot be modified, let alone translated—a translation of the Qur'an is no longer the Qur'an. Nevertheless, something of the power of the poem's imagery can be understood

Fig. 9.4 Left page of double frontispiece to volume VII of the Qur'an of Baybars Jashnagir, from Egypt. 1304–06. Illuminated manuscript, 18½" × 12½". British Library, London. The most elaborate Qur'ans, such as this one, were financed by endowments created by wealthy individuals in support of a mosque and attendant buildings.

in translation. Consider a passage describing paradise from the *Surah* 76, known as "Time" (**Reading 9.1a**):

READING 9.1a

from the Qur'an, *Surah 76*

76.11 Therefore Allah will guard them from the evil of that day and cause them to meet with ease and happiness;

76.12 And reward them, because they were patient, with garden and silk,

76.13 Reclining therein on raised couches, they shall find therein neither (the severe heat of) the sun nor intense cold.

76.14 And close down upon them (shall be) its shadows, and its fruits shall be made near (to them), being easy to reach.

76.15 And there shall be made to go round about them vessels of silver and goblets which are of glass,

76.16 (Transparent as) glass, made of silver; they have measured them according to a measure.

76.17 And they shall be made to drink therein a cup the admixture of which shall be ginger,

76.18 (Of) a fountain therein which is named Salsabil [sal-sa-BEEL].

76.19 And round about them shall go youths never altering in age; when you see them you will think them to be scattered pearls.

76.20 And when you see there, you shall see blessings and a great kingdom.

76.21 Upon them shall be garments of fine green silk and thick silk interwoven with gold, and they shall be adorned with bracelets of silver, and their Lord shall make them drink a pure drink.

76.22 Surely this is a reward for you, and your striving shall be recompensed.

This vision of paradise addresses all the senses—touch, taste, and smell (the fruit so "easy to reach," the drink of ginger), sight ("when you see there, you shall see blessings"), and sound (in the very melody of the verse itself). All is transformed into riches. Even the young people in attendance will appear to be "scattered pearls."

The promise of heaven, so richly described here, is balanced by a moral dimension reminiscent of both the Old and New Testaments of the Christian Bible. Note particularly the call for believers to "let not hatred of a people incite you not to act equitably." Other parts of the Qur'an explicitly appeal to Jews and Christians to accept the teachings of Islam (**Reading 9.1b**):

READING 9.1b

from the Qur'an, *Surah* 5

5.8 O you who believe! Be upright for Allah, bearers of witness with justice, and let not hatred of a people incite you not to act equitably; act equitably, that is nearer to piety, and be careful of (your duty to) Allah; surely Allah is Aware of what you do.

5.9 Allah has promised to those who believe and do good deeds (that) they shall have forgiveness and a mighty reward. . . .

5.68 Say: O followers of the Book! . . .

5.69 Surely those who believe and those who are Jews and the Sabians and the Christians whoever believes in Allah and the last day and does good—they shall have no fear nor shall they grieve. . . .

5.75 The Messiah,[1] son of Marium, is but an apostle; apostles before him have indeed passed away; and his mother was a truthful woman; they both used to eat food. See how we make the communications clear to them, then behold, how they are turned away.

[1]**Messiah:** Jesus.

In the context of the present-day political climate in the Middle East, it is worth remembering that such moral positioning—and apparent tolerance—is fundamental to the Islamic tradition. However, like both Christianity and Judaism, the Qur'an also contains less tolerant messages. In the *surah* "Muhammad," the Prophet calls for his followers to "smite the necks" of those "who disbelieve" (for excerpts from the *surah*, see **Reading 9.1,** page 311). In other words, as is the case with the Bible, what one takes from the Qur'an depends on what one chooses to emphasize.

The Hadith

In addition to the Qur'an, another important source of Islamic tradition is the **hadith** [ha-DEET], meaning "narrative" or "report," which consists of sayings of Muhammad and anecdotes about his life. The story of Muhammad and the Black Rock of the Kaaba comes from the hadith (**Reading 9.2**).

The hadith literature was handed down orally, as was common in Arab society until about 100 years after Muhammad's death, when followers began to write the sayings down.

READING 9.2

from the Hadith

"Actions are but by intention and every man shall have but that which he intended."

"None of you [truly] believes until he wishes for his brother what he wishes for himself."

"Get to know Allah in prosperity and He will know you in adversity. Know that what has passed you by was not going to befall you; and that what has befallen you was not going to pass you by. And know that victory comes with patience, relief with affliction, and ease with hardship."

"If you feel no shame, then do as you wish."

"Everyone starts his day and is a vendor of his soul, either freeing it or bringing about its ruin."

"O My servants, it is but your deeds that I reckon up for you and then recompense you for, so let him who finds good [i.e., in the hereafter] praise Allah, and let him who finds other than that blame no one but himself."

"Renounce the world and Allah will love you, and renounce what people possess and people will love you."

The *Hijra* and Muslim Practice

In 622, Muhammad was forced to flee Mecca when its polytheistic leadership became irritated at his insistence on the worship of only one God. In a journey known as the **hijra** [HIJ-rah] (or *hegira*, "emigration"), he and his followers fled to the oasis of Yathrib [YA-trub], 200 miles north, which they renamed al-Medina, meaning "the city of the Prophet." Here Muhammad created a community based not on kinship, the traditional basis of Arab society, but on common

LEARN MORE Gain insight from a primary source from the Qur'an at **www.myartslab.com**

The *bismillah* consists of the phrase "In the name of Allah, the Beneficent, Ever-Merciful." Every pious Muslim begins any statement or activity with it, and it inaugurates each chapter of the Qur'an. For Arab calligraphers, to write the *bismillah* in as beautiful a form as possible brings the scribe forgiveness for sins, and the phrase appears in the Islamic world in many different forms—even in the shape of a parrot. From the time that Abd al-Malik took control of the Umayyad family in 692, it became an important part of architectural practice as well. It first appears in written form on a band of mosaic script around the interior walls and above the entrance of Dome of the Rock in Jerusalem (see Fig. 9.1). On the next page, the fourteenth-century ceramic tile decoration on a mihrab niche, a design feature in all Islamic mosques commemorating the spot at Medina where Mohammad planted his lance to indicate the direction in which people should pray, gives some indication of how the calligraphic script could blend with floral motifs and geometric designs to create an elaborate ornamental surface.

Ahmed Karahisari. Calligraphic Qur'an frontispiece, from Istanbul. ca. 1550. Ink, gold, and color on paper, 19⅔" × 13¾". Museum of Turkish and Islamic Art, Istanbul. Karahisari (1469–1560) was the most famous calligrapher of his day. He placed the *bismillah* in black script between two square scripts. On top, the words "Praise God" are repeated four times. The bottom block contains the entire text of *Surah* 112 of the Qur'an: "Say: 'He is Allah, the only one [that is, indivisible]. Allah, the eternally Besought of all! He begetteth not nor was begotten. And there is none comparable to Him.'"

The importance of writing in spreading the new faith suggests one reason that Muslim calligraphers were held in such high esteem. Most Westerners think of handwriting as a form of self-expression. But the Muslim calligrapher's style has a much more important role to play: to attract the attention of the reader, eliciting admiration for the beauty of the script, and in turn reflecting the beauty of the Muslim faith. The Muslim calligrapher is considered the medium through which Allah expresses himself. The more beautiful the calligraphic script, the more fully Allah's beauty is realized. Hence, over time, many styles of elaborate cursive script developed, as illustrated on the next page. At the same time, everyday affairs required the development of simpler, less artistic forms, and the *riq'a* script is an example.

Mastering the art of calligraphy was, in this sense, a form of prayer, and it was practiced with total dedication. A famous story about an incident that happened in the city of Tabriz, in northern Iran, during the great earthquake of 1776–77, illustrates this. The quake struck in the middle of the night and buried many in the rubble. Survivors stumbled through the

Bismillah in the form of a parrot, from Iran. 1834–35. Ink on paper under wax coating. Cincinnati Art Museum, Franny Bryce Lehmer Fund. 1977.65. The parrot reads right to left, beginning over the large dot beneath its tail. The word *Allah* appears at the back of its head. The parrot is to humankind as humankind is to Allah. That is, it mimics human language without understanding it, just as humans recite the words of Allah without fully understanding them.

SEE MORE For a Closer Look at the *bismillah* in the Dome of the Rock, go to **www.myartslab.com**

The *Bismillah* and the Art of Calligraphy

Naskh

Thuluth

Muhaqqaq

Nastaliq

© M. Sakkal 2010

Riq'a

Five examples of the *bismillah* in different Islamic cursive scripts. *Naskh*, literally "copying," was developed in the tenth century, and refined into a fine art form in Turkey in the sixteenth century. *Thuluth* evolved over the centuries into a more impressive, stately calligraphic style, often used for titles or epigrams rather than lengthy texts, and often found in many variations on architectural monuments, as well as on glass, metalwork, textiles, and wood. It is the script employed on the mihrab niche below. *Muhaqqaq* emerged in the eleventh century in the art of making manuscripts of the Qur'an. *Nastaliq* developed in Iran in the fourteenth and fifteenth centuries. It is the most fluid and expressive of the scripts presented here, and is used extensively in copying romantic and mystical epics in Persian. *Riq'a*, the simpler style of everyday writing, is very economical and easy to write.

debris looking for signs of life. In the basement of a ruined house, rescuers discovered a man sitting on the floor absolutely absorbed in his work. He did not respond to their yells for him to hurry out before an aftershock buried him. Finally, he looked up and complained that they were disturbing him. They told him that thousands had been killed in an earthquake, and if he did not hurry up, he would be next. "What is all that to me?" he replied. "After many thousands of attempts I have finally made a perfect 'waw' [meaning 'and']." He showed them the letter, indeed a very difficult letter to make. "Such a perfect letter," he exclaimed, "is worth more than the whole city!"

Something to Think About . . .

How might modern technologies—from type to the Internet—pose a challenge to the calligraphic tradition in Islam?

Mihrab niche, Isfahan, Iran. ca. 1354–55. Mosaic of polychrome-glazed cut tiles on fritware body; set into plaster, 135 1/16" × 113 11/16". ©1982 The Metropolitan Museum of Art/Art Resource, NY. Harris Brisbane Dick Fund, 1939. 39.20. The *bismillah* is contained in the rectangle in the center of the niche. The verses surrounding the niche are from the Qur'an, *Surah* 9: 18–22, beginning with this exhortation: "The mosques of Allah shall be visited and maintained by such as believe in Allah."

Fig. 9.5 The Mosque of al-Mutawakkil, Samarra, Iraq. 848–52. The huge dimensions of the mosque can be accounted for by the fact that all worshipers must face the same direction—that is, toward Mecca—arranging themselves in parallel lines to kneel prostrate. Thus, each worshiper requires a good deal of individual space. As early as 670, many mosques were large enough to accommodate as many as 3,000 worshipers.

submission to the will of God. Such submission did not need to be entirely voluntary. Muslims were obligated to pursue the spread of their religion, and they did so by means of the **jihad** [jee-HAAD], the impassioned religious struggle that could take either of two forms: a lesser form, holy war; or a greater form, self-control over the baser human appetites. In order to enforce submission, Muhammad raised an army of some 10,000 men and returned to Mecca, conquering the city and destroying the idols in the Kaaba, with the exception of the Black Stone. Confronted by a Muslim army defined by both piety and zealotry, soon the entire western region of Arabia came under Muslim sway, and by the time of Muhammad's death even Mecca had submitted.

The community of all Muslims would come to be known as the *Umma* [OOM-mah]. It represented such a departure from tradition that its creation required a new calendar. Based on lunar cycles, the Muslim year is about 11 days shorter than the Christian year, resulting in a difference of about three years per century. The calendar began in 622 CE. Thus, in the year 2007, the Muslims celebrated the start of their year 1428.

The Mosque At Medina, Muhammad built a house that surrounded a large, open courtyard, which served as a community gathering place. There the men of the community would gather on Fridays to pray and listen to a sermon delivered by Muhammad. It thus inspired the *masjid* [mahs-JEED], the Arabic word for **mosque**, or "place of prostration." On the north and south ends of the courtyard,

covered porches supported by palm tree trunks and roofed by thatched palm fronds protected the community from the hot Arabian sun. This many-columned covered area, known as a **hypostyle** space (from the Greek *hupostulos* [hye-pos-TOO-lus], "resting upon pillars"), would later become a feature of many Muslim mosques. An important feature was the **qibla** [KIB-lah], a wall that indicated the direction of Mecca. On this wall were both the **minbar** [MIN-bur], or stepped pulpit for the preacher, and the **mihrab** [MEER-uhb], a niche commemorating the spot at Medina where Muhammad planted his lance to indicate the direction in which people should pray.

The Prophet's Mosque in Medina has been rebuilt so many times that its original character has long since been lost. But at Samarra, some 60 miles north of Baghdad on the Tigris River in modern Iraq, the remnants of the Mosque of al-Mutawakkil [al moo-ta-WAK-kul], built in the mid-ninth century, as well as a similar floorplan from a relatively contemporary mosque in Muslim Spain, show how large the mosque would soon develop (Figs. **9.5** and **9.6**). Built between 848 and 852, the mosque measures 800 by 500 feet, an area of over 10 acres. For centuries, it was the largest mosque in the world. It demonstrates the extraordinary popularity of the Muslim religion, since its central courtyard and hypostyle spaces would have been filled with many thousands of worshipers each Friday. About half the site was covered with a wooden roof on 464 supports, under which worshipers could pray. Although in a state of

Hypostyle mosque
Great Mosque, Córdoba, Spain,
after extension by
al-Hakam II

Fig. 9.6 Plan of the Great Mosque, Córdoba, Spain. After its extension ca. 961–976. See Fig. 9.8.

ruin today, the walls of the mosque were originally richly decorated with glass mosaic and marble panels.

The most remarkable feature of the surviving mosque at Samarra is the spiral tower opposite the mihrab. Some speculate that this tower, originally 165 feet tall, is a minaret, the tower from which the *muezzin* [moo-EZ-un] (crier) calls the faithful to prayer. But none of the earliest mosques had minarets, and although the call to prayer has become standard Muslim practice, even the earliest minarets may have been modeled on lighthouses (the root of *minaret* is *nur* [NOOR], meaning "light"), serving as sentinels to guide the faithful across the desert to the mosque. Others theorize that the tower was inspired by the ziggurats of ancient Mesopotamia (see Fig. 2.1).

Women in Islam Although Muslim practice today varies widely, in Muhammad's time, women were welcome in the mosque. In the Qur'an, Muhammad teaches that women and men are equal partners: "The faithful men and the faithful women are protecting friends for each other" (*Surah* 9:7). The husband's honor becomes an integral part of his wife's honor, and vice versa. They share equally in each other's prosperity and adversity. But Muhammad further allowed for Muslim men to have up to four wives, provided that they treated all justly and gave each equal attention. (Polygamy was widely practiced in the Arab world at the time, and marrying the widow of a deceased comrade, for instance, was understood to be an act of protective charity.) Muhammad himself—and subsequently other leaders as well—was exempt from the four-wife limitation. Although he had only one wife for 28 years, after she died when he was 53, he married at least 10 other women. The Qur'an describes the wives of Muhammad—and by extension, the wives of all Muslim men—as "Mothers of the Faithful" whose duty was the education of the *Umma*'s children. They helped them along their spiritual path, transmitting and explaining the teaching of Muhammad in all spheres of life.

One of the most discussed and most controversial aspects of Muslim faith (even among Muslims) is the **hajib** [hih-JAHB], literally "curtain," the requirement that women be covered or veiled. Its origins can be traced to

Islam's Jewish heritage and the principle of *tzenuit* [dzen-WEET], which in Hebrew means "modesty" in both dress and behavior and which requires, among other strictures, that all married women cover their hair whenever non-family members are present. Islamic covering ranges from a simple scarf covering the hair to the **chador** [CHA-dohr], which covers the wearer from head to toe, leaving only her hands and her face (or part of her face) exposed. This full covering is currently popular, especially in Iran. Interestingly, the Qur'an is not explicit about the covering. Women are advised to dress in a way that enables them to avoid harassment by not drawing attention to their beauty, or *zinat* [ZEE-nat], a word that means both physical beauty and material adornment in Arabic. The basic message and instruction expressed in the Qur'an is for Muslims to act modestly and dress modestly, a rule that applies to men and women.

Both men and women are entitled to equal treatment before the law, and justice is considered to be genderless. Both have the right to have disputes settled by an arbiter of *shari'a* [sha-REE-ah], the divine law. In the manuscript page showing a husband complaining about his wife before a state-appointed judge, or *qadi* (Fig. 9.7) [QAH-dee], the wife,

Fig. 9.7 *A Qadi Sits in Judgment,* Baghdad. 1327. 14½″ × 11″. Illuminated manuscript. Bibliothèque Nationale, Paris. The women wear the *hajib,* in this instance, a full-length scarf.

accompanied by two other women who serve as witnesses, points an accusing finger at her husband. In such disputes, the first duty of the *qadi* is to reconcile the couple and avoid divorce, which, though legal in Islam, is discouraged. But all in all, the *shari'a* regulated gender relations in ways that favored males. It defined marriage as a reciprocal relationship in which a man owed his wife material support, and a wife owed her husband unwavering obedience. It asserted the male right of polygamy and outlined the terms in which males were to treat their multiple wives equally. A man could unilaterally repudiate a wife, but a woman could only bargain with her husband to end a marriage. And the *shari'a* affirmed the patrilineal structure of Muslim society by granting mothers only temporary custody of their children after the termination of a marriage, giving ultimate custody to the father or father's family.

Many modern scholars see the *shari'a* as a social revolution providing new rights and security for women in the cultures of the Middle East. But others regard the rules and regulations of the *shari'a* as a stifling suppression of the marriage practices of pre-Islamic Arab society, which was far less patriarchal. Traditional Arab society provided, among other things, for unilateral divorce by women and a woman's right to remain in her own clan and keep her children after divorce. It seems clear as well, that as Islam spread across the Middle East in the eighth and ninth centuries, the *shari'a* was adapted to and modified by local customs and practices. A clear example is the *shari'a*'s stated punishment for adultery. The Qur'an ordains that

adulterers be given 100 lashes. But the standard punishment outlined in the *shari'a* by the early ninth century is death by stoning, justified by a hadith attributed to the prophet but probably originating in pre-Islamic tribal practices.

THE SPREAD OF ISLAM

Following the death of the Prophet in 632, the **caliphs** [KAY-lifs], or successors to Muhammad, assumed political and religious authority, and Islam spread with a rapidity that is almost unimaginable (Map **9.2**). Damascus fell to the caliphs in 634, Persia in 636, Jerusalem in 638, and Egypt in 640. By 710, all of North Africa and Spain were under Muslim rule.

The speed of the conquest can be partially accounted for by the fact that the Byzantine and Persian empires were exhausted by a long war. Soon after the Byzantine emperor Heraclius [heh-RAK-lius] (r. 610–40) captured Egypt, Palestine, Syria, and Asia Minor from the Persians, Muslim armies struck, driving the Byzantine armies out of their newly acquired territories and overrunning most of the Persian Empire as well. Most of the peoples in these territories, although Christian, were of the same linguistic and ethnic background as their new Muslim conquerors. Furthermore, the brand of Greek Orthodox Christianity that the Byzantine rulers had imposed on them was far too conservative for many. From Persia to Egypt, many peoples accepted their Muslim conquerors as preferable to the Byzantine rulers who had preceded them.

Map 9.2 The expansion of Islam to 850.

The successes of Islam must also be attributed to its appeal both as a religion and as a form of social organization. It denied neither Judaism nor Christianity, but merely superseded them. As opposed to the Jewish faith, which was founded on a common ethnic identity, Islam opened its arms to any and all comers—a feature it shared with Christianity. But unlike Christianity, it did not draw any special distinction between the clergy and the laity. It brought people together in the mosque, which served as a community meetinghouse, courthouse, council chamber, military complex, and administrative center. Traders naturally migrated to it, as did poets, artists, and scholars. In fact, the mosque was closer in function to the classical agora than to the Christian tabernacle. The sense of community that the mosque inspired played a central role in the spread of Islam.

By the eleventh century, *madrasas* [mud-RAD-sas], or teaching colleges, were attached to the mosques, and mosques became centers of learning as well. Here students studied the Qur'an, the hadith, and Islamic law, as well as mathematics, poetry, and astronomy. The madrasas eventually contributed to the rise of an intellectual elite, the *ulama* [OO-la-mah] (people possessing "correct knowledge"), a group that functioned more or less in the manner of Christian priests or Jewish rabbis. Yet any man of great religious learning could serve as an *alim* [AA-lum] (the singular form of *ulama*), and *ulama* had the singular role of overseeing the rulers of Islam, guaranteeing that they followed the letter of the law as stated in the Qur'an.

Works of the Umayyad Caliphs: The Great Mosque of Damascus

If, in the Muslim world, Mecca was the center of culture, mosques sprang up everywhere as Islam extended its reach. One of the earliest was in Damascus (Fig. 9.8). Originally, the Muslim community in Damascus shared the site with the Christian community, who worshiped in a Byzantine church enclosed inside a walled compound. But by 705, the Muslim community had grown so large that radical steps had to be taken to accommodate it. The Byzantine church was torn down, leaving a large courtyard, and the compound walls were transformed into the walls of the mosque. A large prayer hall was constructed against the *qibla* wall and decorated with an elaborate facade that faced into the courtyard, while the street side of the mosque was left relatively plain.

The Great Mosque of Damascus was the work of the Umayyad [oo-MAH-yahd] caliphs, a Meccan family who were relatives of the Prophet. The first of the Umayyad family to come to power was Ali, the Prophet's cousin, son-in-law, and first con-

vert to Islam. In 661, a rival faction that opposed Ali's rise to power based solely on his familial connections assassinated him. The leader of the *Umma*, they argued, should simply be the best Muslim, whomever that might be. (This division exists to this day. Those who believe that only descendants of Ali should rule are known as Shiites, and they live largely in Iran and Iraq. A more moderate group, known as Sunnis, who today represent the vast majority of Muslims, believe that religious leaders should be chosen by the faithful. These two groups continue to vie for power in modern-day Islam, especially in Iraq. A more conservative group, the Kharijites [KHA-ree-jytes], who originally supported the assassination of Ali on grounds of his moral weakness, still survives in Oman and North Africa.)

After Ali's assassination, the Umayyad family briefly fell from power until Abd al-Malik [ubd al MAH-luk] (r. 685–705) subdued the family's adversaries in 692. His son, al-Walid [al wah-LEED] (r. 705–715), was responsible for the construction and decoration of the Great Mosque in Damascus. One large section of the original interior decoration survives—a glass mosaic landscape in the covered walkway surrounding the courtyard. The mosaics were probably the work of Christian Byzantine artisans brought to Damascus by al-Walid. Rising in improbable scale above the walkway is an expanse of colonnaded pavilions, towering trees, and arched

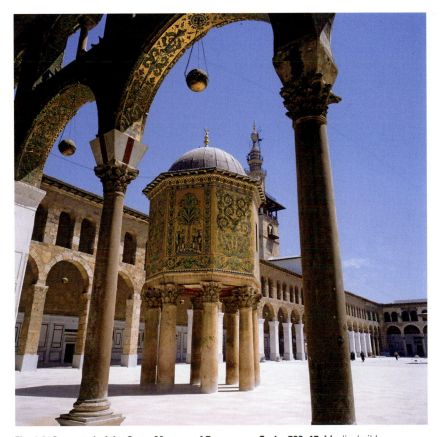

Fig. 9.8 Courtyard of the Great Mosque of Damascus, Syria. 706–15. Muslim builders may have considered the site of this mosque to possess mystical powers. The Byzantine church that had stood here was dedicated to John the Baptist. It had supplanted a Roman temple of Jupiter, which had earlier supplanted a temple dedicated to Haddad, the ancient Ammonite storm god.

bridges (Fig. **9.9**). It has been suggested that this is the Paradise promised by the Prophet in *Surah* 76:14 of the Qur'an (see Reading 9.1a, page 288), but it may be, instead, that this landscape was designed as simply an attractive decorative addition.

Images in Muslim Art

It is worth noting that human figures are notably absent in the Great Mosque's mosaic decoration. Neither are there any animals. In fact, Muslim religious architecture is so notably free of figurative decoration that many people, even some Muslims, assume that representations of "living beings" are forbidden in Islam. As we saw in Chapter 8, the Byzantine emperor Leo III attributed the successes of the Muslim armies to their ban on human figures in their mosques. The following admonition from the Qur'an (5:92) is often cited by Muslims who worry about the role of image-making in Muslim art and decoration: "O believers, wine and arrow-shuffling idols and divining arrows are an abomination, / some of Satan's work; then avoid it." But, it can be argued, "idols" here refers to pagan idols of the kind the Prophet eliminated from the Kaaba in Mecca. Also, at the time, Muhammad had allowed a painting of Mary and the infant Jesus to remain in the building. The hadiths, however, also supported those who opposed image-making. There the Prophet is reported to have warned, "An angel will not enter a house where there is a dog or a painting." Likewise, the Prophet claimed that "those who make these pictures will be punished on the Day of Judgment by being told: Make alive what you have created."

Some religious scholars believed that the ban on representation applied only to "living" things. Thus, the depiction of Paradise, as on the walls of the Great Mosque of Damascus, was acceptable, because Paradise is "beyond the living." Such thinking would also lead the Muslim owner of a Persian miniature representing a prince feasting in the countryside to erase the heads of all those depicted (Fig. **9.10**). Such an act is closely related to Byzantine iconoclasm, as no one could presume to think that figures without heads could possibly be "alive." In fact, as we will see, Muslim artists in Persia took great delight in illustrating literary texts, creating scene after scene depicting people in various forms of action, including lovemaking. Their freedom to do so is partly explained by their distance from more conservative brands of Arabian Islam, but also by their belief that they were not illustrating "living beings" so much as fictive characters.

Whatever an individual Muslim's feelings about image-making might be, all Muslims recognized that it posed a problem. The practical solution to the problem was to decorate without images, and this was especially true for the decoration of both the Qur'an and religious architecture.

Fig. 9.9 Detail of mosaic decoration, Great Mosque of Damascus. 715. The decorative scheme of such panels reflects Byzantine influence, as well as the Roman love of landscape mosaic.

At the heart of Islamic culture was the word, in the form of the recitations that make up the Qur'an. In fact, those who transcribed the Qur'an enjoyed a status higher than that of artists and architects and at least equal to that of poets, whose largely oral works had, from pre-Islamic times, been considered the highest form of art. It is also important to remember that the Qur'an is itself a work of oral poetry.

ISLAM IN AFRICA AND SPAIN

Scholars once believed that the rapid expansion of Islam was entirely due to the determination of the faithful to convert new followers to the faith, but overpopulation of the Arabian peninsula probably also played a role. If faith offered the excuse, the practical result of Islamic expansion was the acquisition of new territories and the wealth they brought with them.

After gaining control of virtually all of the Middle East, the Arabic Muslim armies moved into North Africa in 639. After gaining control of the port of Alexandria, they launched a navy that seized Cyprus and Rhodes and began attacking Italy and Sicily. They moved across North Africa and took Carthage in 698, defeating the native Berber tribes. In 711, Muslim armies, under the command of a freed Berber slave, Tariq [TAH-ruk], crossed into Spain at the Strait of Gibraltar (*Gibraltar* is a corruption of the Arabic words

Fig. 9.10 Page from a copy of Nezami's *Khamseh* (the "Quintet"), illustrating a princely country feast, from Persia (modern Iran). 1574–75. Illuminated manuscript, 9¾" × 6". India Office, London. Nezami's poem, written in the twelfth century, consists of five romantic epics in 30,000 couplets. It became one of the most widely illustrated poems in Persian literature.

meaning "Rock of Tariq") and moved quickly northward, deep into France. They were finally defeated in 732 at the Battle of Poitiers, also known as the Battle of Tours, by the king of the Franks, Charles Martel, and pushed back south of the Pyrenees. In the succeeding centuries, most of Europe became increasingly united in its opposition to Islam. This resulted in a series of military crusades to free the Holy Land, and Jerusalem in particular, of Muslim influence (discussed in Chapter 10). However, the Arabs maintained a dominant presence in Spain, particularly in the southern region of Andalusia [an-duh-LOO-zhee-uh] (*al-Andalus* [al AN-da-loos], in Arabic). There Muslim culture flourished until Christian armies finally expelled the Muslims in 1492, the same year that Columbus set sail for America.

Islamic Africa

The Muslim impact on the culture of North Africa cannot be overstated. Beginning in about 750, not long after

Muslim armies had conquered most of North Africa, Muslim traders, following the trade routes created by the Saharan Berber peoples, began trading for salt, copper, dates, and especially gold with the sub-Saharan peoples of the Niger [NY-jur] River drainage. Gradually they came to dominate the trans-Saharan trade routes (Map 9.3), and Islam became the dominant faith of West Africa. By the ninth century, a number of African states existed in the broad savanna south of the Sahara Desert known as the Sudan [soo-DAN] (which literally means "land of the blacks"). These states seemed to have formed in response to the prospects of trade with the Muslim and Arab world. Ghana [GAHN-uh], which means "war chief," is an early example, and its name suggests that a single chieftain, and later his family, exerted control over the material goods of the region, including gold, salt, ivory, iron, and particularly slaves. Muhammad accepted slavery as the just spoils of war, although no Muslim was ever to enslave another Muslim. Between the ninth and twelfth centuries, the slave trade grew from 300,000 to over a million, and it was so lucrative that the peoples of the Sudan, all eager to enslave each other for profit, fought each other. (There is some reason to believe that many African converts to Islam were initially attracted to the religion as a way to avoid becoming slaves, since the faithful were exempt from servitude.) Finally, the empire of the Mali [MAH-lee] people subsumed Ghana under the leadership of the warrior-king Sunjata [soon-JAH-tuh] (r. 1230–55) and gained control of the great trade routes north out of the savanna, through Timbuktu, the leading trading center of the era.

In 1312, Mansa Moussa [MAHN-sah MOO-sah] (*mansa* is the equivalent of the term "emperor") came to the Malian throne. A devout Muslim, he built magnificent mosques throughout his empire, including the Djingareyber [jin-gah-REY-bur] Mosque in Timbuktu [tim-BUK-too]

Map 9.3 The Trans-Saharan trade routes. ca. 1350. The shaded portion indicates the empire of Mali in the fourteenth century. The dashed lines trace the main trans-Saharan routes of the period.

Fig. 9.11 Djingareyber Mosque, Timbuktu, Mali. ca. 1312. Today the mosque—and the entire city of Timbuktu—is in danger of becoming a desert, as the sands from the Sahara overtake what once was the Mali savanna.

(Fig. **9.11**). Still standing today and made of burnt brick and mud, it dominates the city. Under Moussa's patronage, Timbuktu grew in wealth and prestige and became a cultural focal point for the finest poets, scholars, and artists of Africa and the Middle East. To draw further attention to Timbuktu, and to attract more scholars and poets to it, Mansa Moussa embarked on a pilgrimage to Mecca in 1334. He arrived in Cairo at the head of a huge caravan of 60,000 people, including 12,000 servants, with 80 camels carrying more than two tons of gold to be distributed among the poor. Five hundred of the servants carried staffs of pure gold. In fact, Moussa distributed so much gold in Egypt that the value of the precious metal fell dramatically and did not recover for a number of years. When Moussa returned from the holy cities of Mecca and Medina, he built mosques, libraries, and madrasas throughout his kingdom. He convinced the Arab poet and architect Abu-Ishaq Ibrahim-es-Saheli [aboo iss-HAAK eeb-rah-HEEM es-SAA-heh-lee] to return with him, and it was Ibrahim-es-Saheli who devised the burnt brick and much of the construction techniques for the Djingareyber Mosque.

Such was Mansa Moussa's fame that the Jewish mapmaker Abraham Cresques [AY-bru-hum KREK] prominently represented him in his *Catalan Atlas*, made in 1375 for Charles V of France (Fig. **9.12**). Crowned in gold and enthroned above his capital of Timbuktu, Mansa Moussa holds a golden orb in one hand and a golden scepter in the other. Cresques depicts a river of gold flowing out of Mali eastward to Cairo and Alexandria. The caption to the king's right reads, "So abundant is the gold which is found in his country that he is the richest and most noble king in the land."

Islamic traditions meanwhile continued to exist alongside indigenous African art and music. For instance, the military exploits of the first Malian *mansa*, Sunjata, still survive in an epic poem, the *Sunjata*. The poem was passed down through the generations, much in the way that the Homeric epics must have been passed down in prehistoric Greece. Its transmitters were Malian **griots** [gree-YOH], professional poet/storytellers who chant or sing traditional narratives from memory, generally accompanying themselves on a harp, either a three- or four-stringed **bolon** [boh-LON], or a 21-stringed *kora* [KOH-rah]. The *Sunjata* was not transcribed until the twentieth century. The poem opens with the griot identifying himself (**Reading 9.3a**):

READING 9.3a

from the *Sunjata*, 12th century

I am a griot. . . . We are vessels of speech, we are the repositories which harbor secrets many centuries old. The art of eloquence has no secrets for us; without us the names of kings would vanish into oblivion, we are the memory of mankind; by the spoken word we bring to life the deeds and exploits of kings for younger generations. . . . Listen to my word, you who want to know; by my mouth you will learn the history of Mali.

Fig. 9.12 Abraham Cresques. Map of North Africa, and detail, *The Catalan Atlas*, from Majorca, Spain. 1375. Index, Bibliothèque Nationale, Paris. The map features the Atlas Mountains, Mansa Moussa of Mali, the king of Organa, the king of Nubia, the king of Babylon, and the Red Sea. Note the "River of Gold" that flows across North Africa to Egypt. The mapmaker, Cresques, lived on the Catalan island of Majorca, where a school of nautical mapmakers thrived, their work based on the experience of Mediterranean sailors. The gold used in the map is actual gold leaf.

Later in the poem, Sunjata oversees a festival in celebration of his military exploits, a description that creates a vivid picture of Malian tradition (Reading 9.3b):

HEAR MORE at www.myartslab.com To this day, griots in West Africa perform the *Sunjata* (track **9.1**). The performance features many of the characteristics common to West African music. These include polyrhythmic percussion, featuring as many as five to ten different rhythms simultaneously played on a variety of instruments (such as drums, rattles, and, here, bows and spears knocking together), communal performance, responsive chants, and what in another context might be considered "noise"—shrill cries, for instance—adding to the tonal richness of the whole.

Islamic Spain

Like Islamic Africa, Islamic Spain maintained its own indigenous traditions while it absorbed Muslim ones, thus creating a distinctive cultural and political life. In 750, the Abbasids [AB-ass-eed], a large family that claimed descent from Abbas [AB-bass], an uncle of Muhammad, overthrew the Umayyad caliphs. The Abbasids shifted the center of Islamic power from Damascus, where the Umayyads had centered their power, to a magnificent new capital in Iraq popularly known as Baghdad. In the middle of the ninth century, they moved again, to the complex at Samarra (see Fig. 9.5), 60 miles farther up the Tigris, probably in an attempt to seek more space to build palaces and mosques. Meanwhile, Spain remained under Umayyad control, initially under the leadership of Abd ar-Rahman (r. 756–88) [abd ur rahh-MAN], who had escaped the Abbasid massacre of Umayyads in Syria in 750, arriving in Córdoba [KOR-doh-buh] in 756. For over three centuries, the Spain he encountered had been controlled politically by a Germanic tribe from the north, the Visigoths, who had become Christian. But some 45 years earlier, in about 711 or 712, these Christian Visigoths had been defeated in southern Spain by a force of invading Muslim Arabs and Berbers. Gradually, Abd ar-Rahman solidified Muslim control of the region, first in Córdoba, then in Seville, Toledo (the former Visigothic capital), and Granada.

The Great Mosque of Córdoba In the last years of his reign, secure in his position, Abd ar-Rahman built a magnificent new mosque in Córdoba, tearing down an existing Visigothic church and building his new mosque in its place, for which the Christian church was handsomely reimbursed. Abd ar-Rahman's original design included a double-tiered system of reused Roman and Visigothic columns and capitals supporting horseshoe shaped double arches, all topped by a wooden roof (Fig. **9.13**). The double arches may have served a practical function. The Visigoths tended to build with relatively short, stubby columns. To create the loftier space for the mosque, the architects superimposed another set of columns on top, creating the double tier. But the design also echoes the same double-tiered design found at the Great Mosque at Damascus, which also reuses Roman columns, and the architects may have simply copied the Damascus model. The arches also employ a distinctive design of alternating stone and red brick voussoirs, the wedge-shaped stones used to build an arch (see *Materials & Techniques*, page 196). The use of two different materials is functional as well, combining the flexibility of brick with the strength of stone. The hypostyle plan of the mosque was infinitely expandable, and subsequent Umayyad caliphs enlarged the mosque in 852, 950, 961–76, and 987, until it was more than four times the size of Abd ar-Rahman's original and incorporated 1,200 columns.

Under the Umayyad caliphs, Muslim Spain thrived intellectually. Religious tolerance was extended to all. (It is worth noting that Muslims were exempt from taxes, while Christians and Jews were not—a practice that encouraged conversion.) Spanish Jews, who had been persecuted under the Visigoths, welcomed the Muslim invasion and served as scientists, scholars, and even administrators in the caliphate [KAY-lih-fate]. Classical Greek literature and philosophy had already been translated into Arabic in Abbasid Baghdad. The new School of Translation established

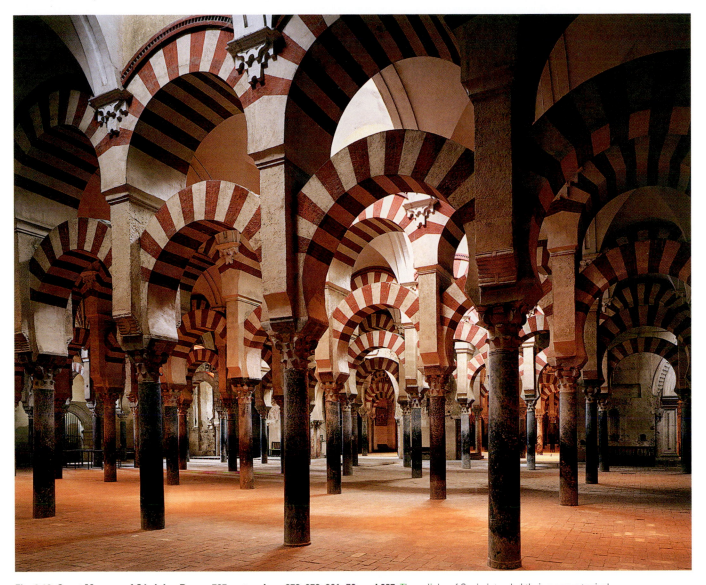

Fig. 9.13 Great Mosque of Córdoba. Begun 785, extensions 852, 950, 961–76, and 987. The caliphs of Spain intended their mosque to rival those in Jerusalem, Damascus, and Iraq. The forestlike expanse of the interior is a result of these aspirations. Even though only 80 of the original 1,200 columns survive, the space appears infinite, like some giant hall of mirrors.

LEARN MORE View an architectural simulation of Islamic arches at **www.myartslab.com**

by the Umayyads in Toledo [toh-LEH-doh] soon was responsible for spreading the nearly forgotten texts throughout the West. Muslim mathematicians in Spain invented algebra and introduced the concept of zero to the West, and soon their Arabic numerals replaced the unwieldy Roman system. By the time of Abd ar-Rahman III (r. 912–61), Córdoba was renowned for its medicine, science, literature, and commercial wealth, and it became the most important center of learning in Europe. The elegance of Abd ar-Rahman III's court was unmatched, and his tolerance and benevolence extended to all, as Muslim students from across the Mediterranean soon found their way to the mosque-affiliated madrasa that he founded—the

earliest example of an institution of higher learning in the Western world.

Outside of Córdoba, Abd ar-Rahman III built a huge palace complex, Madinat al-Zahra, to honor his wife. (Its extensive remains are still being excavated.) Its staff included 13,750 male servants along with another 3,500 pages, slaves, and eunuchs. Its roof required the support of 4,300 columns, and elaborate gardens surrounded the site. As many as 1,200 loaves of bread were required daily just to feed the fish in the garden ponds.

The decorative arts of the era are equally impressive. A famous example is a **pyxis**, a small, cylindrical box with a lid, made for Prince al-Mughira, Abd ar-Rahman III's son (Fig. **9.14**) in 968. Carved in ivory by artisans at Madinat al-Zahra, perhaps to hold the prince's jewelry or toiletries, each of its four sides is decorated with a medallion linked to the others by borders of delicately pierced foliage of an oriental palm. In one of these medallions, a lutist stands between two cross-legged figures, one holding a fan, the other a bottle of a kind associated particularly with the Umayyad caliph. Above them to the right two falconers stand back-to-back—the falcon being the traditional symbol of the Umayyad dynasty. Almost every element in the design has symbolic meaning, especially the oriental palm tree, which symbolizes the exile of the dynasty, banished to the distant land of Spain by the Abbasids.

The city of Córdoba reflected the splendor of its palace. Writers at the time, visiting the caliphate, testify that its population was about 500,000 (compared to 40,000 in Paris at about the same time). There were 1,600 mosques, 900 public baths, and more than 80,000 shops. About half the population had running water and lavatories in their homes. And the main city streets were lighted by torchlight at night.

Jews in Muslim Spain Jews had settled in Spain as early as 586 BCE, when Nebuchadnezzar [neh-boo-kad-NEZ-zur] II conquered Jerusalem and destroyed the First Temple in Jerusalem. The Hebrew word for Spain was *Sepharad* [SEF-ar-ud], and the Spanish Jews were thus known as Sephardim [suh-FAR-deem]. Under Umayyad rule, the Jewish population flourished to such an extent that some scholars refer to the period as the Golden Age of Jewish Culture. Jews served at the highest levels of government and participated in the social and intellectual fervor that marked the Umayyad court. They dedicated themselves to the study of science and medicine. In fact, Abd ar-Rahman III's court physician was the Jewish Hasdai ibn Shaprut [huz-DAH-ee ubun shap-ROOT] (ca. 915–ca. 990). Jewish scholars also de-voted themselves, under Hasdai ibn Shaprut's patronage, to the art of poetry and the study of Hebrew grammar. He was also instrumental in making Córdoba the new center of Jewish theological studies.

The Umayyad caliphate in Spain ultimately collapsed in the eleventh century, when internal politics caused it to break up into small competing states called *taifas*. Taifa Spain was far less tolerant of Judaism than the Umayyads, and persecutions began. The first one was on December 30, 1066, when the Jews were expelled from Granada and 1,500 families who refused to leave were killed. Nevertheless, Jewish culture still thrived, especially in Toledo and

Fig. 9.14 Royal workshop of Madinat al-Zahra, Pyxis of al-Mughira. ca. 968. Elephant ivory, carved and engraved decoration, trace of black inlay, possibly jade, height 6″. Musée du Louvre, former Riano Collection, purchased 1898. OA 4068. The Arabic inscription around the base of the lid reads: "God's blessing, favors, joy, beatitude to al-Mughira son of the Commander of the faithful, may God have mercy upon him, in the year 357 [of the Hegira]."

Córdoba. It was in Córdoba that Moses Maimonides (1138–1204), one of the greatest Jewish scholars, was born, although he and his family were driven out of the country in 1148 by the Almoravids, a Muslim Berber dynasty that had been called into Spain in 1085 from its capital in Marrakesh, in present-day Morocco, in order help the *taifas* drive Christian armies from northern Spain. Maimonides is renowned for being the first person to write a systematic summary of Jewish law, the *Mishneh Torah*. He also produced one of the great philosophical works of Judaism, *Guide to the Perplexed*, a work about the nature of God in general that would influence later Christian thinkers such as Thomas Aquinas (see Chapter 12).

One of the great Jewish poets of the era is Judah Halevi [YOO-dah hah-LEH-fee] (ca. 1075–1141). In Córdoba, he wrote one of the best-known books of the era, *The Book of Argument and Proof in Defense of the Despised Faith*, later known as *The Book of the Kuzari*. This dialogue between a Jewish scholar and the pagan king of the Khazars [khah-ZARS], a seminomadic Turkish people, is considered by many to be one of the most important works of Jewish philosophy. The book argues, among other things, that the Hebrew language is itself divine, that the Torah is supernatural—not just a "gift from God" but the very "presence of God"—and that the special function of the Jewish people in God's plan is to bring about the redemption of the world.

Halevi was a poet of both secular and religious verse, including love songs, drinking songs, and autobiographical lyric poems concerning his faith. One of the most moving of the latter is "My Heart Is in the East." It embodies feelings shared by all Jews of the Diaspora (**Reading 9.4**):

READING 9.4

Judah Halevi, "My Heart Is in the East"

My heart is in the East, and I live at the edge of the West.
I eat. I taste nothing. How can I enjoy it?
How can I fulfill my word to leave
While Zion is locked up in red Edom [EH-dum][1]
and I stand in the ropes of Arabia?
Easily I could give up
all the good wonders of Spain.
Glory would be to see the dust of the Temple,
our ravaged shrine.

[1]**Edom:** a Hebrew word meaning "red" but referring to Esau in the Hebrew Scriptures as well as to the nation tracing its ancestry to him.

Before the end of his life, Halevi did leave his native Spain for Zion, perhaps driven out by the Berbers. He reached Alexandria, where he continued to write, but died six months later.

The Alhambra The collapse of the Umayyad caliphate and the subsequent rise and fall of the various Islamic dynasties was the inspiration for a pioneering work of sociology, the *Muqaddimah* [moo-QAD-dee-ma] (literally "Introduction") of Ibn Khaldun [ubun khal-DOON] (1332–1406), the first volume of a universal history that comprises six books. Originally conceived by its Tunisian-born author as a history of the North African Berber dynasties that rose to power in Spain after the Almoravid arrival in 1085, the work is based on Ibn Khaldun's central concept of *asabiyah* [ah-sa-BEE-ah], or "group feeling." *Asabiyah* is the source of cohesion within a community, and although it occurs almost naturally in small groups, such as families or tribes, religion can greatly expand its effects. Khaldun analyzes how *asabiyah* can carry groups to power, but he also demonstrates how, over time, the power of *asabiyah* dissipates in a group, causing its downfall and its eventual replacement by a new group with a more vital or contemporary sense of itself as a coherent power.

Of all the Berber dynasties in Spain, the Nasrid [nahs-REED] dynasty (r. 1230–1492) represented this new, stronger power, and their architecture embodied their sense of *asabiyah*. On a hill above Granada they erected a magnificent palace and fortress, which flourished as a center for the arts. Named the Alhambra [ahl-HAHM-bra]—from the Arabic word for "red citadel"—after the reddish tone of its walls, it gives us some sense of what the Abd ar-Rahman III's palace complex in Córdoba must have been like.

Within the walls of the Alhambra are palaces, mosques, gardens, quarters for artisans, baths, and tombs. The Palace of the Myrtles served as the official chambers for receiving and hosting visitors. Named after the shrubs planted in its courtyard, it was based on the plan of an urban dwelling in the Arab heartland, where life centered around a sheltered outdoor patio surrounded by doorways leading to the bedrooms, sitting rooms, and storage areas. The Palace of the Lions, named after the fountain in its courtyard surrounded by 12 stone lions, served as a private residence (Fig. **9.15**). The various rooms of the palaces opened into their central courtyards. Poetic texts adorn the palaces, carved into the capitals of their colonnades and inscribed on their walls and **miradors** [MEE-rah-dohrs], projecting rooms with windows on three sides. On a mirador overlooking the gardens of one palace are the words "I am a garden adorned with beauty. Gaze upon my loveliness and you will know this to be true." On another is the poignant phrase "I believe that the full moon has its home here." On the walls beneath the decorated ceilings of the Palace of the Lions, the fourteenth-century court poet Ibn Zamrak [ubun ZAM-rak] outlined the spiritual essence of the architectural traceries and grilles of the palace's arches and domes:

> And how many arches rise up in its vault supported by columns which at night are embellished by light!
> You would think that they are heavenly spheres whose orbits revolve, overshadowing the pillar of dawn when it barely begins to appear after having passed through the night.

The play of light and shadow, and the airy lightness of the stone- and plasterwork that adorn the Alhambra, symbolize the celestial heavens. The ceiling of the Hall of the Abencerrajes [ah-ven-ser-RAKH-ess] is decorated with **muqarnas** [moo-QARR-nass], small nichelike components unique to Islamic architecture that are combined in successive layers to enclose a space and produce surfaces rich

Fig. 9.15 Courtyard of the Palace of the Lions, Alhambra, Granada, Spain. 1354–91. The 12 stone lions supporting the fountain were salvaged from an earlier complex that stood on the Alhambra hill overlooking Granada.

Fig. 9.16 *Muqarnas* dome (plaster ceiling), Hall of the Abencerrajes, Palace of the Lions, Alhambra, Granada. 1354–91. The Hall of the Abencerrajes may have been used as a music room, the elaborate ceiling contributing to its nearly perfect acoustics.

in three-dimensional geometric compositions (Fig. **9.16**). Here they are used to catch the changing light as it moves from window to window across the top of the dome drum. The inescapable conclusion is that the Alhambra was meant to be something akin to heaven on earth, or paradise (from the Persian word for an enclosed park, *faradis* [faa-raa-DEES]), the literal embodiment of what, in the Great Mosque of Damascus, could only be imaged in mosaic (see Fig. 9.9).

The visitor to the Alhambra is struck by one other inescapable reality—there is water everywhere, in gardens, courtyards, and patios. Inscribed on the wall of one courtyard are the words, "The water in the basin in my center is like the soul of a believer who rests in the remembrance of God." But the water in the Alhambra is not merely passive. It flows, gurgles, and bubbles. Everywhere there is the *sound* of water, the essential *melody* of nature.

THE ARTS OF THE ISLAMIC WORLD

Between the eighth and thirteenth centuries, the Islamic world, from Baghdad in the east to Córdoba in the west, developed artistic traditions and practices compared to which the arts in Western Europe simply paled. With the same technical virtuosity that the architects at the Alhambra employed, Islam's musicians, bookmakers, illustrators, and poets crafted beautiful works of complex abstract design.

Music in the Islamic World

Music was central to Islamic culture. Though Muhammad and his followers initially viewed music with some skepticism, believing that it distracted the faithful from their true purpose, within a century of his death, Muslim worship had become a highly musical event. In the call to prayer, each of the call's seven phrases is sung, with a long pause between each phrase and each phrase becoming more melodic than the last. In the daily prayer service and on holy days, verses from the Qur'an are chanted and special songs are sung.

Traditional Arabic music is based on intonations and rhythms closely related to the inflections of words. It uses many more pitch intervals than Western music, breaking what we think of as a given pitch into fractions of semitones and microtones. In addition, Arabic song is "voiced" through the nose as well as the mouth, resulting in a range of distinctly nasal pitches, as in the Andalusian song from the "Nuba 'al'istihlal'" [na-ba aal-iss-teehh-LAAL], "Songs to be sung after sunset" (track **9.2**). **HEAR MORE** at www.myartslab.com These songs were often accompanied, at least outside the mosque, by a range of instruments, including drums, tambourine, flute, oboe, and lute—or oud [ood], from the Arabic for "wood"—a bent-necked, pear-shaped string instrument. As Islam spread, the *oud* became known, throughout North Africa, as the *qitara* [qee-TAH-rah]—the guitar—which achieved its modern form in Islamic Spain. Like Arabic music in general, the *qitara* was believed to be closely connected to nature. Its four strings variously represented the four seasons, the four phases of the moon, the four alchemical elements (hotness, coldness, dryness, and moistness), or the four bodily humors (in the medieval world, the four elemental fluids of the body—blood, phlegm, choler or yellow bile, and melancholy or black bile).

During the Abbasid era (750–1258), only an accomplished musician could be considered a truly educated person. Al-Kindi [al-KIN-dee] (790–874) studied the effects of music on people's feelings and behavior and developed a system of modes, or scales, corresponding to the emotions that the music was meant to evoke. In effect, the Arabs were the first to put into writing the concepts of scale that would become second nature in European theory. (Their notation, like European chant, lacked rhythmic notation until the twelfth to thirteenth centuries.) Many theorize that the new instruments were introduced into Europe from the Middle East, and may have been accompanied by the theoretical ideas behind them. By the ninth century, the renowned musician Ziryab [zeer-YAB] (789–857) arrived in Córdoba from Baghdad and founded the first conservatory of music in Spain. Here, musicians began to experiment with ensemble compositions divided into five or more movements performed by string, wind, and percussion instruments, and often accompanied by a vocal chorus. New instruments were invented—trumpets, viols, and kettledrums. In essence, the elements of the Western orchestra were now in place.

The Art of the Book

Sometime in the eighth century, the art of papermaking was introduced into the Arabic world from China. The process involved extracting cellulose pulp from any of a number of plants, suspending the pulp in water, catching it on a fine screen, and then drying it into sheets. By the first years of the ninth century, most official documents in Baghdad were executed on paper, and soon afterward books, which were more affordable than parchment manuscripts, began to increase in number. Calligraphers and artists created not only scholarly treatises but also romances, epics, and lyric poetry, and most Abbasid cities soon boasted special booksellers' markets. As Jonathan M. Bloom notes in his history of papermaking in the Islamic world, *Paper Before Print*, "Paper . . . became the prime medium of memory." Bloom suggests that although scholars have long recognized "the major achievements of intellectual life under the Abbasids . . . these achievements were not accidental. Rather, they were tied to the introduction of paper: they were a product of both increased intellectual curiosity—itself fostered by the growth of learning made possible by the explosion of books—and attempts to exploit the potential applications of paper." It is likely that the West did not produce paper in any sufficient quantity for another 500 years—until the invention of the printing press—because of its comparative lack of interest in the written word. The richest library in the West by the mid-fourteenth century, for instance, was the college library of the Sorbonne in Paris, which boasted some 2,000 volumes. By contrast, a single tenth-century Andalusian scholar, Ibn Hani al-Andalusi [ubun HAA-nee al an-DA-loo-see], reputedly owned a private library of some 400,000 volumes. Muslim culture, in turn, was slow to adopt the printing press because it so valued the art of calligraphy.

As a result of its book production, Abbasid Baghdad at the height of its influence, from the ninth to the twelfth centuries, was the center of world culture. Trade flourished as silk and porcelain from China, horses from Arabia, cotton from Egypt, and minerals from throughout Europe overflowed its markets. As one late ninth-century visitor remarked, "Goods are brought from India, Sind [i.e., Pakistan], China, Tibet, the lands of the Turks . . . the Ethiopians, and others to such an extent that [the goods] are more plentiful in Baghdad than in the countries from which they come. They can be procured so readily and so certainly that it is as if all the good things of the world are sent there, all the treasures of the earth assembled there, and all the blessings of creation perfected there." There are, he commented further, "none more learned than their scholars, better informed than their tra-ditionists, more cogent than their theologians . . . more literate than their scribes, more lucid than their logicians . . . more eloquent than their preachers, more poetic than their poets." The book made this cultural eloquence manifest and transportable. Islamic learning—and with it, Islamic faith—spread throughout the world.

Nezami's Haft Paykar One of the most widely illustrated poems of the Middle Ages is the Haft Paykar [pay-KAR] ("Seven Beauties"). It is one of five romantic epics in 30,000 couplets that make up Khamseh [KHAM-sa] (Quintet) by the Persian poet considered to be the master of the genre, Nezami [nee-ZAH-mee] (ca. 1141–1203 or 1217), whose full name is Elyas Yusof Nezami Ganjavi [eel-YAS YOO-suf nee-ZAH-mee gan-YAH-vee]. A romantic epic is a poem that celebrates love between a man and woman as a cosmic force for harmony and justice. Thus, the love stories that form the epic's core narrative are also vehicles for treating broader philosophical issues such as just rule, human perfection, and spiritual growth. The Haft Paykar, Nezami's masterpiece, narrates how, one day, the legendary Persian prince Bahram Gur [BAH-ram GOOR] discovers a mysterious pavilion with portraits of seven beautiful princesses decorating its walls (Fig. **9.17**). He falls in love

Fig. 9.17 *Prince Bahram Gur Introduced into the Hall of Seven Images*, from a copy of Nezami's poem *Haft Paykar* ("Seven Beauties"), from *Nezami's Khamseh*, in the *Anthology* of Iskandar Sultan. From Shiraz, Iran. 1410. Illuminated manuscript, 9½″ × 5⅞″. Calouste Gulbenkian Foundation Museum, Lisbon. Another illustration of Nezami's poem is reproduced in Fig. 9.10, but defaced by its owner.

with all of them, marries them, sets up each princess in a separate pavilion of her own, and visits them one by one. Each princess tells him a story—each of about 1,000 couplets, two-line rhymed stanzas—that is meant to instruct him in the art of love and the love of beauty. **Reading 9.5** includes the first 29 couplets of "The Tale of the Black Princess."

READING 9.5
_____

from Nezami, *Haft Paykar*, "The Tale of the Black Princess," 1197

When Bahram pleasure sought, he set
his eyes on those seven fair portraits;
On Saturday, from Shammasi [SHA-ma-see] temple[1] went
in Abbasid black[2] to pitch his tent,
Entered the musk-hued dome, and gave
his greetings to the Indian maid.
Til night he there made merry sport,
burnt aloes-wood,[3] and scattered scent.
When Night in kingly fashion spilled
black grains of musk on whitest silk,
The king from that Kashmiri spring[4]
sought perfume like the dawn breeze brings:
That she might loose some women's words,
sweet stories from her store of pearls,
Those tales for which all hearers long,
and soothe to sleep the drunken man.
That Turk-eyed, Hindu-born gazelle
loosed fragrant musk, her tale to tell.
She said, "May the king's fanfare play
above the moon's high throne; and may
He live as long as turns the world;
may all heads at his threshold bow.
May he gain all his wishes; may
his fortune never flag." This prayer
Concluded, she bowed low, and loosed
from sugared lips sweet aloes-wood.
She told (her eyes cast down in shame)
a tale unmatched by anyone. . . .

[1]**Shammasi temple:** the temple of fire, served by white-robed priests.
[2]**Abbasid black:** the color of the Abbasid caliphs.
[3]**aloes-wood:** incense made of aloe.
[4]**Kashmiri spring:** a reference to the "black princess," who is from India.

The story of Bahram and his seven wives is a narrative device known as a **framing tale**. This form allows the poet to unite different tales—in this case seven—under an overarching narrative umbrella. The Western reader is probably most familiar with the framing tale in *The Thousand and One Nights*, also known as *The Arabian Nights*.

The Thousand and One Nights The Thousand and One Nights is a compilation of prose tales from various sources—Persian, Arabic, and Indian—that were united into a single narrative between the eighth and tenth centuries in Baghdad. It is likely that Nezami knew it well. The framing tale derives from the Indian story of Scheherazade [shuh-hera-ZAAD] (Shahrasad [SHAHH-raa-zaad] in Persian),

who chooses to marry King Shahryar [shahh-ra-YAHR], who so fears the prospect of female infidelity that he kills each new wife on the morning after their wedding night. In a conscious defense of womankind, Scheherazade knows that if she can tell a story each night and carefully construct it so as to reach its climax just after dawn, the king must let her live until the next evening in order to hear the tale's ending. After a thousand nights—and some 250 tales—the king comes to appreciate Scheherazade's beauty, wit, and civilizing power, and so spares her the fate of all his previous wives.

Both the *Haft Paykar* and *The Thousand and One Nights* show the centrality of love and sexuality in Islamic culture. In Islam, erotic sensory satisfaction, love, luxury, sensuality, and enjoyment were manifestations of divine grace. And although both framing tales portray women in almost total subservience to the ruler/husband, the women in each tale assert a certain real authority. In the *Haft Paykar*, women bring the prince Braham Gur to a state of wisdom and spiritual wholeness. In *The Thousand and One Nights*, women's intelligence, wit, and reason at least equal and sometimes surpass that of their male counterparts.

The Thousand and One Nights was extremely popular in the West from the eighteenth century onward, and it exercised a considerable influence on the development of the novel in Western literature. It contains a wealth of stories popular to the present day—the adventures of Sinbad the Sailor, Ali Baba, and Aladdin, to name just a few—but its eroticism and ribald humor have often been sanitized in Western retellings. The stories wind in and out of one another in a seemingly endless pattern of repetition. The famous "Tale of the Fisherman and the Genie" (see **Reading 9.6**, pages 311–313) is a sequence of stories within stories that mirrors the framing technique of the whole, the fisherman telling tales to outwit an angry genie just as Scheherazade tells her tales to outwit the king. The sequence is repeatedly interrupted as dawn approaches and Scheherazade's stories must end for the night.

The Thousand and One Nights embodies a tension that pervades Islamic culture to this day and, it is fair to say, Western culture as a whole. That tension is between the exercise of authoritarian power over women in patriarchal society and the need for women to free themselves of that power—in Scheherazade's case, in order to survive. Related to this is the tendency of patriarchal society to reduce women to sexual objects even as it recognizes their great intellectual capacity. Scheherazade's tales must be understood in this context: They allow her to resist the king whom she entertains nightly, a man who is empowered by the *shari'a* (shah-REE-a) or a like set of laws, who feels no compunction about executing wife after wife, day after day.

The Sufi Tradition

After the 1258 fall of Baghdad to Mongol invaders—the conquering Mongols would themselves become Muslim—the art of bookmaking shifted to Iran, where a thriving literary culture, exemplified by the poetry of Nezami, already existed. Particularly at the provincial capitals of Shiraz and

Fig. 9.18 *Dervishes Dancing*, from a copy of *Sessions of the Lovers*, from Turkey. **Sixteenth century.** Illuminated manuscript, approx. 9″ × 6″. Bodleian Library, Oxford. The Sufi's goal was to achieve direct contact with God through mystical trance, and the ecstatic whirling dance could, the Sufis believed, induce such a trance. In this miniature, the dervishes dance to the accompaniment of flutes and tambourines.

Herat, home to a number of important Persian poets and painters, the art of the book became associated with the mystical practices of the Sufi [SOO-fee] orders. Sufism (from the Arabic word for "wool," *suf*, a reference to the coarse woolen garments worn by Sufi practitioners) embraces a wide range of mystical practices. All of them share a belief in attaining visionary experience and divine inspiration by means of trances achieved in the intense experience of music, poetry, and dance. Thus, the ecstasy of the wild, whirling dervish dance (the Persian word for a Sufi or Muslim mystic is *darvish*) represents the path of the soul as it moves closer to God (Fig. **9.18**). The great Sufi poets—Sa'di [SAA-adi] (ca. 1213–92), Rumi [ROO-mee] (ca. 1207–73), and Jami [JAH-mee] (1414–92) among them—emphasize the pursuit of the beautiful, often in the form of a beautiful woman or, in the case of Rumi, a beautiful man. However, such a pursuit is an allegory for, or figurative representation of, the pursuit of the beauty that is God.

For instance, Jami's version of the "Seduction of Yusuf [YOO-suf] and Zulaykha [zoo-LAY-kuh]" (**Readings 9.7a** and **9.7b**), a story celebrated by several Sufi writers, retells, in elaborate fashion, the story of Joseph and the wife of Potiphar [POT-uh-fur], Zuleika [zoo-LAY-kuh], which appears in both the Bible and Qur'an. Yusuf protests that his love is not sexual but divinely inspired:

READING 9.7a

from Jami, "Seduction of Yusuf and Zulaykha," 1483

I would not passion's victim be,
And turned from sin—but not from thee.
My love was pure, no plant of earth
From my rapt being sprung to birth:
I loved as angels might adore. . . .

His pure adoration leads Yusuf to understand "the great lesson"—"That vice and bliss are wide apart." His love for his lady leads him to the love of God.

In Jami's poem, Zulaykha builds a palace with seven rooms, each decorated with an erotic painting of herself and Yusuf, in order to seduce the beautiful youth. As she leads the unsuspecting Yusuf from room to room, she locks each door behind her. When they reach the last room, she throws herself on Yusuf, who flees as each of the seven doors miraculously opens before him. In Jami's poem, the palace and its decorations stand for the temptations of the material world with its seven climes, the habitable climatic regions of the earth (Fig. **9.19**). Yusuf's beauty, which Zulaykha mistakenly sees as physical rather than spiritual, is comparable to the beauty of God, and his faith in the all-seeing God unlocks the doors to allow his escape. Recalling Yusuf's power over her, Zulaykha then bemoans her loss:

READING 9.7b

from Jami, "Seduction of Yusuf and Zulaykha" (before 1492)

Let me look back to that dark hour
That bound my spirit to thy power—
Thy grateful words, thy glance recall,
My hopes, my love—and curse them all;
Let me thy tender looks retrace,
The glories of thy heavenly face;
Thy brow, where Aden's[1] splendor lies,
And the mild luster of thine eyes:
Yet let my heart no weakness prove,
But hate thee as I once could love.
What fearful eloquence was thine,
What awful anger—just—divine!
Shuddering, I saw my heart displayed
And knew all this I should have said!
'Twas mine to shrink, withstand, in time,
For, while I sinned, I knew my crime.
O wretched, wavering heart!—as vain
Thy wild resentment as thy pain:
One thought alone expels the rest,
One sole regret distracts my breast,
O'ermastering and subduing all—
More than my crime, more than my fall:
Are not shame, fear, remorse, forgot,
In that one thought—he loves me not?

[1]**Aden:** the Garden of Eden.

As we will see in the following chapters, Zulaykha's point of view, and, more powerfully, Yusuf's understanding of love itself, would soon make its way to Europe, particularly in the tradition of "courtly love" championed by the troubadour poets.

Rumi's poetry, especially the *Mathnavi* [MAT-nuh-vee] (Rhymed Discourses), an epic-length verse collection of mystical stories composed of some 27,000 verse couplets, is

Fig. 9.19 Bihzad. *The Seduction of Yusuf,* **from a copy of Sadi's** *Bustan* **("Orchard"), prepared for Sultan Husayn Mirza at Herat, Persia (modern Afghanistan). 1488.** Ink and color on paper, 11⁷⁄₈″ × 8²⁄₃″. National Library, Cairo. Bihzad is one of the most renowned illustrators of the fifteenth century. In illustrating this manuscript, he worked together with Sultan Ali Mashhadi, who was himself the greatest calligrapher of the day. The text of Sadi's version of the Yusuf story is in the cream-colored panels in the top, middle, and bottom of the page.

considered the masterwork of the Sufi tradition—"the Qur'an in Persian," Jami called it. The stories, which invariably end happily, illustrate God's limitless mercy toward humankind, and Rumi invokes the Qur'an's message of hope repeatedly. Indeed, for him hope is virtually synonymous with faith. The stories continually cite the Qur'an and interpret it in terms of human potential for mystical union with God, a potential hinted at in physical union with a lover. This hinted potential is the subject of Rumi's collection of about 30,000 verses entitled *The Divan of Shams of Tabriz.* Rumi thought of Shams (meaning "Sun") of Tabriz [tah-BREEZ] as the "Divine Beloved," the physical incarnation of spiritual love. Rumi met him in 1244, and when Shams disappeared 15 months later, Rumi wrote poems describing the loss of his lover in terms of abandonment by God. Poems like "Love's Body," "Caring for My Lover," and "The Clear Bead at the Center" (see **Reading 9.8**, page 313) are at once carnal and spiritual, erotic and mystical, and they speak of the rebirth of the human spirit through love.

The Islamic Heritage

Islam is often considered outside the Western tradition, but it is a fundamental part of the Western heritage. As we have seen, Western music—indeed, the Western orchestra—originates in Muslim musical traditions. The spiritual depth of the love poem, as it comes to fruition in the work of the medieval troubadour poets and the poets of the Renaissance, is first developed in the Muslim world. Many of the decorative effects achieved in medieval architecture and design reflect the interlace and arabesques that inform Islamic architecture. See, for example, the portal of Saint Michel d'Aiguilhe, in Le-Puy-en-Venay, France (Fig. **9.20**), the first stop on a Christian pilgrimage route to Santiago de Compostela, where the body of the apostle Saint James the Greater lay at rest, a pilgrimage itself modeled in many ways on the Muslim **hajj** to Mecca. The portal incorporates the colored stonework and double arches of the mosque at Córdoba and the intricate design of a mihrab niche.

Fig. 9.20 Portal of Saint Michel d'Aiguilhe, Le-Puy-en-Venay, France. ca. 1162–80. Charles Martel stopped the Arab invasion of France at Poitiers in 792, but decorative work such as this underscores the lasting Islamic influence in Europe (see Chapter 13).

Fig. 9.21 Griffin, from the Islamic Mediterranean, probably Fatimid Egypt. Eleventh century. Bronze, height 3' 6 ⅛". Museo dell'Opera del Duomo, Pisa. The griffin was moved into the museum in 1828 to protect it from the elements.

But in its insistence that Jesus was a "mere" prophet and not the son of God, and in its belief that the Qur'an superseded both the Hebrew and Christian Scriptures, Islam inevitably came into conflict with the Christian West. By the time that Pope Urban II (papacy 1088–99) launched the First Crusade in 1095, gathering over 100,000 people to march on Jerusalem, Islam represented the forces of darkness to European Christians. Their determination to liberate the Holy Land from Muslim domination became a key factor in the history of the late Middle Ages.

A notable symbol of this determination is an Islamic bronze griffin that, from 1100 to 1828, sat atop Pisa Cathedral, itself built to celebrate the victory in 1063 of this Italian city-state over Muslim forces in the western Mediterranean (Fig. **9.21**). Decorated with incised feathers, its back designed to suggest silk drapery, the griffin symbolized to Muslims eaglelike vigilance, lionlike courage, and, perhaps most of all, the rich history of Mesopotamia and Persia. But the Catholic Church appropriated this bronze griffon to different ends and transformed its meaning. From its perch atop Pisa Cathedral it symbolized the dual nature of Christ, his divinity (the eagle) and his humanity (the lion). The composite creature was, in the Church's mind, the image of the Christian victory over Islam. ■

THINKING BACK

What was the message of the Prophet Muhammad?

According to tradition, beginning in 610 the Muslim prophet Muhammad began to recite messages from God, which he dictated to scribes who collected them to form the scriptures of Islam, the Qur'an. At the core of the Qur'an is the concept of "submission" or "surrender" to Allah, the all-merciful, all-seeing, all-powerful God. Other than the Qur'an, what other work forms the basis of Islamic faith? How is the idea of community reflected in the mosque and its attendant rituals? How is it reflected in the idea of the jihad? What are the "lesser" and "greater" forms of the jihad? What is the *shari'a*, and how would you describe traditional relations between men and women as outlined in the *shari'a*?

Why did Islam spread so rapidly?

Islam spread rapidly throughout the Middle East. It was appealing both as a religion that welcomed all converts and as a form of social organization that drew no distinction between clergy and congregation. As the center of the religious community, the mosque serves as meetinghouse, courthouse, and administrative center. What role do the madrasas, or teaching colleges, built at mosques, play?

How did Islam come to Africa and Spain?

In the eighth and ninth centuries, Muslims came to dominate the trans-Saharan trade routes, and Islam became the dominant faith of North and West Africa. Muslims especially traded in salt, gold, and slaves (Muhammad had expressly authorized the practice of enslaving conquered peoples). By 1312, the Malian ruler Mansa Moussa, a devout Muslim, had built the Djingareyber Mosque in Timbuktu and led a pilgrimage to Mecca. The epic of *Sunjata*, detailing the exploits of the first Malian king, reflects this world and is still sung by Malian griots, or professional poets, to this day.

In Spain, the Umayyad caliph Abd ar-Rahman built a magnificent new mosque in Córdoba, and by the middle of the tenth century, under the leadership of Abd ar-Rahman III, Córdoba was the most important center of learning in Europe. How did the Jewish population of Spain fit into this culture? What cultural priorities are reflected in such Spanish Muslim works as the Alhambra in Granada?

What place do the arts hold in the Islamic world?

Many faithful believed that Muhammad had opposed image-making in the hadith. As a result, the art of calligraphy assumed a central place in Islamic visual culture, especially the bismallah, consisting of the phrase "In the name of Allah, the Beneficent, Ever-Merciful," with which every pious Muslim begins any statement or activity. How does iconoclasm manifest itself in Islam? Traditional Arabic music is based on intonations and rhythms closely related to the inflections of words, and it uses many more pitch intervals than Western music, but how does it contribute to the development of Western music?

The art of papermaking transformed Islamic culture, as the book became the prime medium of memory and Baghdad became a major publishing center. One of the most widely illustrated poems of the Middle Ages is Nezami's *Haft Paykar* (*Seven Beauties*), a romantic epic. What is the primary narrative device that it employs? How is this device central to *The Thousand and One Nights*, a prose compilation of Persian, Arabic, and Indian stories told by Scheherazade? After the fall of Baghdad to invading Mongols in 1258, book publishing moved to Iran, where we find the mystical poetry of Sufi poets such as Jami and Rumi. What is the central theme of their work?

PRACTICE MORE Get flashcards for images and terms and review chapter material with quizzes at **www.myartslab.com**

GLOSSARY

bismillah A sacred invocation of the name of Allah.

bolon A three- or four-stringed harp.

caliph A successor of Muhammad.

calligraphy The art of producing artistic, stylized handwriting.

chador A covering worn by Muslim women that covers the wearer from head to toe and most or all of the face.

couplet A two-line rhymed stanza.

framing tale A narrative device that allows a writer to unite different tales under an overarching narrative umbrella.

griot A West African poet/storyteller who chants or sings traditional narratives from memory, generally accompanied by a harp.

hadith The collection of the sayings of Muhammad and anecdotes about his life, accepted as a source of Islamic doctrine.

hajib The Islamic practice of dressing modestly; specifically, the requirement that women be covered or veiled.

hajj A pilgrimage to Mecca made as a religious duty for Muslims.

hijra The flight of Muhammad from Mecca in 622.

hypostyle A vast space filled with columns supporting a roof.

jihad The impassioned religious struggle undertaken by Muslims as a religious duty. The jihad may take one of two forms: the lesser is a holy war; the greater is self-control over the baser human appetites.

mihrab A niche in the wall of a mosque commemorating the spot at Medina where Muhammad planted his lance to indicate the direction in which people should pray.

minbar The stepped pulpit for the preacher on the *qibla* wall of a mosque.

mirador A projecting room with windows on three sides.

mode A series of different scales.

mosque A building used for worship by Muslims.

muqarnas A small, nichelike component unique to Islamic architecture and used in multiple rows to enclose a space.

pyxis A small, cylindrical box with a lid.

qibla The wall of a mosque indicating the direction of Mecca.

Qur'an The sacred text of Islam composed of the revelations of Allah to Muhammad.

romantic epic A poem that celebrates love between a man and woman as a cosmic force for harmony and justice.

Umma The community of all Muslims.

READINGS

READING 9.1

from the Qur'an, *Surah 47*

The Qur'an consists of the revelations said to have been made to Muhammad and preserved in oral traditions by his followers, who used them in ritual prayers. The core of Islamic faith, they were written down and gathered into a single book in 651–52 at the order of Uthman [oot-MAN], the third caliph, or successor to the Prophet. Divided into 114 chapters, or surahs ("units of revelation"), the Qur'an is, very often, a book of remarkable beauty, but in the surah *reproduced here, it reveals itself to be less than tolerant of those who do not accept the Muslim faith.*

Surah 47 Muhammad

In the name of Allah, most benevolent, ever-merciful.

1. (As for) those who disbelieve and turn away from Allah's way, He shall render their works ineffective.

2. And (as for) those who believe and do good, and believe in what has been revealed to Muhammad, and it is the very truth from their Lord, He will remove their evil from them and improve their condition.

3. That is because those who disbelieve follow falsehood, and those who believe follow the truth from their Lord; thus does Allah set forth to men their examples.

4. So when you meet in battle those who disbelieve, then smite the necks until when you have overcome them, then make (them) prisoners, and afterwards either set them free as a favor or let them ransom (themselves) until the war terminates. That (shall be so); and if Allah had been pleased He would certainly have exacted what is due from them, but that He may try some of you by means of others; and (as for) those who are slain in the way of Allah, He will by no means allow their deeds to perish.

5. He will guide them and improve their condition.

6. And cause them to enter the garden which He has made known to them.

7. O you who believe if you help (the cause of) Allah, He will help you and make firm your feet.

8. And (as for) those who disbelieve, for them is destruction, and He has made their deeds ineffective.

9. That is because they hated what Allah revealed, so He rendered their deeds null.

10. Have they not then journeyed in the land and seen how was the end of those before them: Allah brought down destruction upon them, and the unbelievers shall have the like of it.

11. That is because Allah is the Protector of those who believe, and because the unbelievers shall have no protector for them.

READING CRITICALLY

Despite their apparent intolerance for non-Muslims, this *surah* also contains many passages that could be called compassionate and caring. How are the two opposing sentiments reconciled?

READING 9.6

"Tale of the Fisherman and the Genie" from *The Thousand and One Nights* (ca. 800–1300)

The Thousand and One Nights *was assembled sometime between the eighth and tenth centuries from stories of Persian, Arabic, and Indian origin that had circulated orally for hundreds of years. The work itself, consisting of some 250 tales, exists in many versions—often sanitized in English translation, reducing this adult masterpiece to a collection of children's stories. It is a framed tale in which Scheherazade, a woman of great wit and beauty, tells a story each night to her king and husband. He is a man so obsessed with the possibility of female adultery that, until he marries Scheherazade, he has killed each of his new brides the morning after their wedding night. To forestall her own death, Scheherazade cleverly stops her stories each morning before they reach their conclusion. "The Tale of the Fisherman and the Genie," the opening of which is excerpted here, is itself a sequence of tales within a tale, mirroring the structure of the whole, as the fisherman tells his stories in order to forestall the anger of a Genie.*

I have heard, Oh worthy King, that there was once a poor, old Fisherman who had a wife and three children to support. Each day, it was his custom to cast his fishing-net into the ocean exactly four times, and no more. One day, at about noon, he went towards the seashore, where he set his basket down in the sand. Tucking up his shirt and plunging into the water, he cast his net and waited until it settled to the bottom of the sea. Then, he gathered the cords of the net together, and tried to haul it away. But its heaviness overpowered him, and no matter how hard he tried, he could not pull it up. So he carried the ends of the cords to the shore, drove a stake into the sand, and bound the cords tightly to the stake. Then he stripped his clothes from his body and dove into the water, working hard until he finally raised the net from the sea.

Rejoicing, he put his clothes back on and went to examine the net and found a dead jackass inside of it, which had torn all the net's meshes. As he saw this, the Fisherman sadly exclaimed, "There is no majesty, and there is no might except Allah the glorious, the great! But, well, this is a strange sort of daily bread." He paused, considering, and then murmured to himself, "Well, up and at it! I'll finish my fishing now, for I'm very sure of Allah's goodness."

So the Fisherman gazed at the dead ass for a moment, and then pulled it free from the netting. He wrung out the net, and spread it over the sand. Calling out "In Allah's name!" he plunged back into the sea. He cast the net a second time. . . .

[*He casts his net three times, pulling a large earthen pitcher out of the sea the second time, and shards of pottery and glass the third, blessing Allah each time although he catches no fish. On the fourth cast he pulls out* . . .] a cucumber-shaped copper jar, brimming with something mysterious. The mouth of the jar was sealed with lead, and stamped with the seal of our Lord Solomon, David's son, Allah praise them! Seeing this the Fisherman rejoiced and said, "If I sell this in the brass bazaar, I could get ten golden dinars for it!" He shook the jar, and finding it heavy, murmured, "I wish I knew what was in it. I feel as if I must find out—so I'll open it and look inside, and then I'll store it in my bag, to sell at the brass market. Taking out a knife, he pried the lead until he had loosened it from the jar. He set the seal on the ground, and turned the vase upside-down, shaking it and trying to pour out whatever could be inside. Surprisingly, nothing emerged, and the fisherman stood in wonder.

But suddenly, a spiral of smoke burst from the jar, rising toward the heavens. The fisherman marvelled as it was drawn into the air, ascending far above him. As it reached its full height, the thick, vaporous smoke condensed and formed a Genie, so huge that his head brushed the sky, and his feet touched the ground. The Genie's head curved as large as a dome; his hands dangled, big as pitchforks. His legs were long as masts, his mouth as wide as a cave, his teeth like large stones, and his nostril flared like pitchers' spouts. His eyes shone like two lamps, and his face proved fierce and threatening.

Now, when the Fisherman saw the Genie, his muscles quivered, his teeth chattered, and his throat grew too dry to swallow. Paralyzed, clenched with fear, he could do nothing.

The Genie looked at him and cried, "There is no god but *the* God, and Solomon is the prophet of God." He added, "Oh Apostle of Allah, do not slay me. Never again will I oppose you or sin against you."

The Fisherman replied, "Oh Genie, did you say, 'Solomon the Apostle of Allah?' Solomon has been dead for nearly eighteen hundred years, and now we're in the last days of the world! Where have you come from? What's happened to you? Why have you been in that jar?"

When the Evil Spirit heard the Fisherman's words, he answered, "There is no god but *the* God. Be happy, Fisherman!"

"Why should I be happy?" asked the Fisherman.

"Because," replied the Genie, "you must die a terrible death this very hour."

"You deserve heaven's abandonment for your good tidings!" cried the Fisherman. "For what reason should you kill me? What have I done to deserve death? I, who freed you from the jar, dragged you from the depths of the sea, and brought you up to dry land?"

"Ask me only in which way you will die, how I will slaughter you," said the Genie.

"What's my crime?" the Fisherman persisted. "Why such retribution?"

"Hear my story, Oh Fisherman!" cried the Genie.

The Fisherman swiftly answered, "Tell it, but tell it briefly. My heart is in my mouth."

And so, the Genie began his tale. "I am one of the heretical Genie," he explained. "I, along with the famous Sakhr al Jinni, sinned against Solomon, David's son. After this, the Prophet Solomon sent his minister, Asaf son of Barkhiya, to seize me. This minister bound me and took me against my will, bringing me to stand before the Prophet Solomon like a supplicant. When Solomon saw me, he appealed to Allah, and demanded that I embrace the True Faith and obey Allah's commands. I refused; and so he sent for this jar and imprisoned me in it, sealing it with lead and stamping it with the Most High Name. He ordered another spirit to carry me off, and cast me into the center of the ocean. I lived there for a hundred years, and during this time I said in my heart, 'I'll forever reward whoever releases me with the greatest of riches.' But an entire century passed, and when no one set me free, I began the second century saying, 'I'll reveal the secret treasures of the earth to whoever will release me.' Still, no one set me free, and soon four hundred years passed. Then I said, 'I'll grant three wishes to whoever will release me.' Yet again, no one set me free. Then I became angry, so furious, I said to myself, 'From now on, I'll kill whoever releases me, and I'll let him choose what type of death he will die.' And now, as you're the one who's released me, I give you the choice of your death."

The Fisherman, hearing the words of the Genie; exclaimed, "Oh Allah! How could it be that I didn't come to free him before this? Spare my life, Genie, and Allah will spare yours; don't kill me, and Allah will never send anyone to kill you!"

"There is no help for you. You must die," the Genie obstinately explained. . . .

As the Genie spoke, the Fisherman said to himself, "This is a Genie, but I'm a man to whom Allah has given a cunning wit. So now, as he uses his malice to destroy me, I'll use my intelligence and cunning to stop *him*." He turned to the Genie and said, "Have you really resolved to kill me?"

"Of course."

"Even so," exclaimed the Fisherman, "if I ask you a question about a certain matter, will you swear by the Most Great Name, engraved on the seal-ring of Solomon, Son of David, that you'll answer it truthfully?"

The Genie trembled as he heard the Fisherman mention the Most Great Name. "Yes," he promised the Fisherman, though his mind grew troubled. "Yes, ask, but be brief."

The Fisherman said, "How did you fit into this bottle, which doesn't even look big enough to hold your hand, or even your foot? How could it have been big enough to contain all of you?"

"What!" replied the Genie. "You don't believe my whole body was in there?"

"No!" cried the Fisherman. "I'll never believe it until I see all of you inside of it, with my own eyes." 130

And then Scheherazade saw that dawn crept over the edge of the horizon, and so she stopped telling her story. But the next day, when the fourth night came, her sister said to her, "Please finish the story. None of us are sleepy." And so, Scheherazade resumed her storytelling . . . .

READING CRITICALLY

In what way does the Genie mirror the king in both action and attitude?

READING 9.8

from Rumi, *The Divan of Shams of Tabriz* (ca. 1250)

Jalal ad-Din Rumi [jaa-LAAL udd-een ROO-mee] was born in the Persian province of Khorasan [KHOR-uh-sahn] in 1207. After the Mongol invasion of central and western Asia, he settled in Anatolia, a region of Asia Minor known as Rum (Rome in Turkish). Jalal ad-Din means, literally, "Glory of Religion." His entire name means, then, "Roman Glory of Religion." Rumi became a leader of the Sufi community, named sheik, or elder, and received the title "Mevlana," [meh-woo-LAH-nuh] meaning "our master." He is still known by that name throughout the Middle East and India. The four poems below are from a collection of lyrics entitled The Divan of Shams of Tabriz, which contains about 30,000 verses celebrating the poet's physical love for Shams ad-din [SHAM-ss add-EEN] of Tabriz, who represented for him the physical incarnation on earth of the spiritual love of God.

LOVE'S BODY

The moon and a batallion of stars came
and the sun, a lonely horseman, dissolved.
The moon lives beyond the night, beyond the day.
What eye can see him?
The sightless eye is a minaret.
How can it make out the bird on the minaret?
Sometimes the cloud in our heart is tight
because we love the moon.
Sometimes it falls away.
When you began to love your passion died 10
and though you had a thousand things to do,
you did nothing,
but since one day granite becomes a ruby,
it isn't lazy.
If in the market of love you see decapitated heads
hanging from butcher hooks,
don't run off. Come in. Look closely.
The dead are alive again.

CARING FOR MY LOVER

Friends, last night I carefully watched my love
sleeping by a spring circled with eglantine.[1]

The houris[2] of paradise stood around him,
    their hands cupped together
between a tulip field and jasmines.
Wind tugged softly in his hair.
His curls smelled of musk and ambergris.[3]
Wind turned mad and tore the hair right off
    his face
like a flaming oil lamp in a gale.
From the beginning of this dream I told myself
    go slowly, wait
for the break into consciousness. Don't breathe. 10

THE CLEAR BEAD AT THE CENTER

The clear bead at the center changes everything.
There are no edges to my loving now.
I've heard it said there's a window that opens
from one mind to another,
but if there's no wall, there's no need
for fitting the window, or the latch.

READING CRITICALLY

Explain, in your own words, the argument of "The Clear Bead at the Center."

[1]**eglantine:** sweetbrier, a fragrant pink climbing rose.
[2]**houris:** beautiful virgins provided in paradise to faithful Muslims.

[3]**musk and ambergris:** perfumes.

10

Fiefdom and Monastery, Pilgrimage and Crusade

The Early Medieval World in Europe

THINKING AHEAD

What does Anglo-Saxon art and literature say about Anglo-Saxon culture?

Who was Charlemagne?

What was the Ottonian Empire?

What event is depicted in the Bayeux Tapestry?

What is a pilgrimage church?

Why did the Crusades occur?

What was troubadour poetry?

Sutton Hoo lies near the modern city of Ipswich, England, in the county of Suffolk, East Anglia (Map **10.1**). There, a burial mound contains the remains of a wealthy and powerful Anglo-Saxon man, probably a seventh-century king. (Coins found at the site date to the late 630s.) The burial mound concealed a ship, 90 feet long and 14 feet wide, a little larger than a similar burial ship excavated in 1904 from Oseberg, just outside Oslo, Norway (Fig. **10.1**). The burial ship at Sutton Hoo had been dragged up a 100-foot hill—or "hoo"—above the river Deben and laid in a trench. Midway between the ship's bow and stern, a house had been constructed. Inside the house was the coffin, accompanied by a treasure horde of richly decorative ornaments and armor, gold coins from France, silver spoons and bowls from the Eastern Mediterranean, and a wooden harp. The trench was filled in and a mound was raised over it. For 1,300 years it remained untouched, high above the Deben estuary, as if the dead warrior were standing perpetual guard over East Anglia, looking eternally out to sea.

First excavated in 1939, only two objects discovered at the site show any evidence of Christian culture—two silver spoons inscribed with the names Saulos and Paulos in Greek lettering. The names might refer to the biblical King Saul of the Hebrew Bible and St. Paul of the New Testament. Christianity had, in fact, almost completely disappeared in England shortly after the Romans left in 406. Over the next 200 years, Germanic and Norse tribes—Angles, Saxons, Jutes, and Frisians—invited in as mercenaries by Romanized British leaders, began to operate on their own. Their Anglo-Saxon culture, steeped in Germanic and Norse values and traditions, soon came to dominate cultural life in Britain. Nevertheless, at the time of the Sutton Hoo burial, the late 630s, Christianity had begun to reassert itself in England. There is some speculation that the elaborate Sutton Hoo burial ceremony, which included cremation—forbidden by Christianity—and apparent human and animal sacrifice, represented an open defiance of Christian practices.

At the time of its seventh-century burials, Sutton Hoo was, at best, a remote outpost of Anglo-Saxon culture, but no other archeological site has revealed more about the Anglo-Saxons. Whoever was buried there was a lord or chief to whom his followers owed absolute loyalty, the basis of the feudal societies that would later dominate European life in the Middle Ages. **Feudalism** is related to the Roman

◀ **Fig. 10.1 Burial ship, from Oseberg, Norway. ca. 800.** Wood, length 75′ 6″. Vikingskiphuset, Universitets Oldsaksamling, Oslo, Norway. This ship served as a burial chamber for two women. They were laid out on separate beds in a cabin containing wooden chests (empty, but probably once filled with precious objects) and several wooden, animal-head posts.

HEAR MORE Listen to an audio file of your chapter at **www.myartslab.com**

Map 10.1 Anglo-Saxon England and Celtic Ireland.

custom of patronage (see Chapter 6), under which a patron, usually a lord or nobleman, provided protection to a person who worked for him in exchange for his loyalty. In the Middle Ages, this relationship developed into an agriculturally based economic system, in which the tenant was obligated to serve the nobleman (often militarily) and pay him with goods or produce in exchange for use of a piece of land—called a **fief** [feef]—and the nobleman's protection.

The rudiments of this system were in place in sixth-century England. The Anglo-Saxons comprised only about one-tenth of a total population of roughly 1 million; the remainder were Britons. The Anglo-Saxons controlled the land while the Britons largely worked it, and the wealth the Anglo-Saxons extracted from this relationship is everywhere apparent in the treasures discovered at Sutton Hoo. The nobles in control of their various fiefdoms in turn owed allegiance to their king, who was overlord of all the fiefdoms in his kingdom. In return for their loyalty, the king rewarded his nobles with gold, weaponry, and elaborately decorated items of personal adornment, like the artifacts buried at Sutton Hoo.

When Christianity was reintroduced to Anglo-Saxon England, the Church adapted the principles of feudalism. Instead of the tenant owing allegiance to his nobleman and the nobleman to his king, all owed allegiance to the Christian God. Briton and Anglo-Saxon alike might make gifts to the Church, and in return the Church offered them not protection, but salvation. As a result, the Church quickly became wealthy. To decorate its sanctuaries, the

Church promoted the same refined and elaborate handiwork as the feudal lords had commissioned for their personal use, incorporating Christian themes and imagery into the animal and interlace styles of Germanic and Norse culture. And it acquired large parcels of property overseen by a clergy who were feudal lords themselves. These properties soon developed into large working monasteries, where like-minded individuals gathered in the pursuit of religious perfection. The monasteries in turn became great centers of learning.

These monasteries soon began to promote the idea of doing penance for one's sins by embarking on religious pilgrimages. Part of the reason seems to have been the increasing urbanization of Europe, and with it, worsening hygienic conditions that spread disease. Believing that disease was related to sinfulness, pilgrims sought to atone for their sins, saving themselves from sickness and contagion on earth and perpetual damnation in the afterlife. Political and religious motives also played a role. The pilgrimage to Mecca had played an important role in Islamic tradition, and the economic benefits realized by that relatively remote city on the Arabian peninsula were not lost on Rome. But more important, the religious value of a Christian pilgrimage to Jerusalem—the most difficult and hence potentially most rewarding of Christian pilgrimages—demanded that the Western church eliminate Muslim control of the region, a prospect the Church frankly relished. By 1100, thousands of pilgrims annually were making their way to Jerusalem, which Christian forces retook in 1099 in the First Crusade, and to Rome, where the remains of Saints Peter and Paul were housed. Large numbers of pilgrims traveled across Europe to Santiago de Compostela [san-tee-AH-go day kom-poh-STEL-uh], in the northwest corner of modern Spain, where the body of the apostle Saint James the Greater lay at rest, and in England, pilgrims would soon journey to Canterbury to worship at the shrine of Saint Thomas à Becket, the Archbishop of Canterbury, who had staunchly defended the authority of the Church over that of the English throne, resulting, in 1170, in his assassination.

This chapter outlines the rise to power of feudal society and the adaptation of feudal practices by the medieval kings and emperors and by the Christian Church. Perhaps the most important ruler to codify and adopt these practices was Charlemagne [SHAR-luh-mane], who dreamed not only of unifying Europe under his rule, but also of unifying church and state in a single administrative and political bureaucracy. Although Charlemagne's empire dissolved with his death in 843, subsequent rulers, such as the Ottonian kings in Germany, followed his example by building a tightly knit political bureaucracy and championing the arts. But the Church competed with the kings for the loyalty of the people, and in its architecture, in its art, and in the music of its liturgy, the Church sought to appeal to the emotions of the people, calling on them to reject the worldly aspirations of the court and seek the rewards of heaven.

Fig. 10.2 Purse cover, from Sutton Hoo burial ship. ca. 625. Gold with Indian garnets and cloisonné enamels, originally on an ivory or bone background (now lost), length 8". © The Trustees of the British Museum/Art Resource, NY. This elaborate purse lid would have been attached to the owner's belt by hinges. In the Sutton Hoo burial mound, the purse contained gold coins and ingots.

SEE MORE For a Closer Look at the purse cover from the Sutton Hoo burial ship, go to **www.myartslab.com**

ANGLO-SAXON ARTISTIC STYLE AND CULTURE

A purse cover from the Sutton Hoo site (Fig. 10.2) is a fine example of the artistic style of this non-Christian Germanic culture. It is a work of **cloisonné** [kloy-zun-AY], a technique in which strips of gold are set on edge to form small cells. The cells are then filled with a colored enamel glass paste and fitted with thin slices of semiprecious stones (in this case, garnet). At the top of the purse cover shown here, two hexagons flank a central motif of **animal interlace**. In this design, two pairs of animals and birds, facing each other, are elongated into serpentine ribbons of decoration, a common Scandinavian motif. Below this, two Swedish hawks with curved beaks attack a pair of ducks. On each side of this design, a male figure stands between two animals. This **animal style** was used in jewelry design throughout the Germanic and Scandinavian world in the era before Christianity. Notice its symmetrical design, its combination of interlaced organic and geometric shapes, and, of course, its animal motifs. Throughout the early Middle Ages, this style was imitated in manuscripts, stone sculpture, church masonry, and wood sculpture.

In many ways, the English language was shaped by Anglo-Saxon traditions. Our days of the week are derived from the names of Saxon gods: Tuesday and Wednesday are named after two Saxon gods of war, Tiw and Woden.

Thursday is named after Thor, the god of thunder, and Friday after Frigg, Woden's wife. Similarly, most English place-names have Saxon origins. *Bury* means fort, and Canterbury means the fort of the Cantii tribe. *Ings* means tribe or family; Hastings is where the family of chief Haesta lived. *Strat* refers to a Roman road; Stratford-on-Avon designates the place where the Roman road fords the river Avon. *Chester* means Roman camp, as in Dorchester; *minster* means monastery, as in Westminster; and *ham* means home, as in Nottingham.

Society, Law, and Family Life

The survival of Anglo-Saxon names in modern English suggests the degree to which this culture dominated even medieval English life. Earlier Anglo-Saxon culture revolved around the king and his thanes (lords). The king possessed his own large estate, as did each of his thanes, and the king and his retinue moved continually among the estates of the thanes, who owed hospitality and loyalty to the throne. Aside from these few powerful persons, feudal society was composed of peasants. Some were *ceorls*, or churls, free men who owned farms of 90 to 100 acres. Others rented land from the thanes, usually in lots of 20 acres. They paid their lords in goods—sheep or grain—and worked his fields two or three days per week. All employed serfs (day laborers) and thralls (slaves), often captives of wars. (Evidence suggests that by the eighth century, the Anglo-Saxons were routinely marketing slaves abroad, in France and Rome

Dumquid adheret tibi fedes iniqui
tatis: qui fingis laborem in precepto.
Captabunt in animam iufti: ÷san
guinem innocentem condempnabūt.

Fig. 10.3 **Farmers using a moulboard plow and harnessed oxen, from the Luttrell Psalter. ca. 1325–1340.** British Library, London. Add. MS 42130. The Luttrell Psalter is a decorated (illuminated) manuscript from the Middle Ages. It was written and illuminated from about 1325 for a landowner and knight, Sir Geoffrey Luttrell of Irnham in Lincolnshire (England).

particularly.) Runaway slaves were punished by death, as were those convicted of disloyalty to their thanes.

Anglo-Saxon law was based on the idea of the *wergeld*, or "life-price" of an individual. A thane's value was roughly six times that of a churl, and a thrall had no value at all. If a thane were killed (or injured), his family (or in the case of injury, he himself) was entitled to be compensated at the highest fixed rate. But a thane could kill or injure a thrall with no *wergeld* due at all. The *wergeld* for men and women was identical, although a pregnant woman was worth as much as three times the usual rate, and a woman's potential as a bearer of children could raise her value even if she were not pregnant.

The medieval fief averaged from 3,000 to 5,000 acres and included one or more manor houses occupied by the lord. The manor house was surrounded by a small village that included as many as 50 families, a common mill, a wine press, an oven, and a church. Surrounding the village were fields and pasture. Oats, corn, barley, wheat, and rye were the largest crops, and over time, serfs developed the heavy-wheeled plow for cultivating sandy soil and the moulboard plow for plowing clay soils. The tandem four-oxen harness helped them in their work (Fig. **10.3**). They also learned to offset soil depletion by crop rotation, allowing one-third of their fields to lie fallow each year to recover their fertility. They made beer from barley and kept pigs, cattle, goats, and sheep.

Anglo-Saxon law provided women with considerable legal status, including the right to own property and the right to sell it or even give it away without male consent. They could act in their own defense in a court of law and testify to another person's truthfulness, male or female. Women could not marry against their will, nor could they be sold for money. Most of these rights would be lost after the 1066 invasion of England by the Normans, who believed that in marrying a woman they acquired her property as well. Under the Normans, women themselves became property; their function was to serve their husbands.

Fig. 10.4 **A fourteenth-century English manuscript, the Luttrell Psalter. ca. 1325–40.** British Library, London. These illustrations show women at their daily tasks: carrying jugs of milk from the sheep pen, feeding the chickens, carding and spinning wool.

Family life in Anglo-Saxon England consisted largely of work, though there seems to have been a clear division of labor between men and women. In Anglo-Saxon wills, the male line was referred to as the *wœpnedhealf*, "weapon half" or *sperehealf*, "spear half," and the female line the *wifhealf*, "wife half" or *spinelhealf*, "spindle half." Whether this division of labor between warrior and housekeeper extended into the peasant classes is debatable. It seems likely that among the lower classes, all household members worked in the fields, although food preparation and cloth-making remained women's work as well (Fig. 10.4). In fact, the Anglo-Saxon *lorg*, or weaver's beam, later known as the distaff, became the universal symbol of women's side of the family.

Beowulf, the Oldest English Epic Poem

This rigidly hierarchical society is celebrated in the oldest English epic poem, *Beowulf*. In the poem, a young hero, Beowulf [BAY-uh-wolf], comes from afar to rid a community of monsters that have been ravaging it. A treasure very much like that found in the Sutton Hoo ship burial is described just 26 lines into the poem, when the death of Danish king Shield Sheafson is described (**Reading 10.1a**).

READING 10.1a

Beowulf, trans. Seamus Heaney

Shield was still thriving when his time came
and he crossed over into the Lord's keeping.
His warrior band did what he bade them
when he laid down the law among the Danes:
they shouldered him out to the sea's flood,
the chief they revered who had long ruled them.
A ring-whorled prow rode in the harbour,
ice-clad, outbound, a craft for a prince.
They stretched their beloved lord in his boat,
laid out by the mast, amidships,
the great ring-giver. Far-fetched treasures
were piled upon him, and precious gear.
I never heard before of a ship so well furbished
with battle tackle, bladed weapons
and coats of mail. The massed treasure
was loaded on top of him: it would travel far
on out into the ocean's sway.
They decked his body no less bountifully
with offerings than those first ones did
who cast him away when he was a child
and launched him alone out over the waves.
And they set a gold standard up
high above his head and let him drift
to wind and tide, bewailing him
and mourning their loss. No man can tell,
no wise man in hall or weathered veteran
knows for certain who salvaged that load.

The ship described here probably looked very much like the one excavated in 1904 from Oseberg, just outside Oslo, Norway (see Fig. 10.1). Its prow rises to a spiral that corresponds to the "ring-whorled prow" described above. A thick layer of blue clay, nearly impenetrable by water or air and topped with turf, preserved the ship and the other objects of wood, leather, and textiles discovered in it. As *Beowulf* suggests ("No man can tell . . . for certain who salvaged that load"), it seems likely that burial mounds were commonly looted and that the Oseberg mound was plundered in ancient times. No jewelry, gold, or silver was found in the grave.

The findings at Sutton Hoo and Oseberg suggest that *Beowulf* accurately reflects many aspects of life in the northern climates of Europe in the Middle Ages. The poem was composed in Anglo-Saxon, or Old English, sometime between 700 and 1000 CE, handed down first as an oral narrative and later transcribed. Its 3,000 lines represent a language that predates the merging of French and English tongues after 1066, when William the Conqueror, a Norman duke, invaded England. The poem survived in a unique tenth-century manuscript, copied from an earlier manuscript and itself badly damaged by fire in the eighteenth century. It owes its current reputation largely to J. R. R. Tolkien, author of *The Lord of the Rings*, who in the 1930s argued for the poem's literary value. The source of Tolkien's attraction to the poem will be obvious to anyone who knows his own great trilogy.

Beowulf is an English poem, but the events it describes take place in Scandinavia. One of its most notable literary features, common to Old English literature, is its reliance on compound phrases, or **kennings**, substituted for the usual name of a person or thing. Consider, for instance, the following line:

> *Hwœt we Gar-Dena in gear-dagum*
> So. The Spear-Danes in days gone by

Instead of saying "the past," the poem says *gear-dagum*, which literally means "year-days." Instead of "the Danes," it says *Spear-Danes*, implying their warrior attributes. The poet calls the sea the *fifelstréam*, literally the "sea-monster stream," or "whale-path," and the king, the "ring-giver." A particularly poetic example is *beado-leoma*, "battle-light," referring to a flashing sword. In a sense, then, these compound phrases are metaphoric riddles that context helps to explain. *Beowulf* contains many such compounds that occur only once in all Anglo-Saxon literature—*hapax legomena*, as they are called, literally, "said or counted once"—and context is our only clue to their meaning.

The poem opens with Beowulf's arrival among the Danes to rid them of the monster Grendel [GREN-dl]. The monsters in the poem, it becomes clear, are in some sense metaphors for fate and the destructive forces of nature. When Beowulf and his troops meet a Dane guarding the coast, they are undaunted by the prospect of confronting these forces (**Reading 10.1b**):

READING 10.1b

Beowulf, trans. Seamus Heaney

"So tell us if what we have heard is true
about this threat, whatever it is,

---

this danger abroad in the dark nights [Grendel],
this corpse-maker mongering death
in the Shieldings' country. I come to proffer
my wholehearted help and counsel.
I can show the wise Hrothgar a way
to defeat his enemy and find respite—
if any respite is to reach him, ever.
I can calm the turmoil and terror in his mind.
Otherwise, he must endure woes
and live with grief for as long as his hall
stands on the horizon, on its high ground."
Undaunted, sitting astride his horse,
the coast-guard answered, "Anyone with gumption
and a sharp mind will take the measure
of two things: what's said and what's done.
I believe what you have told me: that you are a troop
loyal to our king. So come ahead
with your arms and your gear, and I will guide you. . . ."
So they went on their way. The ship rode the water,
broad-beamed, bound by its hawser
and anchored fast. Boar-shapes flashed
above their cheek guards, the brightly forged
work of goldsmiths, watching over
those stern-faced men. They marched in step,
hurrying on till the timbered hall
rose before them, radiant with gold.
Nobody on earth knew of another
building like it. Majesty lodged there,
its lights shone on many lands.

The Danish king Hrothgar [ROTH-gar] is described elsewhere in *Beowulf* as "the best of earthly kings . . . the best of those who bestowed gold." Like all Anglo-Saxon rulers, he relied on his wealth to guarantee the loyalty of his followers—and, interestingly, a gold boar-shaped helmet crest such as the one described here has been unearthed in England. (Fig. **10.5**).

Beowulf keeps his word and kills Grendel. Subsequently, Grendel's mother attacks in an even more fearsome battle, which again Beowulf wins. But Hrothgar reminds him of life's fragility (**Reading 10.1c**):

READING 10.1c

Beowulf, trans. Seamus Heaney

O flower of warriors, beware . . .
Choose, dear Beowulf, the better part,
eternal rewards. Do not give way to pride.
For a brief while your strength is in bloom
but it fades quickly; and soon there will follow
illness or the sword to lay you low,
or a sudden fire or surge of water
or jabbing blade or javelin from the air
or repellent age. Your piercing eye
will dim and darken; and death will arrive,
dear warrior, to sweep you away.

With these words in mind, Beowulf returns home to Sweden with his men and rules well, but 50 years later, he meets the dragon, or "hoard-guard," who teaches him Hrothgar's lesson. Resigned to the fact that only he of all warriors can defeat the dragon that is menacing his loyal people, he exhibits the courage and loyalty to his vassals that define the warrior's world in the Middle Ages (**Reading 10.1d**).

READING 10.1d

Beowulf, trans. Seamus Heaney

"I would rather not
use a weapon if I knew another way
to grapple with the dragon and make good
    my boast
as I did against Grendel in days gone by.
But I shall be meeting molten venom
in the fire he breathes, so I go forth
in mail-shirt and shield. I won't shift a foot
when I meet the cave-guard: what occurs on the wall
between the two of us will turn out as fate,
overseer of men, decides. I am resolved.
I scorn further words against this sky-borne foe. . . ."
Then he drew himself up beside his shield.
The fabled warrior in his warshirt and helmet
trusted in his own strength entirely
and went under the crag. No coward path.
Hard by the rock-face that hale veteran,
a good man who had gone repeatedly
into combat and danger and come through,
saw a stone arch and a gushing stream
that burst from the barrow blazing and wafting
a deadly heat. It would be hard to survive
unscathed near the hoard, to hold firm
against the dragon in those flaming depths.
Then he gave a shout. The lord of the Geats
unburdened his breast and broke out
in a storm of anger. Under grey stone
his voice challenged and resounded clearly.
Hate was ignited. The hoard-guard recognized
a human voice, the time was over
for peace and parlaying. Pouring forth
in a hot battle-fume, the breath of the monster
burst from the rock. There was a rumble under ground.
Down there in the barrow, Beowulf the warrior
lifted his shield: the outlandish thing
writhed and convulsed and viciously
turned on the king, whose keen-edged sword,
an heirloom inherited by ancient right,
was already in his hand. Roused to a fury,
each antagonist struck terror in the other. . . .
That final day was the first time
when Beowulf fought and fate denied him
glory in battle. . . . Beowulf was foiled
of a glorious victory. The glittering sword,
infallible before that day,
failed when he unsheathed it, as it never should have.
    . . . so every man must yield
the leasehold of his days.

Some have interpreted Hrothgar's admonition to Beowulf to value "eternal rewards" over earthly glory as evidence that the poem is a Christian allegory. And although Beowulf does

Fig. 10.5 Crest of the Benty Grange Helmet, Derbyshire. Late seventh century. Hollow bronze, approx. 3 $1/2$″. Courtesy of Sheffield Galleries & Museums Trust. Boar-crested helmets such as this are described in *Beowulf*. The boar evidently symbolized both ferocity and courage.

indeed give "thanks to Almighty God," and admit that his victory over Grendel would not have been possible "if God had not protected me," there is nothing in the poem to suggest that this is the Christian God. There are no overtly Christian references in the work. At Beowulf's tragic end, he passes "into the Lord's keeping," but "No man can tell . . . for certain" where death will carry him. The poem teaches its audience that power, strength, fame, and life itself are fleeting—a theme consonant with Christian values, but by no means necessarily Christian. And although Beowulf, in his arguably foolhardy courage at the end of the poem, displays a Christ-like willingness to sacrifice himself for the greater good, the honor and courage he exhibits are fully in keeping with the values of feudal warrior culture.

The Merging of Pagan and Christian Styles

Whatever *Beowulf*'s relation to Christian tradition, it is easy to see how the poem might have been read, even in its own time, in Christian terms. Other clearly Christian poems survive from the era, among them *The Dream of the Rood*, in which a poet recounts his dream of a conversation with the wooden cross (the *rood*) upon which Jesus was crucified. Jesus is portrayed as if he were a Germanic king willing to die, like Beowulf, for the greater good. Another is the short poem known as *Caedmon's Hymn*, written by the Anglo-Saxon monk, Caedmon [KAD-mun], probably in the 670s or 680s (**Reading 10.2**). It is the only surviving text of what was reportedly a large body of vernacular religious poetry by Caedmon. Tradition holds that the monk was unable to sing, but one night he heard himself singing his poem in a dream, and he miraculously awoke with the ability to sing it. So that you can see how remote the Anglo-Saxon is from the English translation, here is the original text following the translation.

READING 10.2

from *Caedmon's Hymn*

Now we must praise heaven-kingdom's guardian,
the Measurer's might and his mind-plans,
the work of the Glory-father, when he of wonders of every one,
eternal Lord, the beginning established.
He first created for men's sons
heaven as a roof, holy Creator;
then middle-earth, mankind's Guardian,
eternal Lord, afterwards made
for men earth, Master almighty.

Nu scylun hergan   hefaenricaes uard
metudæs maecti   end his modgidanc
uerc uuldurfadur   sue he uundra gihuaes
eci dryctin   or astelidæ
he aerist scop   aelda barnum
heben til hrofe   haleg scepen
tha middungeard   moncynnæs uard
teci dryctin   æfter tiadæ
firum foldu   frea allmectig

The poem makes traditional use of kennings—*modgidanc*, "mind-plans," for instance, means wisdom. But perhaps what is most notable is that Caedmon's word for "Lord," *dryctin*, is the West Saxon version of the secular and military Germanic word, *truhtin*, "warlord." In Caedmon's use of this word we see the merging of Christian and pagan traditions.

Caedmon's *Hymn* is the product of a gradual re-Christianization of the British Isles that had begun in the fifth century. After the Romans withdrew from Britain in 406, Christianity had survived only in the westernmost reaches of the British Isles—in Cornwall, in Wales, and in Ireland, where St. Patrick had converted the population between his arrival in 432 and his death in 461. Around 563, an Irish monk, Columba, founded a monastery on the Scottish island of Iona. He traveled widely through Scotland and converted many northern Picts, a Scottish tribe, to Christianity. In about 635, almost simultaneous with the pagan burial at Sutton Hoo, in which only a few if any Christian artifacts were discovered, a monk from Iona built another monastery at Lindisfarne [LIN-dis-farn], an island off the coast of Northumbria [north-UM-bree-uh] in northeast England. The "re-Christianization" of Britain was under way.

The Celtic [KELL-tik] Christian Church differed from Roman Christianity in several important ways. It celebrated Easter on the vernal equinox and believed that Mary, mother of Jesus, was exempt from original sin. It invented private confession. The office of bishop was a ceremonial position, and authority rested instead with abbots and abbesses, giving women an important role in the

Fig. 10.6 Bishop Eadfrith, Carpet page, from the *Lindisfarne Gospels* **from Northumbria, England. ca. 698.** Tempera on vellum, 13 ¹/₂″ × 9 ³/₄″. British Library, London. An inscription on the manuscript identifies Eadfrith as its scribe and decorator, Ethelwald as its binder, Billfrith as the monk who adorned it with gems, and Aldred as its translator into Anglo-Saxon: "Thou living God be mindful of Eadfrith, Ethelwald, Billfrith, and Alfred a sinner; these four have, with God's help, been engaged upon this book."

Church. And the Celtic cross is itself unique, symmetrical and superimposed upon a circle.

These differences would later cause considerable difficulty, but meanwhile, in 597, Pope Gregory I (papacy 590–604) sent a mission to England of 40 monks, headed by the Benedictine [ben-uh-DIK-teen] prior Augustine (d. 604)—not the same Augustine who had written *The Confessions* and *The City of God*—to convert the pagan Anglo-Saxons. Augustine met with the Anglo-Saxon king Aethelberht [ETH-el-bert] (r. 560–616) on the island of Thanet, in Kent. The encounter is described by the eighth-century historian Bede [beed] (ca. 672–735) in his *History of the English Church and People*, written in 731:

> After some days, the king came to the island and, sitting down in the open air, summoned Augustine and his companions to an audience. But he took precautions that they should not approach him in a house; for he held an ancient superstition that, if they were practicers of magic, they might have opportunity to deceive and master him. But the monks were endowed with power from God, not from the devil, and approached the king carrying a silver cross as their standard and the likeness of our Lord and Savior painted on a board.

The story narrates the confrontation, in other words, of two distinct styles of thought and art—the animal style, with which Aethelberht was at home, and the Christian icon (see Chapter 8); pagan superstition and Christian faith; an oral, illiterate culture and a text-based one. Although Aethelberht was slow to convert, he allowed Augustine to build a cathedral at Canterbury on the site of an old Roman church and, soon after, a church in London dedicated to St. Paul.

Manuscript Illustration: Blending of Anglo-Saxon and Christian Traditions

In 601, Gregory sent Augustine a letter urging him not to eliminate pagan traditions overnight, but to incorporate them into Christian practice: "For it is certainly impossible to eradicate all errors from obstinate minds at one stroke, and whoever wishes to climb a mountain top climbs gradually step by step, and not in one leap." This is one reason that the basic elements of the animal style, evident in the purse cover from Sutton Hoo (see Fig. 10.2), appear in a manuscript page from the *Lindisfarne Gospels*, designed by Bishop Eadfrith of Lindisfarne in 698 (Fig. **10.6**). Notice particularly how the geometric grids in the border decoration of the purse cover are elaborated in the central circle of the Lindisfarne **carpet page** (a descriptive term, not used in the Middle Ages, that refers to the resemblance between such pages and Turkish or Islamic carpets). The animal interlace of the purse cover reappears in the corner designs that frame the central circle of the carpet page, where two birds face outward and two inward. And the beasts that turn to face one another in the middle of the cover are echoed in the border figures of the carpet page, top and bottom, left and right. The pre-Christian decorative vocabulary of the Sutton Hoo treasure, created to honor a pagan king, has been transformed to honor the Christian conception of God.

This carpet page is an example of a Celtic cross. Legend has it that while preaching to a group of the soon-to-be converted, St. Patrick had been shown an ancient standing stone monument with a circle carved onto it, symbolic, he was told, of the moon goddess. Patrick reportedly made the mark of a Latin cross through the circle and blessed the stone, thereby making the first Celtic cross. The story is probably only a legend—the circle with a cross through it antedates Patrick's arrival in Ireland, where it probably symbolized, in pagan culture, the sun and moon, male and female, unity and balance in all things—but the legend speaks to the *syncretism* [SIN-krih-tiz-um] (the combining of different practices and principles) of the age.

The syncretic [sin-KRET-ik] style of art that flourished in England and Ireland during the early Middle Ages is called *Hiberno-Saxon* (*Hibernia* [hy-BUR-nee-uh] is the Latin name for Ireland). Hiberno-Saxon manuscript illustration is notable particularly for its unification of Anglo-Saxon visual culture with the textual tradition of Christianity. In the monastic *scriptoria* (singular **scriptorium**)—the halls in which monks worked to copy and decorate biblical texts—artists soon began to decorate the letterforms themselves, creating elaborate capitals at the beginning of important sections of a document. One of the most beautiful capitals is a page from the *Book of Kells*, made at Iona in the late eighth century (Fig. **10.7**). The basis of the design consists of the Greek letters *chi* [ky], *rho* [roe], and *iota* [eye-OH-tuh] (X, P, and I, or *chri*), an abbreviation of *Christi*. In this instance, the text begins *Christi autem generatio*, "Now this is how the birth of Jesus Christ came about," quoting Matthew 1:18. The dominant letterform is *chi*, a giant unbalanced X much larger on the left than on the right. Below the right side of the *chi* is *rho*, which curves around and ends with the head of a red-haired youth, possibly a depiction of Christ, which also dots the *I*. Not long after Ionan monks completed this manuscript, Vikings began to threaten the Scottish coast, and the monks retreated to Kells in the interior of Ireland. So great was the renown of the book they had created that in 1006 it was referred to as "the chief relic of the Western world."

The task of Christian missionaries in England was to transfer the allegiance of the people from their king, or thane, to God. They could not offer gold, or material wealth, but only salvation, or spiritual fulfillment. They had to substitute for the great treasure at Sutton Hoo the more subtle treasures of faith and hope. The missionaries' tactic was simple—they bathed the spiritual in material splendor. They illuminated their manuscripts with a rich

Fig. 10.7 *Chi Rho Iota* page, *Book of Matthew*, *Book of Kells*, **probably made at Iona, Scotland. Late eighth or early ninth century.** Tempera on vellum, 13″ × 9 ½″. Trinity College Library. Dublin, MS58 (A.1.6.), fol. 34v. While the abbreviation for *Christi*—*XPI* or *Chri*—dominates the page, the remainder of the verse from Matthew is at the bottom right. *Autem* appears as an abbreviation resembling the letter *h*, followed by *generatio*, which is fully written out. So common were abbreviations in manuscript illumination, saving both time and space, that the scribes were often given the title of official court "abbreviator."

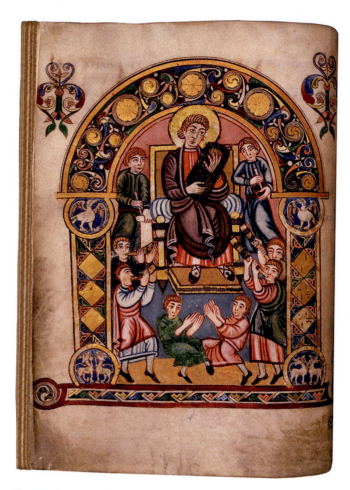

Fig. 10.8 Page with *David and Court Musicians*, now fol. 30b, but likely once the frontispiece of the *Vespasian Psalter*, Canterbury, England. First half of eighth century. British Library, MS Cotton Vespasian A.i. A psalter is a book of psalms. One of the most interesting aspects of this illustration is that it suggests that instrumental music may have played a role in Christian liturgy long before the twelfth century, when instrumentation is usually thought to have been introduced.

decorative vocabulary. They adorned Christianity in gold and silver, jewels and enamel, and placed it within an architecture of the most magnificent kind. And they transplanted pagan celebrations to the context of the Christian worship service.

A manuscript page probably created at Canterbury in the first half of the eighth century is revealing on this last point (Fig. **10.8**). It depicts an enthroned David, author of the Psalms, surrounded by court musicians. The scene could as easily illustrate an episode in *Beowulf* when a great celebration takes place in Hrothgar's hall after Beowulf defeats the monster Grendel:

> They sang then and played to please the hero,
> words and music for their warrior prince,
> harp tunes and tales of adventure:
> there were high times on the hall benches
> and the king's poet performed his part. . . .
>
> *Beowulf, ll. 1062–66*

David, indeed, is a Judeo-Christian version of "the king's poet," only his king is the Christian God. More to the

point, the harp that David plays in the manuscript illustration is very like the six-stringed wooden harp discovered at Sutton Hoo. As the animal-style frames and borders of the scene suggest, this is a celebration any Anglo-Saxon noble would have recognized. In the centuries to come, Christianity would create its own treasure trove, its own celebratory music, its own great halls (the cathedrals), and its own armored warriors fighting their own heroic battles (the Crusades). Beowulf's Grendel would become the infidel Muslim, and his king, his Lord God.

CAROLINGIAN CULTURE

Although England was slow to Christianize, the European continent was not. Christianity was firmly established in 732, at Poitiers [PWAH-tee-ay], France, just south of Tours [toor] in the Loire Valley. There Charles Martel [sharl mar-TELL], king of the Franks, defeated the advancing Muslim army, which had entered Spain in 711 and had been pushing northward ever since. The Arabs retreated south, beyond the Pyrenees, and settled into Spain. The Franks were one of many Germanic tribes— like the Angles and Saxons in England—that had moved westward beginning in the fourth century CE. Most of these tribes adopted most of the Christian beliefs of the Roman culture they conquered, most notably the Ostrogoths in Italy, the Visigoths in southern Gaul (France) and Spain, the Vandals in North Africa, and the Franks, who controlled most of modern France. Unlike the other Germanic tribes, the Franks were Orthodox, or Catholic, Christians, the result of the conversion in 496 of Clovis (ca. 466–511). Clovis was the founder of the first Frankish dynasty, the Merovingians [MER-uh-VIN-gee-uns]. Within a hundred years, the Franks would come to control most of Western Europe.

During the Merovingian era, the Franks attempted to establish order across a broad area that included three major regions: Neustria (western France), Austrasia (roughly comparable to central Germany), and Burgundy (Map **10.2**). They did this by making pacts with the local noble landowners and creating a new royal office, the count. Frankish kings gave land to the counts in return for their loyalty. But by the seventh century, counts and noblemen alike ruled their small territories like petty tyrants, paying little or no heed to the king. Real power rested with the head of each of the three regions, who held the office of mayor of the palace.

With the rise of Pepin I (d. 639) to the position of mayor of the palace in Austrasia, the family which would come to be known as the Carolingians [kar-oh-LIN-gee-uns] gradually assumed complete power. Pepin II's son, Charles Martel (r. 714–41), not only defeated the Muslim army at Poitiers, but also bestowed more property on already landed gentry. These parcels of land, or fiefdoms, were confiscated from the Church, which depended on the Franks for protection and so had little choice in the matter.

Map 10.2 The empire of Charlemagne to 814.

Legend:
The Frankish Empire, 768
} Charlemagne's Kingdom to 814
Tributary Peoples, 814
Possessions of the Byzantine Empire

Fig. 10.9 Equestrian statue of Charlemagne. Early ninth century. Bronze with traces of gilt, height 9 1/2" Musée du Louvre, Paris. Charlemagne stood 6' 3 1/2" tall, remarkably tall for the time.

In 751, with the pope's blessing, the Carolingian nobility elected Martel's son, Pepin the Short, as their king. Three years later, a new pope traveled to Saint-Denis [san duh-NEE], near Paris, where he anointed Pepin protector of the Church and the Carolingians "kings by the grace of God." In return, Pepin led an army south into Italy and crushed the Lombards [LOM-bards], a Germanic people who had invaded Italy nearly 200 years earlier and established a kingdom in the Po valley. Pepin turned the territory over to the pope; the land became known as the Papal States.

Pepin the Short's son, Charlemagne, "Charles the Great" (r. 768–814), had even greater imperial ambitions than his father (Fig. 10.9). (It is for him that historians have labeled this the Carolingian era, from *Carolus*, Latin for Charles.) Charlemagne brought one after another pagan tribe to submission, forcing them to give up their brand of Christianity and submit to Rome's Nicene Creed. Charlemagne's kingdom grew to include all of modern-day France, Holland, Belgium, Switzerland, almost all of Germany, northern Italy and Corsica, and Navarre, in northern Spain. Even larger areas paid him tribute. In return for his Christianization of this vast area, Pope Leo III crowned him emperor on Christmas Day, 800, creating what would later be known as the Holy Roman Empire.

The *Song of Roland*: Feudal and Chivalric Values

Charlemagne's military might was the stuff of legend. For centuries after his rule, tales of his exploits circulated throughout Europe in cycles of poems sung by *jongleurs* [zhohn-GLER], professional entertainers or minstrels who moved from court to court and performed *chansons de geste* [shahn-SOHN deh zhest] ("songs of heroic deeds"). The oldest of these, and the most famous, is the *Song of Roland*, a poem built around a kernel of historical truth transformed into legend and eventually embellished into an epic. Four thousand lines long, composed of ten-syllable lines grouped in stanzas, it was transmitted orally for three centuries and finally written down in about 1100, by which time the story of a military defeat of little consequence had become an epic drama of ideological importance. The *jongleurs* sang the poem accompanied by a lyre. The only surviving musical notations to the poem are the letters *AOI* that end some verses. The exact meaning of this phrase is unclear, but it probably indicates a musical refrain, repeated throughout the performance. Most likely, the poem was sung in a **syllabic** setting, one note per syllable, in the manner of most folk songs even today. Its melody was probably also **strophic**—that is, the same music repeated for each stanza of the poem.

The *Song of Roland* tells the story of an event that occurred in 778, when Charlemagne's rear guard, led by his nephew Roland, Roland's friend Oliver, and other peers, was ambushed by Muslim forces as Charlemagne's army returned from his invasion of Spain. (In fact, it was Basque [bask] Christians who ambushed Charlemagne, and he had actually been invited into Spain by Muslim Saracens [SAR-uh-senz] to help them fight other Muslims. However, over time, the story's villains were transformed from Basque Christians into Muslims for political and propagandistic purposes, as armies were organized to fight in the Middle East for the liberation of Jerusalem from Islam.)

The story is a simple one: The heroic Roland's army is betrayed by Ganelon, who tells the Saracen Muslim army of Roland's route through Roncevaux [ROHNS-voh], where his 20,000 soldiers are attacked by 400,000 Muslims. Roland sounds his ivory horn, alerting Charlemagne to the Saracen presence, but by then the Frankish guard has been defeated. Discovering Roland and his army dead, Charlemagne executes the treacherous Ganelon, and an epic battle between Charlemagne and the Muslims ensues. Charlemagne is victorious—but not without divine intervention. Charlemagne's prayer keeps the sun from setting, allowing his army time to defeat the Saracens.

Roland as the Ideal Feudal Hero The poem embodies the values of feudalism, celebrating courage and loyalty to one's ruler above all else, in this case Roland's loyalty to Charlemagne. Although the feudal obligation of the vassal to his lord had long been established in Germanic culture—among the Anglo-Saxons, for instance—its purest form was probably Carolingian. Roland is an ideal feudal hero, courageous and loyal, but he possesses—or is possessed by—a sense of pride that inevitably leads to his demise, just as Beowulf's self-confidence leads to his. In the following reading (Reading 10.3), Roland's companion, Oliver, counsels Roland that the Muslim (Saracen) army is so great that he ought to use his horn, Oliphant, to call Charlemagne to help him, but Roland's pride prevails.

READING 10.3
Song of Roland

81 Count Oliver has climbed up on a hill;
From there he sees the Spanish lands below,
And Saracens assembled in great force.
Their helmets gleam with gold and precious stones,
Their shields are shining, their hauberks[1] burnished gold,
Their long sharp spears with battle flags unfurled.
He tries to see how many men there are:
Even battalions are more than he can count.
And in his heart Oliver is dismayed;
Quick as he can, he comes down from the height,
And tells the Franks what they will have to fight.

82 Oliver says, "Here come the Saracens—
A greater number no man has ever seen!
The first host carries a hundred thousand shields,
Their helms are laced, their hauberks shining white,
From straight wood handles rise ranks of burnished spears.
You'll have a battle like none on earth before!
Frenchmen, my lords, now God give you the strength
To stand your ground, and keep us from defeat."
They say, "God's curse on those who quit the field!
We're yours till death—not one of us will yield." AOI

83 Oliver says, "The pagan might is great—
It seems to me, our Franks are very few!
Roland, my friend, it's time to sound your horn;
King Charles will hear, and bring his army back."
Roland replies, "You must think I've gone mad!
In all sweet France I'd forfeit my good name!
No! I will strike great blows with Durendal,[2]
Crimson the blade up to the gilt of gold.
To those foul pagans I promise bitter woe—
They are all doomed to die at Roncevaux. AOI

84 Roland, my friend, let the Oliphant[3] sound!
King Charles will hear it, his host will all turn back,
His valiant barons will help us in this fight."
Roland replies, "Almighty God forbid
That I bring shame upon my family,
And cause sweet France to fall into disgrace!
I'll strike that horde with my good Durendal;
My sword is ready, girdled here at my side,
And soon you'll see its keen blade dripping blood.
The Saracens will curse the evil day
They challenged us, for we will make them pay." AOI

85 "Roland, my friend, I pray you, sound your horn!
King Charlemagne, crossing the mountain pass,
Won't fail, I swear it, to bring back all his Franks."
"May God forbid!" Count Roland answers then.
"No man on earth shall have the right to say
That I for pagans sounded the Oliphant!
I will not bring my family to shame.

I'll fight this battle; my Durendal shall strike
A thousand blows and seven hundred more.
You'll see bright blood flow from the blade's keen steel,
We have good men; their prowess will prevail,
And not one Saracen shall live to tell the tale."

86 Oliver says, "Never would you be blamed;
I've seen the pagans, the Saracens of Spain.
They fill the valleys, cover the mountain peaks;
On every hill, and every wide spread plain,
Vast hosts assemble from that alien race;
Our company numbers but a few."
Roland replies, "The better, then, we'll fight!
If it please God and His angelic host,
I won't betray the glory of sweet France!
Better to die than learn to live with shame—
Charles loves us more as our keen swords win fame."

87 Roland is brave, and Oliver is wise;
Both are so brave men marvel at their deeds.
When they mount chargers, take up their swords and
   shields,
Not death itself could drive them from the field.
They are good men; their words are fierce and proud.

¹**hauberks:** long coats of chain mail.
²**Durendal:** Roland's sword.
³**Oliphant:** Roland's horn, made of elephant tusk.

The loyalty of the Franks—and of Roland and Oliver in particular—to Charlemagne is expressed in these words, uttered by Roland a moment later:

> "In his lord's service, a man must suffer pain,
> Bitterest cold and burning heat endure;
> He must be willing to lose his flesh and blood. . . .
> And if I die, whoever takes my sword
> Can say its master has nobly served his lord."

It is out of a sense of duty that Roland turns to face the Saracens—duty to Charlemagne, his lord, and by extension, duty to the Christian God in the battle against Islam. Roland's insistence that he "will strike great blows with Durendal" (his sword is itself a gift from Charlemagne) expresses the Christian nature of the combat. Durendal's golden hilt conceals four relics (venerated objects associated with saints or martyrs), including hairs of St. Denis, the patron saint of France whose name the Franks shout as a battle cry. Thus, each blow is a blow for Christendom. The reward for such dutiful combat is, as he says, the love of his king. But it is also the love of the whole Christian world, demonstrated by the many visual retellings of episodes from the epic in church art and in manuscripts. Indeed, Roland ultimately sacrifices all for his king and his God. Mortally wounded in combat, he "knows that death is very near / His ears give way, he feels his brain gush out." Explicit and vivid language heightens the intensity of the moment, and the directness lends credence to characters who are otherwise reduced to stereotypes ("Roland is brave,

and Oliver is wise"). But, finally, in his slow and painful death—"Count Roland feels the very grip of death / Which from his head is reaching for his heart"—he becomes a type for Jesus, sacrificing himself for all of Christendom.

The Chivalric Code The *Song of Roland* is one of the earliest expressions of feudalism's **chivalric code**. The term *chivalry* (from the French *chevalier* [shuh-VAHL-ee-ay], "horseman") expressed the qualities of an ideal knight, and may in fact more nearly reflect the values of the eleventh century (when the poem was written down) than the eighth-century practices of Charlemagne's day. Nevertheless, something very like this set of values already exists in *Beowulf*. The chevalier was a **knight** (from the German *knecht*, "young soldier"), and he was guided by a strict, though unwritten, code of conduct: courage in battle, loyalty to his lord and peers, and a courtesy verging on reverence toward women. Although in practice these values often broke down, feudalism and chivalry were powerful mechanisms for maintaining social order and political harmony throughout medieval Europe.

Promoting Literacy

Across Europe, the Church had traditionally served as the chief guardian of culture. In its monastic centers, the Roman love of learning had been maintained, especially in the manuscripts transcribed by monastic copyists. But literacy was anything but widespread. Charlemagne sought to remedy this situation at his court at Aachen (modern Aix-la-Chapelle [ex-lay-shah-PELL]), which soon attracted leading scholars and artists, whose efforts Charlemagne rewarded handsomely. Chief among these was an Englishman, perhaps even of Anglo-Saxon origin, Alcuin [AL-kwin] of York (735–804), who in 782 became head of Charlemagne's court school. One of the foremost grammarians and theologians of the period, Alcuin served as Charlemagne's personal tutor.

Alcuin's main purpose in Aachen was to create a curriculum to promote literacy that could be disseminated throughout the Carolingian Empire. Schools designed to teach children basic skills in reading and writing and some further study in the liberal arts and theology were established in Lyon [lee-OH], Orléans [or-lay-AH], Mainz [mynts], Tours, Laon [lan], and Metz, which was a center for singing and liturgy (see Map 10.2). By 798, a decree from Aachen ordered prelates and country clergy throughout the empire to start schools for children. The emphasis was on educating males. The work of the state bureaucracy would fall to them, and by receiving a Christian education, they would lead in accordance with Church principles. But there is evidence that girls, especially those of noble birth, were also admitted to the local schools created by Alcuin.

There was also a religious purpose in educating the people. Charlemagne believed that to spread the gospel, people should be able to read aloud and sing in church, to say nothing of grasping the fundamental truth believed to be

Fig. 10.10 Page with end of Psalm 111 and Psalm 112, *Utrecht Psalter*, **from Benedictine Abbey at Hautvilliers, France. ca. 825–50.** Ink on vellum or parchment, 13″ × 9 ⅛″. Bibliotheek der Rijksuniversiteit, Utrecht, the Netherlands, MS. 32 if. 65 v.

Fig. 10.11 Page in Carolingian miniscule with Psalm 111, from the *Harley Psalter*, **written in Christ Church, Canterbury, England. 1010–1030.** Ink on vellum, 15″ × 12 ¼″. 73 fols. © The British Library Board: Harley 603, f.57v. In the late tenth century, the *Utrecht Psalter* (see Fig. 10.10) made its way to Canterbury, where scribes copied it in the new writing style developed at Charlemagne's court.

revealed in the Bible. Education thus furthered the traditional role of the Church. It provided a means for the Church—and Charlemagne's state as agent of the Church—to insert itself into the lives of every individual. Alcuin published a book of Old and New Testament passages to be read during Mass, as well as a book of prayers and rites that was made obligatory for all churches in the empire in 785. The last eight years of Alcuin's life were dedicated to producing a corrected version of the Latin Vulgate Bible that would become the standard text throughout the Middle Ages.

A New Style of Writing All of this was made possible by one of the less heralded but most important accomplishments of Charlemagne's court—a standardized, legible style of writing. Until this time, manuscripts had employed a Roman script made up entirely of capital letters with no space between the words, a style still evident in the famous *Utrecht Psalter*, made in Reims [rhanz] during Carolingian times (Fig. 10.10). But Charlemagne, who demanded written documentation of his holdings by his vassals, required a more uniform and legible writing style, and Alcuin helped him develop it. The new style, known as *Carolingian minuscule*, was characterized by clearly formed lowercase letters, linked into individual words, with clearly delineated spaces

between each word, and capital letters beginning each sentence. The page from the *Harley Psalter* (Fig. 10.11) is an example of Carolingian minuscule, and except for the writing style, it is a direct copy of the text from the *Utrecht Psalter* shown in Figure 10.10.

The importance of this script to our cultural history cannot be overstated: It is the ancestor of the modern alphabet. All subsequent writing and type fonts derive from this model, and it made written material accessible not only to generations of learned scholars and teachers, but eventually, in the print era, to laypeople throughout Europe.

The Medieval Monastery

The monastery was a central part of Carolingian culture, arguably its most important institution. Before the Carolingian era, monastic life varied widely across Europe. In Italy, the rule of solitude (the Greek word *monos*, from which *monasticism* derives, means "alone") was barely enforced, and life in a monastery could be positively entertaining. If, in Ireland, more austere conditions prevailed, still the lively intellectual climate of the monastery attracted men and women seeking a vocation. Even from monastery to monastery, different conditions and rules prevailed.

Charlemagne imposed on all monasteries in the Frankish kingdom the rule of Benedict of Nursia [NOOR-she-uh], an Italian monk who had lived two centuries earlier (ca. 480–547). The Rule of St. Benedict defined monastic life as a community of like-minded individuals, all seeking religious perfection, under the direction of an abbot elected by the monks. Monks were to live a family life in the pursuit of religious perfection. They were to possess nothing of their own, accepting worldly poverty. They were to live in one place and not wander, guaranteeing the community's stability. And they were never to marry, acknowledging their chastity. Each day was divided into eight parts, the *horarium* [hor-AR-ee-um] (from the Latin *hora*, "hour"). The *horarium* is the daily prayer schedule of liturgical praise called the **Divine Office** (the word *Office* comes from the Latin *officium*, meaning "duty"), marked by recitations of the psalms and the chanting of hymns and prayers at eight specific times of the day, from early morning until bedtime. Between services, the monks studied, worked, and ate a light breakfast and heartier dinner. They lived by the motto of their order: "Pray and work."

The Ideal Monastery: St. Gall The Swiss monastery of St. Gall, near Lake Constance, was Charlemagne's ideal monastery (Figs. **10.12** and **10.13**); its functional, orderly plan was used in many Benedictine monasteries. As medieval historian Walter Horn pointed out in the 1970s, the original plan was laid out in modules, or standard units, of 2 1/2 feet, and the entire complex was composed of multiples or parts of this standard unit. The nave and the transept of the church, each 40 feet wide, are composed of 16 modules. The area where they cross is a perfect square with 16 modules on a side. Each arm of the transept is equal to the crossing square—that is, 16 modules square. The area between the transept and the apse is also one crossing square. And the nave is 4 1/2 crossing squares long—or 56 modules. The rest of the monastery is built on this rational and orderly plan. The length of each monk's bed was to be 2 1/2 modules, the width of each garden path 1 1/4 modules, and so on. This systematic arrangement reflects an increasing tendency in medieval thinking to regard Christianity as a logical and rational philosophy of life, based on carefully constructed arguments and precise definition of parts as orderly as the "rule" of the day in the *horarium*.

Fig. 10.12 Plan for a monastery at St. Gall, Switzerland. ca. 820. Redrawn from an original in red ink on parchment (inscriptions translated into English from Latin). 28″ × 44 1/8″. Stiftsbibliothek, St. Gall, Switzerland.

Fig. 10.13 Reconstruction model of the monastery of St. Gall, after the plan, by Walter Horn. 1965. The monastery builders did not follow this plan exactly; nevertheless, the plan was widely influential. Many of the surviving cathedrals of Europe discussed in the next chapters were originally surrounded by monasteries constructed on this model.

Adjacent to the church, with its imposing westwork, is a **cloister**, or rectangular courtyard, typically arcaded and dedicated to contemplation and reflection. Beside it, on the east side, are the monks' dormitories, latrines, and baths, and on the west, storage cellars. To the south of the cloister is the **refectory**, or dining hall. Further to the south, and to the west and east, behind and adjacent to the refectory are outbuildings housing all the facilities necessary to support a community of approximately 100 monks—a kitchen, a brewery, a bakery, a mill, workshops for artisans, barns for various animals, a vegetable garden (with its own gardener), and an orchard that doubles as a cemetery. Surrounding the entire complex were fields in which the brothers worked. This side of the monastery was reserved for the members of the community.

The general public could enter the north side of the monastery. Here, beside the entrance to the church, we find a hostel, or inn, for housing less-well-to-do visitors, as well as a guesthouse for nobility, and between them a special kitchen (St. Benedict had directed that monasteries extend hospitality to all visitors). Directly to the north of the church is the monastery school, dedicated, by imperial decree, to educating the youth of local nobility. Another school, the novitiate, to the east of the church, was dedicated to the education and housing of young novices—those hoping to take vows and become brothers. In the northeast corner of the monastery was a public hospital, including an herb garden for remedies, the physician's quarters, and a facility for bloodletting—in the Middle Ages and until the nineteenth century the most common means of curing severe illness.

Women in Monastic Life Although the religious life offered women an alternative to life as housewife or worker, life in the convent or nunnery was generally available only to the daughters of aristocrats. Within the monastic system, women could achieve significant prestige. St. Benedict himself had a sister, Scholastica (d. ca. 543), who headed a monastery not far from his own. Hilda, abbess of Whitby (614–80), ran one of the most prominent Anglo-Saxon monasteries, a community of both monks and nuns. One of her most important acts was to host a Council at Whitby in an attempt to reconcile Celtic and Latin factions of the Church in England. It was to Hilda that the poet Caedmon first sang his *Hymn* (see Reading 10.2). She is one of the first women who rose to a prominent position within the largely male medieval Church.

Roswitha [ros-VEE-tah] of Gandersheim [GAHN-durs-hime] (ca. 935–75) never achieved Hilda's political prominence, but she was one of the notable playwrights of her day. Forgotten until the late fifteenth century, her plays concentrate on women heroines whose personal strength and sense of self-worth allow them to persevere in the face of adversity and challenges to their modesty and chastity.

One of the foremost women of the age was Hildegard [HIL-dug-gard] of Bingen [BING-un] (1098–1179), who ran the monastery at Bingen, near Frankfurt, Germany. She entered the convent at the age of eight and eventually became its abbess. Extraordinarily accomplished—she wrote tracts on natural science, medicine, and the treatment of disease, an allegorical dialogue between the vices and virtues, as well as a significant body of devotional songs (see the next section on monastic music)—she is best known as the first in a long line of female Christian visionaries and mystics, a role anticipated in Western culture by the Delphic priestesses (see Chapter 5). Her visions are recorded in the *Scivias*, a work whose title derives from the Latin *Scite vias domini*, "Know the ways of the Lord" (**Reading 10.4a**). The *Scivias* was officially designated by the pope as divinely inspired. A zealous advocate for Church reform, she understood that this recognition lent her the authority to criticize her secular and Church superiors, including the pope himself, and she did not hesitate to do so.

Hildegard of Bingen, *Scite vias domini*

In the year 1141 of the incarnation of Jesus Christ the Son of God, when I was forty-two years and seven months of age, a fiery light, flashing intensely, came from the open vault of heaven and poured through my whole brain. . . . And suddenly I could understand what such books as the psalter, the gospel and the other catholic volumes of the Old and New Testament actually set forth.

Indeed, from the age of girlhood, from the time that I was fifteen until the present, I had perceived in myself, just as until this moment, a power of mysterious, secret, and marvelous visions of a miraculous sort. . . . I have not perceived these visions in dreams, or asleep, or in a delirium, or with my bodily eyes, or with my external mortal ears, or in secreted places, but I received them awake and looking attentively about me with an unclouded mind, in open places, according to God's will.

The page from the *Scivias* reproduced here (Fig. **10.14**) illustrates this passage. Hildegard is shown recording her divine revelation, as her copyist waits to transcribe her words. Such images were directly supervised by Hildegard herself.

Later in the *Scivias*, Hildegard has a vision of the devil (**Reading 10.4** on pages 353–354), embodied as a monstrous worm who oversees a marketplace full of material goods. After describing her vision, she interprets some of the key images. Hildegard's impulse to interpret her own words is typical of religious literature in the Middle Ages: Its primary purpose was to teach and instruct. But, more than that, Hildegard's *Scivias* shares with other visionary and mystical writing of the period an impulse to make the unknowable vividly present in the mind's eye of her audience. Like the Delphic priestess, she directly encounters the divine through revelation and vision.

Monastic Music Hildegard is responsible for more surviving compositions than any other musician, male or female, who worked before the early fourteenth century. Her *Ordo virtutum* (*Play of the Virtues*) is a composition of texts and 82 melodies that dramatizes the conflict between good and evil. In it the devil, who never sings but shouts all his lines, confronts a personification of each of the 16 Virtues. Hildegard

collected all of her liturgical works in a *Symphonia armonie electium revelationum* (*Symphony of the Harmony of Celestial Revelations*). Like her *Scivias*, Hildegard's music is designed to illuminate spiritual truths. She believed that in singing and playing music, the mind, heart, and body become one, that discord among celebrants is healed, and the harmony of the heavens is realized on earth.

By the time that Hildegard was composing, the liturgy, and particularly its music, had become remarkably unified. This had been accomplished at Charlemagne's insistence. Although we have no written melodies from Charlemagne's time, most scholars agree that he adopted a form that later became known as **Gregorian chant**—named after Pope Gregory I, the same pope who sent Augustine to England in 597. Called *cantus planus*, plainsong or **plainchant**, it consisted of **monophonic** songs (that is, songs for one or many voices singing a single melodic line with no harmony). The style of Gregorian chant probably originated in the way that ancient Jews sang the Psalms. In its simplest form, the chant is sung **a capella** (that is, without musical

Fig. 10.14 Facsimile of page with *Hildegard's Vision*, *Liber Scivias*. ca. 1150–1200. Hildegard wrote 33 visionary tracts, collected in *Liber Scivias,* which were acknowledged by the Church as divine. The original manuscript was lost during World War II.

accompaniment) and performed in a syllabic style (a single note for each syllable). Often the final word of each phrase is emphasized by the addition of one or two other notes:

1. Di-xit Dóminus Dómino mé- o : *Séde a déxtris mé- is.

Dixit dominus from Psalm 109

This is the opening line of Psalm 109 ("The Lord said to my Lord: sit on my right hand"). Its four-line staff would become the traditional Gregorian notation, with each note, or **neume** [noom], indicated by a small square. Neumatic chant derives its name from these notes. In **neumatic** [noo-MAT-ik] chant, HEAR MORE at the syllabic style gives way to a form in which each www.myartslab.com syllable is sung to two or three notes (track **10.1**). In later medieval chant, a single syllable may be sung to many HEAR MORE at notes, a practice known as **melismatic** [mel-uz-www.myartslab.com MAT-ik] chant (track **10.2**):

Ky - - ri - e———————— e - - le - i - son

Kyrie Eleison from opening of mass

The Mass Since the earliest times, the celebration of the Mass was a central rite of the Christian Church. It is a celebration of the Eucharist, the fulfillment of Jesus's instruction (recorded in 1 Corinthians 11:24–25) to do in memory of him what he did for his disciples at the Last Supper—that is, Jesus gave his disciples bread, saying, "This is my body," and wine, saying, "This is my blood." Christians generally recognized, in its celebration, the presence of Christ. In the medieval Mass, the *Kyrie* [KIR-ee-ay], which is either the first or second element in every Mass, consists of three phrases: *Kyrie eleison* [ih-LAY-ih-son] ("Lord, have mercy") is sung three times, followed by *Christe* [KRIS-tay] *eleison* ("Christ, have mercy"), likewise sung three times, and then another *Kyrie eleison*, set to different music, repeated three times again. The repetition of three phrases three times each is deeply symbolic, the number three referring to the Trinity, and the three squared (three times three) signifying absolute perfection.

The plainchant composed by Hildegard of Bingen is unique in the range of musical effects it employs. In contrast to the rather narrow scope of most chants of her day, she uses extremes of register to create "soaring arches" that, she believed, brought heaven and earth together. Although traditional plainchant rarely employed intervals greater than a second or third (one or two notes apart on a keyboard), Hildegard regularly used wider intervals such as fourths and fifths, again to create a sense of moving between the divine and mundane. Her melodies ascend rapidly upward as if toward the heavens. She combines neumatic and melismatic passages; the former seem grounded in the everyday, while the latter suggest the joy of salvation. Her unique style

can be more readily appreciated by comparing HEAR MORE at (track **10.3**) to the more traditional approaches www.myartslab.com to plainchant represented in tracks **10.1** and **10.2**.

The most important single element in determining the nature of a given plainchant melody is its function in the liturgy, which remained consistent from the time of Charlemagne through the sixteenth century. Certain chants, focusing on the Psalms, were composed specifically for the eight *horarium* (hours) of the Divine Office and sung exclusively by cloistered monks and nuns. The Rule of St. Benedict required that the entire 150 Psalms be recited each week.

The Mass had its own repertoire of plainchant. It was celebrated once each day, between 6 AM and 9 AM in every church, convent, and monastery, and was open to any baptized member of the community or congregation. Some elements were performed at every Mass, including the Credo, a musical setting of the Nicene Creed (see Chapter 8), while others were sung only on special Sundays or feast days of the liturgical year. The liturgical year revolves around two major feast days, Christmas and Easter; each is preceded by a season of penitence.

Charlemagne standardized the liturgy by creating several singing schools, including one at St. Gall, where plainchant was taught to choirmasters from throughout the empire. "In every bishop's see," he ordered in the Law of 789, "instruction shall be given in the psalms, musical notation, chant, the computation of the years and seasons, and grammar."

THE OTTONIAN EMPIRE

Charlemagne's empire dissolved in 843 when his son Louis the Pious (r. 814–40) divided the kingdom among his own feuding sons, Lothar [LOH-tar], the eldest of the three; Louis the German; and their half-brother, Charles the Bald. To the east, Louis the German ruled most of what is today modern Germany and Austria. To the west, Charles the Bald ruled most of what is now modern France. And between the two was Lothar, whose kingdom extended in a narrow band from the North Sea to Italy. When Lothar died in 855, his kingdom was partitioned among his three sons. With this middle territory thus weakened, Charles the Bald to the west and Louis the German to the east began to fight over it, a contest between the German and French Frankish kingdoms. By the end of the tenth century, two powerful kingdoms—one German, the other French—had emerged.

The German kingdom was led by Duke Otto I (r. 936–73). Otto came to the rescue of Pope John XII in 961, and in return, the pope crowned Otto emperor on February 2, 962. Nevertheless, the pope lost control of the Church, as Otto made it clear that the Church depended on his military support. When John refused to accept the situation, Otto deposed him and proclaimed that the pope ruled at the pleasure of the emperor. Although the Ottonian Empire was a conscious reinvention of the Carolingian dream, unifying church and state in a single administrative and political bureaucracy, it was built on the exercise of power, not consensus, and it collapsed in the eleventh century, as the Church retaliated against secular power.

Ottonian Art

The art created under the five Ottonian rulers (936–1024) is distinguished by its spiritual expressiveness. The so-called *Gero Crucifix*—the oldest surviving large-scale crucifix in carved wood—was commissioned by Archbishop Gero of Cologne [kuh-LONE], in 970 (Fig. **10.15**). It is intensely emotional, focusing on Christ's suffering, not his triumph. The tendons in his chest are drawn tight, and his abdomen protrudes as the weight of his body sags downward in death. That the *Gero Crucifix* is slightly larger than life size adds to its expressive force. It seems less sculpture than real flesh, an object designed to inspire pity and awe in the viewer. Sagging, emaciated, and bloodied, it seems the very opposite of the triumphant Christ of the Resurrection (compare, for instance, Fig. 8.23). It announces a new, powerful expressiveness that would be passed on to the artists of the Romanesque period, discussed in the following pages.

CONTINUITY & CHANGE

Transfiguration of Christ, **p. 269**

CAPETIAN FRANCE AND THE NORMAN CONQUEST

To the west of the Ottonian Empire, the Frankish territory formerly controlled by Charles the Bald was invaded in the middle of the ninth century by Normans—that is, "Northmen"—Viking warriors from Scandinavia. The Viking onslaught was devastating, as they plundered and looted across the north European seas, targeting especially isolated but wealthy monasteries such as Lindisfarne, which they had attacked even earlier, in 793. The Viking invasions fragmented the former empire and caused nobility, commoners, and peasants alike to attach themselves to anyone who might provide military protection—thus cementing the feudal system. By the tenth century, they had raided, explored, and settled territories from North America, which the explorer Leif [leef] Eriksson reached about the year 1000, to Iceland, Greenland, the British Isles, and France. In France, they besieged Paris in 845 and gained control of the lower Seine [sen] valley. In 915, the Frankish king Charles III (r. 893–923) was forced to grant the Norse leader Rolf, or Rollo, permanent control of the region. Rollo became the first duke of Normandy.

The rest of the western Carolingian Empire, now called France, remained fragmented, with various counts and

Fig. 10.15 *Gero Crucifix*, Cologne Cathedral, Germany. ca. 970. Painted and gilded oak, height of figure, 6′ 2″. This is one of the few surviving pieces of wooden sculpture from the period and certainly one of the largest. It is the most powerful representation of Christ as a tortured martyr in the early Middle Ages. A cavity in the back of the head was made to hold a piece of communion bread, the Host. Thus, the crucifix not only represents the body of the dying Jesus, but contains within it the body of Christ obtained through the sacrament of the Eucharist.

dukes competing for power. Finally, in 987, Hugh Capet [KAY-pit], lord of the Île de France [eel deh-frahns], a relatively small domain stretching from Paris and its environs south to Orléans in the Loire [lwahr] Valley, was selected to serve as king. Hugh began a dynasty of Capetian [kuh-PEE-shun] kings that ruled for the next 350 years. From the beginning, the Capetians concentrated their energies on building a tightly knit administrative bureaucracy. Their most contentious relationship was with the dukes of Normandy, who were fiercely independent, going so far as to claim England for themselves, independent of Capetian influence.

The Normans invaded England in 1066, a story narrated in the famous Bayeux [BY-yuh] Tapestry (see Closer Look on pages 336–337). England and northern France thus became one country, with one king, William I, the Conqueror, and a small group of barons who owned estates on both sides of the English Channel. To both pacify and defend themselves against the Saxons, the Normans constructed **motte and bailey** castles (Fig. 10.16). A motte is a raised earth mound, and a bailey is the enclosed courtyard at its base. Archeologists estimate that the Normans built about 500 of them between 1066 and 1086, or one every two weeks. Such fortifications could be built in as little as eight days. In time, elaborate stone castles would replace these fire-prone wooden fortifications.

Fearing an invasion from Denmark, William I ordered a complete survey of the country so that he could more ac-

curately determine how much tax he could raise to provide a new army. Known as the Domesday [DOOMZ-day] (or "Judgment") Book, it measured the population of England at about 1 million, with fully three-quarters of the country's wealth resting in the hands of the king and 300 landowners. Two hundred of these were French nobles, and only two were English. The other hundred were archbishops, bishops, and the heads of monasteries. The rest of the land was in the hands of small farmers, and 90 percent of the population worked on the land. Some were freemen, but most owed at least partial allegiance to a local lord. Ten percent of the people were serfs, who owned no land at all. The Domesday Book gives us a remarkable view of medieval society and of the great gulf between rich and poor upon which it was based.

PILGRIMAGE CHURCHES AND THE ROMANESQUE

Throughout the Middle Ages, it was customary for Christians to go on religious pilgrimages to holy places or sites containing sacred objects. People believed that their prayers for forgiveness, healing, fertility, or anything else would have a better chance of being fulfilled if they were able to get physically close to a holy object, person, or site. The pilgrimage was also an act of piety, demonstrating the pilgrim's faith, and, in part, an act of penance. As Europe became increasingly urbanized, worsening hygienic conditions spread disease. Believing that disease was related to sinfulness, pilgrims sought to atone for their sins, saving themselves from sickness and contagion on earth and perpetual damnation in the afterlife.

Perhaps because it was closer to Northern Europeans than either Jerusalem or Rome, Santiago de Compostela was by far the most popular site of pilgrimages in the eleventh through thirteenth centuries. It had also developed a reputation for repeated miracles, and by the mid-twelfth century, a Pilgrim's Guide to Santiago de Compostela had appeared. Written in Latin, probably by monks in southern France, it describes and illustrates the towns and monuments on the major pilgrimage routes through France and Spain (Map 10.3).

Specific routes soon developed that allowed pilgrims to visit other sacred sites along the way. These sites housed the **relics**—bones, clothing, or other possessions—of Christian saints and martyrs. Relics arrived, virtually by the boatload, from the Middle East, where Crusaders, fighting the Muslims

Fig. 10.16 Motte and bailey castle. When Normans first landed in England, they constructed mounds, called mottes, upon which they built a square wooden tower called a keep. First used as a lookout tower and elevated fighting point, the keep later became an accommodation for the lord of the castle. At the foot of the motte was a flat area called a bailey, surrounded by a wooden stockade. Domestic buildings, including stables, kitchens, and servants' quarters, were located in the bailey. A moat, or trench filled with water, often surrounded the castle—a natural result of digging dirt for the motte.

Map 10.3 The pilgrimage routes.

for control of Jerusalem and other sites sacred to Christianity, purchased them for resale in the West. The resale of these artifacts, whose authenticity was often questionable, helped to finance the Crusades. What was reputed to be the tunic that the Virgin Mary wore when she gave birth to Christ was housed at Chartres [shart]. At Vézelay [VAYZ-lay], the starting point of one of the four routes to Santiago de Compostela, pilgrims could pray to what were asserted to be the bones of Mary Magdalene.

The Abbey Church of Sainte-Foy [sant fwah] at Conques [cohnk] is the oldest of the major pilgrimage churches (Fig. 10.17). The Abbey Church is one of the earliest examples of a style that art historians have come to call the **Romanesque** [roh-mun-ESK], "in the manner of the Romans," because it revives elements of Roman architectural tradition. The basilica tradition that extends back to the Roman Basilica Nova (see Fig. 6.32) became the model for the Romanesque church floor plan, although the wooden ceilings of churches like Old Saint Peter's (see Figs. 8.10 and 8.11) were replaced by much more fire-resistant barrel vaults.

Fig. 10.17 Abbey Church of Sainte-Foy, Conques, Auvergne, France. ca. 1050–1120. Sainte-Foy was the second church on the route to Santiago de Compostela that began at Le Puy (see Fig. 9.20).

The *Bayeux Tapestry*—actually a 231-foot-long embroidery—was sewn between 1070 and 1080, almost certainly by women at the School of Embroidery at Canterbury, in Kent, England—one of the few surviving works by women we have from the period. The embroiderers of the *Bayeux Tapestry* worked with twisted wool, dyed in eight colors, and used only two basic stitches. It was commissioned by Bishop Odo of Bayeux, half-brother of William, Duke of Normandy, whose conquest of England in 1066 it narrates in both pictures and words (in Latin). Like the Column of Trajan (see Figs. 6.22 and 6.23), its story is both historical and biased. The tapestry was designed to be hung around the choir of Odo's Bayeux Cathedral—an unabashed act of self-promoting propaganda on the part of the Normans.

When the English king Edward the Confessor died on January 5, 1066, without an heir, William, Duke of Normandy, claimed the throne, swearing that Edward had promised William the English throne when Edward died. But on his deathbed, Edward named Harold of Wessex king, while two other contenders, Harold Hardrada of Norway and Tostig, Earl of Northumbria, also laid their claims. Battle was inevitable.

William was particularly unhappy with Harold of Wessex's claim to the throne. Harold had visited Normandy, sometime between 1064 and the end of 1065, at the insistence of King Edward. In fact, the *Bayeux Tapestry* begins at this point. The tapestry narrates the Norman point of view, so its reliability is uncertain, but according to both the tapestry and other Norman sources, during his stay, Harold recognized William as Edward's heir. Whether Harold did so willingly is debatable—even the tapestry shows Harold being taken prisoner by a vassal of William.

Harold was back in England before Edward died on January 5, 1066, and he became king, abrogating whatever oath he may have sworn to William. The tapestry shows him in February with Halley's Comet in the sky—interpreted by the Anglo-Saxons as a portent of disaster and resulting, the tapestry implies, from his having broken his oath. Ghost ships, perhaps from a dream, decorate the border below the troubled king, foreshadowing the invasion to come.

As William prepared to invade England from the south, Harold Hardrada and the Norwegians prepared to press their own claims from the north. The weather determined the course of battle. Strong northerly winds kept William

The *Bayeux Tapestry*. 1070–80. Embroidered wool on linen, height 20". Entire length of fabric, 231'. Musée de la Tapisserie, Bayeux, France/With special authorisation of the city of Bayeux/The Bridgeman Art Library. This, the first section of the tapestry, depicts King Edward the Confessor talking to Harold, Earl of Wessex, his wife's brother. He is sending Harold on a mission to France, ostensibly to tell William, Duke of Normandy, that he will be Edward's successor.

The *Bayeux Tapestry*. 1070–80. Musée de la Tapisserie, Bayeux, France/With special authorisation of the city of Bayeux/The Bridgeman Art Library. Harold swears allegiance to William, his right hand on the altar between them, and his left on a chest presumably housing sacred objects from the Cathedral at Bayeux.

The *Bayeux Tapestry*. 1070–80. Musée de la Tapisserie, Bayeux, France/With special authorisation of the city of Bayeux Giraudon/The Bridgeman Art Library. The Normans sail for England. Note the animal-head prow of the ship, which underscores the Norse origins of the Normans.

The *Bayeux Tapestry*. 1070–80. Musée de la Tapisserie, Bayeux, France/With special authorisation of the city of Bayeux/The Bridgeman Art Library. Having returned to England just before Edward's death and having assumed the throne, Harold is disturbed by the arrival of a comet with a fiery tail, visible in the top border.

The *Bayeux Tapestry*. 1070–80. Erich Lessing/Art Resource, NY. Harold, with the green shield, receives an arrow to the eye at the Battle of Hastings. Immediately to the right, a Norman soldier slays him. Note the soldiers stripping armor from the dead in the bottom border.

docked in Normandy, but the same winds favored the Norwegians, who soon landed on the north coast. Harold met them at Stamford Bridge, near York, on September 25, 1066, and defeated them. By then, the winds had changed, and William sailed from the south, landing in Sussex. Harold turned his troops southward, but exhausted from both battle and the hurried march, they were defeated by William's army at Hastings on October 14, 1066. Harold died in the battle. The embroidery ends with a simple statement—"and the English turned and fled"—as if there is nothing more to say.

For seven centuries, the tapestry was cared for at Bayeux Cathedral, where it was hung round the nave on feast days and special occasions. It escaped destruction in the French Revolution in 1789, and was taken to Paris in the early eighteenth century when Napoleon exhibited it in his own propaganda campaign as he prepared to invade England.

Something to Think About . . .

Looking more closely at the sections of the narrative reproduced here, in what ways does the tapestry reveal itself to be a work of propaganda?

SEE MORE For a Closer Look at the *Bayeux Tapestry,* go to **www.myartslab.com**

Fig. 10.18 Reliquary effigy of Sainte-Foy. Made in the Auvergne region, France, for the Abbey Church of Sainte-Foy, Conques, France. Mostly 983–1013 with later additions. Gold and silver over a wooden core, studded with precious stones and cameos, height 34". Church Treasury, Conques. This jewel-encrusted reliquary survived because monks hid it in the wall of the church when Protestants burned the abbey in 1568. It was not discovered until restoration of the church in the 1860s.

The portals of new pilgrimage churches were modeled after the triumphal arches of Rome, but they celebrate the triumph of the Christian God, not a worldly leader. Such a revival of architectural tradition, reaching back for almost an entire millennium, represents in part a lack of technological innovation rather than a philosophical return to Roman traditions. However, the Christian adoption of Roman architectural styles also underscores the long-standing Christian rejection of its Judaic heritage—the Temple and the synagogue—as well as a growing identification with the Greco-Roman West. As this identification took hold, religious fervor came to define the age.

CONTINUITY&CHANGE

The Arch of Titus, **p. 197**

The Abbey Church at Conques housed the relics of Saint Foy ("Saint Faith" in English), a child who was martyred in 303 for refusing to worship pagan gods. Her remains were contained in an elaborate jeweled **reliquary** (Fig. **10.18**), a container used to protect and display sacred relics. It stood in the choir of the church, where pilgrims could view it from the ambulatory. The head of the reliquary, which is disproportionately large, was salvaged from a late Roman wooden mask and covered with gold foil. Many of the precious stones that decorate the reliquary were gifts from pilgrims. The actual remains of the saint were housed in a recess carved into the back of the reliquary, and below it, on the back of her throne, was an engraving of the Crucifixion, indicating the connection between Saint Foy's martyrdom and Christ's.

Like the largest of the pilgrimage churches, Sainte-Foy was constructed to accommodate large numbers of visitors. Its west portal was large and opened directly into the nave (Figs. **10.19** and **10.20**). Wide aisles skirted the nave and continued around the transept, choir, and apse, creating the ambulatory. A second-story gallery was built over the side aisles; it both accommodated still more people and served structurally to support the extra weight of the arched stone ceilings.

The **barrel vault** that rises above the nave of Sainte-Foy is one of the distinctive features of Romanesque architecture. As we saw in Chapter 6, barrel vaults are elongated arched masonry structures spanning an interior space and shaped like a half cylinder. In Romanesque churches, the space created by such vaults was designed to raise the worshipping pilgrims' eyes and thus direct their thoughts to heaven. An especially interesting example of this effect can be seen in the groin vaults of the Romanesque church of Sainte-Madeleine [sant-mad-LEN] at Vézelay (Fig. **10.21**). As at Sainte-Foy, the nave is divided into sections, called **bays**, by the round arches of the vault. But at Vézelay, these arches are constructed of alternating pink and gray stone voussoirs [voo-SWAR], the wedge-shaped stones that form the arch,

CONTINUITY&CHANGE

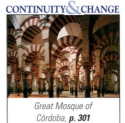

Great Mosque of Córdoba, **p. 301**

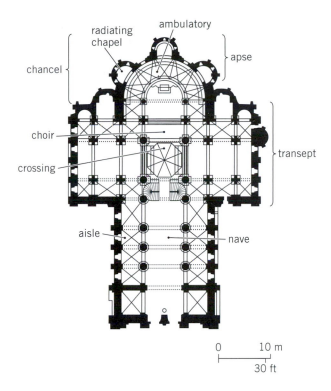

Figs. 10.19 and 10.20 Floor plan and interior of the nave, Sainte-Foy, Conques. ca. 1050–1120. Some of the innovations of the Romanesque cathedral can be explained, at least in part, by the need to allow pilgrims to pass through the church without disturbing the monks as they attended to their affairs at the main altar in the choir. Thus, an ambulatory extended around the transept and the apse where pilgrims could walk.

quarried locally. The effect is similar to the interior of the Great Mosque at Córdoba [KORD-uh-buh] (see Fig. 9.13), built 300 years earlier, although it remains uncertain if they were influenced by the Islamic mosque. This alternation of brick and stone is a fairly common building technique in Roman architecture, and in fact it may be the case that the architects at Córdoba were themselves imitating Roman models. The effect of the alternating voussoirs at Vézelay, as at Córdoba, is to lighten the visual impact of the arches, giving them an almost airy height.

The pilgrimage churches evidently competed with one another in decorating their basilicas. Writing in the eleventh century, the French Benedictine monk Raoul Glaber [rah-ool-glay-bear] noted, "throughout the world, especially in Italy and Gaul, a rebuilding of church basilicas [is occurring], . . . each Christian people striving against the others to erect nobler ones." The portals to the churches were of special importance. Not only was the portal the first thing the visitor would see, it also marked the boundary between secular and sacred space. The space created under the portal arch, called the **tympanum** [TIM-puh-num], was filled with sculptural relief.

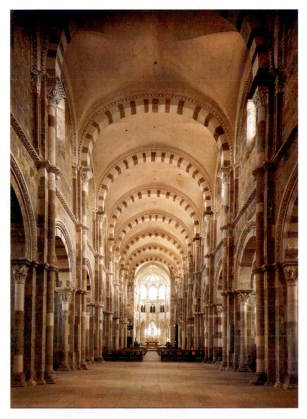

Fig. 10.21 Interior of the nave, Church of Sainte-Madeleine, Vézelay, France. ca. 1089–1206. The nave of this church is extremely long, nearly 200 feet, giving pilgrims a sense of ever-increasing majesty as they moved from the portal at the western, "dark" end of the church toward the choir and reliquary at the eastern end, toward the light of salvation. Vézelay was extensively restored in the nineteenth century.

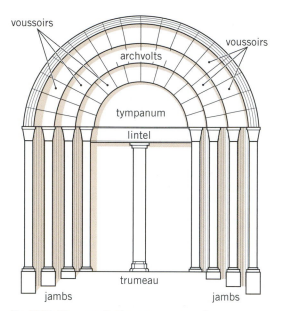

voussoirs

voussoirs

archvolts

tympanum

lintel

trumeau

jambs

jambs

Fig. 10.22 Diagram of a Romanesque portal.

Fig. 10.23 *Last Judgment*, **tympanum and detail of west portal, Sainte-Foy, Conques. ca. 1065.** This depiction of the Last Judgment uses composition subtly and effectively to distinguish the saved from the damned. To Christ's left, the action is chaotic—figures twist and turn in often unpredictable directions. To his right, on the other hand, everyone stands upright under orderly arrangements of arches.

Fig. 10.24 Detail of west portal tympanum of Sante-Foy, Conques. Showing, in lower register, Satan meting out punishments and torture.

LEARN MORE View an architectural simulation of the Romanesque portal at **www.myartslab.com**

All of the elements of Romanesque portals were equally subject to decorative relief (see diagram, Fig. 10.22): the lintel, **jambs** (the vertical elements on both sides of door supporting the lintel or arch), **trumeau** [troo-MOH] (the column or post in the middle of a large door helping to support the lintel), and the **archivolt** [AR-ki-volt] (the curved molding formed by the voussoirs making up the arch). The tympanum of Sainte-Foy at Conques depicts *The Last Judgment* (Figs. **10.23** and **10.24**). At the center of the tympanum, Christ raises his right arm to welcome those who are saved. His lowered left hand points to hell, the destination of the damned. He sits enthroned in a **mandorla**, an almond-shaped oval of light signifying divinity, a motif imported to the Western world from the Far East, through Byzantium (see Fig. 8.23), and one widely used by Romanesque artists. Below Christ's feet, the weighing of souls is depicted as a contest between the archangel Michael and a desperate demon who cheats by pressing his forefinger onto the pan, nevertheless failing to overcome the goodness of the soul in question.

The lintel is divided into two parts: on the left, heaven, and on the right, hell. The two are divided by a partition: An angel welcomes the saved, while on the other side, a demon armed with a bludgeon shoves the damned into hell's monstrous jaws. Situated frontally under the arches of heaven, the saved give the appearance of order and serenity, while all is confusion and chaos on hell's side. Satan stands in the center of the right lintel (see Fig. 10.24), presiding over an astonishing array of tortures. On Satan's left, a figure symbolizing Pride is thrown from his high horse, stabbed through with a pitchfork. Next to them, a bare-breasted adulteress and her lover await Satan's wrath. A figure symbolizing Greed is hung from on high with his purse round the neck and a toad at his feet. A demon tears the tongue out of Slander. In the small triangular space at the right above Satan, two fiendish-looking rabbits roast a poacher on a spit. In the corresponding triangular space to the left, a devil devours the brain of a damned soul who commits suicide by plunging a knife into his throat. Close by, another hunchbacked devil has just grabbed the harp of a damned soul and tears his tongue with a hook. Such images were designed to move the pilgrim to the right hand of Christ, not the left.

These themes are the focus of perhaps the most famous sermon of the Middle Ages, *On the Misery of the Human Condition*. Pope Innocent III (papacy 1198–1216) wrote this tract before his ascension to the papacy; on his election, the Church cardinals unanimously approved it as official Church doctrine. In the sermon, Innocent rails at length on the wretchedness and worthlessness of human beings, their weaknesses, folly, selfishness, vileness, their crimes, and their sins. He describes the human body as putrid in both life and death: "In life, [man] produced dung and vomit; in death he produces rottenness and stench." But perhaps most dramatically, he catalogues the fate that awaits them in hell (**Reading 10.5**):

READING 10.5

from Pope Innocent III, *On the Misery of the Human Condition*

There shall be weeping and gnashing of teeth, there shall be groaning, wailing, shrieking and flailing of arms and screaming, screeching, and shouting; there shall be fear and trembling, toil and trouble, holocaust and dreadful stench, and everywhere darkness and anguish; there shall be asperity, cruelty, calamity, poverty, distress, and utter wretchedness; they will feel an oblivion of loneliness and namelessness; there shall be twistings and piercings, bitterness, terror, hunger and thirst, cold and hot, brimstone and fire burning, forever and ever world without end. . . .

Such imagery is meant to strike terror into the soul of listeners by serving as a **memento mori** [mi-MENT-oh MORE-ee], a "reminder of death." Faced with such prospects, pilgrims were willing to endure the physical hardship and considerable danger their journeys entailed. Some brought great sums of money with them—gold, silver, jewelry, at least enough money to pay for their lodging and meals. If they inaugurated a new economy of hospitality in their travels, they also invited larceny, even murder, and bandits plagued the pilgrimage routes.

Cluny and the Monastic Tradition

One of the most influential of the Romanesque pilgrimage churches was the Abbey of Cluny. Like Charlemagne's Saint-Gall (see Figs. 10.12 and 10.13), Cluny, founded in about 910, was a reformed Benedictine monastery. The Cluniac [KLOO-nee-ak] order enjoyed a special status in the Church hierarchy, reporting directly to the pope and bypassing all feudal or ecclesiastic control. No secular ruler could exercise any control over the monastery (the origin of our modern insistence on the separation of Church and State). Furthermore, the Cluniac order insisted on the celibacy of its monks and nuns—the Church was to be their only lord and spouse. Celibacy was not the rule elsewhere, and was not officially imposed on Catholic priests until 1139.

Perhaps the most important role of the Cluniac order was its sense of culture as wider than local traditions. Its monks preserved and translated classical texts. They rediscovered, particularly, Latin and Roman antecedents. The plan of their church mimicked Old St. Peter's in Rome. They were lovers of knowledge and of beauty (both considered chief attributes of the Almighty), and of classical means of representation. The naturalism we associate with Greek and Roman art gradually began to find favor once again.

Cluny's abbot was among the most powerful men in Europe; Abbot Hugh de Semur, who ruled the abbey from 1049 to 1109, was the most influential of these. In 1088,

Fig. 10.25 Reconstruction drawing of the Abbey Church (Cluny III), Cluny, Burgundy, France. 1088–1130. View from the east (after Conant).

Hugh began work on a new church for the abbey, supported financially by King Alfonso VI of León [lay-OHN] and Castile [kah-STEEL], in northern Spain. Known as Cluny III (Fig. 10.25) because it was the third church built on the site, it was described by a contemporary as "shining on the earth like a second sun." Today only a portion of its south transept and tower remain—the rest was destroyed in the late eighteenth century by French revolutionaries.

The entire arrangement reflects the ideal Carolingian monastery at Saint-Gall. Originally, the barrel-vaulted ceiling of Cluny III soared to a height of nearly 100 feet. It had a five-aisled nave and a double transept. From the portal to the end of the apse, the interior space stretched 415 feet—twice as long as Vézelay's impressive nave. The interior of the church was richly decorated. The floor was paved with mosaic, and an elaborate sculpture scheme, most of which was painted in brilliant colors, lined the walls. Over 1,200 carved capitals topped the interior columns. Of these, some of the most interesting crowned a semicircular group surrounding the high altar, among them a pair that depicts the eight tones of the sacred psalmody (Fig. 10.26). They indicate the impor-

tance of the liturgy to the Cluniac order and the centrality of music to that liturgy. The rich decoration, the soaring space of the stone architecture (which naturally enhanced the sound of the monks' chants), and music itself showed the faithful, according to the monk Theophilus, writing in the first decades of the twelfth century, "something of the likeness of the paradise of God."

Choral Music Benedictine monks at Cluny introduced choral music into the liturgy sometime in the first half of the tenth century. Odo of Cluny (879–942), the monastery's second abbot, was an important musical theorist. He is often credited with developing one of the first effective systems of

Fig. 10.26 *The Third Tone of the Sacred Psalmody*, ambulatory capital from the Abbey Church (Cluny III), Cluny, Burgundy, France. 1088–1130. Farinier Museum of the Abbey at Cluny. The inscription reads: "The third [tone] strikes, and represents the resurrection of Christ." The lyre, with its strings stretching upward to the horizontal frame, was thought to resemble the cross.

musical notation, used to teach choral music to other monasteries in the Cluniac fold. The method used the letters A through G to name the seven notes of the Western scale. Working from Odo's example, 100 years later Guido [GWEE-doh] of Arezzo [ah-RET-soh] (ca. 990–ca. 1050) introduced the idea of depicting notes on a staff of lines so that the same note always appears on the same line. With this innovation, modern musical notation was born.

Choral music introduces the possibility of **polyphony** [puh-LIF-uh-nee]—two or more lines of melody—as opposed to the monophonic quality of Gregorian chant (see Chapter 12). The earliest form of this new polyphonic music was called **organum**. It simply consists of voices singing note-to-note in parallel. Probably the first instance of this would have been adult monks singing a monophonic chant in parallel with boys' voices singing the same melody at a higher pitch. Soon the second voice began to move in contrary motion to the bass chant (**free organum**), or to add numerous notes to individual syllables above the bass chant (**melismatic organum**). An excellent example of melismatic organum is the "Alleluia, dies sanctificatus" by the composer Léonin, who worked from 1163 to 1190 at Notre-((•• **HEAR MORE** at Dame [noh-truh-dahm] Cathedral in Paris www.myartslab.com (track **10.4**). The movement of the two voices could be diagrammed as shown here:

Diagram of melismatic organum from Léonin's "Halleluia, dies sanctificatus."

The lower voices hold unusually long notes, while the upper voices move more rapidly and freely, creating two independent musical lines. One can only imagine how music like this, performed by as many as 100 voices, might have sounded in Cluny III, which was famous for its acoustics.

The Cistercian Challenge

Not everyone supported the richness of the Cluniac liturgy and its accompanying music, art, and architecture. From the point of view of Bernard, abbot of Clairvaux [clair-VOH], such artistic excess—in other words, beauty—was an affront to the monastic mission. Chief spokesperson for a new order of Cistercian [sis-TUR-shun] monks, Bernard of Clairvaux (1091–1153) advocated a rigorous application of the rule of Saint Benedict. Cistercians were to be self-sufficient, living off their own cultivation of the land (this proved impossible in practice). They were to live a simple life of self-imposed poverty symbolized by the undyed wool of their habits. And their plain, undecorated churches stand in stark contrast to the grandeur and opulence of the rest of Romanesque

architecture. Can it be, Bernard asks in his *Apologia for Abbot William*, that the riches of such large and sumptuous churches as Cluny and others are meant to stimulate financial donations to the Church? Is it really true, he asks, that if "their eyes are feasted with relics . . . their purse strings are loosed"? Bernard is denouncing not beauty itself, but the use of beauty for monetary profit. He also objects to the fact that it distracts attention from prayer. The Cistercians belong to a long tradition of thought that challenges the role of art in religion, extending back to the early years of Islam and the iconoclasts in Byzantium, although they do not oppose the use of imagery. They simply discourage using imagery in an ostentatious way.

THE CRUSADES

On November 25, 1095, at the Council of Clermont [KLER-mohn] (modern Clermont-Ferrand [fuh-RAHND]), Pope Urban II (papacy 1088–1099) preached the First Crusade. The pope had received his training as a monk at Cluny, under the direct tutelage of Hugh de Semur. What motivated the First Crusade is difficult to say. We know that throughout Christendom there was a widespread desire to regain free access to Jerusalem, which had been captured by the Arabs in 638. In part, however, the aim was to bring peace to Europe. Because of the feudal **primogeniture** system, by which the eldest son in a family inherited all of its property, large numbers of aristocratic younger brothers were disinherited and left to their own devices. They had taken to feuding with one another (and with their elder brothers) and raiding other people's land. The Crusades organized these disenfranchised men with the promise of reward, both monetary and spiritual: "Jerusalem," Urban preached, "is the navel of the world; the land is fruitful above all others, like another paradise of delights. . . . Undertake the journey [also] for the remission of your sins, with the assurance of the imperishable glory of the kingdom of heaven." The pope also presented the Crusades as a Holy War.

> A race from the kingdom of the Persians, an accursed race, a race utterly alienated from God . . . has invaded the lands of the Christians and has depopulated them by the sword, pillage and fire. . . . They destroy the altars, after having defiled them with their uncleanness. . . . When they wish to torture people by a base death, they perforate their navels, and dragging forth the extremity of the intestines, bind it to a stake; then with flogging they lead the victim around until the viscera having gushed forth the victim falls prostrate upon the ground. . . . What shall I say of the abominable rape of the women? . . . On whom therefore is the labor of avenging these wrongs and of recovering this territory, if not upon you?

It was convincing rhetoric. Nearly 100,000 young men signed on.

The First Crusade was thus motivated by several forces: religious zeal, the desire to reduce conflict at home by sending off Europe's feuding aristocrats, defending Christendom from barbarity, the promise of monetary reward otherwise unavailable to the disenfranchised young nobility, and, not least of all, that nobility's own hot blood and sense of adventure. The First Crusade was a low point in Christian culture. Late in the year 1098, having destroyed the city of Antioch [AN-tee-ok], the Frankish army (called the *Franj* by the Muslims) attacked the city of Ma'arra (modern Ma'arrat an Nu'man in Syria). "For three days they put people to the sword," the Arab historian Ibn al-Athïr wrote, "killing more than a hundred thousand people and taking many prisoners." This is undoubtedly an exaggeration, since the city's population was then something under 10,000, but the horror of what happened next somewhat justifies Ibn al-Athïr's numbers. As reported by Frankish chronicler Radulph of Caen, "In Ma'arra our troops boiled pagan adults in cooking pots; they impaled children on spits and devoured them grilled." In an official letter to the pope, the commanders explained: "A terrible famine racked the army in Ma'arra, and placed it in the cruel necessity of feeding itself upon the bodies of the Saracens." An anonymous poet of Ma'arra lamented: "I know not whether my native land be a grazing ground for wild beasts or yet my home!" Descriptions of the slaughter of the citizens of Jerusalem, when the Crusaders finally took that city on July 15, 1099, are no less gruesome. One important account of the First Crusade is the *Deeds of the Franks*, a history written anonymously about 1100–1101 (**Reading 10.6**, pages 354–355)

The Muslim peoples of the Middle East were not the only victims of the Crusades. During the early days of the First Crusade in 1096, Count Emicho of Leiningen, in present-day Germany, making his way down the Rhine to embark for Jerusalem, robbed and murdered all the Jews he could find, killing 800 in Worms and wiping out the entire Jewish population of both Mainz and Cologne. Emicho seems to have been motivated by the need for funds to support his army, but his was a religious war as well. In his eyes,

Map 10.4 The Crusades. 1096–1204. The First Crusade was predominantly over land, but the subsequent efforts were all by sea.

Fig. 10.27 **Krak des Chevaliers, Syria. First occupied 1109.** Two lines of defense made the castle virtually impenetrable. An aqueduct brought water to the castle. Water was stored in huge cisterns beneath the outer ward. If during siege the water supply was cut off, the knights could hold out for several months.

the Jews, like the Muslims, were the enemies of Christ. Local bishops, to their credit, attempted to stop the carnage, and Bernard of Clairvaux would later preach against the persecution of Jews, but in the Middle East, once Jerusalem was taken, Jews were burned alive or sold into slavery. The small number who survived did so by converting to Christianity.

The First Crusade was militarily successful. But by the middle of the eleventh century, Islamic armies had recaptured much of the Middle East, prompting a Second Crusade from 1147 to 1149, and then a Third in 1189 (see Map **10.4**). Politically and religiously, the first three Crusades were failures. Rather than freeing the Holy Land from Muslim influence, they cemented it more firmly than ever. But they did succeed in stimulating Western trade with the East. Merchants from Venice, Genoa, and Pisa followed the Crusaders into the region, and soon new wealth, generated by these new markets, flowed into Europe. The Fourth Crusade in 1202 was motivated almost entirely by profit as Venice agreed to transport some 30,000 Crusaders in return for their destroying its commercial rivals in the Adriatic and Aegean, particularly Constantinople.

Krak des Chevaliers and the Medieval Castle Krak des Chevaliers [krahk day shuh-VAHL-yay] (Fig. **10.27**), in northern Syria, was first occupied by Crusaders in 1109, and, beginning in 1142, it was occupied by the Knights Hospitaller, whose mission was to care for the sick and wounded. During the Crusades, it was besieged 12 times, finally falling to Berber invaders in 1271.

Krak des Chevaliers was modeled on the castle-fortresses built by the Normans in England and northern France. When the Normans arrived in England in the twelfth century, they needed defenses against the Saxons. To provide protection, they built mounds, or mottes, topped with a wooden tower, or keep (see Fig. 10.16). Beginning in 1078, stone castles gradually replaced these wooden fortifications (Fig. **10.28**). The sheer weight of the stone keep required that it be built on solid ground. So, unless a natural hill presented itself, the motte (the mound on

Fig. 10.28 **Stone castle.** Surrounded by a moat, a trench filled with water, the stone castles that replaced motte and bailey castles were eminently defensible, comparatively immune from fire, and rising as high as 100 feet, imposing symbols of Norman power.

which the older wooden towers had been built) was eliminated. Now the keep served as the main residence of the lord and included a main hall, a chapel, and a dungeon. Workshops, kitchens, and storehouses surrounded the bailey. Most stone castles had a well for fresh water in case of siege, a great advantage over the aqueduct supplying Krak des Chevaliers.

ELEANOR OF AQUITAINE AND THE ART OF COURTLY LOVE

In the Second Crusade, Eleanor of Aquitaine [ak-wuh-TAIN] (ca. 1122–1204) accompanied her husband, King Louis [LOO-ee] VII, into battle in the Middle East, along with 300 ladies of similar mind, all dressed in armor and carrying lances. Her intent was to help the sick and wounded. The women, most of whom eventually returned safely to Europe, never engaged in battle, but theirs was an act of uncommon personal and social bravery. They were widely chided by contemporary commentators, but their actions underscore the changing role of women in medieval society.

Perhaps most notably, women, especially women of noble birth, were becoming increasingly literate. This was the time in which the great oral poems of the first millennium—poems like *Beowulf* and *Song of Roland*—were first written down. Furthermore, over 2,600 poems survive as texts composed by the **troubadour** poets of Eleanor's own day, and some of these survive with the accompanying music for the poems as well. In the decade that she lived at Poitiers, from 1170 to 1179, Eleanor and her daughter by Louis VII, Marie, Countess of Champagne, established that city as the center of a secular culture and literary movement that celebrated the art of courtly love.

Troubadour poetry originated in the south of France, in Provence, the area around the lower Rhone Valley, and slightly later spread north (the Northern poets are sometimes called *trouvère* poets to distinguish from their Southern forebears—and far more *trouvère* music survives than troubadour). The troubadour poets, most of them men, though a few were women, usually accompanied themselves on a lyre or lute, and in their poems they can be said to have "invented" romantic love as we know it today—not the feelings and emotions associated with love, but the conventions and vocabulary that we use to describe it. The primary feeling is one of longing, of a knight or nobleman for a woman (usually unattainable because married or of a higher status), or, when the troubadour was a woman—a **trobairitz**—the reverse. Thus, to love is to suffer, to wander aimlessly, unable to concentrate on anything but the mental image of the beloved, to lose one's appetite, to lie sleepless at night—in short, to give up life for a dream. There was, in addition, a quasi-religious as-

Fig. 10.29 Casket with scenes of courtly love, from Limoges. ca. 1180. Champlevé enamel, $3\frac{5}{8} \times 8\frac{1}{2} \times 6\frac{3}{8}$". © The Trustees of the British Museum/Art Resource, NY. At the left, a lady listens, rather sternly, as a troubadour poet expresses his love for her. In the center is a knight, sword in one hand and key to the lady's heart in the other. On the right, the knight kneels before the lady, his hands shaped in a heart; a rope around his neck, held by the lady, signifies his fidelity to her.

pect to courtly love. Recognizing that he is beset by earthly desires, the lover sees his ability to resist these temptations and rise above his own base humanity as evidence of his spiritual purity. Finally, in the courtly love tradition, the smitten knight or nobleman must be willing to perform any deed to win his lady's favor. In fact, the loyalty that he once conferred upon his lord in the feudal system is, in courtly love, transferred to his lady (who is often, in fact, his lord's wife), as the scenes on a jeweled twelfth-century casket make clear (Fig. **10.29**). If the courtly love tradition reduced women to little more than objects of male desire, in some measure it also allowed them to share in the power enjoyed by their husbands. The thirteenth-century poet Guiraut Requier [GEAR-oh reh-KEY-ay] wrote that four ranks of musicians existed. The lowest was the *jongleurs*, musicians who not only sang but also engaged in acrobatics, animal tricks, and other like entertainments. *Minstrels* were next on the ladder, full-time musicians of lesser station than troubadours because they did not write their own material. The *troubadours* composed their own music and lyrics and performed their own songs, most often at court. The highest rank of musician was *doctores de trobar* (*trobar* means "to invent" and is the root of *troubadour*), the most outstanding composers of the day.

Bernard de Ventadour One of these *doctores de trobar* was Bernard de Ventadour [VON-tuh-door] (d. 1195?). His poems, composed in honor of Eleanor, became staples of court society. Bernard apparently first met Eleanor at Anjou and accompanied her to England after she became queen. Thus, it is likely that his music influenced English song as well as French. Bernard's work is remarkable in that 41 of his surviving songs are musically notated, so that they can be performed today more or less as they were originally. "The Skylark" is typical (track **10.5**, **Reading 10.7**).

((• HEAR MORE at www.myartslab.com

chronicler, wrote "many good songs" dedicated to him. Of the four of these late-twelfth- or early-thirteenth-century songs that survive, only one, "A chantar" ("Song"), still has its music (track **10.6**). Each line of the poem has its own musical phrase, and, as is true for most secular song, the music is strophic—the same music repeats in each stanza.

HEAR MORE at www.myartslab.com ●))

Beatriz's "Cruel Are the Pains I've Suffered" is an example of the remarkable freedom of expression that a *trobairitz* could enjoy. She clearly regrets her choice to remain true to her husband, and in fact the poem reads as a frank invitation to adultery (**Reading 10.8**):

READING 10.7

Bernard de Ventadour, "The Skylark," verses 1–4 and 7

Now when I see the skylark lift
His wings for joy in dawn's first ray
Then let himself, oblivious, drift
For all his heart is glad and gay,
Ay! such great envies seize my thought
To see the rapture others find,
I marvel that desire does not
Consume away this heart of mine.

Alas, I thought I'd grown so wise;
In love I had so much to learn:
I can't control this heart that flies
To her who pays love no return.
Ay! now she steals, through love's sweet theft,
My heart, my self, my world entire;
She steals herself and I am left
Only this longing and desire.

Losing control, I've lost all right
To rule my life; my life's her prize
Since first she showed me true delight
In those bright mirrors, her two eyes.
Ay! once I'd caught myself inside
Her glances, I've been drowned in sighs,
Dying as fair Narcissus died
In streams that mirror captive skies.

Deep in despair, I'll place no trust
In women though I did before;
I've been their champion so it's just
That I renounce them evermore;
When none will lift me from my fall
When she has cast me down in shame,
Now I distrust them, one and all,
I've learned too well they're all the same.

Since she, my Lady, shows no care
To earn my thanks, nor pays Love's rights
Since she'll not hear my constant prayer
And my love yields her no delights,
I say no more; I silent go;
She gives me death; let death reply.
My Lady won't embrace me so
I leave, exiled to pain for aye.

Beatriz de Dia We know of 12 or so *trobairitz*, or woman troubadour poets. Of these, one of the best is Beatriz de Dia, wife of William, Count of Poitiers. While married, Beatriz fell in love with a knight and, according to a contemporary

---

READING 10.8

Comtessa de Dia's "Cruel Are the Pains I've Suffered," from *Lark in the Morning: The Verses of the Troubadours*

Cruel are the pains I've suffered
For a certain cavalier
Whom I have had. I declare
I love him—let it be known forever.
But now I see that I was deceived:
When I'm dressed or when I languish
In bed, I suffer a great anguish—
I should have given him my love.

One night I'd like to take my swain
To bed and hug him, wearing no clothes—
I'd give him reason to suppose
He was in heaven, if I deigned
To be his pillow! For I've been more
In love with him than Floris was
With Blanchefleur: my mind, my eyes
I give to him; my life, *mon cor*.*

When will I have you in my power,
Dearest friend, charming and good?
Lying with you one night I would
Kiss you so you could feel my ardor.
I want to have you in my husband's
Place, of that you can rest assured—
Provided you give your solemn word
That you'll obey my every command.

*Mon cor means "my heart" and alludes to a popular French romance, *Floris et Blanchefleur.*

That poems such as this survived, let alone that they became well known, underscores the remarkable personal freedom of court women of the age. In fact, we know that aristocratic women, particularly in France, gained many rights during the period, among them the right to hold property, administer estates, and create wills—all at least partially attributable to the need for women to manage their husbands' estates while the men were fighting in the Crusades or other wars. That they also felt free to confess to loving men other than their husbands suggests that Eleanor's notorious relationship with Henry II was hardly unique.

CHAPTER 10 *Fiefdom and Monastery, Pilgrimage and Crusade* **347**

Fig. 10.30 Page with *Lancelot Crossing the Sword Bridge and Guinevere in the Tower*, from *Romance of Lancelot*. ca. 1300. 13 1/2″ × 10″. © The Pierpont Morgan Library/Art Resource, NY. In this trial, Lancelot crosses a raging stream, cutting himself on a long, sharpened sword, but "even his suffering is sweet to him" with Guinevere in sight.

The Romance: Chrétien de Troyes's *Lancelot*

Because the poetry of the courtly love tradition was written in the vernacular—the common language of everyday life—and not in the Latin of the highly educated, a broader audience was able to enjoy it. And longer forms, like the *Song of Roland*, also began to circulate widely, some of them in prose. A remarkable example is the work of Marie de France. Though born in France, she wrote in the English court, and in the late twelfth century, she published a collection of over 100 *Fables*, many of which were her own. Marie also published another collection of 12 *Lais* [lay], folktales that deal, in a variety of forms and lengths, with matters of love. A *lai* is technically a short romance that combined supernatural elements and the courtly love tradition; typically they were sung by minstrels, accompanied by a harp or lyre. In *Bisclavret* (see **Reading 10.9, pages 355–357**), she tells the story of a werewolf who is unjustly betrayed by his "loving" wife but ultimately saved by a more loving king.

One of the most popular works of the day, Chrétien de Troyes's [kray-tee-EN duh trwah] *Lancelot*, appeared around

1170. Centered on the adventures of Lancelot, a knight in the court of the legendary King Arthur of Britain, and focusing particularly on his courtly love-inspired relationship with Guinevere, Arthur's wife, the poem is an example of the **medieval romance**. The term "romance" derives from the Old French term *romans*, which referred to the vernacular, everyday language of the people as opposed to Latin. The medieval romance was designed to entertain a broad audience with stories of adventure and love, while it pretended to be an actual historical account of Charlemagne, King Arthur, or Roman legend.

Lancelot, subtitled *The Knight of the Cart*, opens with a challenge offered to King Arthur and his court on Ascension Day by a knight named Sir Meleagant of Gorre. Sir Meleagant claims to hold many of Arthur's knights in prison, but offers to free them if any knight dares to escort the beautiful Queen Guinevere [GWEN-uh-veer] into the forest and defend her against him. Arthur's brother Kay asks to take on the mission, and Arthur agrees. Knowing Kay to be a poor knight, Sir Gawain [guh-WAIN] and the other knights of the Round Table quickly chase after him into the forest. Too late, they come upon Kay's riderless horse, all that remains of a scene of recent combat. Lancelot takes one of Gawain's horses and charges off after Meleagant, who has abducted Guinevere. Gawain catches up to Lancelot, finds the horse he has lent him dead, the victim of a fierce battle, and then discovers Lancelot on foot, having overtaken a cart of the kind used to take criminals to their execution. The cart is driven by a dwarf, who has told Lancelot that if he boards the cart, he will soon know Guinevere's fate. To board such a cart is a great dishonor, but Lancelot reluctantly agrees, and the next day, Lancelot and Gawain learn the way to Meleagant's kingdom of Gorre from a damsel standing at a fork in the road.

Both forks lead to Gorre, one by way of the perilous Underwater Bridge, the other by the even more perilous Sword Bridge. Gawain takes the first, Lancelot the second. Lancelot faces many challenges and temptations but finally arrives at the Sword Bridge, which he crosses by virtue of his love for Guinevere (Fig. **10.30**). He subsequently defeats Meleagant but spares his life at Guinevere's behest. Guinevere, to his dismay, behaves coldly toward him, offended at his earlier hesitation to enter the cart. He should not have put his own honor before love, she explains. After reuniting with Gawain, who was preparing to take on Meleagant himself in Lancelot's absence, Lancelot overcomes Meleagant once and for all, and he and Guinevere are reconciled.

CONTINUITY & CHANGE

Sufi poetry, **p. 307**

Guinevere agrees to meet Lancelot in Meleagant's castle secretly at night. There he kneels before her, "holding her more dear than the relic of any saint," a scene in which the "religion of love"—so marvelous in its physical joy that the narrator cannot tell of it, "for in a story it has no place"—is confounded with spiritual ecstasy. This feature is surely indebted to Islamic notions of physical love as a metaphor for the love of God, as found in Sufi poetry (see Chapter 9) and in the love songs popular in the Islamic Spanish courts, where the bilingual minstrels who inaugurated the troubadour tradition first flourished.

The love of woman celebrated in medieval romance and troubadour poetry was equated in the Christian mind with love for the Virgin Mary. As Mother of Heaven and of Christ, as the all-compassionate mediator between the Judgment seat and the horrors of hell, Mary was increasingly recognized as the spiritual equivalent of the lady of chivalry, crowned the Queen of Heaven, overseeing her heavenly court. Songs were sung to her, cathedrals built in her honor (all cathedrals named Notre Dame, "Our Lady," are dedicated to her), and a Cult of the Virgin developed around her.

Lancelot was written at the request of Eleanor of Aquitaine's daughter, Marie—herself named after the Virgin—as its laudatory prologue, a standard feature of the form, attests (**Reading 10.10**):

READING 10.10

from Chrétien de Troyes, *Lancelot*

Since my lady of Champagne wishes me to undertake to write a romance, I shall very gladly do so, being so devoted to her service as to do anything in the world for her, without any intention of flattery. But if one were to introduce any flattery upon such an occasion, he might say, and I would subscribe to it, that this lady surpasses all others who are alive, just as the south wind which blows in May or April is more lovely than any other wind. But upon my word, I am not one to wish to flatter my lady. I will simply say: "The Countess is worth as many queens as a gem is worth of pearls and sards." Nay I shall make no comparison, and yet it is true in spite of me; I will say, however, that her command has more to do with this work than any thought or pains that I may expend upon it. Here Chrétien begins his book. . . . The material and the treatment of it are given and furnished to him by the Countess, and he is simply trying to carry out her concern and intention.

Chrétien presents himself as the servant of Marie who devotes his writer's skill to doing her bidding, just as the knight Lancelot serves Queen Guinevere with his knightly skill, and as the Christian serves the Virgin Mary. Similarly, Chrétien's story transforms the heroism of the *Song of Roland*, which is motivated by feudal loyalty to king and country, to a form of chivalry based on the allegiance of the knight to his lady. In a medieval romance, the knight is driven to heroic action not so much by the lure of greater glory as by his own desire for his lady. To the knight, the lady is a prize to be won, an object to be possessed. Beyond the drama of his exploits and his lady's distress, the conflict between the sexual desires of both knight and lady and the hypothetical purity of their "spiritual" love gives the story its narrative power. In a medieval romance, as well as in the troubadour poem, perhaps the greatest test the lovers face is their own sexuality—an almost sure-fire guarantor of the form's popularity.

Toward a New Urban Style: The Gothic

Romanesque art and architecture thrived, especially along the pilgrimage routes in the south of France, from roughly 1050 to 1200. But in the 1140s, a new style began to emerge in the North that today we call Gothic. New cathedrals—at Saint-Denis, just outside Paris, and at Chartres—were dominated by soaring spires and stained-glass windows. Decorative sculpture proliferated. Pointed arches, as opposed to the rounded arches of the Romanesque barrel vault, lifted interior spaces to new heights. All of these new elements were anticipated in the Romanesque, in the magnificent stained glass at Poitiers, in the sculpture of the pilgrimage route church portals, and in the pointed arches of Fontenay Abbey. And like their Romanesque forebears, most of the new Gothic cathedrals were built to house precious relics and to accommodate large crowds of pilgrims.

The Romanesque style was a product of rural monastic life, separated from worldly events and interactions, but the Gothic style was a creation of the emerging city—of the craft guilds and artisans, merchants, lawyers, and bankers who gathered there. It represents the first step in a gradual shift in the West from a spiritually centered culture to one with a more secular focus. No longer was religion—worshiping at a pilgrimage church or fighting a Crusade—the dominant motive for travel. Instead, trade was. Merchants and bankers grew in importance. Craftsmen flourished. Secular rulers became more ambitious. In fact, personal ambition and success would increasingly be defined in worldly, rather than spiritual, terms.

The Gothic does not, however, abandon the spiritual. The new masonry architecture that developed resulted in intricate stonework that was almost skeletal in its lightness, soaring ever higher to create lofty interior spaces that inevitably caused the viewers' eyes, upon entering the space, to raise heavenward. These extraordinarily high spaces

Fig. 10.31 *Angel Subduing Demon*, decorated column capital, Church of Sainte-Madeleine, Vézelay, France. ca. 1089–1206.

Fig. 10.32 *The Angel of the Annunciation*, west front portal, Reims Cathedral, Reims, France. ca. 1245–55 (detail of Fig. 12.16).

were lit, furthermore, by stained glass that purposefully evoked the miraculous light of the Creator himself. Although the architecture was intended to invoke intensely spiritual feelings, we also see the beginning of a renewed interest in worldly things. This shift is evident in two images of angels. The flattened, distorted features of the angel on the Romanesque capital from Vézelay (Fig. 10.31) contrast dramatically with the heightened naturalism of the angel from the portal at Reims (Fig. 10.32). The Romanesque angel is depicted in profile, its wings flattened behind it. The folds of the drapery covering its body are realized by a parallel bands of shallowly incised lines. But freed from the stone backdrop of relief sculpture, the Gothic angel steps forward with an amazingly lifelike gesture. Where the gender of the Romanesque angel is indeterminate, the Reims sculpture is so lifelike—and clearly feminine—that it seems to have been modeled on a real person. Nothing of the formulaic vocabulary of Romanesque sculpture remains. The winsome smile and delicate figure of the Gothic angel are, finally, more worldly than angelic. In fact, she seems so much a part of our world that we hardly miss the halo that identifies her Romanesque forebear. ■

THINKING BACK

What do Anglo-Saxon art and literature say about Anglo-Saxon culture?

The burial mound at Sutton Hoo has revealed more about the art and culture of Anglo-Saxon England than any other archeological site. Buried in the mound was a lord or chief to whom his followers owed absolute loyalty. Can you describe the nature of the economic relationship between the lord and his followers? How is this relationship reflected in the epic poem *Beowulf*? How does it compare to the Roman system of patronage?

Although by no means a Christian poem, *Beowulf*'s themes are consonant with Christian values, teaching its audience that power, strength, fame, and life itself are transitory. Christianity survived the end of Roman control over Britain only in the farthest reaches of the British islands—in Cornwall, Wales, and Ireland. But in 597, Pope Gregory I sent a mission to England, headed by the Benedictine prior Augustine, to convert the pagan Anglo-Saxons. The pope urged Augustine not to try to eliminate pagan traditions but to incorporate them into Christian practice. How is this reflected in the manuscripts produced in the monasteries?

Who was Charlemagne?

Charlemagne gained control of most of the European continent, creating what would later be known as the Holy Roman Empire. Charlemagne's exploits were celebrated in many poems, chief among them the *Song of Roland*. What feudal values are reflected in this poem? How do they differ from those of *Beowulf*? Why do we call the Song of Roland's values system a "chivalric code"?

In keeping with his stature as head of the largest feudal empire since Roman times, Charlemagne charged the scholars working in his capital of Aachen, chief among them Alcuin of York, with creating a curriculum that would promote literacy throughout the empire. How did writing contribute to this aim? Arguably the most important institution of the Carolingian era was the monastery. Charlemagne imposed the Rule of St. Benedict on all monasteries and created what he believed to be the ideal monastery at St. Gall. What is the Rule of St. Benedict? What role does music play in monastic life? What role did women have in monastic life, and how was Hildegard of Bingen unique among them?

What was the Ottonian Empire?

Although the Ottonian Empire was a conscious reinvention of the Carolingian dream, unifying church and state in a single administrative and political bureaucracy, it was built on the exercise of power, not consensus, and it eventually collapsed in the eleventh century. How would you characterize the art created in this period?

What event is depicted in the Bayeux Tapestry?

The Frankish territory to the west of the Ottonian Empire was invaded by the Normans, Viking warriors from Scandinavia, in the tenth century. As illustrated in the famous *Bayeux Tapestry*, the Normans subsequently also invaded England from their stronghold in northern France, defeating the English at the Battle of Hastings on October 14, 1066. England and northern France thus became one country, with one king, William I, the Conqueror. Why did William immediately order a survey of the country, called the Domesday Book?

What is a pilgrimage church?

Churches such as the Abbey Church of Sainte-Foy in Conques, France, became the focus of Western culture in the Middle Ages as Christians began to do penance for their sins by undertaking pilgrimages to churches housing the relics of venerated saints. The churches were Romanesque. How would you define this architectural style?

Most of the pilgrimage churches were controlled by the Abbey of Cluny. Cluny's abbot was among the most powerful men in Europe, and the church at Cluny was a model for all pilgrimage churches. Music was central to the Cluniac liturgy. Can you describe the musical practices at Cluny? How do they differ from those of Charlemagne's time? Why did Bernard, abbot of the Cistercian monastery at Clairvaux, object to Cluniac practice?

Why did the Crusades occur?

On November 25, 1095, Pope Urban II, who had been trained at Cluny, preached the First Crusade, pleading with Christians to retake Jerusalem from the Muslims. Nearly 100,000 young men signed on out of religious zeal, and for the sake of adventure and a chance to get away from troubles at home. In the Middle East the Crusaders built giant fortresses like the Krak des Chevaliers, modeled on the fortresses built by the Normans in England. In general, how would you describe the outcome of the first and the three subsequent Crusades?

What was troubadour poetry?

Eleanor of Aquitaine accompanied her husband, King Louis VII of France, on the Second Crusade. At Poitiers, Eleanor and her daughter, Marie de Champagne, championed a literary movement that celebrated the art of courtly love. These values are reflected in medieval romances and in the work of troubadour poets like Bernard de Ventadour and Beatriz de Dia. How does courtly love reflect feudal traditions? How does it also reflect certain religious ideals?

PRACTICE MORE Get flashcards for images and terms and review chapter material with quizzes at **www.myartslab.com**

GLOSSARY

a capella Without instrumental accompaniment.

animal interlace A type of decorative motif featuring elongated animals interlaced into serpentine ribbons.

animal style A style of decoration featuring symmetrical design, interlaced organic and geometric shapes, and animal motifs.

archivolt A curved molding formed by the voussoirs making up the arch.

barrel vault An elongated arched masonry structure spanning an interior space and shaped like a half cylinder.

bay A main section of a nave formed by the round arches of a vault.

carpet page A descriptive term that refers to the resemblance between highly decorated pages of medieval manuscripts and Turkish or Islamic carpets.

chanson de geste A type of French medieval epic poem; literally "song of heroic deeds."

chivalric code The code of conduct for a knight: courage in battle, loyalty to his lord and peers, and courtesy toward women.

cloisonné A style of decoration in which strips of gold are set on edge to form small cells, which are filled with colored enamel glass paste and fitted with thin slices of semiprecious stones.

cloister A rectangular courtyard, typically arcaded and dedicated to contemplation and reflection.

Divine Office The duty of daily prayer recited by priests and other religious orders.

feudalism The economic system that prevailed in medieval Europe; it was related to the Roman custom of patronage and was based on land tenure and the relationship between the tenant and the landowner.

fief A piece of land.

free organum A type of polyphony in which the second voice moves in contrary motion to the bass chant.

Gregorian chant A type of liturgical chant popularized during the time of Charlemagne and still widely used until the twentieth century.

jamb The vertical elements on both sides of a door that support the lintel or arch.

jongleur A professional entertainer or minstrel who performed from court to court.

kenning A compound phrase used in poetry to substitute for the name of a person or thing.

knight A chevalier guided by a strict unwritten code of conduct; see *chivalric code*.

lai A short romance fusing supernatural elements and the courtly love tradition, sung by minstrels and accompanied by a harp or lyre.

mandorla An almond-shaped oval of light signifying divinity.

medieval romance A story of adventure and love that pretended to be a true historical account of Charlemagne, King Arthur, or Roman legend.

melismatic In later medieval chant, the practice of singing a single syllable to many notes.

melismatic organum A type of polyphony in which the second voice moves in contrary motion to the bass chant or adds numerous notes to individual syllables above the bass chant.

memento mori A reminder of death.

monophonic A song in which one or many voices sing a single melodic line with no harmony.

motte and bailey A type of castle consisting of a raised earth mound (motte) and the enclosed courtyard at its base (bailey).

neumatic A simple chant form in which each syllable is sung to two or three notes.

neume A note in traditional Gregorian notation, usually indicated by a small square.

organum A type of polyphonic music consisting of voices singing note-to-note in parallel.

plainchant Plainsong; a liturgical chant.

polyphony Music with two or more lines of melody.

primogeniture In the feudal system, the right of the eldest son to inherit all property.

refectory A dining hall.

relic An object (bones, clothing, or other possessions) venerated because of its association with a Christian saint or martyr.

reliquary A container used to protect and display *relics*.

Romanesque An art historical period so called because the architecture incorporated elements of Roman architectural tradition.

scriptorium The hall in which monks worked to copy and decorate biblical texts.

strophic The same music repeated for each stanza of a poem.

syllabic One note per syllable.

trobairitz A woman *troubadour*.

troubadour A class of poets that flourished in the eleventh through thirteenth centuries in southern France and northern Italy.

trumeau The column or post in the middle of a large door opening to aid in supporting the lintel.

tympanum The space created under the portal arch, often filled with sculptural relief.

READINGS

READING 10.4

Hildegard of Bingen, *Scivias*

Hildegard of Bingen's remarkable Scivias *("Know the Ways of the Lord") is a compilation of her visions and her analyses of them. The following is her vision of the devil. After describing her vision, she analyzes it line by line, and in so doing creates a vision of Hell sufficient to frighten any soul into accepting a Christian calling. Such visions of the devil would become commonplace in the art of her time (see Figure 10.24), but hers is one of the earliest and most powerful presentations.*

Then I saw a burning light, as large and as high as a mountain, divided at its summit as if into many tongues. And there stood in the presence of this light a multitude of white-clad people, before whom what seemed like a screen of translucent crystal had been placed, reaching from their breasts to their feet. And before that multitude, as if in a road, there lay on its back a monster shaped like a worm, wondrously large and long, which aroused an indescribable sense of horror and rage. On its left stood a kind of market-place, which displayed human wealth and worldly delights and various sorts of merchandise; and 10 some people were running through it very fast and not buying anything, while others were walking slowly and stopping both to sell and to buy. Now that worm was black and bristly, covered with ulcers and pustules, and it was divided into five regions from the head down through the belly to its feet, like stripes. One was green, one white, one red, one yellow and one black; and they were full of deadly poison. But its head had been so crushed that the left side of its jawbone was dislocated. Its eyes were bloody on the surface and burning within; its ears were round and bristly: its nose and mouth were those 20 of a viper, its hands human, its feet a viper's feet, and its tail short and horrible.

And around its neck a chain was riveted, which also bound its hands and feet and this chain was firmly fastened to a rock in the abyss, confining it so that it could not move about as its wicked will desired. Many flames came forth from its mouth, dividing into four parts: One part ascended to the clouds, another breathed forth among secular people, another among spiritual people, and the last descended into the abyss. And the flame that sought the clouds was opposing the people who wanted to 30 get to Heaven. And I saw three groups of these. One was close to the clouds, one in the middle space between the clouds and the earth, and one moved along near the earth; and all were shouting repeatedly, "Let us get to Heaven!" But they were whirled hither and thither by that flame; some did not waver, some barely kept their balance and some fell to the earth but then rose again and started toward Heaven. The flame that breathed forth among secular people burned some of them so that they were hideously blackened and others it transfixed so that it could move them anywhere it wanted. Some escaped 40 from the flame and moved toward those who sought Heaven, reiterating shouts of "O you faithful, give us help!" But others remained transfixed. Meanwhile, the flame that breathed forth among spiritual people concealed them in obscurity; but I saw them in six categories. For some of them were cruelly injured by the flame's fury; but when it could not injure one of them, it burningly breathed on them the deadly poison that flowed from the worm's head to its feet, either green or white or red or yellow or black. But the flame that sought the abyss contained in itself diverse torments for those who had worshiped Satan in 50 place of God, not washed by the font of baptism or knowing the light of truth and faith. And I saw sharp arrows whistling loudly from its mouth, and black smoke exhaling from its breast, and a burning fluid boiling up from its loins, and a hot whirlwind blowing from its navel, and the uncleanness of frogs issuing from its bowels; all of which affected human beings with grave disquiet. And the hideous and foul-smelling vapor that came out of it infected many people with its own perversity. But behold, a great multitude of people came, shining brightly; they forcefully trod the worm underfoot and severely tormented it, but could not be injured by its flames or its poison. And I heard again the voice from Heaven, saying to me . . . : 60

3. The deceptions of the Devil lie in the path humans take in this world

And before that multitude, as if in a road, there lies on its back a monster shaped like a worm, wondrously large and long. This means that the ancient serpent is well-known to humanity in the course of the pilgrimage of the good and the bad through the world, not in that visible form but in its inner meaning. Its mouth is gaping upward 70 in order to pull down by deception those who are tending toward the celestial regions; but it is lying down, because the Son of God destroyed so much of its strength that it cannot stand up. **And it arouses an indescribable sense of horror and rage;** for the mental capacity of mortal humans is insufficient to understand the manifold variations of its poisonous fury and malicious exertions.

4. The Devil offers fraudulent riches and delights, and some buy them

On its left stands a kind of marketplace, which dis- 80 **plays human wealth and worldly delights and various sorts of merchandise.** For the left hand of the destroyer signifies death, and there is seen a marketplace composed of Death's evil works: pride and vainglory in corruptible riches, licentiousness and lust for transitory pleasures, and trafficking in all kinds of earthly desires. Thus those who would be terrified by the horror of the Devil if they met it openly are deceived by these things; they are lightly offered persuasions to vice as a merchant displays his diverse wares to people, and delighted by the display so that they 90 buy what is offered. So the Devil offers humanity his lying arts; and those who desire them buy them. How? They throw away a good conscience as if selling it, and they collect deadly wounds in their souls as if buying them. . . .

6. The Devil labors to deceive the five senses of humanity

But you see that **that worm is black and gristly, covered with ulcers and pustules.** This shows that the ancient serpent is full of the darkness of black betrayal, and the bristles of concealed deception, and the ulcers of impure pollution, and the pustules of repressed fury. **And it is** 100 **divided into five sections from the head down through the belly to its feet, like stripes;** for from the time of his first deception when he tried to put himself forward until the final time when his madness will end, he does not cease to inspire the five human senses with the desire for vices. Simulating a deceitful rectitude he draws people to the downward slopes of his unclean arts. One is green, one white, one red, one yellow, and one black and they are full of deadly poison. The green indicates worldly melancholy; the white, improper irreverence; the red, deceptive glory; the yellow, biting envy; and 110 the black, shameful deceit, with all other perversities that bring death to the souls of those who consent to them. . . .

8. What the eyes and ears and nostrils of the serpent signify

Its eyes are bloody on the surface and burning within; because his wicked intent outwardly inflicts harm on human bodies and inwardly drives a fiery dart into their souls. **Its ears are round and bristly;** for the bristles of his arts pierce a person all around, so that if he finds anything that is his in that person, he may quickly throw him down. **Its nose and mouth are those of a viper;** for he shows 120 people unbridled and vile behavior, through which transfixing them with many vices, he may cruelly slay them.

9. Its hands and feet and tail and what they signify

Its hands are human, for he practices his arts in human deeds; its feet a viper's feet, because he ceaselessly ambushes people when they are journeying and inflicts devilish lacerations on them; **and its tail short and horrible,** for it signifies his power in the short but most evil time of the son of perdition, whose desire to run wild exceeds his power to do it.

READING CRITICALLY

In her third point of analysis, Hildegard says that "the mental capacity of mortal humans is insufficient to understand the manifold variations of its poisonous fury and malicious exertions." What is her rhetorical strategy here? In other words, why does she say this, and what effect does she think it will have on the reader?

READING 10.6

from "The Fall of Jerusalem" from the *Gesta Francorum* (*Deeds of the Franks*)

The Gesta Francorum *is an anonymous account of the First Crusade (1096–99). It is an extraordinary account not only of military matters—tactical operations, supply and provision operations, and so on—but also of the psychological mood of the Crusaders. The knight who wrote it was, apparently, an average soldier, and he gives us something of the unprejudiced point of view of the army as a whole.*

At length, our leaders decided to beleaguer the city with siege machines, so that we might enter and worship the Saviour at the Holy Sepulchre.[1] They constructed wooden towers and many other siege machines. Duke Godfrey made a wooden tower and other siege devices, and Count Raymond did the same, although it was necessary to bring wood from a considerable distance. However, when the Saracens saw our men engaged in this work, they greatly strengthened the fortifications of the city and increased the height of the turrets at night. On a certain Sabbath night, the leaders, after having decided which parts of the wall were weakest, dragged the tower and the machines to the eastern side of the city. Moreover, we set up the tower at earliest dawn and equipped and covered it on the first, second, and third days of the week. The Count of St. Gilles erected his tower on the plain to the south of the city.

[1]**Holy Sepulchre** The church built at the site where Jesus was believed to be buried and where he rose from the dead.

While all this was going on, our water supply was so limited that no one could buy enough water for one *denarius*[2] to satisfy or quench his thirst. . . . Early on the sixth day of the week we again attacked the city on all sides, but as the assault was unsuccessful, we were all astounded and fearful. However, when the hour approached on which our Lord Jesus Christ deigned to suffer on the Cross for us, our knights began to fight bravely in one of the towers—namely, the party with Duke Godfrey and his brother, Count Eustace. One of our knights, named Lethold, clambered up the wall of the city, and no sooner had he ascended than the defenders fled from the walls and through the city. Our men followed, killing and slaying even to the Temple of Solomon, where the slaughter was so great that our men waded in blood up to their ankles. . . .

[Finally] the pilgrims entered the city, pursuing and killing the Saracens up to the Temple of Solomon, where the enemy gathered in force. The battle raged throughout the day, so that the Temple was covered with their blood. When the pagans had been overcome, our men seized great numbers, both men and women, either killing them or keeping them captive, as they wished. . . . Afterward, the army scattered throughout the city and took possession of the gold and silver, the horses and mules, and the houses filled with goods of all kinds.

[2] ***Denarius*** A silver coin of the Roman Empire.

Rejoicing and weeping for joy, our people came to the Sepulchre of Jesus our Saviour to worship and pay their debt [i.e., fulfill crusading vows by worshiping at the Sepulchre]. At dawn our men cautiously went up to the roof of the Temple and attacked Saracen men and women, beheading them with naked swords. Some of the Saracens, however, leaped from the Temple roof. . . .

Then our leaders in council decided that each one should offer alms with prayers, that the Lord might choose for Himself whom He wanted to reign over the others and rule the city. They also ordered all the Saracen dead to be cast outside because of the great stench, since the whole city was filled with their corpses; and so the living Saracens dragged the dead before the exits of the gates and arranged them in heaps, as if they were houses. No one ever saw or heard of such slaughter of pagan people, for funeral pyres were formed from them like pyramids, and no one knows their number except God alone.

READING CRITICALLY

This account of the fall of Jerusalem amounts to a description of what might be called, from a contemporary point of view, a war crime. Why does the writer not see it in those terms?

READING 10.9

from Marie de France, *Bisclavret* (*The Werewolf*)

We actually know almost nothing about Marie de France, except that she was a marvelous storyteller. At the end of her collection of Fables, *she tells us, "I'll give my name, for memory: / I am from France, my name's Marie"—and that about sums up what we know of her. Some speculate that she worked in Henry II's court, and that she was Henry II's half-sister, since Henry's father had an illegitimate daughter named Marie who subsequently became abbess of Shaftesbury about 1180.*

The following lai *represents one of the darker of the 12 she wrote. Combining the stuff of medieval folk superstition and the chivalric tradition, it is a perfect example of the growing popular appeal of literary works in the Romanesque world.*

Since I am undertaking to compose *lais*,
I don't want to forget Bisclavret;
In Breton, the *lai's* name is *Bisclavret*—
the Normans call it *Garwaf* [The Werewolf].
In the old days, people used to say—
and it often actually happened—
that some men turned into werewolves
and lived in the woods.
A werewolf is a savage beast;
while his fury is on him   10
he eats men, does much harm,
goes deep in the forest to live.
But that's enough of this for now:
I want to tell you about the Bisclavret.
In Brittany there lived a nobleman
whom I've heard marvelously praised;
a fine, handsome knight
who behaved nobly.
He was close to his lord,
and loved by all his neighbors.   20
He had an estimable wife,
one of lovely appearance;

he loved her and she him,
but one thing was very vexing to her:
during the week he would be missing
for three whole days, and she didn't know
what happened to him or where he went.
Nor did any of his men know anything about it.
One day he returned home
happy and delighted;   30
she asked him about it.
"My lord," she said, "and dear love,
I'd very much like to ask you one thing—
if I dared;
but I'm so afraid of your anger
that nothing frightens me more."
When he heard that, he embraced her,
drew her to him and kissed her.
"My lady," he said, "go ahead and ask!
There's nothing you could want to know,   40
that, if I knew the answer, I wouldn't tell you."
"By God," she replied, "now I'm cured!
My lord, on the days when you go away from me
I'm in such a state—

so sad at heart,
so afraid I'll lose you—
that if I don't get quick relief
I could die of this very soon.
Please, tell me where you go,
where you have been staying.   50
I think you must have a lover,
and if that's so, you're doing wrong."
"My dear," he said, "have mercy on me, for God's sake!
Harm will come to me if I tell you about this,
because I'd lose your love
and even my very self."
When the lady heard this
she didn't take it lightly;
she kept asking him,
coaxed and flattered him so much,   60
that he finally told her what happened to him—
he hid nothing from her.
"My dear, I become a werewolf:
I go off into the great forest,
in the thickest part of the woods,
and I live on the prey I hunt down."
When he had told her everything,
she asked further
whether he undressed or kept his clothes on [when he
became a werewolf].   70
"Wife," he replied, "I go stark naked."
"Tell me, then, for God's sake, where your clothes are."
"That I won't tell you;
for if I were to lose them,
and then be discovered,
I'd stay a werewolf forever.
I'd be helpless
until I got them back.
That's why I don't want their hiding place to be known."
"My lord," the lady answered,   80
"I love you more than all the world;
you mustn't hide anything from me
or fear me in any way:
that doesn't seem like love to me.
What wrong have I done? For what sin of mine
do you mistrust me about anything?
Do the right thing and tell me!"
She harassed and bedeviled him so,
that he had no choice but to tell her.
"Lady," he said, "near the woods,   90
beside the road that I use to get there,
there's an old chapel
that has often done me good service;
under a bush there is a big stone,
hollowed out inside;
I hide my clothes right there
until I'm ready to come home."
The lady heard this wonder
and turned scarlet from fear;
she was terrified of the whole adventure.   100
Over and over she considered
how she might get rid of him;
she never wanted to sleep with him again . . .
[The lady asks a knight who has always loved her to find Bisclavret and kill him, but they never find him, and the two marry.
But one day some hunters find him.]

[T]he hunters and the dogs
chased him all day,
until they were just about to take him
and tear him apart,
at which point he saw the king   110
and ran to him, pleading for mercy.
He took hold of the king's stirrup,
kissed his leg and his foot.
The king saw this and was terrified;
he called his companions.
"My lords," he said, "come quickly!
Look at this marvel—
this beast is humbling itself to me.
It has the mind of a man, and it's begging me for mercy!
Chase the dogs away,   120
and make sure no one strikes it.
This beast is rational—he has a mind.
Hurry up: let's get out of here.
I'll extend my peace to the creature;
indeed, I'll hunt no more today!"
Thereupon the king turned away.
Bisclavret followed him;
he stayed close to the king, and wouldn't go away;
he'd no intention of leaving him.
The king led him to his castle;   130
he was delighted with this turn of events,
for he'd never seen anything like it.
He considered the beast a great wonder
and held him very dear.
He commanded all his followers,
for the sake of their love for him, to guard Bisclavret well,
and under no circumstances to do him harm;
none of them should strike him;
rather, he should be well fed and watered.
They willingly guarded the creature;   140
every day he went to sleep
among the knights, near the king.
Everyone was fond of him;
he was so noble and well behaved
that he never wished to do anything wrong.
Regardless of where the king might go,
Bisclavret never wanted to be separated from him;
he always accompanied the king.
The king became very much aware that the creature loved him.
Now listen to what happened next.   150
The king held a court;
to help him celebrate his feast
and to serve him as handsomely as possible,
he summoned all the barons
who held fiefs from him.
Among the knights who went,
and all dressed up in his best attire,
was the one who had married Bisclavret's wife.
He neither knew nor suspected
that he would find Bisclavret so close by.   160
As soon as he came to the palace
Bisclavret saw him,
ran toward him at full speed,
sank his teeth into him, and started to drag him down.
He would have done him great damage
if the king hadn't called him off,
and threatened him with a stick.

Twice that day he tried to bite the knight.
Everyone was extremely surprised,
since the beast had never acted that way   170
toward any other man he had seen.
All over the palace people said
that he wouldn't act that way without a reason:
that somehow or other, the knight had mistreated Bisclavret,
and now he wanted his revenge.
And so the matter rested
until the feast was over
and until the barons took their leave of the king
and started home.
The very first to leave,   180
to the best of my knowledge,
was the knight whom Bisclavret had attacked.
It's no wonder the creature hated him.
Not long afterward,
as the story leads me to believe,
the king, who was so wise and noble,
went back to the forest
where he had found Bisclavret,
and the creature went with him.
That night, when he finished hunting,   190
he sought lodging out in the countryside.
The wife of Bisclavret heard about it,
dressed herself elegantly,
and went the next day to speak with the king,
bringing rich presents for him.
When Bisclavret saw her coming,
no one could hold him back;
he ran toward her in a rage.
Now listen to how well he avenged himself!
He tore the nose off her face.   200
What worse thing could he have done to her?
Now men closed in on him from all sides;
they were about to tear him apart,
when a wise man said to the king,
"My lord, listen to me!
This beast has stayed with you,
and there's not one of us
who hasn't watched him closely,
hasn't traveled with him often.
He's never touched anyone,   210
or shown any wickedness,
except to this woman.
By the faith that I owe you,
he has some grudge against her,
and against her husband as well.
This is the wife of the knight
whom you used to like so much,
and who's been missing for so long—
we don't know what became of him.
Why not put this woman to torture   220
and see if she'll tell you
why the beast hates her?
Make her tell what she knows!
We've seen many strange things
happen in Brittany!"
The king took his advice;
he detained the knight.
At the same time he took the wife
and subjected her to torture;

out of fear and pain   230
she told all about her husband:
how she had betrayed him
and taken away his clothes;
the story he had told her
about what happened to him and where he went;
and how after she had taken his clothes
he'd never been seen in his land again.
She was quite certain
that this beast was Bisclavret.
The king demanded the clothes;   240
whether she wanted to or not
she sent home for them,
and had them brought to Bisclavret.
When they were put down in front of him
he didn't even seem to notice them;
the king's wise man—
the one who had advised him earlier—
said to him, "My lord, you're not doing it right.
This beast wouldn't, under any circumstances,
in order to get rid of his animal form,   250
put on his clothes in front of you;
you don't understand what this means:
he's just too ashamed to do it here.
Have him led to your chambers
and bring the clothes with him;
then we'll leave him alone for a while.
If he turns into a man, we'll know about it."
The king himself led the way
and closed all the doors on him.
After a while he went back,   260
taking two barons with him;
all three entered the king's chamber.
On the king's royal bed
they found the knight asleep.
The king ran to embrace him.
He hugged and kissed him again and again.
As soon as he had the chance,
the king gave him back all his lands;
he gave him more than I can tell.
He banished his wife,   270
chased her out of the country.
She went into exile with the knight
with whom she had betrayed her lord.
She had several children
who were widely known
for their appearance:
several women of the family
were actually born without noses,
and lived out their lives noseless.
The adventure that you have heard   280
really happened, no doubt about it.
The *lai* of Bisclavret[1] was made
so it would be remembered forever.

READING CRITICALLY

How does Marie's story suggest the conflict between
bestiality and civilization in human behavior? What values does it most uphold?

---

[1] Until this point, "Bisclavret" is a common noun; hereafter it is used as the werewolf's name.

11 | Centers of Culture
Court and City in the Larger World

THINKING AHEAD

How did poetry, art, and architecture of the Tang and Song dynasties reflect the values of the Chinese state?

What religions shaped Indian and Southeast Asian civilization?

Why did the Japanese capital move to Asuka, Nara, Heian-kyo, and Kamakura?

What shapes did civilization take in Africa?

Where did culture thrive in Mesoamerica?

Who were the Moche and the Inca?

Buddhism lies at the heart of culture in Asia during the period that in the West we call the Middle Ages. Between the first and third centuries CE, Buddhist missionaries from India had carried the religion over the Silk Road (see *Continuity & Change*, page 235, Chapter 7) into Southeast Asia and north into China and Korea. By 600 CE, Buddhism had reached all the way to Japan (Map **11.1**).

The first Chinese Buddhist monk to set out on the Silk Road in search of Buddhist scripture to translate into Chinese was Zhu Shixing [joo shih-hsing] of Hunan province. His journey dates from about 260 CE. At the same time, far away on the Silk Road, a resident of Dunhuang [doon-hwahng] began his life's work as a translator of Buddhist texts. One of the most telling manifestations of the religion's spread is the appearance everywhere of images of Buddha (Fig. **11.1**). In early Buddhist art, the Buddha was never shown in figural form. It was believed to be impossible to represent the Buddha, since he had already passed to nirvana. Instead, his presence was symbolized by such things as his footprints, the banyan tree (see Chapter 7), the wheel (representing *dharma*, or the Wheel of Law), or elephants (see Fig. 7.19).

By the fourth century, during the reign of the Gupta rulers in India, the Buddha was commonly represented in human form. Typically his head is oval, framed by a halo. Atop his head is a mound, symbolizing his spiritual wisdom, and on his forehead is a "third eye," symbolizing his spiritual vision. His demeanor is gentle, reposed, and meditative. His elongated ears refer to his royal origins, and his hands are set in one of several symbolic gestures, called **mudra**. At Bamiyan, on the Silk Road in present-day Afghanistan, two massive Buddhas, 175 and 120 feet tall, were carved into a cliff face in the third century CE. These figures were completely destroyed by the fundamentalist Islamic Taliban in 2001. However, many surviving replicas from the Silk Road era suggest that the hands of these Buddhas, which succumbed to natural forces long ago, were held up in the *Dharmachakra* mudra [dahr-mah-chahk-rah mood-rah], the teaching pose. This mudra symbolizes intellectual debate and is often associated with Buddhist centers of learning. Painted gold and studded with jewels, and surrounded by caves decorated with Buddhist wall paintings, these enormous images reflect the magnitude of Buddha's eternal form, at which the earthly body can barely hint.

◄ **Fig. 11.1 Colossal Buddha, Bamiyan, Afghanistan. ca. third century CE.** Stone, height 175′. This sculpture thus embodies the spread of ideas across Asia during the period of the European Middle Ages. Buddhism would spread, through China, to Japan by 600 CE. Indian Hinduism would, in turn, spread across Southeast Asia. This and another colossal sculpture of Buddha nearby were destroyed in February 2001 by the fundamentalist Islamic Taliban, who evidently felt that as false idols they were an affront to Mohammed.

HEAR MORE Listen to an audio file of your chapter at **www.myartslab.com**

Fig. 11.2 *Large Seated Buddha with Standing Bodhisattva*, **from cave 20, Ungang, Shaanxi, China, Northern Wei dynasty. ca. 460–70 CE.** Stone, height 44'. By the last half of the fifth century, when this sculpture was carved, the Chinese Wei rulers, who lived near the eastern end of the Silk Road, had become acquainted with the Indian Buddhist religion.

A seated Buddha from another cave, in Ungang, Shaanxi, China (Fig. **11.2**) exhibits the *Dhyana* mudra [duh-YAH-nuh mood-rah], a gesture of meditation and balance. The lower hand represents the physical world of illusion, the upper, nirvana. Together they symbolize the path to enlightenment. The bodhisattva—a person of near total enlightenment who has vowed to help others achieve it—standing next to him is exhibiting the *Abhaya* mudra [uh-BAH-yah mood-rah], a gesture of reassurance, blessing, and protection.

This chapter traces the development of five great centers of culture during the period that coincides with Europe's Middle Ages: China, India, Japan, Africa, and the Americas. It was a period of great cross-fertilization in Asia, as the example of Buddhism demonstrates. Chinese technological innovation was unrivaled in the world, and Chinese art and literature flourished as well. In India, Buddhists, threatened by invading Muslims from Persia, retreated into the Himalayan Mountains, even as the Hindu religion regained prominence and spread across Southeast Asia. In Japan, a feudal, military society vied with Buddhist teaching for pre-eminence. Across the African continent, sophisticated peoples rose to dominate their regions. Similarly, in the Americas, cultures in Mesoamerica and Peru achieved similar levels of complexity and sophistication without the kind of contact with other great cultures that marked

development in Asia. This chapter's overview of these cultures puts the Western Middle Ages in a broader perspective. During these years, the growing globalization of culture was just beginning to assert itself on the Silk Road. As we will see, the world's centers of culture were never again to be isolated from each other.

DEVELOPMENTS IN CHINA

After the fall of the Han dynasty in 220 CE (see Chapter 7), China entered an uneasy period. Warring factions vied for control of greater or lesser territories, governments rose to power and fell again, civil wars erupted, and tribes from Central Asia continuously invaded. During this time, Buddhism began to spread through the culture. The Confucian ethical system (see Chapter 7) seemed to have resulted in civil and cultural dysfunction. In contrast, Buddhism offered an ethical system based less on social and civic duty and more on each person's responsibility for his or her actions. Especially in its emphasis on meditation and enlightenment, Buddhism was compatible with Daoism (also discussed in Chapter 7). By the seventh century CE, Chinese leaders had learned to take the best from all three—Confucianism, Buddhism, and Daoism—and the culture was once again unified.

Map 11.1 The spread of Buddhism, 500 BCE–eleventh century CE.

Arrives in Tibet 6th and 7th centuries CE but only gains a foothold in 11th century

Arrives in Korea 4th and 5th centuries CE

JAPAN

KOREA

Arrives in China 1st and 2nd centuries CE

TIBET

CHINA

Arrives in Japan around 520–550 CE

Bodh Gaya

Arrives in Burma and Thailand in 1st century CE

Starts 500 BCE

BURMA

INDIA

N

500 km

500 miles

THAILAND

LAOS

VIETNAM

CAMBODIA

Arrives around 3rd century BCE

SRI LANKA

→ Spread of Buddhism

The Tang Dynasty in Chang'an, "The City of Enduring Peace" (618–907 CE)

In 618, the Tang dynasty reestablished a period of peace and prosperity in China that, except for a brief period of turmoil in the tenth century, would last for 660 years. The Tang dynasty the product of the largest and most organized government in the world in the last half of the first millennium. Its capital was the eastern end of the Silk Road, Chang'an, "City of Enduring Peace" (present-day Xi'an, which is about one-seventh the size of the Tang capital). The city had served as the capital of the Han dynasty as well, but as the Tang restored trade along the Silk Road, they created elaborate plans to restore the city, too. By the eighth century, its population was well over 1 million, living inside a walled perimeter nearly 26 miles in length and enclosing almost 42 square miles. Outside the walls lived perhaps as many as another million people. Among its inhabitants were Korean, Japanese, Jewish, and Christian populations, and its emperors maintained diplomatic relations with Persia.

Chang'an was the largest city in the world, laid out in a carefully conceived grid that dramatized the Tang commitment to social order and mirrored, they believed, the order of the cosmos (Fig. **11.3**). Each of the city's 108 blocks was itself a miniature walled city, with its own interior streets and gates that locked at night. Astronomers laid out the streets by aligning them with the shadow of the sun at noon and the position of the North Star at night, thereby orienting the city to the four cardinal directions. The imperial palace was located at the north end, facing south, thus symbolizing the emperor looking out over his city and,

by extension, his empire. Traditionally, Chinese emperors turned their backs to the north, from where, it was believed, evil spirits (not to mention Huns) came. Government buildings occupied the space in front of the imperial palace. A 500-foot-wide avenue led from these directly to the southern gate.

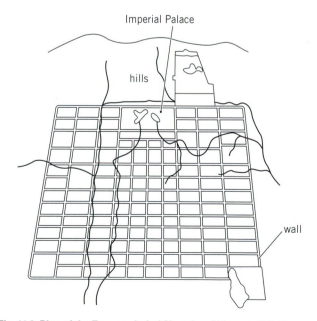

Fig. 11.3 Plan of the Tang capital of Chang'an, China. ca. 600. The location of the capital had been determined in Han times by the practice of *feng shui*, literally "wind and water," which assesses the primal energy that flows through a particular landscape. In this case, the hills to the north of the city and the streams running through it were understood to protect the precinct. *Feng shui* is still practiced to this day.

Imperial Palace

hills

wall

Tang Art and Architecture Like all great Chinese dynasties, the Tang were great builders. One of their most important accomplishments was to build the Grand Canal on the Yellow River, just downstream from Chang'an, to the Hangzhou Bay, at the mouth of the Yangzi River, thus uniting northern and southern China. The Chinese had developed iron- and steel-casting during the Han dynasty in the third century BCE, and by the sixth or seventh century CE, the technique had become commonplace, used to construct not only suspension bridges but also **pagodas**. (Equally sophisticated iron- and steel-casting would not develop in the West until the eighteenth century.) The pagoda is a multistoried structure of successively smaller, repeated stories, with projecting roofs at each story. The design derives from Han watchtowers and Indian stupas (see Fig. 7.17), which had become more and more towerlike in the sixth century CE. The pagoda was understood to offer the temple a certain protection. Of the few surviving buildings in China that predate 1400, the Great Wild Goose Pagoda at Ci'en [tseh-ehn] Temple in Chang'an is one of the most magnificent (Fig. **11.4**). It was built—entirely of masonry, not iron or steel—in 645 for the monk Xuanzang [shoo-ehn-tsahng], who taught and translated the materials he brought back with him from a 16-year pilgrimage to India. In its simplicity and symmetry, it represents the essence of Tang architecture.

Tang Poetry The Tang valued education above all. The imperial college at Chang'an trained all civil servants (women were excluded), and intellectual achievement was held in high esteem. Confucian and Daoist philosophy dominated the arts, particularly poetry, where two Tang poets, the Daoist Li Bai (701–62) and the Confucian Du Fu (712–70), achieved special prominence. Both relied for inspiration on *The Book of Songs* (see Chapter 7) but extended its range considerably. Their different temperaments are expressed in two short poems (**Reading 11.1a**):

Fig. 11.4 Great Wild Goose Pagoda at Ci'en Temple, Xi'an, Shanxi. Tang dynasty, first erected 645 CE. The Temple was rebuilt in the eighth century, when two stories were added to the original five.

READING 11.1a

Poems by Li Bai and Du Fu

"Summer Day in the Mountains" by Li Bai
Lazy today, I wave my white feather fan.
Then I strip naked in the green forest,
untie my hatband and hang it on a stone wall.
Pine wind sprinkles my bare head.

"Broken Lines" by Du Fu
River so blue the birds seem to whiten.
Flowers almost flame on the green mountainside.
Spring is dying yet again.
Will I ever go home?

Li Bai is famous for the self-examination in his poems, his colloquial speech, and his frank celebration of his own sensuality. We see these characteristics, too, in his poem, "Drinking Alone by Midnight," addressed to the moon (see **Reading 11.1** on page 397).

The poems of Du Fu are sometimes full of pathos. He wrote "Dreaming of Li Bai" when his friend was in exile in the south. The two belonged to a group called the Eight Immortals of the Wine Cup, famous for gathering in a garden of peach and plum trees on moonlit spring nights, where they drank wine to unleash their poetic temperaments. Like all the Immortals of the Wine Cup, Li Bai and Du Fu were equally expert in poetry, calligraphy, and painting—as well as statesmanship and philosophy. They present a model of what 500 years later the West would come to call the "Renaissance Man," the perfectly rounded individual, at home in any arena. They also embody the complex characteristics of Tang culture—at once strong and vigorous as well as passionate and sympathetic, simultaneously realistic and idealistic, intensely personal even while dedicated to public service.

The Song Dynasty and Hangzhou, "The City of Heaven" (960–1279 CE)

"The most splendid city in the world"—so the Venetian explorer Marco Polo (1254–1324) described Hangzhou, the capital of China's Southern Song dynasty (1127–1279) when Polo first visited it in 1274. Although Hangzhou was now the world's largest city—home to about 2 million people—no other Westerner had ever seen it. Marco Polo's father and uncle had a successful trading business with the East, and Polo lived with them in China for 17 years.

He wrote at length about his journey to Hangzhou in his *Travels*, first published in 1299. He claimed that he first visited the city as the ambassador of Kublai Khan. Northern Song China was already in Kublai Khan's hands, conquered in 1271, but he would not conquer the Southern Song on the Yangzi River until 1279. So when Polo first saw Hangzhou, it was still a Song city. Its lakes and parks were so beautiful, filled with floating teahouses from which passengers could view the palaces, pagodas, and temples that dotted the shore, that the city was known as Kinsai [KEEN-sa-hee], or the "City of Heaven." The entire city, some 200 square miles, was protected by a 30-foot-high wall, with even higher watchtowers rising above it. Inside the walls, a system of canals, which must have reminded Polo of his native Venice, was crisscrossed by some 12,000 bridges. These canals were fed by the most famous and probably most beautiful lake in China, the so-called West Lake, a popular resort. Beautiful women and pleasure-seekers gathered on houseboats on its waters, and writers and artists congregated in the tranquil libraries and monasteries on its shores.

"In this city," Polo would write, "there are 12 guilds of different crafts, and each guild has 12,000 houses in the occupation of its workmen. Each of these houses contains at least 12 men, while some contain 20 and some 40, including the apprentices who work under the masters. All these craftsmen had full employment since many other cities of the kingdom are supplied by this city." In fact, each guild was formed around people from the same province. In Hangzhou, tea and cloth merchants hailed from the eastern province of Anhwui, carpenters and cabinetmakers from the city of Ningbo, and so on. All came together to enjoy the benefits of trade and commerce in the capital. Foodstuffs, silks, spices, flowers, and books filled the markets (**Reading 11.2**):

READING 11.2

from Marco Polo, *Travels*

Those markets make a daily display of every kind of vegetable and fruit; and among the latter there are in particular certain pears of enormous size, weighing as much as ten pounds apiece, and pulp of which is white and fragrant like a confection, besides peaches in their season both yellow and white, of every delicate flavor. . . .

From the Ocean Sea also come daily supplies of fish in great quantity, brought 25 miles up river, and there is also great store of fish from the lake, which is the constant resort of fishermen, who have no other business. Their fish is of sundry kinds, changing with the season; and it is remarkably fat and tasty. Anyone who should see the supply of fish in the market would suppose it impossible that such a quantity could ever be sold; and yet in a few hours the whole shall be cleared away; so great is the number of inhabitants who are accustomed to delicate living.

These citizens "accustomed to delicate living" apparently lived remarkably well: "The houses of the citizens are well built and elaborately finished," Polo claims, "and the delight they take in decoration, in painting and in architecture, leads them to spend in this way sums of money that would astonish you." In other words, Hangzhou was a center of Asian culture that no one in the West, save Marco Polo, could even dream existed, in many ways exceeding anything the West had realized.

The Song dynasty enjoyed tremendous prosperity. It was the world's greatest producer of iron, and its flourishing merchant class traded not only along the Silk Road (see Chapter 7) but also throughout the Southeast Asian seas by boat. The government was increasingly controlled by this wealthy merchant class. Crucial to their rise was the development of movable type, which allowed the Song to begin printing books on paper. The printing press revolutionized the transmission of knowledge in China. (Gutenberg's movable-type printing press, which, in the West, we commonly credit with revolutionizing the transmission of knowledge, was 400 years in the future.) The children of the thriving merchant class attended public, private, and religious schools, where they could study the newly printed books—including *The Book of Songs*, required reading for all Chinese civil servants, and various encyclopedias—as they prepared for government examinations. This new class of highly educated government officials restored Confucianism to dominance and strengthened it with relevant additions from Daoism and Buddhism. Buddhism was officially rejected as foreign, but its explanation of the universe provided an invaluable metaphysical element to Confucianism. As a result, these new officials brought to government a deep belief, based on neo-Confucian teaching, that the well-run society mirrored the unchanging moral order of the cosmos.

Chan Buddhism Especially important to artists and literati in the Song era was the development of Chan Buddhism. "Chan" (better known in the West as "Zen," as it is pronounced in Japanese) derives from the Sanskrit word *dhyana*, meaning "meditation." Like Daoism, Chan Buddhism teaches that one can find happiness by achieving harmony with nature. By using yoga techniques and sitting meditation, the Chan Buddhist strives for oneness with the Dao ("the Way") and the Confucian *li*, the principle or inner structure of nature. The Chan Buddhists thought that the traditional scriptures, rituals, and monastic rules of classical Buddhism were essentially beside the point, because Buddha's spirit was innate in everyone, waiting to be discovered through meditation. Thus, the poets and artists who practiced Chan Buddhism considered themselves instruments through which the spirit of nature expressed itself.

Song Painting This essential "rightness" of the Song world is manifested especially in Chinese painting of the Song era, when landscape painting became the principal and most esteemed means of personal and philosophic expression in the arts. The landscape was believed to embody the underlying principle behind all things, made manifest in the world through its material presence. Closely akin to the spiritual quest of the Dao, the task of the artist was to reveal the unifying principle of the natural world, the eternal essence of mountain, waterfall, pine tree, rock, reeds, clouds, and sky. Human figures are dwarfed by the landscape, insignificant in the face of nature. Over and over again, the paintings of the period rise from foreground valleys to high mountaintops, the eye following paths, cascading waterfalls, rocky crags, and tall pines pointing ever higher in imitation of "the Way," the path by which one leaves behind the human world and attains the great unifying principle (see *Closer Look*, pages 366–367).

The Yuan Dynasty (1279–1368)

Throughout the period known as the medieval era in the West, China was threatened from the north by nomadic tribes. The Northern Song capital of Bianjing [beehn-geeng] had fallen to tribes from Manchuria in 1126, forcing the Song to retreat south to Hangzhou. Finally, the Song dynasty succumbed to the Mongol leader Kublai Khan in 1279. Kublai Khan ruled from a new capital at present-day Beijing, transforming it into a walled city constructed on a grid plan and extending the Grand Canal to provision the city.

Calling themselves the Yuan dynasty, the Mongols under Kublai Khan and his descendants controlled the highest posts in the government, but they depended on Chinese officials to collect taxes and maintain order. The Chinese understood the need to cooperate with the Mongols, but they viewed the Mongols as foreigners occupying their homeland. (Remember, foreigners were banned from entering the Forbidden City.)

Not long after Marco Polo's arrival in China, the scholar-painters of the Chinese court, unwilling to serve under foreign domination, were retreating from public life. But while in exile, they created an art symbolic of their resistance. Paintings of bamboo, for instance, abound, because bamboo is a plant that might bend, like the Chinese themselves, but never break. Painted in 1306, Cheng Sixiao's [chehng-sih-she-how] *Ink Orchids* (Fig. **11.5**),

Fig. 11.5 Cheng Sixiao, *Ink Orchids.* **Yuan dynasty, 1306.** Ink on paper, 10 1/8″ × 16 3/4″. Municipal Museum of Fine Art, Osaka, Japan. Artists of the Yuan dynasty such as Cheng Sixiao painted for their fellow artists and friends, not for the public. Thus, Cheng Sixiao could feel comfortable describing his political intentions in the text accompanying this painting.

Map 11.2 **India and Southeast Asia.**

according to its inscription, is meant to protest the "theft of Chinese soil by the invaders." Orchids, in fact, can live without soil, in rocks or in trees, sustained by the moisture in the air around them, even as Sixiao the painter thrives. The Mongols were finally overthrown in 1368, when Zhu Yuanzhang (r. 1368–98) drove the last Yuan emperor north into the Gobi desert and declared himself first emperor of the new Ming dynasty. China was once again ruled by the Chinese.

INDIAN AND SOUTHEAST ASIAN CIVILIZATIONS

By 1200, Indian civilization was among the world's oldest, and it asserted broad influence over all of Southeast Asia (Map **11.2**). Its history during the centuries before and after 1200 was largely determined by competing religious forces, especially Buddhism, Islam, and Hinduism. Buddhism, which flourished in India from about 100 to 600 CE, had steadily waned in influence. It was further diminished when Muslim invaders entered northern India in the eleventh and twelfth centuries, destroying centers of worship in their path. Many of the Buddhist monks fled north into Nepal and across the Himalayas into Tibet or eastward into present-day Myanmar (formerly Burma). The Muslim invaders, who established their capital at Delhi, brought with them new forms of art and architecture rooted in Persian court traditions. Meanwhile, Hinduism became increasingly popular, and it gradually asserted itself as the dominant Indian religion. Well into the fifteenth and sixteenth centuries, India was ruled by Hindu dynasties, especially in the south, where the culture was relatively isolated from the influence of the Delhi sultans. Hinduism spread throughout Southeast Asia, where Cambodian monarchs constructed magnificent temples inspired by Indian prototypes.

CLOSER LOOK

The human presence in nature goes almost unnoticed in Guo Xi's [gwoh hsee] hanging scroll, *Early Spring*. Nature, embodied by the mountain, is all-embracing, a powerful and imposing symbol of eternity. The composition of Guo Xi's painting is based on the Chinese written character for mountain. The fluid gestures of the calligrapher's hand are mirrored in Guo Xi's painting, both in the organization of the whole and in the individual brush-and-ink strokes that render this ideal landscape. Like the calligrapher, Guo Xi is interested in the balance, rhythm, and movement of his line.

A court painter during the reign of the Emperor Shenzong [shehn-tsohng] (r. 1068–85), Guo Xi was given the task of painting all the murals in the Forbidden City, the imperial compound in Beijing that foreigners were prohibited from entering. His ideas about landscape painting were recorded by his son, Guo Si [gwoh seh], in a book entitled *The Lofty Message of the Forests and Streams*. According to this book, the central peak here symbolizes the emperor himself and its tall pines the gentlemanly ideals of the court. Around the emperor the masses assume their natural place, as around this mountain the trees and hills fall into the order and rhythms of nature.

Guo Xi, *Early Spring*. Song dynasty, 1072.
Hanging scroll, ink and slight color on silk, length 5′. Collection of the National Palace Museum, Taipei, Taiwan, Republic of China. Everything has its proper place in the Chinese universe, and thus the painting possesses multiple points of view. Accordingly, each part of this painting is constructed at the appropriate "distance."

Chinese character for "mountain."

Something to Think About . . .

In the West, landscape painting did not become a popular genre until the eighteenth century. What differences in attitude between East and West during the Middle Ages might account for this?

Barely noticeable, two figures get out of their boat at the bottom left, and another figure stands on the shoreline at the right. Two waterfalls cascade down the hillside behind this second figure, and a small village can be seen nestled on the mountainside above the falls.

SEE MORE For a Closer Look at Guo Xi's *Early Spring*, go to **www.myartslab.com**

The central mountain is painted so that we gaze up to it in the "high distance," as we would gaze up at the emperor.

On the left side of the painting, we gaze far off into a "level distance," creating a sense of limitless, eternal space.

In the humbling "deep distance" of the foreground, far below our point of view, we see images that reflect our own insignificance in nature.

Fig. 11.6 *Manjushri, thangka* **from Central Tibet. Thirteenth century.** Gouache on cotton, height 22".
Private collection. At the base of the *thangka* are three images of Manjushri wielding swords with four arms,
representing his ability to cut through ignorance.

Fig. 11.7 Jungle filled with ancient temples and pagodas, Bagan, Myanmar (formerly Burma).
1057–1287. The temple complex at Bagan covers an area of approximately 16 square miles. © Keren Su/Corbis. All Rights Reserved.

Buddhist Art and Architecture

High in the isolated valleys of the Himalayas in Nepal and Tibet, Buddhist monks adapted Buddhism to the native Tibetan mystical religion known as Bon [bohn]. The local religious leaders, known as *lamas* (meaning "none superior"), considered themselves the reincarnation of earlier deceased lamas and Buddhist bodhisattvas. The chief lama, the Dalai (meaning "ocean"), was believed to be the reincarnation of the bodhisattva Avalokiteshvara [avah-lo-kee-TESH-varah], the embodiment of compassion in this new form of Buddhism. Enlightenment, not simply nirvana, is the goal of this version of Buddhism, generally known as Mahayana, and the vow of every bodhisattva is to help others achieve enlightenment before they themselves cross over into paradise.

Among the artistic expressions of this faith were rolled-up cloth paintings, known as *thangkas* [TAHN-kas]. As monks traveled from one monastery to another, they would unroll *thangkas* as aids to instruction. Painted on the *thangkas* were images representing Buddhist figures of authority, including lamas, bodhisattvas, and the Buddha himself, which, the Tibetans believed, were manifest in their images. The *thangka* reproduced here (Fig. 11.6) represents Manjushri [MAHN-joo-shree], a bodhisattva associated with a great historical teacher, thus symbolizing wisdom.

In Myanmar, Anawratha [eh-nuh-YAH-thah], the first king of the Bagan Empire (r. 1044–1077), was a devout Buddhist. His capital at Bagan became a center of Buddhist learning, attracting monks from across Southeast Asia, especially from India, as Muslims gained control of the subcontinent. There he built the Shwesandaw Paya, or "Sunset Temple," in 1057 (visible at the top left of Fig. 11.7), a five-terraced structure topped by a circular stupa that, legend has it, contains the hairs of Buddha. For the next two centuries, until Bagan was overrun by the army of Kublai Khan in 1287, Anawratha's heirs built more than 13,000 temples, pagodas, and other religious structures, of which some 2,200 temples remain standing.

Hindu Art and Architecture

As we saw in Chapter 7, Hindu religion and art are infused with a deep respect for sexuality, evident even in the architecture. The Kandarya [KAHN-dahr-yah] Mahadeva temple (Fig. 11.8) at Khajuraho, the capital of the Chandella [chan-deh-lah] dynasty, represents the epitome of northern Indian Hindu architecture. Its rising towers are meant to suggest the peaks of the Himalayas, home of the Hindu gods, and this analogy would have been even clearer when the temple was painted in its original white gesso. The plan (Fig. 11.9) is a double cross, with arms extending north and south from the east–west axis. At the first crossing is the *mandapa* [MAHN-dah-pah], the columned assembly hall. At the second crossing is the *garbhagriha* [GARB-hah-gree-hah], or "womb chamber," the symbolic sacred cavern at the heart of the sacred mountain/temple. Here rests the cult image of the Brahman, in this case the *lingam*, or symbol of male sexuality, of Shiva, the first, or formless emanation of the Brahman. (Recall from Chapter 7 that the Brahman is the creator and the universal soul.) Although it is actually almost completely dark, the *garbhagriha* is considered by Hindu worshippers to be filled with the pure light of the Brahman. The towers of the temple rise from east to west, as if gathering around the central tower, known as the *shikara* [SHEE-kah-rah], that rises to a height of over 100 feet above the *garbhagriha*. As the height increases, the temple seems to gather the energy of the Hindu religion to a single rising point, soaring with the spirit of the worshipper.

By the twelfth century, Hinduism had spread from India southeast into present-day Cambodia, where Hindu art achieved a monumental imperial grandeur. In Cambodia, the Khmer monarchy established its capital at Angkor, about 150 miles northwest of present-day Phnom Penh. Covering about 70 square miles, the city was crossed by broad avenues and canals and filled with royal palaces and temples. The largest of these temples, Angkor Wat (Fig. 11.10), was created by Suryavarman [suhr-YAH-vahr-mahn] II (r. 1113–ca. 1150). Five central towers, representing the five peaks of Mount Meru, the center of the Hindu cosmos, rise above a moat surrounding the complex. The approach to the galleries at the towers' base is from the west, crossing a long bridge

Fig. 11.8 Kandarya Mahadeva temple, Khajuraho, Madhya Pradesh, India. Chandella dynasty, ca. 1025–50. The temple's formal design, like that of all Hindu temples, was prescribed in the *shastras*, a body of ancient Hindu writing that sets out the principles of poetry, music, dance, and the other arts. By the second millennium, most temples followed the *shastras* only loosely, freely elaborating on the basic plan.

Fig. 11.9 Plan of Kandarya Mahadeva temple, Khajurabo, India. ca. 1025–50. The temple's main features are the *garbhagriha,* the cult image, and the *mandapa*.

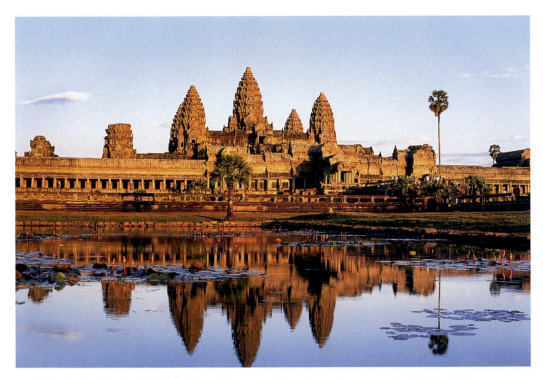

Fig. 11.10 Angkor Wat, Cambodia. Early twelfth century. The entire complex was constructed in the short span of about 30 years.

over the moat, which symbolizes the oceans surrounding the known world. On June 21, the summer solstice and the beginning of the Cambodian solar year, a visitor to the temple arriving through the western gate would see the sun rise directly over the central tower. In this way, the symbolic evocation of the cosmos, so fundamental to Hindu temple architecture, is further elaborated in astronomical terms.

There are literally miles of relief sculptures decorating the walls of Angkor Wat, including images of the *apsaras*, mythological goddesses whose dances were used by the gods to seduce mortals, and *devatas*, guardian spirits who stand individually or in groups with an air of refined elegance (Fig. **11.11**). They are uniformly bare-breasted and wear both a crown and a pleated *sampot* (a wrapped skirt), rolled at the top below the belly to open like a flower. The ubiquity of such figures underscores the important role of goddess worship in Hindu culture (see Chapter 7).

Hindu artists also mastered the art of bronze-casting. In the Tamil Nadu [TA-mul NAH-doo] region of southern India, artists began making large bronze editions of Shiva in his manifestation as Shiva Nataraja [nah-tuh-RAH-juh], Lord of the Dance, as early as the tenth and eleventh centuries. Such images were commissioned as icons for the region's many temples. Since Shiva embodies the rhythms of the universe, he is also a great dancer. All the gods were present when Shiva first danced, and they begged him to dance again. Shiva promised to do so in the hearts of his devotees as well as in a sacred grove in Tamil Nadu itself.

Fig. 11.11 *Devata*, Angkor Wat, Cambodia. Early twelfth century. There are over 2,000 devatas at Angkor Wat.

Fig. 11.12 *Shiva Nataraja, Lord of the Dance,* **from Southern India. Eleventh century CE.** Copper, height 43 $\frac{1}{8}$″. © The Cleveland Museum of Art. Purchase from the J. H. Wade Fund, 1930.331. In his back left hand, Shiva carries fire, representing the destructive energy of his dance at the end of each cosmic age, which cleanses sins and removes illusion from the world. In his back right hand, he holds an hourglass-shaped drum, which represents the rhythmic sound of his dance as he ceaselessly re-creates the universe.

As he dances, he is framed in a circle of fire, symbolic of both creation and destruction, the endless cycle of birth, death, and reincarnation (Fig. **11.12**).

The Rise of Court Life in Japan

Although Buddhism may have been known in Japan earlier, it is commonly believed that it arrived in the Yamato period (see Chapter 1) from Korea and China. According to the *Chronicles of Japan*, a statue of Buddha and a collection of sacred Buddhist texts were given to Japanese rulers by the king of the Baekje region of Korea in 552. Chinese calligraphy was already the basis of the Japanese written language, and to some, Buddhism seemed equally amenable to Japanese adaptation. But Buddhism was by no means welcomed by all. Of the three rival clans then most powerful in Yamato Japan—the Soga, Mononobe, and Nakatomi, each tied to the imperial family through marriage to the emperor—both the Mononobe, who were in charge of the emperor's military, and the Nakatomi, in charge of Shinto ritual, opposed the introduction of Buddhism into the country. But the Soga, managers of imperial estates who were in constant contact with the Koreans and Chinese, were deeply attracted to the religion, and the Yamato emperor allowed them to practiced it within their own clan. As the Soga gained more and more power over the last decades of the sixth century, they eventually defeated the Mononobe and Nakatomi in a civil war, and the head of the Soga clan, Umako, installed his 39-year-old daughter, Suiko, as empress and declared her 29-year-old nephew, Shotoku [SHOH-toh-koo] (r. 593–622), her regent and crown prince. The capital was moved inland from Osaka on the coast to the Soga homeland in the Asuka valley in the central Yamato plain.

Shotoku, whose name means "Wise and Virtuous," emphasized the importance of the Chinese model of civil administration, and introduced Confucianism to the court. When he built a new palace at Ikaruga [ee-KAH-roo-gah], in the central Asuka plain, he constructed a Buddhist temple next to it. Others were built during his administration, and over 1,300 Buddhist monks and nuns were ordained. But Buddhism was in fact practiced only by a small number of aristocracy around the Asuka capital.

The Coming of the Fujiwara

In 645, the Nakatomi, who had been forced to tolerate Buddhism even as they continued to maintain Shinto ritual at court, rebelled, executing the Soga clan. Anyone else who showed resistance to their rule was executed as well. Nakatomi no Kamatari (614–669) was awarded the surname of Fujiwara by Emperor Tenji for his part in crushing the Soga and placing Tenji on the throne. The Fujiwara clan, thus directly descended from the Nakatomi, would become the greatest noble clan of classical Japan, ruling it for 500 years.

In 708, the Fujiwara oversaw the construction of a new capital at Hojeikyo, commonly called Nara after its location in the Nara plain, some 15 miles to the northwest of Asuka (see Map 11.3). It was laid out according to the principles of Chinese city planning as a walled city on the model of Chang-an (see Fig. 11.3), 2.7 miles from east to west and about 3.1 miles from north to south, with a broad avenue running north and south in its center culminating at the Heijo Palace. And although the Nakatomi/Fujiwara clan had despised the Buddhist-leaning Soga the century before, at Nara, they officially accepted Buddhism as the state religion. Magnificent temples and monasteries were constructed, including what would remain, for a thousand years, the largest wooden structure in the world, the Todaiji temple (Fig. 11.13). It houses a giant bronze, known as the Great Buddha, over 49 feet high and weighing approximately 380 tons. According to ancient records, as many as 2.6 million people were required to aid in its construction, although that number represents approximately half of Japan's population at the time and is probably a

Map 11.3 Japan. Isolated from the Asian mainland, Japan was both slow to develop and susceptible to the influence of the more advanced cultures once it became aware of them.

gross exaggeration. The original temple was twice destroyed by warring factions, in 1180 and again in 1567. The current Buddha is in fact a 1691 reconstruction of the original, and the Todaiji temple is itself a reconstruction of 1709. The restored temple is considerably smaller than the original, approximately two-thirds its size, and now stands 188 feet in width and 156 feet in height.

Fig. 11.13 Todaiji Temple, Nara, Japan. 752. The temple's sweeping horned roof is typical of Japanese architecture

The Heian Period: Courtly Refinement

The acceptance of Buddhism by the Fujiwara clan at Nara suggests that the conflict between the clans in the earlier Yamato period was probably as much about power as it was religion. But it is also true that by the seventh century Buddhist doctrine and Shinto had begun to influence each other. The Great Buddha at Nara became identified with the Shinto goddess Amaterasu (see Chapter 1), and Buddhist ceremonies were incorporated into Shinto court ritual. But between 784 and 794, the capital of Japan was moved to Heian-kyo—modern-day Kyoto—which quickly became the most densely populated city in the world. According to records, the move occurred because the secular court needed to distance itself from the religious influence of the Buddhist monks at Nara. Indeed, one of these monks had risen to power as the lover of the Empress Koken (r. 749–59, 765–70).

Like Nara, Heian-kyo was modeled on Chang'an, the capital of the Tang dynasty, and, also as at Nara, the ordered grid of its streets was a conscious bow to Chinese philosophy and its reflection in the workings of government. Between the late eleventh and the middle of the twelfth century at Heian-kyo, scholars estimate that the royal family regularly dedicated new Shinto shrines and new Buddhist temples.

Life of the Nobility At Heian-kyo, the arts flourished in an atmosphere of elegance and refinement. The nobility numbered around 100,000, and they lived in residential complexes that extended across several acres with multiple single-story pavilions and secondary halls tied together by covered walkways. The entire complex usually encircled a garden with a pond and small streams crossed by bridges, the whole surrounded by an earthen wall (Fig. 11.14). As in traditional Shinto shrines, the roofs of the complex were made of cypress-bark shingles. This style of architecture is known as *shinden-zukuri* [SHEEN-dehn SOO-koo-ree], after its main hall, or *shinden*, and *zukuri*, "style." Following Chinese tradition, it was oriented to the south. It was large enough to accommodate the nobleman's several wives—limited polygamy was practiced by the high aristocracy, permitting a nobleman to have one or two lesser wives who could bear him fully recognized children. Theoretically at least, these lesser wives enjoyed less prestige in the court. Behind the *shinden*, in a separate hall to the north, lived the main wife, known as the *kita no kata*, "the person to the north." Secondary wives lived in pavilions to the east and west. Each hall could open into the gardens by means of latticed shutters that could be raised to take advantage of good weather.

Life in the Heian court was determined by gender. Men lived public lives; women much more private ones. In fact, women were rarely visible. An aristocratic woman might make a public excursion to a Buddhist temple, but she would remain out of public view. She might receive a male visitor, but the two would converse through a portable set of curtain panels. Women were, however, highly educated, and they were expected to contribute to the aesthetic of the Heian court. They were judged on their looks—although it is striking to note that there are almost no detailed descriptions of a woman's face or body in Heian writing—on the arrangement of their many layers of silk robes, on their perfumes, on the beauty of their calligraphy, and on their ability to compose poetry at a moment's notice. As opposed to a man's identity, which was regularly displayed in public settings, a woman's identity was defined particularly by her speech, her correspondence, and her poetry and other writings.

Literature and Calligraphy Although many court gatherings took place for the purpose of poetry competitions, in which both men and women participated, poems were generally composed for a single recipient—a friend or lover—and a reply was expected. In her *Diaries*—or *Nikki* in Japanese—

Fig. 11.14 Reconstruction drawing of a *shinden-zukuri* mansion. No original mansions of the nobility survive in present-day Kyoto. Drawings such as this one are based on the ample literary description of these elaborate residences, as well as their representation in illustrated scrolls.

Murasaki Shikibu (973/8–aft. 1014), one of the most accomplished women of the Heian court, a lady-in-waiting to the Empress Shoshi [SHOH-shee] (988–1074), describes just such an exchange (**Reading 11.3**):

Something of the flavor of court life is captured in this brief passage, in the private space of the gentlewoman's world, her relation to the gentlemen of the court, the attention of the two poets to natural beauty, and the expression of that beauty as a means of capturing personal feeling.

Diaries, or *nikki*, comprised an important literary form that tell us much about court life in the Heian period. Murasaki's poems—indeed her entire text—are written in a new, purely Japanese writing system, known as **hiragana** [HEER-ah-gah-nah]. Beginning in the early ninth century, *hiragana* gradually replaced the use of Chinese characters and enabled writers to spell out the Japanese language phonetically. The university curriculum remained based on Chinese classics and history, and the formal workings of state and government still required the use of Chinese. Chinese was the language of the world of men. Since the Heian court strongly discouraged displays of education in Chinese by women, they were taught the *hiragana* script, even though many court women actually knew Chinese quite well.

The popularity of *hiragana*, even among men, who recognized its convenience, encouraged the development of new Japanese forms of poetry, especially the **waka** [WAH-kah] (literally the "poetry of Wa," or Japan). A *waka* consists of 31 syllables in 5 lines on a theme drawn from nature and the changing of seasons. Here is a *waka* by one of the great poets of the Heian period, Ki no Tomonori [KEE noh TOH-moh-noh-ree] (act. 850–904) (**Reading 11.4**):

The tension here, between the calm of the day and the restlessness of the cherry blossoms, is meant to mirror a similar tension in the poet's mind, suggesting a certain sense of anticipation or premonition. *Waka* serves as a model for other Japanese poetic forms, particularly the famous **haiku**, the 3-line, 17-syllable form that developed out of the first three lines of the *waka*.

Sei Shonagon's *Pillow Book* Aside from poetry and diaries, the women of the Japanese court also created a new literary form, the *zuihitsu* [ZU-EE-heet-soo] (literally, "by the line of the brush"), random notes or occasional writings. The first of these was the *Pillow Book* by Sei Shonagon [SAY SHOH-nah-gohn] (ca. 965–aft. 1000), lady-in-waiting to the imperial consort Teishi [TAY-shee] (970–1001) and head of a literary salon that openly competed against that of Murasaki Shikibu, a rivalry that helped to inspire the literary innovation of the period. The clarity of Sei Shonagon's observation in the *Pillow Book* is captured in her short list of "Elegant Things" (**Reading 11.5a**):

Another, longer list, entitled "Hateful Things" (see **Reading 11.5** on pages 398–399), gives the reader a remarkable overview of daily life in the Heian court. Sei Shonagon looks at the entirety of her world, from its insects to the palace dog.

The First Novel: *The Tale of Genji* Murasaki Shikibu, whose *Diaries* we discussed previously, is more famous as the author of a long book of prose and poetry (over 1,000 pages in English translation), including many exchanges of poetry of the type recorded in her *Diaries*. Many consider it the world's first novel—certainly no fiction in the Western world matches its scope until the eighteenth century. Called *The Tale of Genji*, it tells the story of Genji, an imperial prince, born to the favorite wife of the emperor, though she is too low in rank for her son to be an heir to the throne. Much of the action takes place in the homes and gardens of Heian-kyo, and besides being a moving romantic story covering 75 years of the hero's life, from his birth to his death, the novel presents us with a vivid picture of life in Japanese society at the turn of the millennium. As opposed to the *Diaries*, the stories related in *The Tale of the Genji* are, of course, fiction, but, as Genji says at one point in the *Tale*: "Among these lies there certainly are some plausible touching scenes, convincingly told; and yes, we know they are fictions, but even so we are moved."

Soon after it was written, *The Tale of Genji* was illustrated in a handscroll that was an ensemble of more than 100 excerpts from the *Tale*, written in elegant calligraphy on decorative paper probably at court. The paintings, of which only 20 of the original 100 survive, have been attributed to Takayoshi (Fig. **11.15**). Most are focused on intimate episodes of high narrative tension, and of the 20 paintings that survive, 17 depict events happening either in the outer corridor or on the veranda or outer corridor of a *shinden*.

As the scroll was unwound, the viewer would have first seen the right side of Fig. 11.15, the courtyard (now brown but originally silver), and then, at a sharp angle, the veranda and curtain wall of a house in which a deeply moving scene is unfolding in the outer corridor. As a young man, Genji had fallen in love with his father's youngest wife, Fujitsubo [foo-JEE-tsoo-boh], and fathered a son by her. Genji's own father, the emperor, acknowledged the child as his own, and the boy eventually became emperor himself. Genji came to understand the human consequences of his youthful actions only when his own youngest wife bore a son by another man and Genji was forced to acknowledge the child as his own, just as his father had accepted Genji's son. Depicted here is the moment of Genji's acceptance of his wife's son.

The scene is depicted from an aerial perspective just above the roof, which has been "blown off" (a technique known as *fakinaki yatai*) in order to provide a view of the interior. The result is a highly chaotic composition in which geometrical lines of the architecture play off against the figures and their clothing. Genji holds the child in his arms. Beside him to the right, half hidden by the curtains, bowls of food are placed for the ritual celebration. Ladies-in-waiting, one dressed in black, sit below, and at the extreme upper left, the child's mother is indicated by a heap of fabric. Genji knows that the attendants understand that he is not the child's father, and yet he fully understands his duty.

Although Genji is the hero of the book, Murasaki Shikibu gives the women of the Heian court full treatment, chief among them the tellingly named Murasaki, whose own life, from childhood to death, is fully narrated. She is Genji's greatest love, and she receives his lavish attentions. And yet, given the polygamous nature of Japanese society, she suffers much. She is unable to bear Genji a child, and Genji must turn elsewhere for an heir. Likewise, her social status is not high enough to qualify her as his principal wife. Thus, despite her wit and intelligence, her beauty and charm, she is condemned to second-class status.

Fig. 11.15 Attributed to Takayoshi. Illustration to the Azumaya chapter of *The Tale of Genji* by Murasaki Shikibu. Late Heian period, twelfth century. Handscroll, ink and color on paper, height 8 1/2". Tokugawa Art Museum, Nagoya, Japan. Of the original illustrations of *The Tale of Genji*, only 20 pictures survive.

***Yamato-e* and *Omna-e* Painting** The *Genji* scroll has often been described as an example of *yamato-e* [yah-MAH-toh ay] painting, a term coined during the Heian period to distinguish between Japanese and Chinese (*kara-e*) [KAH-rah ay] painting styles. This distinction announces a movement away from traditional Chinese styles to one characterized by Japanese literary themes, native subject matter, and landscapes evocative of traditional poetry. But recently scholars have suggested that *yamato-e* refers more specifically to large-scale landscape paintings generally executed on walls, sliding doors, and folding screens, and that the *Genji* illustrations are, rather, examples of *omna-e* paintings, "women's pictures." *Omna-e* pictures are not necessarily works done exclusively by women, but are rather pictures appropriate to the space of women's lives at court. By the time of the Genji scrolls, *omna-e* paintings were executed by professional artisans at court.

The Kamakura Period (ca. 1185–1392): Samurai and Shogunate

During the Heian period, the emperors had increasingly relied on regional warrior clans—**samurai** (literally, "those who serve")—to exercise military control, especially in the countryside. Over time these clans became more and more powerful, until, by 1100, they had begun to emerge as a major force in Japanese military and political life, inaugurating the Kamakura Period, which takes its name from the capital city of the most prominent of these clans, the Minamoto. Their newfound power in many ways represented a resurgence of the familial clan-based system of authority that had been deeply engrained in Japanese society since at least the time of the Yamato emperors, but almost inevitably, their rise also resulted, as it had among the Yamato clans, in intense rivalry and, eventually, warfare.

Pure Land Buddhist Art As war spread across the country, many Japanese felt that it announced the coming of *Mappo*, the so-called Third Age of Buddha, often translated as the "Age of Dharma Decline." Prophesied to begin 2,000 years after the death of Sakyamuni Buddha, it would last, so it was believed, for 10,000 years. During this period no one would be able to attain enlightenment and society would descend into a condition of degeneracy and corruption. Pure Land Buddhism seemed to offer a way out. Pure Land Buddhism had originated in the late sixth century in China as a particular form of Mahayana Buddhism. The Mahayana Buddhists believed the compassion for all beings is the foundation of faith and that not nirvana but buddhahood is one's ultimate goal. They recognized Buddhas other than Sakyamuni, among them Amitabha Buddha, the Buddha of Infinite Light and Life who dwells in a paradise known as the Western Pure Land. This Pure Land Buddhism had been introduced to Japan as early as the seventh century, the Chinese Amitabha Buddha becoming Buddha Amida. Particularly attractive to the Japanese was the Pure Land belief that by chanting *Namu Amida Butsu* [nah-moo ah-MEE-dah boots(u)] ("Hail to the Buddha Amida"), the faithful would be reborn into the Western Pure Land paradise, where the enlightenment impossible to achieve in the world might finally be attained.

One of the early practitioners of the Pure Land chant was the monk Kuya [koo-yah] (903–972), who traveled on foot around the countryside chanting and doing charitable deeds. His enduring popularity is underscored by the fact that more than 200 years after his death, his likeness would be represented in a sculpture by the Kamakura artist Kosho [koh-shoh] (Fig. 11.16). His staff is topped by deer horns, symbolic of his slaying of a deer, the violence of whose death converted him to Buddhism. The most remarkable feature of the sculpture, however, is Kosho's representation of the chant. It consists of six small buddhas, emanating from Kuya's mouth. Each buddha represents one syllable of the *Namu Amida Butsu* chant (the final "u" of which is silent).

Fig. 11.16 Kosho. *Kuya Preaching*. Kamakura period, before 1207. Painted wood with crystal inlaid eyes, height 46 ¹/₂″. Rokuhara Mitsu-ji, Kyoto. Kuya wears a gong held to his chest by a yoke over his shoulders. The gong would have accompanied him as he danced while chanting.

The Arts of Military Culture The Kamakura period actually began when the Minamoto clan defeated its chief rival, the Taira, in 1185, but the contest for power between the two dominated the last years of the Heian period. The complex relationship between the Fujiwara of the Heian era and the samurai clans of the Kamakura is embodied in a long handscroll narration of an important battle of 1160, from the *Scrolls of Events of the Heiji Period*, painted by an unknown artist in the thirteenth century perhaps 100 years after the events themselves (Fig. **11.17**). In 1156, Go Shirakawa [goh sheer-ah-kah-wah] (1127–1192; r. 1156–1158) ascended to the throne, with the Fujiwara to serve in what had become their traditional role as regent to the emperor, the highest position in the government. But Go Shirakawa resisted the Fujiwara attempt to take control of the government, and in 1157, they recruited one of the two most powerful samurai clans, the Minamoto, to help them stage a coup and imprison the emperor. *Night Attack on the Sanjo Palace* depicts the moment troops led by Fujiwara Nobuyori attacked the emperor's palace in the middle of the night, taking him prisoner and burning his palace to the ground. The chaos and violence of the events are captured by the sweeping linear ribbons of flame and smoke rising to the upper right and the confusion of horsemen, warriors, fleeing ladies, the dead, and the dying in the foreground, all framed by an architecture that falls at a steep diagonal to the bottom left. The samurai warriors, dressed in elaborate iron armor, were master horsemen and archers. In this scene, many hold their bows, the lower portions of which are smaller than the top in order that they might pass over a horse's neck. As it turned out, this was a brief moment of triumph for the Minamoto. The rebellion was quickly quashed by the second of the powerful clans, the Taira, and for the next 20 years, the Taira managed to control the Japanese imperial court with the abdicated emperor Go Shirakawa's blessing. But in 1185, the Minamoto samurai army, led by Minamoto Yoshitusune (1159–1189), defeated the Taira, killing virtually all male members of the Taira clan and large numbers of their wives and children.

Yoshitusune's brother, Yoritomo (1147–1199), had sat out the war in Kamakura, and as soon as the war was ended, he quickly disposed of all samurai rivals in the region, including his own brother, whom he hunted down, but who managed to commit suicide rather than be captured. Yoritomo demanded that all other samurai lords pledge allegiance to him or risk the fate of his brother, and he soon

Fig. 11.17 *Night Attack on the Sanjo Palace*, detail, from the *Scrolls of Events of the Heiji Period*. **Kamakura period, late thirteenth century.** Handscroll, ink and colors on paper, 16 ¼" × 275 ½". Courtesy, Museum of Fine Arts, Boston. Reproduced with permission. © 2006 Museum of Fine Arts, Boston. All Rights Reserved. Fenollosa-Weld Collection (11.4000). This is the central scene of the scroll, which begins with the moving toward the palace from the right and ends with it leaving in triumph to the left.

controlled most of the Japanese archipelago. He established his rule at Kamakura, and thus removed Japanese government from the influence of both the aristocratic court at Heiankyo and the Buddhist stronghold at Nara. Interestingly, Yoritomo never tried to assume the imperial throne, and neither did any of the subsequent samurai rulers. Instead, he considered himself the emperor's servant, much as the Fujiwara had served the Heian emperors. But, in 1192, the imperial court granted him the title of Seiitai Shogun, literally "Barbarian-subduing General," and as **shogun**— that is, general-in-chief of the samurais—his military form of government, known as the shogunate, ruled the country for 150 years.

Yoritomo's shogunate was, in many ways, defined by land reforms that he immediately instituted. In essence, he granted the country estates that had belonged formerly to his enemies as gifts to his followers. These new landholders came to be officially known as *daimyo*, literally "great name," by the fifteenth century. They defined themselves first by the absolute allegiance to the shogun, and then by their devotion to military arts and their concern for their "great name"—by extension, their honor, their fame, and their pride in their family or clan. Eventually, when Japan enjoyed an extended period of peace, from 1600 until the mid-nineteenth century, these values were codified and expanded upon by a *daimyo* class—whose militarism seemed increasingly irrelevant—into a well-defined code of conduct, **bushido**, "the way of the warrior," which continues to influence many aspects of Japanese society to this day.

THE CULTURES OF AFRICA

Just as in Europe and Asia, all over Africa, powerful kingdoms arose during this period. Several large kingdoms dominated the western African region known as the Sahel, the grasslands that serve as a transition between the Sahara desert and the more temperate zones to the west and south. Among the most important is the kingdom of Mali, discussed in Chapter 9, which shows the great influence Islam had come to have on much of northern Africa long before the end of the first millennium CE. Farther south, along the western coast of central Africa, were the powerful Yoruba state of Ife [EE-fay] and the kingdom of Benin [buh-NEEN]. On the eastern side of Africa, the Zagwe dynasty continued long Christian traditions in the Horn of Africa, while the Arab Swahili culture thrived along the central east coast. Farther south, near the southeastern tip of Africa, the ancient Shona civilization produced urban centers represented today by the ruins of "Great Zimbabwe" (Map **11.4**).

Ife Culture

The Ife culture is one of the oldest in West Africa. It developed beginning around the eighth century along the Niger River, in what is now Nigeria. It was centered in the city of Ife. By 1100, it was producing highly naturalistic, sculptural, commemorative portraits in clay and stone, probably depicting its rulers, and not long after, elegant brass sculptures as well.

An example of Ife brasswork is the *Head of a King* (or *Oni* [OH-nee]) (Fig. **11.18**). The parallel lines that run down the face represent decorative effects made by scarring—**scarification**. A hole in the lower neck suggests that the head may have been attached to a wooden mannequin, and in memorial services, the mannequin may have worn the royal robes of the Ife court. Small holes along the scalp line suggest that hair, or perhaps a veil of some sort, also adorned the head. But the head itself was, for the Ife, of supreme importance. It was the home of the spirit, the symbol of the king's capacity to organize the world and to prosper. Ife culture depended on its kings' heads for its own welfare. Since the Ife did not leave a written record of their cultural beliefs, we can best understand their ancient culture by looking at their contemporary descendants.

Yoruba Origin Myths The Yoruba people, whose population today is about 11 million, trace their ancestry directly to Ife

Map 11.4 Africa. ca. 1350, including predominant forms of economic activity.

culture. The Yoruba cosmos consists of the world of the living (*aye* [aye-yeah]) and the realm of the gods (*orun* [oh-ROON]). The gods are themselves called *orisha* and among them are the primordial deities, who created the world, as well as forces of nature, such as thunder and lightning, and ancestral heroes who have risen to immortality. Linking these two worlds is the king, who serves as the representative in this world of those existing in *orun*. The king's head is thus sacred, and his crown, or *ade* [ah-DEH] (Fig. **11.19**), rising high above his head, symbolizes his majesty and authority. Rows of beads fall over his face to shield viewers from the power of his gaze. Imagery on the crown varies, but often refers to Ife myths of origin, similar to myths of origin found throughout the world (see Chapter 1). The first Yoruba king, Oduduwa [oh-DOO-doo-wah], from whom all subsequent kings descend, is frequently represented. According to leg-

end, Oduduwa was ordered to create a land mass out of the watery reaches of Earth so that it might be populated by people. Oduduwa lowered himself down onto the waters, the legend continues, and emptied Earth from a small snail shell onto the water. He then placed a chicken on the sand to spread it and make land. Finally he planted some palm kernels. It was at Ife that he did this, and Ife remains the most sacred of Yoruba sites.

Fig. 11.18 Head of an *Oni* (King). Ife culture, Nigeria. ca. thirteenth century. Brass, height, 11 $^7/_{16}$″. Museum of Ife Antiquities, Ife, Nigeria. The metal used to cast this head is an alloy of copper and zinc, and therefore not technically bronze, but brass.

Fig. 11.19 *Ade*, or beaded crown, Yoruba culture, Nigeria. Late twentieth century. Beadwork, height, 6′1 $^1/_4$″. © The Trustees of the British Museum/Art Resource, NY. Today, approximately 50 Yoruba rulers wear beaded crowns and claim descent from Oduduwa.

Benin Culture

Sometime around 1170, the city-state of Benin, some 150 miles southeast of Ife, also in the Niger basin, asked the *oni* of Ife to provide a new ruler for their territory, which was, legend has it, plagued by misrule and disorder. The *oni* sent Prince Oranmiyan [oh-RHAN-mee-yan], who founded a new dynasty. Oranmiyan was apparently so vexed by the conditions he found that he named his new state *ibini,* "land of vexation," from which the name Benin derives. After some years, Oranmiyan returned home, but not until after he had impregnated the Benin princess. Their son Eweka [eh-WEE-kah] would become the first king, or *oba,* as the Benin culture called their ruler, ruling from 1180 to 1246.

Already in place at the capital, Benin City, were the beginnings of a massive system of walls and moats that would become, by the fifteenth century, the world's largest human-built earthwork. According to archeologist Phillip Darling, who has studied the wall and moat system for several decades, they total some 10,000 miles in length, or some four to five times the length of the main Great Wall of China. These earthworks consist of moats, the dirt from which was piled alongside them to make walls up to 60 feet high. They were probably first dug over a thousand years ago to protect settlements and their farmlands from the nocturnal raids of the forest elephant. But as Benin grew, linear earth boundaries demarcated clan or family territories and symbolically signified the boundary between the real physical world and the spirit world. When the British arrived in the late nineteenth century, the walls were still largely intact (Fig. **11.20**), but they were soon destroyed by British forces, and what remains of them have been increasingly consumed by modern urbanization.

Like the Ife to the north, the Benin rulers also created life-like images of their ancestor rulers. In the first half of the twentieth century, recognizing that many of the oral traditions of Benin culture were in danger of being lost, the Benin court historian, Chief Jacob Egharevba (1893–1981), recorded as many traditional tales and historical narratives as he could find and published them in his *Short History of Benin.* This is his account of the origins of brass-casting (see *Materials & Techniques,* page 40 in Chapter 2) of *oba* heads in Benin culture (**Reading 11.6**):

READING 11.6

from Jacob Egharevba, *A Short History of Benin*

Oba Oguola [r. 1274–1287] wished to introduce brass casting into Benin so as to produce works of art similar to those sent him from Ife. He therefore sent to the Oni of Ife for a brass-smith and Iguegha was sent to him. Iguegha was very clever and left many designs to his successors, and was in consequence deified, and is worshipped to this day by brass-smiths. The practice of making brass-castings for the preservation of the records of events was originated during the reign of Oguola.

The artists, members of the royal casters' guild, lived in their own quarters just outside the palace in Benin, where they are located to this day. Only the *oba* could order brass-work from them. These commissions were usually memorial heads, commemorating the king's royal ancestors in royal costume (Fig. **11.21**). (The head shown in Figure **11.21** was made in the mid-sixteenth century, but heads like it were made in the earliest years of bronze production in the culture.) As in Ife culture, the *oba*'s head was the home of the spirit and the symbol of the *oba*'s capacity to organize the world and to prosper.

This power could be described and commemorated in an oral form known as a **praise poem**. Praise poems are a major part of West African culture. By praising something—a

Fig. 11.20 Drawing of Benin City as it appeared to an unknown British officer in 1891. The network of walls and moats visible in this drawing covers an area of over 2,500 square miles.

Fig. 11.21 Head of an Oba. Nigeria; Edo, Court of Benin. ca. 1550. Brass, 9 1/4 × 9 5/8 × 9″. Image copyright © The Metropolitan Museum of Art/Art Resource, NY. Such heads were usually commissioned upon the death of an *oba* by his successor, so that the deceased leader might continue to influence his community.

king, a god, a river—the poet was believed to gain influence over it. Almost everyone in West African culture has praise poems associated with them. These poems often use a poetic device known as **anaphora** [un-NAF-uh-ruh], a repetition of words and phrases at the beginning of successive sentences that, owing to the particularities of the West African languages, is almost impossible to duplicate in translation. But the poems are intended to create a powerful and insistent rhythm that rises to a crescendo.

West African Music

The rhythm-driven crescendo of the Benin praise poem shares much with African music as a whole. In fact, the poem may have been accompanied by music. African music is part of the fabric of everyday life, accompanying work, poetry, ceremony, and dance, and often evoked by visual art. The Western idea that music can be isolated from everyday experience is almost incomprehensible to the African sensibility. Typically consisting of a single line of melody without harmony, African music is generally communal in nature, encouraging a sense of social cohesion by promoting group activity. As a result, one of the most universal musical forms throughout Africa is **call-and-response** music, in which a caller, or soloist, raises the song, and the community chorus responds to it.

Call-and-response music is by no means simple. The Yoruba language, for instance, is tone-based; any Yoruba syllable has three possible tones and this tone determines its meaning. The Yoruba reproduce their speech in the method of musical signaling known as **talking drums** (track **11.1**), performed with three types of batá drums, which imitate the three tones of the language. In ritual drumming, the drums are played for the Yoruba gods and are essentially praise poems to those gods. Characteristic of this music is its polyrhythmic structure. Here as many as five to ten different "voices" of interpenetrating rhythms and tones, often repeated over and over again in a call-and-response form, play off against one another. This method of playing against or "off" the main beat is typical of West African music and exists to this day in the "off-beat" practices of Western jazz.

HEAR MORE at www.myartslab.com

Fig. 11.22 **Beta Ghiorghis (House of Saint George), Lalibela, Ethiopia. Thirteenth century.** Saint George Church is one of more than 1,500 stone carved churches that can still be seen in Ethiopia.

East Africa: The Zagwe Dynasty

Ironically, one of the dynasties of greatest cultural importance in medieval East Africa was also one of the shortest lived and least revered. In the region of today's Ethiopia, the Zagwe dynasty reigned for approximately 150 years, from the early twelfth century (when the declining Aksumite Empire fell), to 1270, when the last Zagwe ruler was deposed. The new ruling family claimed descent from King Solomon, and in order to give the impression that their family had a dazzling and unbroken chain of legitimate power reaching back into biblical times, they embarked on a campaign to discredit the Zagwe dynasty as usurpers and their reign as a disgrace. Nevertheless, the Zagwe rulers had already ensured their survival as a respected part of Ethiopian history by the rock churches they left behind.

The most famous of these was commissioned by the emperor Lalibela. In the town now known by his name, he ordered the construction of a series of churches. Unlike most buildings, instead of being built up from the ground, the churches at Lalibela were carved downward through the soft rocks at the site (Fig. **11.22**). Engineers had to conceive of the completed building in advance, including decorative details, because subtractive techniques such as carving do not allow for repair of mistakes. Once the shell of the building was carved, the interior was hollowed out into rooms for use in Christian worship and study.

The Swahili Coast

In the medieval era, Christian places of worship were rare in Africa. In the trading centers of the north and west, Islam was the dominant nonindigenous religion. East Africans had traded with Arab sailors since before the beginning of the common era, from trade depots along a narrow coastal strip ranging from today's Somalia through Mozambique (see Map 11.4). When these traders embraced Islam, the people the Arabs called Swahili, from the Arabic word for "shore," were quick to follow. From Mogadishu in the north to Sofala in the south, a region known as the Swahili Coast, Arabs and Africans blended their customs to create one of the most vibrant cultures in Africa. They also created a new language—Swahili, an African language with many borrowings from Arabic.

Looking directly out onto the Indian Ocean, Swahili ports played a key role in trade with all of Asia from the medieval era onward. The great Chinese explorer Zheng He (see Chapter 18) reached the Swahili coast, trading Chinese porcelain and other goods for African products such as spices and wild animals to take back to the Chinese emperor.

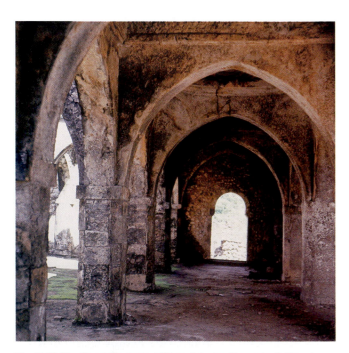

Fig. 11.23 **The Great Mosque at Kilwa, interior, Tanzania.** Built and remodeled over the centuries, it was completed with barrel vaulting and domes by the mid-fifteenth century.

The Swahili were renowned for their architecture. Using local materials such as fossilized coral limestone, they built mosques and other buildings, carving trims and decorations directly into the stone in floral designs, arabesques, and other patterns like those in the Qur'an (see Chapter 9). So beautiful were these works that, upon visiting Kilwa, medieval explorer Ibn Battuta pronounced it "the most beautiful of cities." The mosque at Kilwa (Fig. **11.23**) would have been where Ibn Battuta stopped to pray. Constructed of pieces of fossilized coral bound together by cement made from sand, the pillars, arches, and walls of the mosque were coated in a glossy plaster also made from coral, into which patterns were excised.

Great Zimbabwe

In embracing Islam, the people of the Swahili Coast transformed their society, but the influence of the new faith did not spread far inland. West of Sofala, at a port at the southern end of the Swahili Coast, the Shona people built an entirely indigenous African civilization in the region of today's Zimbabwe. The Shona people, who still occupy the region today, are thought to have first come to the region by 1100 CE. At first the Shona relied on their advanced skills at mining, animal husbandry, and agriculture to sustain their communities in the rocky grasslands of the region, but as the Swahili Coast became more and more lucrative as a center of trade, the Shona positioned themselves as an inland hub of trade to which coastal traders could travel to procure goods for export. From surrounding regions, they mined or imported copper and gold, and in return received exotic goods such as porcelain and glass from Asia and the Middle East.

Between the thirteenth and fifteenth centuries, the Shona erected the massive stone buildings and walls of a city known today as Great Zimbabwe. (The word *zimbabwe* is thought to refer to "palaces of stone.") A huge city for its time, the ruins cover one square mile and are believed to have housed a population of somewhere between 10,000 and 20,000. Great Zimbabwe has several distinct areas. The oldest of these, a hilltop enclosure known as the Hill Ruin, probably served as a lookout, but may also have been set apart for religious ceremonies or initiation rites. Built around 1250, it has a perimeter wall of smooth stone blocks that follows the contours of the hilltop. Inside this wall are several smaller enclosures with floors of clay that were hardened and polished to a shine. The enclosures also had ceremonial platforms decorated with carved geometric patterns and tall rock monoliths topped by carved birds, possibly representing messengers from the spirit world (Fig. **11.24**).

Below the Hill Ruin stands the Great Enclosure, a group of structures also encircled by a tall stone wall (Fig. **11.25**). This part of Great Zimbabwe was built approximately a century later, using a different style for the perimeter wall. Here, Shona craftsmen built a double wall with a space between the two walls only wide enough to allow single-file

Fig. 11.24 Bird carved from soapstone, Great Zimbabwe, Zimbabwe. ca. 1200–1400 CE. Height 14.5″, atop a stone monolith (total height: 64″). Great Zimbabwe Site Museum, Zimbabwe. One of eight such decorative monoliths at Great Zimbabwe, the bird is not a recognizable species and includes certain human features such as toes instead of talons. This has led to speculation that the figure may represent deceased Shona rulers who were believed to have the power to move between the spirit and human worlds. A crocodile, possibly another symbol of royalty, climbs up the front of the monolith.

Fig. 11.25 Double perimeter wall and remains of two towers that resemble Shona granaries in the Great Enclosure, Great Zimbabwe. ca. 1200–1400 CE. The skill of the craftsmen who built these structures was extraordinary. They used no mortar, but instead fit the stones together so tightly that the walls reached 30 feet in height and were so sturdy that most of them are intact today. Only the clay smoothed over the walls, and the wooden roofs over some of the structures, have eroded away in the last eight centuries.

passage. They tapered the walls inward from a 17-foot-thick base for greater strength and stability, and topped the exterior wall with an alternating diagonal pattern of dark and light-colored rocks. This decoration may have been meant to represent lightning, or perhaps the zebra, an animal frequently depicted in Shona art. These decorative stripes are echoed inside the courtyard of the enclosure, where a large platform similar to those in the Hill Ruin was constructed. One other notable feature of the Great Enclosure is two conical structures that interrupt passage around the perimeter wall. These are likely to have been ancient granaries, for the Shona people today still use similar structures.

The remainder of Great Zimbabwe consists of clusters of smaller buildings known as the Valley Ruin. Historians and archeologists presume from this that most of the population lived in the valley and that the Great Enclosure was probably a royal residence. One intriguing mystery, how-

ever, is the reason for the massive walls of the Great Enclosure and Hill Ruin. Despite the turrets and lookout spots, the walls do not appear to have been meant for defense, and from this, scholars have surmised that the walls may have existed primarily to serve as a buffer between royalty and the common people, and as a constant reminder of their power and status.

THE CULTURES OF MESOAMERICA IN THE CLASSIC ERA

The cultures of pre-Columbian Mesoamerica, comprising modern-day Nicaragua, Honduras, Guatemala, Belize, and southern Mexico, possessed a great sense of their own history. They were fully aware that cultures at least as great as themselves—the Olmec in particular (see Chapter 1)—

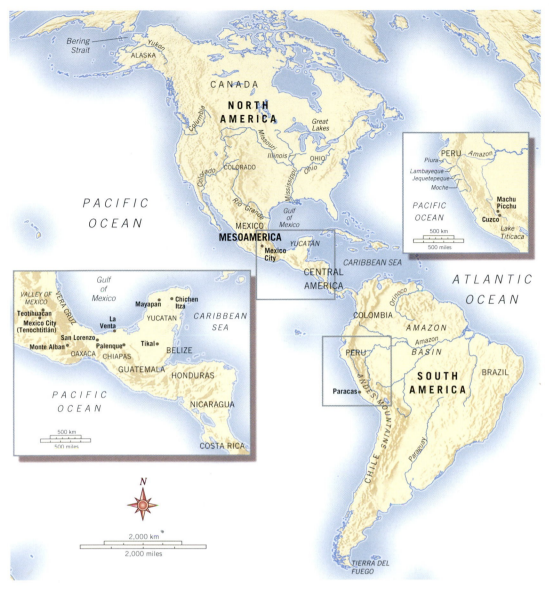

Map 11.5 The Americas. The two chief centers of cultural development in pre-Columbian times in the Americas were Mesoamerica, the semicircular land mass extending from central Mexico south and east through Guatemala and the Yucatan peninsula, and the central Andes of South America in modern-day Peru.

had preceded them. But during a period of about a thousand years, roughly 250 BCE to 900 CE, which archeologists call the Classic Era, the cultures of Mesoamerica flourished. "Pre-Columbian" refers to the era before Columbus arrived in the Americas in 1492, and the title "Classic Era," borrowed from Greco-Roman culture, designates what historians consider to be the high point of pre-Columbian culture in the Americas. Three great cultures thrived in Mesoamerica during the Classic Era: the Zapotec culture in the state of Oaxaca; the somewhat mysterious but enormously influential civilization centered at Teotihuacán, just north of Tenochtitlán (present-day Mexico City); and to the south, the Maya culture in the states of Yucatan, and Chiapas, and the countries of Belize, and Guatemala

(Map **11.5**). These cultures were at once highly developed and, from a Western point of view, seemingly backward, astronomically sophisticated, with two separate but extraordinarily accurate calendars, yet lacking both a domesticated beast of burden capable of carrying an adult. Even more astonishing, they lacked one of the most fundamental tools of civilization—the wheel. Although they used wheels on children's toys, they never enlarged them for use on wagons or carts. These civilizations never discovered how to process bronze or iron, yet they moved and cut stones weighing in excess of 100 tons and built enormous temples, the centerpieces of cities rivaling any in Europe or Asia. But what they lacked, they probably did not need, and what they developed was extraordinary.

Monte Albán and Zapotec Culture

Zapotec culture, which occupied the territory later controlled by the Mixtec, was centered at Monte Albán in Oaxaca. The Zapotecs had themselves been closely tied to the Olmecs (see Chapter 1), but instead of living in the alluvial lowlands of the Gulf coast, they built their capital atop a mountain overlooking the three major valleys of central Oaxaca. It seems likely that they were the first Mesoamerican people to use the 260-day calendar, and they possessed a writing system, although, with the exception of names, dates, and places, it remains largely undeciphered. Like the Olmec before them, they valued jade above all other precious stones or metal—more than gold and silver. Jade would remain the most treasured material through the entire history of the cultures of Mesoamerica, from the Olmecs to the Aztecs. The translucent green color of jade symbolized water, fertility, and vegetation—in short, the life force. Large stones were very rare, and specimen pieces were passed down from generation to generation. A particularly fine example is a bat god from Monte Albán, discovered in the grave of an early Zapotec king (Fig. **11.26**). Worn as the symbol of his power, its eyes, made of shell, stare fiercely out at any who would have approached him.

Teotihuacán

Teotihuacán thrived from about 50 to 750 CE. By the fourth century CE, it was a center of culture comparable to Constantinople in the Old World. In contrast to the later Mayan cities, many of which were quickly forgotten and overgrown in the jungle, Teotihuacán remained, for the Maya, the Aztecs, and other Mesoamerican civilizations, a holy site, the manifestation on Earth of Tollan, the Mesoamerican mythic place of origin. Even a thousand years after it flourished, the most important Aztec rulers made pilgrimages to it.

The city is laid out in a grid system, the basic unit of which is 614 square feet, and every detail is subjected to this scheme, conveying a sense of power and mastery. A great, broad avenue, known as the Avenue of the Dead, runs through the city (Figs. **11.27** and **11.28**). It links two great pyramids, the Pyramids of the Moon and the Sun, both surrounded by about 600 smaller pyramids, workshops and numerous plazas, and a giant market area. There are some 2,000 known apartment complexes—more are likely to be excavated—nearly all adorned with complex murals related to ritual life. Their size, location (nearer or farther from the center), and their quality of construction is indicative of the social status of the inhabitant. The Pyramid of the Sun is oriented to mark the passage of the sun from east to west and the rising of the stellar constellation, the Pleiades, on the days of the equinox. Each of its two staircases contains 182 steps, which, when the platform at its apex is added, together total 365. The pyramid is thus an image of time. This representation of the solar calendar is

Fig. 11.26 Jade pendant, Zapotec, Monte Albán, State of Oaxaca, Mexico. Late pre-Classic (200 BCE–100 CE). Jade with shell inlays, 11′ × 6 3/4″. National Museum of Anthropology, Mexico. Though found at Monte Albán, where it was discovered in a tomb, this piece may well have been passed down from the Olmecs. It represents a bat god.

echoed in another pyramid at Teotihuacán, the Temple of the Plumed (or Feathered) Serpent, which is decorated with 364 serpent fangs.

At its height, in about 500 CE, about 200,000 people lived in Teotihuacán, making it one of the largest cities in the world. Scholars believe that a female deity, associated with the moon, as well as cave and mountain rituals, played an important role in Teotihuacán culture. The placement of the Pyramid of the Moon, in front of the dead volcano Cerro Gordo (see Fig. **11.28**), supports this theory. It is as if the mountain, seen from a vantage point looking north up the Avenue of the Dead, embraces the pyramid in its flanks. And the pyramid, in turn, seems to channel the forces of nature—the abundant water on the mountain in particular—into the heart of the city.

Fig. 11.27 **Teotihuacán, Mexico, as seen from the Pyramid of the Moon, looking south down the Avenue of the Dead, the Pyramid of the Sun at the left. ca. 350–650 CE.** One of the largest cities in the world by the middle of the first millennium, Teotihuacán covered an area of nearly 9 square miles.

LEARN MORE View an architectural simulation of Teotihuacán at **www.myartslab.com**

Fig. 11.28 **The Pyramid of the Moon, looking north up the Avenue of the Dead.** Beginning at the southern end of the city, and culminating at the Pyramid of the Moon, the Avenue of the Dead is 2 $\frac{1}{2}$ miles long.

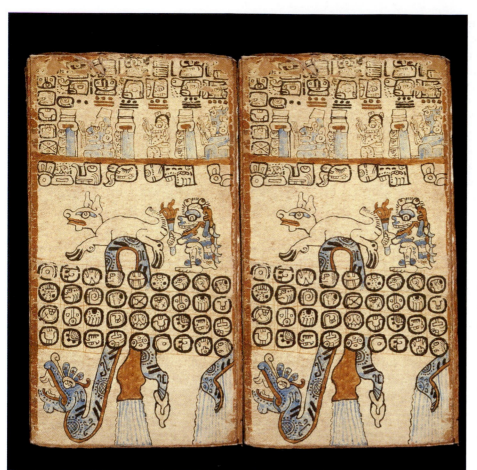

Fig. 11.29 Madrid Codex, leaves 13–16. ca. 1400. Amatl paper, 56 leaves, painted on both sides and screenfolded. Museo de América, Madrid. Diviners would have used this text to predict events such as flood, drought, or an abundant harvest.

Mayan Culture

To the south, another culture, that of the Maya, both pre-dated and post-dated that of Teotihuacán. The Maya occupied several regions: the highlands of Chiapas and Guatemala; the Southern lowlands of Guatemala, Honduras, El Salvador, Belize, and the Northern lowlands in the states of Yucatan, Campeche, and Quintano Roo. They were never unified into a single political entity, but rather consisted of many small kingdoms that engaged in warfare with one another over land and resources.

An elaborate calendar system enabled them to keep track of their history—and, evidence suggests, predict the future. It consisted of two interlocking ways of recording time, a 260-day calendar and a 365-day calendar. The 260-day calendar probably derives from the length of human gestation, from a pregnant woman's first missed menstrual period to birth. When both calendars were synchronized, it took exactly 52 years of 365 days for a given day to repeat itself—the so-called calendar round—and the end of each cycle was widely celebrated.

The Mayan calendar was put to many uses. An example is the Madrid Codex (Fig. **11.29**), one of the four surviving Mayan codices. It consists of 56 stucco-coated bark-paper leaves, painted, with the exception of one page, on both sides. Over 250 separate "almanacs" that place events of

both a sacred and secular nature within the 260-day Mesoamerican ritual calendar fill its pages. It records events concerning particularly the activities of daily life (planting, tending crops, the harvest, weaving, and hunting), rituals, astronomic events, offerings, and deities associated with them. The four horizontal rows in the lower half of each panel are composed of the glyphs of the 20 named days recycling 13 times. Sky serpents who send the rain and speak in thunder are shown weaving around the rows of glyphs. In the shorter top two leaves, standard numerology can be seen. The Mayans wrote numbers in two ways, as a system of dots and bars, seen here, and in a set of pictorial variants. Twenty was expressed with a glyph of the moon, and zero with a shell glyph, a number, incidentally, used widely in Mesoamerica many centuries before Hindu mathematicians "discovered" it in India.

The City of Palenque Among the most important Mayan cities is Palenque, one of the best-preserved of all Mayan sites. Lost in the jungle for centuries following its decline, which occurred around the year 850, Palenque was rediscovered in 1746 by a Spanish priest who had heard rumors of its existence. The Temple of Inscriptions, facing into the main courtyard of the so-called Palace, which may have been an administrative center rather than a royal residence, rises in nine steps, representing the nine levels of the Mayan Underworld (Fig. **11.30**). It is inscribed with the history of the Palenque kings, who were associated with the jaguar. The first recorded king is K'uk B'alam [k'oohk-b'ahl-um—the apostrophes indicate glottal stops], "Quetzal Jaguar," who, so the inscriptions say, founded the city on March 11, 431. Palenque's most powerful king was K'inich Janaab' Pakal I (Great Sun Shield), known as Pakal [pah-CAL] (603–83), who ruled for 67 years, and the Temple of Inscriptions was erected over his grave.

In 1952, Alberto Ruz, a Mexican archeologist, discovered the entrance to the tomb of Lord Pakal, under the pyramid. It was hidden under large stone slabs in the floor of the temple at the top of the pyramid. Ruz had to clear the passage down to Pakal's tomb, at the very base of the structure, which had been back-filled with stone debris. When he reached the tomb, he found that Pakal's face was covered with a jade death mask. A small tube connected the tomb with the upper level, thus providing the dead king with an eternal source of fresh air. It also functioned as a form of communication between the living and the ancestor. Pakal was buried in a large uterus-shaped stone sarcophagus weighing over five tons and covered with jade and cinnabar.

The *Popol Vuh* The *Popol Vuh* [po-pole voo] is a Mayan book of creation. It was written in Quiché, a surviving Mayan dialect still spoken in the Guatemalan highlands, and produced between 1554 and 1558 by a Guatemalan Indian. Despite its late date, it probably represents Mayan belief systems that date back over a thousand years. Sometime in about 1700, a Dominican priest, Francisco Ximénez [hee-may-nez] copied the manuscript, adding a Spanish translation in a column paralleling the Quiché original. The original has since disappeared. Over a hundred years later, the Ximenez copy was found in the archives of San Carlos University in Guatemala City by Brasseur de Bourbourg, who brought it to Paris and published a version of it in 1858. It was subsequently sold to the Newberry Library in Chicago, along with other documents from the Brasseur collection, where it remained uncatalogued and unknown until 1941. The *Popol Vuh* is in four parts, beginning with the deeds of Mayan gods in the darkness of a primeval sea (**Reading 11.7**):

READING 11.7

from *Popol Vuh: The Great Mythological Book of the Ancient Maya*

Before the world was created, Calm and Silence were the great kings that ruled. Nothing existed, there was nothing. Things had not yet been drawn together, the face of the earth was unseen. There was only motionless sea, and a great emptiness of sky. There were no men anywhere, or animals, no birds or fish, no crabs. Trees, stones, caves, grass, forests, none of these existed yet. There was nothing that could roar or run, nothing that could tremble or cry in the air. Flatness and emptiness, only the sea, alone and breathless. It was night; silence stood in the dark.

In this darkness the Creators waited, the Maker, Tepeu, Gucumatz, the Forefathers. They were there in this emptiness, hidden under green and blue feathers, alone and surrounded with light. They are the same as wisdom. They are the ones who can conceive and bring forth a child from nothingness. And the time had come. The Creators were bent deep around talk in the darkness. They argued, worried, sighed over what was to be. They planned the growth of the thickets, how things would crawl and jump, the birth of man. They planned the whole creation, arguing each point until their words and thoughts crystallized and became the

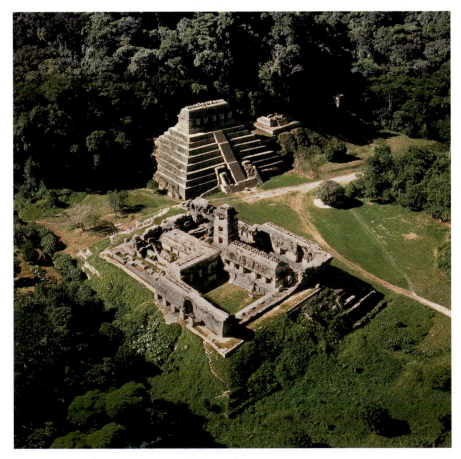

Fig. 11.30 "Palace" (foreground) and Temple of Inscriptions (tomb pyramid of Lord Pakal), Palenque, Mexico. Maya culture. 600–900 CE. These two buildings, along with two other temples not seen in this view, formed the central complex of Palenque. Another complex to the north is composed of five temples and a ball court, and a third group of temples lies to the south. Palenque was the center of a territory that may have been populated by as many as 100,000 people.

LEARN MORE Gain insight from an extended primary source from *Popol Vuh* at **www.myartslab.com**

same thing. Heart of Heaven was there, and in the darkness the creation was planned.

Then let the emptiness fill! they said. Let the water weave its way downward so the earth can show its face! Let the light break on the ridges, let the sky fill up with the yellow light of dawn! Let our glory be a man walking on a path through the trees! "Earth!" the Creators called. They called only once, and it was there, from a mist, from a cloud of dust, the mountains appeared instantly. . . .

The gods try three times to create mankind, once out of animals, a second time out of mud, and a third time out of wood. Wood proves most successful, though the wooden men are killed off as well, and their descendants become monkeys. The rest of Part 1 and all of Part 2 deal with two sets of twins—the Hero Twins, Hunhapu [hoon-AH-poo] and Xbalanque [shibah- LEN-kay]; and their half-brothers, the Monkey Twins, Hun Batz´ [hoon-bahts] and Hun Chouen [hoon-choo-en]. Both sets of twins are ballplayers. Summoned to Xibalba [shibahl-bah] (the Underworld), Hunhapu and Xbalanque undergo a series of tests, transformations, and resurrections.

The connection of the traditional Mesoamerican ballgame to forces of life and death, evidenced so substantially in the *Popul Vuh*, underscores its significance to the culture. Almost all major sites had ball courts (Fig. **11.31**). Players directed a heavy, solid rubber ball with their heads, thighs, or knees, padded to absorb the impact, through the opponent's ring high on the wall on each side of an I-shaped court. The game was closely associated with Mayan myths of origin and had deep religious significance. The ball represented the sun, and the duty of the players was to keep it from falling to earth as it passed through day and night (the games often lasted for several days). The sharply angled walls of the court itself were associated with the crack in the top of Creation Mountain described in the *Popul Vuh*

(the Mayan word for crevice, *hom* [hahm], is also the word for ball court), and play was intimately tied to the gods themselves. The losing team was believed to have betrayed both the sun and the gods. Evidence suggests that the post-Classic Maya decapitated the losing team and displayed their heads on poles surrounding the ball court, and later on wooden scaffolds or stone monuments called "skull racks."

By 900 CE, Mayan culture had collapsed as a result of a wide variety of events, including overpopulation and accompanying ecological degradation, political competition, and war. Its peoples, who survive in large numbers to this day, returned to simple farming around the ruins of their once-great cities.

The Post-Classic Era: Toltecs and Aztecs

In the north, after the decline of Teotihuacán, the Toltec culture rose to power. Centered in Tula in the modern state of Hidalgo, in terms of architecture, symbols, planning, and narrative programs, the Toltecs were a bridge between Teotihuacán and the Aztecs. When, in the twelfth century, Tula was burned and its inhabitants scattered, one of these surviving groups was the Mexica. Later known as the Aztecs, they wandered into the Valley of Mexico in about 1325 and built a village on the shores of Lake Texcoco. There they saw an eagle perching on a prickly pear cactus (*tenochtli*) [teh-nok-tlee], a sign that their wandering was over. They dug canals and drained the shallow areas of the lake, converting them into fertile fields, and there, as well, they built the city of Tenochtitlán on an island in the lake's center.

Blood sacrifice was central to Aztec culture, merging perfectly with the warrior traditions inherited from the Toltecs. The Aztecs believed that the sun, moon, and earth all depended upon human blood for their sustenance. Their chief activity, as a result, was war, and the chief goal of war was to capture sacrificial victims, as well as acquire territory and exact tribute to buttress the life of the elites, including quetzal feathers, copal resin for incense, and cotton for warrior uniforms. At puberty, boys were placed under jurisdiction of a local warrior house and trained for war, where they learned that success in life equaled the number of enemies captured alive for later ritual killing. Death itself, when realized in the pursuit of such honor, was the greatest honor an Aztec male could achieve.

Centered at Tenochtitlán, Aztec culture would survive until the arrival of the Spanish in 1519. In only a few years it was almost totally destroyed, its vast quantities of magnificent goldwork looted and returned to Europe to be melted down to support the warring ways of the European kings (see Chapter 18).

Fig. 11.31 Ball court at Copán, Honduras, Maya Culture. ca. **711-736 CE.** This is the second-largest ball court in Mesoamerica. The largest is at Chichen Itza.

THE CULTURES OF SOUTH AMERICA

As in Mesoamerica, complex cultures developed in South America during the period corresponding to the Middle Ages in Europe, particularly in the area of present-day Peru (see Map 11.5). The region is one of dramatic contrast. The snow-capped peaks and high grasslands of the Andes mountains capture rainfall from the Pacific Ocean, creating rivers that drop quickly to the sea across one of the most arid deserts in the world.

The Moche

In these river valleys, which are essentially oases in the coastal desert, Moche culture flourished for a thousand years, from about 200 BCE to 800 CE. The Moche built large mound temples made entirely of **adobe** bricks, sunbaked blocks of clay mixed with straw. The largest, located in the Moche Valley, from which the culture takes its name, is the so-called Pyramid of the Sun. It is over 1,000 feet long and 500 feet wide and rises to a height of 59 feet. In these pyramids, people buried their dead, accompanied by gold earrings, pendants, necklaces, and other ornaments, as well as elaborately decorated ceramic bowls, pots, and bottles.

The most distinctive bottles depict scenes representative of Moche culture as a whole, usually on bottles with distinctive stirrup spouts that curve elegantly away from the body of the vessel (Fig. 11.32). The list of the subjects depicted is almost endless—animals of all kinds, from seals to owls, warriors, plants, musicians, homes, children at play, women weaving, couples engaged in sex, a man washing his hair—as if the culture was intent on representing every facet of its daily life. Recent research suggests, however, that every one of these scenes has a ritual or symbolic function. This figure, for instance, may well represent the Warrior priest who presided over Moche sacrifice ceremonies, in which prisoners captured in battle were sacrificed and their blood drunk by elaborately dressed warriors.

The Inca

In about 800 CE, the Moche suddenly vanished, many believe as a result of floods brought about by a series of weather events related to El Niño. This major temperature fluctuation of the waters of the Eastern Pacific Ocean results in substantial changes in rainfall levels both regionally and worldwide. The resulting political vacuum lasted for over 400 years until, around 1300, Inca culture emerged. One of many farming cultures in the southern Peruvian highlands, the Inca took advantage of the Andean camelids—llamas, alpacas, vicuñas, and guanacos, beasts of burden unknown to the cultures of Mesoamerica—to forge trading networks that eventually united the southern highlands and northern coastal lowlands under their rule. Large irrigation projects transformed both the river valleys and the desert between them into rich agricultural regions.

Fig. 11.32 *Moche Lord with a Feline,* **from Moche Valley, Peru. Moche culture. ca. 100 BCE–500 CE.** Painted ceramic, height 7 1/2". Buckingham Fund. 1955-2281. Photograph © 2006, The Art Institute of Chicago. All Rights Reserved. Vessels of this kind, depicting almost every aspect of Moche life, were buried in large quantities with Moche rulers.

The Inca were, above all, masterful masons. Working with stone tools and without mortar, they crafted adjoining granite blocks that fit so snugly together that their walls have, for centuries, withstood earthquakes that have destroyed many later structures. Few of the blocks are the same size, and some have as many as 30 faces. Still, the joints are so tight that even the thinnest knife blade cannot be forced between the stones. Cuzco (meaning "navel of the earth"), the capital of the Inca Empire, was laid out to resemble a giant puma, and its masonry, much of which still survives, is unmatched anywhere in the world. At Machu Picchu (Fig. 11.33, on page 394), stone buildings, whose thatched and gabled roofs have long since collapsed, are set on stone terraces in a setting that was designed, recent research has shown, as a royal retreat for the Inca ruler, Pachacuti Inka Yupanqui [pah-chah-coo-tee ink-ah yoo-pahn-kee], who built the complex between 1460 and 1470 to get away from the noise and congestion of the capital.

About 1,200 people lived in Machu Picchu's approximately 170 residences, most of them women, children, and priests. The Inca also created an extraordinary network of roads, ranging from as wide as 50 feet to as narrow as 3 feet, and extending from desert to Andes peaks for some 15,000 miles. Nearly a thousand lodgings were built along the routes, and relay runners could carry news across the region in less than a week.

The Inca were especially attracted to textiles, which apparently they valued even more than gold or other minerals, at least in part because of the extremely high, and cold, elevations at which they lived. The exact meaning of the design of an Inca weaving that survives from the time of the Spanish conquest is unclear, but scholars believe it is largely

Fig. 11.33 Machu Picchu, Inca culture, Peru. ca. 1450. Machu Picchu survived destruction by the Spanish when they invaded in 1532, partly because of its remote location, high in the Andes, and partly because, compared to the Inca capital of Cuzco, it probably seemed small and comparatively insignificant. Nevertheless, by about 1537 it was abandoned as Inca civilization collapsed, victim not only of the Spanish conquistadores, but also of disease, especially smallpox.

symbolic (Fig. **11.34**). Most Inca tunics include only a few examples of the small square units, called *t'o-qapu*, that cover this one entirely. In fact, no other known tunic incorporates such a large number and wide variety. Each of these *t'oqapu* may have held special meaning or significance, referring to specific peoples, places, or things. It seems likely that this particular tunic was worn by the ruler himself, its large number of *t'oqapu* conveying the message that he controlled an enormously diverse culture.

Llamas were the source of wool for the Inca. One was sacrificed in Cuzco each morning and evening, and a white llama was kept at Cuzco as a symbol for the Inca as a whole. According to Spanish commentators, the Cuzco llama was paraded through the streets of the city during celebrations of the coming planting season each April, dressed in a red tunic and wearing gold jewelry. These processions also included life-size gold and silver images of llamas, people, and various Inca gods.

Melted for currency by the Spanish throne, none of these large objects survive. Small objects of gold and silver, which symbolized to the Inca the sun and the moon, were once scattered through the central plaza of Cuzco. The plaza—in Incan times twice as large as it is today—was excavated to a depth of between 6 and 12 inches, its sacred soil carried away to each of the four quadrants of Tahuantinsuyu [ta-WAHN-tin-SOO-yah], as the Inca called their homeland, "Land of the Four Quadrants." The plaza was then refilled with sand brought from the ocean, in which offerings of gold and silver llamas and human figures were distributed. The plaza thus symbolized a great body of water, at once the Pacific Ocean and Lake Titicaca, from which the Inca creator deity, Ticsivirachocha [TIC-see-VEER-ah-COH-cha], had emerged after the great flood to repopulate the world. It was thus, for the Inca before the arrival of the Spanish, the very center of the world.

Fig. 11.34 Tapestry–weave Inca tunic, south coast of Peru. ca. 1440–1540. Camelid fiber and cotton, $35\frac{1}{8}$" × 30". Dunbarton Oaks Research Library and Collections, Washington, D.C. Each square represents a specific group, or an individual's identity, and functions much like a heraldic device or a logo.

The Spanish and the Fate of the Inca and Aztec Capitals

One of the most elaborately decorated of all Inca sites was Cuzco's Coricancha [KORE-eh-KAHN-cha] (literally, "the corral of gold"), the Inca Temple of the Sun facing the plaza (Fig. **11.35**). Dedicated to Inti [in-tee], the sun god, the original temple was decorated with 700 sheets of gold studded with emeralds and turquoise and designed to reflect the sunlight admitted through its windows. Its courtyard was filled with golden statuary—"stalks of corn that were of gold—stalks, leaves and ears," the Spanish chronicler Pedro de Cieza de León reported in the mid-sixteenth century. "Aside from this," he continued, there were "more than twenty sheep [llamas] of gold with their lambs and the shepherds who guarded them, all of this metal."

After their conquest of Peru, the Spanish quickly adapted the foundations of the Inca temple to their own purposes, constructing a Dominican church and monastery on the original Inca foundations. The Inca traditionally gathered to worship at the curved, circular wall of the Coricancha, and thus the apse of Santo Domingo was purposefully constructed above it to emphasize Christian control of the native site. This story—of European control over former native sites and resources—would be all too common in the continuing history of the Western hemisphere, as we will discover in Chapter 18.

But where the Spanish in Peru incorporated Inca stone masonry into their own colonial architecture—the streets

Fig. 11.36 **Serpent heads in the archeological zone of the Templo Mayor, Mexico City, Mexico.** Aztec culture.

of Cuzco are lined to this day with original stone walls—in Mexico, they would obliterate the Aztec capital of Tenochtitlán altogether. Even the giant temple in the heart of the city, the Templo Mayor, was brought to ruin, the Spanish building the capital of what they called New Spain atop its rubble (see Chapter 23). Not until 1978, when workers digging for the electric company excavated a huge disk over 10 feet in diameter and weighing 8.5 tons (see Fig. 18.2), did researchers determine where the temple originally stood, just to the northeast of the Zócalo, the main square of modern Mexico City. In order to accommodate excavation, 13 buildings had to be demolished, four dating from the nineteenth century, the others from the 1930s. The pyramid was composed of four sloped stairways, one on each side, topped by a great platform upon which stood two shrines, one dedicated to Tlaloc, the god of rain and agriculture, and one to Huitzilopochtli, god of war. Each stairway was defined by railings that flanked the stairs terminating, at the base, in menacing serpent heads (Fig. **11.36**). Today the Museum of the Templo Mayor supervises continuing archeological work at the site and houses the more than 7,000 artifacts discovered there. ∎

Fig. 11.35 **Original Inca stone wall of the Coricancha with a Dominican monastery rising above it, Inca culture, Cuzco, Peru.**

THINKING BACK

How did poetry, art, and architecture of the Tang and Song dynasties reflect the values of the Chinese state?

Between the first and third centuries CE, Buddhism spread from India north into China, and with it came images of the Buddha. During the Tang dynasty, trade on the Silk Road flourished. As reflected in the plan of their capital Chang'an, the Tang were committed to social order. The Tang valued the arts—they were especially gifted ceramic artists—and education. Confucian, Buddhist, and Daoist philosophy informed government affairs. How did these philosophies inform the poetry of writers like Li Bai and Du Fu as well? When Marco Polo visited Hangzhou in 1274, it was still the capital city of the Southern Song dynasty. It enjoyed tremendous prosperity, controlled in no small part by a thriving merchant class whose sons had benefited from the invention of the printing press at schools that prepared them for government examinations. What did these students learn from studying the Chinese classics? Many poets and artists of the period practiced the neo-Confucian Chan Buddhism. How were these beliefs reflected in their work? In 1279, the Song fell to the Mongol leader Kublai Khan, who ruled China from Beijing as founder of the Yuan dynasty. The scholar-painters of the Chinese court, unwilling to serve under foreign domination, retreated into exile. How did their artworks reflect their resistance?

What religions shaped Indian and Southeast Asian civilization?

During the era known as the Middle Ages in the West, the history and art of India and Southeast Asia were dominated by the interaction of Buddhism, Islam, and Hinduism. Forced out of northern India by invading Muslims, the Buddhists retreated north into Nepal and across the Himalayas into Tibet or eastward into present-day Myanmar (formerly Burma). In Tibet, a new brand of Buddhism developed under the local religious leaders—the lamas, and the chief lama—the Dahlai. How would you describe Tibetan Buddhism? Meanwhile Hinduism continued to thrive especially in southern India and Cambodia. Distinct Hindu temple styles developed, the chief example of which is the Kandarya Mahadeva temple at Khajurabo which mirrored the Hindu cosmos. As Hinduism spread into Cambodia, enormous temple complexes were constructed, especially at Angkor Wat. What does the sculpture program at Angkor Wat suggest about the Hindu religion?

Why did the Japanese capital move to Asuka, Nara, Heiankyo, and Kamakura?

The end of the Yamato period in Japan was marked by strife between the imperial Sago clan, who were deeply attracted to Buddhism, and the Mononobe, who were in charge of the emperor's military, and the Nakatomi, in charge of Shinto ritual, both of whom opposed the introduction of Buddhism into the country. Prince Shotoku moved the capital to Asuka and introduced Confucian principles into court affairs, but his descendants were executed. Factions continued to fight even after the imperial capital was moved again to nearby Nara and then Heian-kyo (modern Kyoto). During the more stable Heian period, conflicts continued. Nevertheless, the Heian court was one of the greatest elegance and refinement. Noble women lived in extreme seclusion, but could distinguish themselves through their correspondence and verse. Instead of writing in the official Chinese writing style, these women wrote in a new, distinctly Japanese writing system, *hiragana*. Among the most important writers at the Heian court were the Lady Ise, the earliest female master; Sei Shonagon, author of *The Pillow Book*; and Murasaki Shikibu, whose *Diaries* are surpassed only by her monumental fictional narrative, *The Tale of Genji*. How would you describe the style of the scroll illustrations of *The Tale of Genji*? When, again, conflicts among various clans led to the downfall of the Heian dynasty, warriors known as samurai took over the country. The most powerful samurai, Minamoto Yoritomo, took the title of shogun and inaugurated the first shogunate, the Kamakura dynasty. He isolated his government from both the imperial court at Heian-kyo and the Buddhist monks at Nara. But both the court and Buddhism still thrived. What form of Buddhism became increasingly popular? Why?

What shapes did civilization take in Africa?

By 1100, the Yoruba civilization, centered in the west African city of Ife, was producing highly naturalistic commemorative portraits in clay and stone, probably depicting their rulers, and not long after, elegant brass sculptures as well. In Benin, a huge complex of moats and walls developed at the capital. The art of lost-wax casting was perfected there as well. What was the purpose of these sculptures? How are these same purposes reflected in praise poems? In East Africa, Ethiopia was developing monumental architecture in the form of carved rock Christian churches, while farther down the coast the Swahili culture, a hybrid of indigenous African and Arab Muslim customs and languages, fostered cosmopolitan port cities.

Who were the Moche and the Inca?

Moche culture arose in the river valleys of the coastal plains of Peru in about 200 BCE. It produced elaborate ceramic stirrup-spouted bottles that depicted every aspect of Moche life. How might we account for the disappearance of the Moche around 800 CE? Over four hundred years later, the Inca emerged, with their capital at Cuzco in the high Andes, but their influence extended to the coastal plains as well. They were extraordinary masons, and they were especially attracted to textiles. The llama, from which they derived the wool to make their textile wares, was sacred to them. They decorated their temples freely with gold. What did gold represent to them? What about silver? How did all their artworks in precious metals disappear?

PRACTICE MORE Get flashcards for images and terms and review chapter material with quizzes at **www.myartslab.com**

GLOSSARY

adobe A sun-baked block of clay mixed with straw.

anaphora A repetition of words and phrases at the beginning of successive sentences intended to create a powerful and insistent rhythm that rises to a crescendo.

bushido The somewhat mythologized code of conduct practiced by the samurai.

call-and-response A form of music in which a caller, or soloist, raises the song, and the community chorus responds to it.

daimyo The head of a *samurai* clan and landholder.

haiku A form of Japanese poetry consisting of three lines containing usually five, seven, and five syllables.

hiragana A purely Japanese writing system that developed in the early ninth century.

mudra A symbolic gesture.

negative space The space around or between the main objects in a composition.

pagoda A multistoried structure of successively smaller, repeated stories, with projecting roofs at each story.

praise poem A poem in praise of something designed to gain influence over it.

samurai The regional warrior clans of Japan.

scarification Decorative effects made on the face or body by means of intentional scarring.

shogun The general-in-chief of the samurai.

talking drums In Africa, a form of musical signaling.

waka A form of Japanese poetry consisting of 31 syllables in 5 lines on a theme drawn from nature and the changing of seasons.

READINGS

READING 11.1

Poems by Li Bai and Du Fu

Li Bai and Du Fu are generally considered the greatest poets of the Tang dynasty. The two became close friends after Li Bai was summoned to the capital at Chang'an by the Emperor Xuanzong [shoo-ehn-tsahng] in 742. They wrote many poems to one another, a good example of which is the second of the two poems below, while the first poem below underscores his sense of isolation and loneliness after he was expelled from court in 762. After the collapse of the Tang court in the mid-750s, Du Fu wandered down the Yangtze River, finding patrons and dreaming of his return to Chang'an, until his death in 770.

LI BAI, "DRINKING ALONE BY MOONLIGHT"

A pot of wine in the flower garden,
but no friends to drink with me.
So I raise my cup to the bright moon
and to my shadow, which makes us three,
but the moon won't drink
and my shadow just creeps about my heels.
Yet in your company, moon and shadow,
I have a wild time till spring dies out.
I sing and the moon shudders.
My shadow staggers when I dance.   10

We have our fun while I can stand
then drift apart when I fall asleep.
Let's share this empty journey often
and meet again in the milky river of stars.

DU FU, "DREAMING OF LI BAI"

I've swallowed sobs from the lost dead,
but this live separation is chronic grief.
From the malarial south of the river
no news comes of the exiled traveler,

but you visit my dream, old friend,
knowing I ache for you.
Are you a ghost?
No way to tell with the long road between us.
Your spirit comes through the green maple woods
slips home past darkening border fortresses.   20
You are caught in the law's net,
so how can your spirit have wings?
The sinking moon pours onto the rafters
and your face glows in my mind.

The water is deep, the waves are wide.
Don't let the dragons snatch you!

READING CRITICALLY

Both poems develop the image of moonlight. Traditionally, in China, the full moon is a symbol of good luck, harmony, and abundance. How does this symbol inform
these two poems?

READING 11.5

from Sei Shonagon, *The Pillow Book*, "Hateful Things"

We know almost nothing about Sei Shonagon except what she writes about herself in The Pillow Book. *"Hateful Things"
is one of 164 such lists in Sei Shonagon's* Pillow Book. *Others include "People Who Look Pleased with Themselves,"
"Insects," "Things without Merit," and so on. But lists are not her only subject. She continually turns her attention to
minute observations of court life, in entries such as "The Cat Who Lived in the Palace" or "The Women's Apartments
along the Gallery."*

One is in a hurry to leave, but one's visitor keeps chattering
away. If it is someone of no importance, one can get rid of him
by saying, 'You must tell me all about it next time'; but, should
it be the sort of visitor whose presence commands one's best
behaviour, the situation is hateful indeed.

One finds that a hair has got caught in the stone on which
one is rubbing one's inkstick, or again that gravel is lodged in
the inkstick, making a nasty, grating sound.

Someone has suddenly fallen ill and one summons the exorcist. Since he is not at home, one has to send messengers to   10
look for him. After one has had a long fretful wait, the exorcist
finally arrives, and with a sigh of relief one asks him to start his
incantations. But perhaps he has been exorcizing too many evil
spirits recently; for hardly has he installed himself and begun
praying when his voice becomes drowsy. Oh, how hateful!

A man who has nothing in particular to recommend him dis-
cusses all sorts of subjects at random as though he knew
everything.

An elderly person warms the palms of his hands over a
brazier and stretches out the wrinkles. No young man would   20
dream of behaving in such a fashion; old people can really be
quite shameless. I have seen some dreary old creatures actually resting their feet on the brazier and rubbing them against
the edge while they speak. These are the kind of people who in
visiting someone's house first use their fans to wipe away the
dust from the mat and, when they finally sit on it, cannot stay
still but are forever spreading out the front of their hunting
costume[1] or even tucking it up under their knees. One might
suppose that such behaviour was restricted to people of hum-
ble station; but I have observed it in quite well-bred people,   30
including a Senior Secretary of the Fifth Rank in the Ministry of
Ceremonial and a former Governor of Suruga.

I hate the sight of men in their cups who shout, poke their fin-
gers in their mouths, stroke their beards, and pass on the wine
to their neighbours with great cries of 'Have some more! Drink
up!' They tremble, shake their heads, twist their faces, and ges-
ticulate like children who are singing, 'We're off to see the Governor.' I have seen really well-bred people behave like this and I
find it most distasteful.

To envy others and to complain about one's own lot; to   40
speak badly about people; to be inquisitive about the most triv-
ial matters and to resent and abuse people for not telling one,
or, if one does manage to worm out some facts, to inform
everyone in the most detailed fashion as if one had known all
from the beginning—oh, how hateful!

One is just about to be told some interesting piece of news
when a baby starts crying.

A flight of crows circle about with loud caws.

An admirer has come on a clandestine visit, but a dog
catches sight of him and starts barking. One feels like killing the   50
beast.

One has been foolish enough to invite a man to spend the
night in an unsuitable place—and then he starts snoring.

A gentleman has visited one secretly. Though he is wearing
a tall, lacquered hat[2], he nevertheless wants no one to see him.
He is so flurried, in fact, that upon leaving he bangs into something with his hat. Most hateful! It is annoying too when he lifts
up the Iyo blind[3] that hangs at the entrance of the room, then lets
it fall with a great rattle. If it is a head-blind, things are still worse,
for being more solid it makes a terrible noise when it is dropped.
There is no excuse for such carelessness. Even a head-blind does   60
not make any noise if one lifts it up gently on entering and leaving
the room; the same applies to sliding-doors. If one's movements
are rough, even a paper door will bend and resonate when
opened; but, if one lifts the door a little while pushing it, there
need be no sound.

One has gone to bed and is about to doze off when a mos-
quito appears, announcing himself in a reedy voice. One can actually feel the wind made by his wings and, slight though it is,
one finds it hateful in the extreme.

A carriage passes with a nasty, creaking noise. Annoying to   70
think that the passengers may not even be aware of this! If I
am travelling in someone's carriage and I hear it creaking, I dis-
like not only the noise but also the owner of the carriage.

One is in the middle of a story when someone butts in and
tries to show that he is the only clever person in the room. Such
a person is hateful, and so, indeed, is anyone, child or adult,
who tries to push himself forward.

One is telling a story about old times when someone breaks in with a little detail that he happens to know, implying that one's own version is inaccurate—disgusting behaviour!

Very hateful is a mouse that scurries all over the place. 80

Some children have called at one's house. One makes a great fuss of them and gives them toys to play with. The children become accustomed to this treatment and start to come regularly, forcing their way into one's inner rooms and scattering one's furnishings and possessions. Hateful!

A certain gentleman whom one does not want to see visits one at home or in the Palace, and one pretends to be asleep. But a maid comes to tell one and shakes one awake, with a look on her face that says, 'What a sleepyhead!' Very hateful.

A newcomer pushes ahead of the other members in a 90 group; with a knowing look, this person starts laying down the law and forcing advice upon everyone—most hateful.

A man with whom one is having an affair keeps singing the praises of some woman he used to know. Even if it is a thing of the past, this can be very annoying. How much more so if he is still seeing the woman! (Yet sometimes I find that it is not as unpleasant as all that.)

A good lover will behave as elegantly at dawn as at any other time. He drags himself out of bed with a look of dismay on his face. The lady urges him on: 'Come, my friend, it's getting light. 100

You don't want anyone to find you here.' He gives a deep sigh, as if to say that the night has not been nearly long enough and that it is agony to leave. Once up, he does not instantly pull on his trousers. Instead he comes close to the lady and whispers whatever was left unsaid during the night. Even when he is dressed, he still lingers, vaguely pretending to be fastening his sash.

Presently he raises the lattice, and the two lovers stand together by the side door while he tells her how he dreads the coming day, which will keep them apart; then he slips away. The lady watches him go, and this moment of parting will 110 remain among her most charming memories.

Indeed, one's attachment to a man depends largely on the elegance of his leave-taking. When he jumps out of bed, scurries about the room, tightly fastens his trouser-sash, rolls up the sleeves of his Court cloak, over-robe, or hunting costume, stuffs his belongings into the breast of his robe and then briskly secures the outer sash—one really begins to hate him.

READING CRITICALLY

During the Heian period, the finest writers of the day were by and large aristocratic women of middle rank like Sei Shonagon. How does "Hateful Things" reflect the prominence of women in court?

---

[1]**Hunting costume:** men's informal outdoor costume, originally worn for hunting.
[2]**Eboshi (tall, lacquered hat):** black, lacquered head-dress worn by men on the top of the head and secured by a mauve silk cord that was fastened under the chin; two long black pendants hung down from the back of the hat. The *eboshi* was a most conspicuous form of headgear and hardly suited for a clandestine visit.

[3]**Iyo blind:** a rough type of reed blind manufactured in the province of Iyo on the Inland Sea.

12 The Gothic Style
Faith and Knowledge in an Age of Inquiry

THINKING AHEAD

What do we mean by Gothic style?

How did music develop in the Gothic cathedral?

How did cathedrals affect the development of learning?

What is the Radiant style?

How was the Gothic mood expressed in Italy?

On June 11, 1144, King Louis VII, his queen, Eleanor of Aquitaine, and a host of dignitaries traveled a few miles north of Paris to the royal Abbey of Saint-Denis, where they dedicated a new choir for the royal church. It would be the crowning achievement of the king's personal domain, the Île-de-France [eel duh frahns] (see Map **12.1**). Designed by Abbot Suger [soo-ZHER] of Saint-Denis, the choir would quickly inspire a new style of architecture and decoration that came to be known as **Gothic**. *Gothic* was originally a derogatory term, adopted in sixteenth-century Italy to describe the art of northern Europe, where, it was believed, classical traditions had been destroyed by Germanic invaders—that is, by the Goths. In its own time, this style was known as *opus modernum* (modern work) or *opus francigenum* (French work). These terms highlight the style's decidedly new and contemporary flavor as well as its place of origin.

By the end of the twelfth century and the beginning of the thirteenth, town after town across northern France would imitate Suger's design at Saint-Denis. At Chartres, just to the west of the Île-de-France on the Eure [ur] River (Fig. **12.1**), to the north at Rouen [roo-ON], Amiens [ah-mee-EN], and Beauvais [boh-VAY], to the east at Laon and Reims, to the south at Bourges [boorzh], and in Paris itself, Gothic cathedrals sprang up with amazing rapidity. Much of the rest of Europe would soon follow suit.

With the rise of this new Gothic style came a new standard of beauty in Western architecture and decoration. A new masonry architecture developed, eventually resulting in intricate stonework that was almost skeletal in its lightness and soaring ever higher to create lofty interior spaces. Gothic architecture matched the decorative richness of stained glass with sculptural programs that were increasingly inspired by classical models of naturalistic representation. A new, richer liturgy developed as well, and with it, polyphonic music that by the thirteenth century was accompanied by a new instrument—the organ. The Île-de-France was the center of all these developments. It was there, as well, at the University of Paris, founded in 1200, that a young Dominican monk named Thomas Aquinas initiated the most important theological debates of the age, inaugurating a style of intellectual inquiry that we associate with higher learning to this day.

◀ **Fig. 12.1 Chartres Cathedral, the Cathedral of Notre-Dame, Chartres, France. ca. 1140–1220.**
Chartres Cathedral rises majestically, crowning the town surrounding it. Such cathedrals were the cultural centers of their communities, the source of the community's pride and prestige.

HEAR MORE Listen to an audio file of your chapter at **www.myartslab.com**

SAINT-DENIS AND CHARTRES CATHEDRALS

Even as a pupil at the monastery school, Abbot Suger had dreamed of transforming the Abbey of Saint-Denis into the most beautiful church in France. The dream was partly inspired by his desire to lay claim to the larger territories surrounding the Île-de-France. Suger's design placed the royal domain at the center of French culture, defined by an architecture surpassing all others in beauty and grandeur.

After careful planning, Suger began work on the abbey in 1137, painting the walls, already almost 300 years old, with gold and precious colors. Then he added a new facade with twin towers and a triple portal. Around the back of the ambulatory he added a circular string of chapels (Figs. **12.2** and **12.3**), all lit with large stained-glass windows (Fig. **12.4**), "by virtue of which," Suger wrote, "the whole would shine with the miraculous and uninterrupted light."

This light proclaimed the new Gothic style. In preparing his plans, Suger had read what he believed to be the writings of the original Saint Denis. (We now know that he was reading the mystical tracts of a first-century Athenian follower of Saint Paul.) According to these writings, light is the physical and material manifestation of the Divine Spirit. Suger would later survey the accomplishments of his administration and explain his religious rationale for the beautification of Saint-Denis:

> Marvel not at the gold and the expense but at the craftsmanship of the work.
> Bright is the noble work; but being nobly bright, the work
> Should brighten the minds, so that they may travel, through the true lights,
> To the True Light where Christ is the true door.

The church's beauty, therefore, was designed to elevate the soul to the realm of God.

When Louis VII and Eleanor left France for the Second Crusade in 1147 (see Chapter 10), just three years after Suger's dedication of his choir, they also left the abbot without the funds necessary to finish his church. It was finally completed a century after he died in 1151. Much of its original sculptural and stained-glass decoration was destroyed in the late eighteenth century during the French Revolution. Although partially restored in the nineteenth and twentieth centuries, only five of its original stained-glass windows remain, and we must turn to other churches modeled on its design to comprehend its full effect. Chief among these is the Cathedral of Notre-Dame [noh-truh dahm] at Chartres, which, like the other Gothic cathedrals in both the Île-de-France and its surrounding territories, drew its inspiration from Paris.

The cathedral's spires can be seen for miles in every direction, lording over town and countryside as if it were the very center of its world (Fig. **12.5**, on page 404). Chartres was, in fact, located in the heart of France's grain belt, and its economy thrived as France exported grain throughout the Mediterranean basin. But more important, Chartres was the spiritual center of the cult of the Virgin, which throughout

Map 12.1 The growth of the kingdom of France. 1180–1314. As France grew during the Gothic era, the Gothic style spread with it.

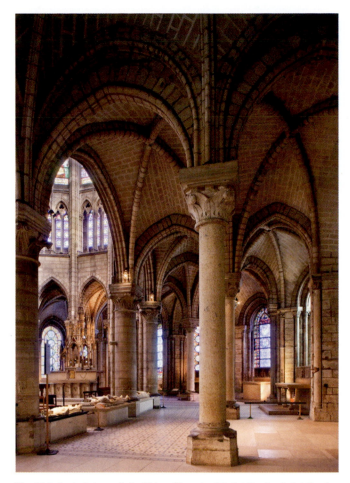

Fig. 12.2 Ambulatory choir, Abbey Church of Saint-Denis, Saint-Denis, France. 1140–44. In Abbot Suger's design, the ambulatory and radiating chapels around the apse were combined, so that the stained-glass windows—two in each chapel—fill the entire choir with light.

Fig. 12.3 Plan of the ambulatory choir, Abbey Church of Saint-Denis, Saint-Denis, France. 1140–44. By supporting the arches over the choir with columns instead of walls, Suger created a unified space reminiscent of the hypostyle space of the Mosque of Córdoba.

Fig. 12.4 Moses window, Abbey Church of Saint-Denis, Saint-Denis, France. 1140–44. This is the best-preserved of the original stained-glass windows at Saint-Denis. Scholars have speculated that Moses was a prominent theme at the royal Abbey of Saint-Denis because his leadership of the Israelites was the model for the French king's leadership of his people.

Fig. 12.5 West facade, Chartres Cathedral, Chartres, France. ca. 1134–1220; south spire ca. 1160; north spire, 1507–13. The different designs of the two towers reflect the Gothic dismissal of Romanesque absolute balance and symmetry as well as the growing refinements of the Gothic style. The later, north tower (left) was much more elaborately decorated and, in the more open framework of its stonework, more technically advanced.

the twelfth and thirteenth centuries assumed an increasingly important role in the religious life of Western Europe. The popularity of this cult contributed, perhaps more than any other factor, to the ever-increasing size of the era's churches. Christians worshipped the Virgin as the Bride of Christ, Personification of the Church, Queen of Heaven, and prime Intercessor with God for the salvation of humankind. This last role was especially important, for in it the Virgin could intervene to save sinners from eternal damnation. The cult of the Virgin manifested itself especially in the French cathedrals, which are often dedicated to *Notre Dame*, "Our Lady."

Soon after the first building phase was completed at Chartres, between about 1140 and 1150, pilgrims thronged to the cathedral to pay homage to what the Church claimed was the Virgin's tunic, worn at Jesus's birth. This relic was housed in the cathedral and was believed to possess extraordinary healing powers. But in 1194, the original structure was destroyed by fire, except for the west facade, a few stained-glass windows, including one of the most beautiful, known as *Notre-Dame de la Belle Verrière* [noh-truh dahm duh la bel vair-ee-AIR] ("Our Lady of the Beautiful Window"), and the tunic of the Virgin. The survival of the window and the tunic was taken as a sign of divine providence, and a massive reconstruction project was begun in gratitude. Royalty and local nobility contributed their financial support, and the local guilds gave both money and work.

Behind the more or less Romanesque west facade, with its round-arch windows, rose what many consider the most magnificent of all Gothic cathedrals, its stained glass unrivaled in Europe.

Stained Glass

The stained-glass program at Chartres is immensely complex. The innovative engineering that marks Gothic architecture (to be discussed later in this chapter) freed the walls of the need to bear the weight of the structure. It also freed the walls to contain glass (see *Materials & Techniques*, page 407, and *Closer Look*, pages 408–409).

The purpose of the stained-glass programs in all Gothic cathedrals was to tell the stories of the Bible in a compelling way to an audience that was largely illiterate. The art allowed them to read the scriptural stories for themselves. At Chartres, 175 glass panels, containing more than 4,000 figures, are carefully designed, in Abbot Suger's words, "to show simple folk . . . what they ought to believe." Two windows are notable for their role in the cult of the Virgin. *Notre-Dame de la Belle Verrière* (Fig. **12.6**), whose central panel survived the fire of 1194, embodies the shift in style that occurred in the twelfth century as the Gothic supplanted the Romanesque. The Virgin and Child in the middle are almost Byzantine in their stiffness, their feet pointed downward, their pose fully frontal, the drapery of their clothing almost flat (see Figure 8.28, Emperor Justinian). But the angels

CONTINUITY&CHANGE

*Emperor Justinian, **p. 272***

Fig. 12.6 *Notre-Dame de la Belle Verrière* **(Our Lady of the Beautiful Window) window, Chartres Cathedral. Central portion, twelfth century; surrounding angels, thirteenth century.** This window is renowned for its stunning combination of red and blue stained glass.

on the side, which are thirteenth-century additions, are both less stiff and more animated. The swirls and folds of their gowns flow across their limbs, revealing the anatomy beneath them.

The second window depicts the so-called Tree of Jesse (Fig. 12.7). Jesse trees are a common motif in twelfth- and thirteenth-century manuscripts, murals, sculpture, and stained glass, and their associated traditions are still celebrated by Christians during the season of Advent. They were thought to represent the genealogy of Christ, since they depict the Virgin Mary as descended from Jesse, the father of King David, thus fulfilling a prophecy in the book of Isaiah (11:1): "And there shall come forth a rod out of the stem of Jesse and a Branch shall grow out of his roots." Most Jesse trees have at their base a recumbent Jesse with a tree growing from his side or navel. On higher branches of the tree are various kings and prophets of Judah. At the top are Christ and Mary. Sometimes the Virgin holds the infant Jesus, but here, as in a similar window at Saint-Denis, Mary appears in the register below Jesus. Since Jesse trees portray Mary as descending from royal lineage, they played an important role in the cult of the Virgin.

Gothic Architecture

As the Gothic style developed, important architectural innovations contributed to the goal of elevating the soul of worshipers to the spiritual realm. Key among these innovations was rib vaulting. The principles of rib vaulting were known to Romanesque architects, but Gothic architects used these techniques with increasing sophistication (see *Materials & Techniques*, page 407). Rib vaulting allowed for the massive stonework of the Romanesque style to be replaced, inside and out, by an almost lacy play of thin columns and patterns of ribs and windows, all pointing upward in a gravity-defying crescendo that carries the viewer's gaze toward the heavens. Extremely high naves—Chartres's nave is 120 feet high, Reims's nave is 125, and the highest of all, Beauvais's, is 157, the equivalent of a 15-story building—add to this emphasis on verticality, contributing a sense of elevation that is both physical and spiritual. The nave of the Cathedral of Notre-Dame at Amiens is perhaps the supreme statement of this architectural verticality (Figs. 12.8 and 12.9). The nave is only 48 feet wide, but it soars to three times that height, 144 feet, and this narrowly proportioned space cannot help but create a sense of exaggerated height in the visitor.

The preponderance of pointed rather than rounded arches contributes to this feeling as well. The pointed arch, in fact, possesses structural properties that contribute significantly to the Gothic style—the flatter or rounder an arch is, the greater outward thrust or pressure it puts on the supporting walls. By reducing outward

Fig. 12.7 *The Tree of Jesse* window, Chartres Cathedral. ca. 1150–70. Jesse was the father of King David, who, according to the Gospels, was an ancestor of Mary. At the base of the window lies the body of Jesse, a tree growing out of him. The tree branches into the four kings of Judea, one on each row. Mary is just below Christ. Seven doves, representing the seven gifts of the Holy Spirit, encircle Christ. In half-moons flanking each section of the tree stand the 14 prophets.

Materials & Techniques

Rib Vaulting

Rib vaults are a form of groin vault (see *Materials & Techniques*, Chapter 6, page 196). They are based on the pointed arch, which can reach to a greater height than a rounded arch. At the groins, structural moldings called *ribs* channel the vault's thrust outward and downward. These ribs were constructed first and supported the scaffolding upon which masonry webbing was built. These ribs were essentially a "skeleton" filled with a lightweight masonry "skin." Throughout the late Middle Ages, more and more intricate and complex versions of this scheme were developed.

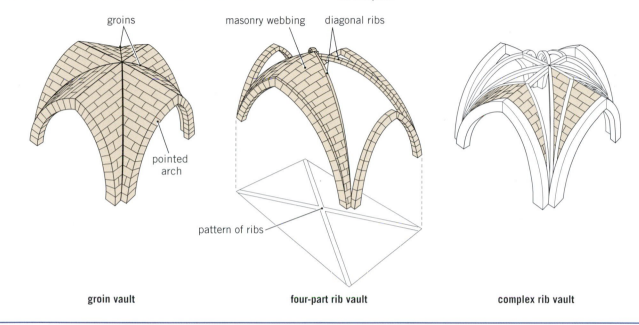

groins

masonry webbing   diagonal ribs

pointed arch

pattern of ribs

groin vault   four-part rib vault   complex rib vault

Figs. 12.8 and 12.9 Nave and vaults above the choir of Amiens Cathedral, Amiens, France. 1220–1288. Note how thin the traceries of stone between the windows at the top of the choir become, an effect that contributes further to the sense of soaring space.

LEARN MORE View an architectural simulation of rib vaulting at **www.myartslab.com**

CLOSER LOOK

The stained glass at Chartres covers more than 32,000 square feet of surface area. Although the illustration below lacks detail, we can imagine the overall effect of so many windows. The windows were donated by the royal family, by noblemen, and by merchant guilds. On an average day, the light outside the cathedral is approximately 1,000 times greater than the light inside. Thus the windows, backlit and shining in the relative darkness of the nave, seem to radiate with an ethereal and immaterial glow, suggesting a spiritual beauty beyond the here and now.

To create the windows, a variety of different colored glass was blown by artisans and rolled out into square pieces. These pieces were broken or cut into smaller fragments and assembled over a drawing marked out in chalk dust. Features of people were painted on in dark pigments, and the fragments were joined by strips of lead. The whole piece was then strengthened with an armature of iron bands, at first stretching over windows in a grid, but later shaped to follow the outlines of the design itself.

Incarnation **window, Chartres Cathedral. ca. 1150.** The program for this window reads left to right, bottom to top, beginning with the Annunciation at bottom left. Next is the Visitation, showing Mary meeting her cousin Elizabeth. In the next row up, shepherds view the Star of Bethlehem on the left; on the right are the three wise men. The life of Christ continues up the window.
Just below the arch at the top, Christ enters Jerusalem on a white donkey. The window culminates in the arch with an enthroned Mary and the Christ child in a mandorla, with angels on each side.

Tree of Jesse window, see Fig. **12.7**.

The Labyrinth
Actually not a maze, but a continuous path that winds back and forth, the so-called labyrinth on the floor of the nave was designed for the pilgrim to re-create a pilgrimage— it was commonly called the Road to Jerusalem—by moving along the path while saying prayers.

The Stained Glass at Chartres

Rose window and lancets, north transept, Chartres. ca. 1150–80. A **rose window** is a round window with mullions (framing elements) and traceries extending outward from its center in the manner of the petals of a rose. It is symbolic of the Virgin Mary in her role as the Mystic Rose—the root plant, it was believed, of the Jesse Tree. This rose window measures 42 feet in diameter. The small windows between the lancets and the rose window contain the French royal coat of arms. They remind the viewer that the windows decorating the north transept were donated by Blanche, the queen mother.

Notre-Dame de la Belle Verrière
(Our Lady of the Beautiful Window), see Figure **12.6**.

Something to Think About. . .

While literacy was increasingly common in the Middle Ages, still large numbers of people remained illiterate. How might the stained glass windows at Chartres have served the masses who were unable to read?

SEE MORE For a Closer Look at the stained glass at Chartres Cathedral, go to **www.myartslab.com**

thrust, the pointed arch allows for larger windows and lighter **buttresses**, pillars traditionally built against exterior walls to brace them and strengthen the vault. **Flying buttresses** (Figs. **12.10** and **12.11**, and visible as well on the exterior of Chartres Cathedral, Fig. 12.1) allow for even lighter buttressing and more windows. They extend away from the wall, employing an arch to focus the strength of the buttress's support at the top of the wall, the section most prone to collapse from the outward pressure of the vaulted ceiling. A flying buttress is basically a huge stone prop that pushes in against the walls with the same force with which the vaults push out. The thrust of the vaulted ceilings still come down the piers and walls, but also move down the arms of the flying buttresses, down the buttresses themselves, and into the ground. The flying buttresses help spread the weight of the vaults over more supporting stone, allowing the walls to be thinner while still supporting as much weight as earlier, thicker walls. As the magnificent flying buttresses at Notre-Dame Cathedral in Paris demonstrate, they also create a stunning visual spectacle, arching winglike from the building's side as if defying gravity.

During the thirteenth century, architects began to adorn the exteriors of their cathedrals with increasingly elaborate decoration. Stone **crockets**, leaflike forms that curve outward, their edges curling up, were added to the pinnacles, spires, and gables of the cathedrals. These were topped by **finials**, knoblike architectural forms also found on furniture. The textural richness of these forms is evident in the comparison of Chartres Cathedral (see Fig. 12.5), where they are relatively absent, and Amiens Cathedral, where they are abundant (Fig. **12.12**). The facade of Amiens is also elaborately decorated with sculpture. Most were made in a twenty-year period by a large workshop in Amiens itself, lending the entire facade a sense of unity and coherence.

The Gothic style spread rapidly across Europe. It was especially well received in England, which, after all, was dominated by French Normans, and in Germany, where a fragmented conglomeration of independent cities,

Figs. 12.10 and 12.11 Flying buttresses, Cathedral of Notre-Dame, Paris, France. 1211–90. Romanesque architects used buttressing, but concealed it under the aisle roofs. Moving the buttresses to the outside of the structure created a sense of light bridgework that contributed to the aesthetic appeal of the building as much as to its structural integrity.

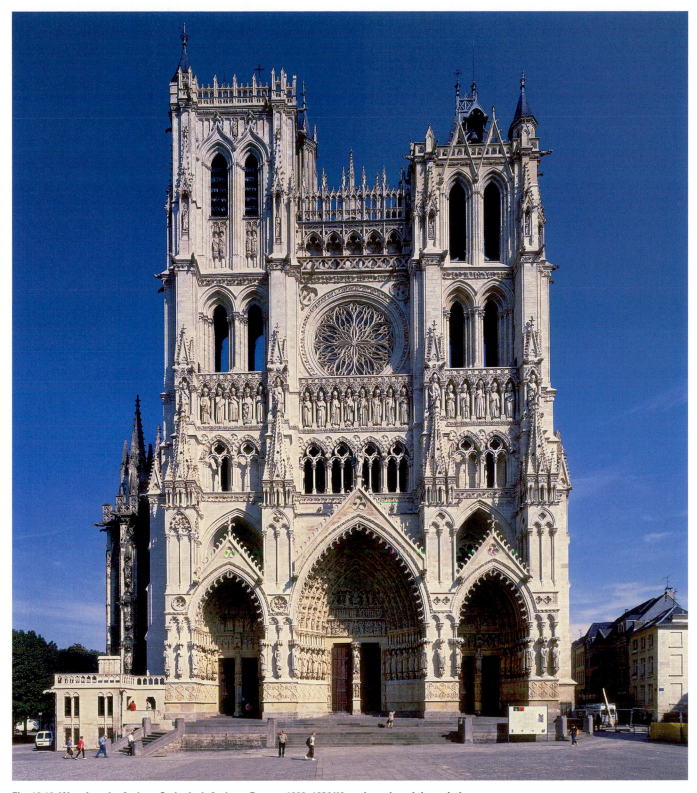

Fig. 12.12 West facade, Amiens Cathedral, Amiens, France. 1220–1236/40, and continued through the fifteenth century. The sculptors who decorated the facade quickly became famous and traveled across Europe, carrying their style to Spain and Italy.

principalities, and bishoprics all sought to imitate what they conceived as the style of the French court. Wells Cathedral is one of the finest Gothic cathedrals built in England in the thirteenth century (Fig. **12.13**, on page 412).

Gothic Sculpture

If we look at developments in architectural sculpture from the time of the decoration of the west portal of Chartres Cathedral (1145–70) to the time of the sculptural plan of

Fig. 12.13 West facade, Wells Cathedral, Wells, England. 1230–50. This cathedral exemplifies the preference for pattern and decoration in English Gothic architecture. The portal has become less important, and the rhythmic structure of the wide facade takes precedence. Life-size sculptures occupy each of the niches—originally 384 of them—representing the Last Judgment.

Fig. 12.14 Jamb statues, west portal, Chartres Cathedral. 1145–70. The decorative patterns at the bottom of these jamb columns are, interestingly, reminiscent of Islamic designs in Spain.

the south transept portal (1215–20), and, finally, to the sculptures decorating the west front of Reims Cathedral (1225–55), we can see that, in a little over 100 years, Gothic sculptors had begun to reintroduce classical principles of sculptural composition into Western art.

Although they seem almost Byzantine in their long, narrow verticality, feet pointing downward, the jamb sculptures on the west portal of Chartres mark a distinct advance in the sculptural realization of the human body (Fig. 12.14). These, and five more sets, flank the three doorways of the cathedral's Royal Portal. The center tympanum of the Portal depicts Christ Enthroned in Royal Majesty, the north tympanum the Ascension of Christ, and the south the Virgin and Child Enthroned. The jamb sculptures represent figures from the Hebrew Bible considered to be precursors of Christ. These works have little in common with Romanesque relief sculpture, typified by the *Last Judgment* tympanum on the Cathedral of Sainte-Foy in Conques (see Fig. 10.24). While the Chartres figures remain contained by the form of the colonnade behind them, they are fully rounded and occupy a space in front of the column itself.

When Chartres was rebuilt after the fire of 1195, a new sculptural plan was realized for the transept doors. The figures stand before a colonnade, as do the jamb figures on the west portal, but their form is hardly determined by it (Fig. 12.15). Now they stand flat-footed. Their faces seem animated, as if they see us. The monk just to the right of the dividing column seems quite concerned for us. The portrait of the knight Saint Theodore, to the

CONTINUITY & CHANGE

Doryphoros, p. 125

left of the column, is particularly remarkable. For the first time since antiquity, the figure is posed at ease, his hip thrusting slightly to the right, his weight falling on his right foot. He stands, in other words, in a *contrapposto* position. (Recall the Greek sculptures of the fifth century BCE, carved in that posture, such as the *Doryphoros* [*The Spear Bearer*], Figure 5.4.) The weight of his sword belt seems to have pulled his cloak off to the right. Then, below the belt, the cloak falls back to the left. The strict verticality of the west portal is a thing of the past.

The sculptures at Reims break even further from Romanesque tradition. They are freed of their backdrop (Fig. 12.16; see also Fig. 10.32). The Angel of the Annunciation tells Mary (the figure next to the angel on the left) that she is with child. The next two figures, to the right, represent the Visitation, when Mary tells her cousin Elizabeth that she is with child and Elizabeth in turn announces the divinity of the baby in Mary's womb. Note how the drapery adorning the pair on the left, with its simple, soft folds, differs profoundly from the drapery of the pair on the right, whose robes are Roman in their complexity. The earlier Mary bears little, if any, resemblance to the other Mary, the first probably carved by a sculptor trained in Romanesque traditions, the latter by one acquainted with Classical models.

The two pairs are as different, in fact, as the two towers of Chartres Cathedral (see Fig. 12.5), which reflect both a weakening of the Romanesque insistence on balance and

Fig. 12.15 Jamb statues, south transept portal, Chartres Cathedral. ca. 1215–20. The statue of Saint Theodore, on the left, is meant to evoke the spirit of the Crusades.

Fig. 12.16 *Annunciation* and *Visitation*, **central portal, west facade, Reims Cathedral, Reims, France. Angel of the Annunciation, ca. 1245–55; Virgin of the Annunciation, 1245; Visitation group, ca. 1230–33.** If these sculptures seem more naturalistic than any for nearly a thousand years, it is partly because they engage one another. It is as if, looking at them, we can overhear their conversation. Note that the most naturalistic sculpture, the Angel of the Annunciation, dates from 15 or 20 years after the Visitation group, suggesting an extraordinary advance, and preference for, naturalism in a very short span of years.

symmetry as well as the fact that both were done at different times. And yet the two pairs of sculptures share a certain emotional attitude—the good-humored smile of the angel, the stern but wise concern of Elizabeth. Even the relative ages of the persons depicted are apparent, where age would have been of no concern to a sculptor working in the Romanesque tradition. These are, in short, the most fully human, most natural sculptures since Roman times. During the Gothic period, artists developed a new visual language. The traditional narratives of biblical tradition could no longer speak through abstracted and symbolic types, but instead required believable, individual bodies to tell their stories. This new language invests the figures of Jesus, Mary, the saints, and even the Angel of the Annunciation with personality.

Music in the Gothic Cathedral: Growing Complexity

With its vast spaces and stone walls, the Gothic cathedral could be as animated by its acoustics as by its light, or, as at Reims, the liveliness of its sculpture. Ecclesiastical leaders were quick to take advantage of this quality in constructing their liturgy. At the School of Notre-Dame, in Paris, the first collection of music in two parts, the *Magnus Liber Organi* [MAG-nus LEE-bur or-GAN-ee] (*The Great Book of Polyphony*), was widely distributed in manuscript by about 1160. Among its

many anonymous composers was Léonin [lay-OH-nen] (see track **10.4**). The *Magnus Liber Organi* was arranged in song cycles to provide music for all the feast days of the Church calendar. The *Magnus Liber* was created at a time when most polyphony was produced and transmitted only orally. What makes it so significant is that it represents the beginning of the modern sense of "composition"—that is, works attributable to a single composer.

HEAR MORE at www.myartslab.com

At the end of the century, Léonin's successor, Pérotin [pay-roh-TEN], revised and renotated the *Magnus Liber*. One of his most famous works is *Viderunt Omnes* ("All Have Seen"), a four-part polyphonic composition based on the traditional plainchant of the same name, meant to be sung in the middle of the Christmas Mass at Notre-Dame Cathedral in Paris (track **12.1**). Throughout the piece, the choir sings a smooth, monophonic plainchant, while three soloists sing the second, third, and fourth melodic lines in **counterpoint**, that is, in opposition, to the plainchant. The clear but intertwined rhythms of the soloists build to a crescendo of sustained harmony and balance that must have inspired awe in the congregation. The music seems to soar upward, imitating the architecture of the cathedral and elevating the faithful to new heights of belief.

HEAR MORE at www.myartslab.com

The words are simple, but because each syllable is sung across a range of notes and rhythms, the music takes almost 12 minutes to perform. What follows is the Latin and translation:

Viderunt omnes fines terrae salutare Dei nostri. Jubilate Deo omnis terra.	All the ends of the earth have seen the salvation of our God. Praise God all the earth.
Notum fecit Dominus salutare suam. Ante conspectum gentium revelavit justitiam suam.	The Lord has made known his salvation. Before the face of the people he has revealed his justice.

The complexity of such rhythmic invention mirrors the growing textural complexity of the facade of Gothic cathedrals, with their spires, gables, crockets, and finials. The tenor—from the Latin *tenere*, "to hold"—generally maintained a traditional line based on ecclesiastical chant. The tenor line might be sung or played instrumentally, perhaps by the organ, which began to replace the choir in the performance of many of these songs. In some ways, this was a practical gesture, since large choirs of the caliber needed to perform the liturgical songs were not easy to organize. The origins of the organ date back to as early as the fourth to third centuries BCE in Greece, with the invention of the hydraulis, which used water pressure to push air through the pipes. By the ninth century CE, the instrument had been modified to use air pressure, supplied by manually operated bellows, to push the air through the pipes. At any rate, the rich tones of the organ, resonating through the nave of the cathedral, gained increasing favor through the Middle Ages, and the organ became necessary to every large cathedral. In the motet, above the tenor line, two or three voices sang interweaving melodies.

Developing from this polyphony was an even more complex musical form, the **motet** [moh-TET], consisting of three (sometimes four) voices. By the late thirteenth century, a motet might be sung in either Latin or vernacular French, and either or both parts might be hymns or troubadour love songs. All these competing lines were held together like the complex elements of the Gothic facade—balanced but competing, harmonious but at odds. They reflected, in short, the great debates—between church and state, faith and reason—that defined the age.

These debates raged at centers of higher learning, where music was part of the regular liberal-arts curriculum. It was studied as a branch of the **quadrivium** [kwah-DRIV-ee-um] (the mathematical arts), alongside arithmetic, geometry, and astronomy, all fields dependent upon proportion and universal harmony. (The other liberal arts constituted the **trivium** [TRIV-ee-um], the language arts, which included grammar, rhetoric, and dialectic.) At the cathedral School of Notre-Dame in Paris, whose purpose was to train clergy, music was emphasized as an all-important liturgical tool. But by the middle of the twelfth century, cathedral schools began allowing nonclerical students to attend lectures. In 1179, a papal degree ordered the schools to provide for the teaching of the *laity* [LAY-ih-tee] (nonclerics), the decree that would eventually give rise to the university as an institution.

THE RISE OF THE UNIVERSITY

The first university was founded in Bologna [buh-LOHN-yuh], Italy, in 1148. Two hundred years earlier, in Spain, Islamic institutions of higher learning were generally attached to mosques, since learning was considered sacred. At first, the term *university* meant simply a *union* of students and the instructors with whom they contracted to teach them. *Universitas* was an umbrella term for *collegia*, the groups of students who shared a common interest or, as at Bologna, hailed from the same geographic area. The University of Bologna quickly established itself as a center for the study of law (Fig. **12.17**), an advanced area of study for which students prepared by mastering the seven liberal arts.

Proficiency in Latin was mandatory, and students studied Latin in all courses of their first four years of study. They read the writings of the ancient Greeks—Aristotle, Ptolemy, Euclid—in Latin translation. Augustine of Hippo's *On Christian Doctrine* was required reading, as were Boethius's writings on music and arithmetic. To obtain their bachelor of arts (BA) degree, students took oral exams after three to five years of study. Further study to acquire mastery of a special field led to the master of arts (MA) degree and might qualify a student to teach theology or practice medicine or law. Four more years of study were required to acquire the title of *doctor* (from the Latin, *doctus* [DOK-tus], learned), culminating in a defense of a thesis before a board of learned examiners.

The University of Paris was chartered in 1200, and soon after came Oxford and Cambridge universities in England. These northern universities emphasized the study of theology. In Paris, a house or college system was organized, at first to provide students with housing and then to help them focus their education. The most famous of these was organized by Robert de Sorbon in 1257 for theology students. The Sorbonne, named after him, remains today the center of Parisian student life.

Heloise and Abelard The quality of its teaching most distinguished the University of Paris. Because books were available only in handwritten manuscripts, they were extremely expensive, so students relied on lectures and copious note-taking for their instruction. Peter Abelard [AB-uh-lahr] (1079–ca. 1144), a brilliant logician and author of the treatise *Sic et Non* ("Yes and No"), was one of the most popular lecturers of his day. Crowds of students routinely gathered to hear him. He taught by the **dialectical method**—that is, by presenting different points of view and seeking to reconcile them. This method of teaching originates in the Socratic method, but whereas Socratic dialogue consisted of a wise teacher who was questioned by students, or even fools, Abelard's dialectical method presumed no such hierarchical relationships. Everything, to him, was open to question. "By doubting," he famously argued, "we come to inquire, and by inquiring we arrive at truth."

Needless to say, the Church found it difficult to deal with Abelard, who demonstrated time and again that various Church Fathers—and the Bible itself—held hopelessly opposing views on many issues. Furthermore, the dialectical method itself challenged the unquestioning faith in God and the authority of the Church. Abelard was particularly opposed by Bernard of Clairvaux, who in 1140 successfully prosecuted him for heresy. By then, Abelard's reputation as a teacher had not faded, but his moral position had long been suspect. In 1119, he had pursued a love affair with his private student, Heloise [HEL-oh-eez]. Abelard not only felt that he had betrayed a trust by falling in love with her and subsequently impregnating her, but he was further humiliated by Heloise's angry uncle, in whose home he had tutored and seduced the girl. Learning of the pregnancy, the uncle hired thugs to castrate Abelard in his bed. Abelard retreated to the monastery at Saint-Denis, accepting the protection of the powerful Abbot Suger. Heloise joined a convent and later served as abbess of Paraclete [PAR-uh-kleet], a chapel and oratory founded by Abelard.

The Romance of the Rose The relationship of Heloise and Abelard would be celebrated in what is undoubtedly the most extensively illuminated and popular vernacular poem of the age, the *Roman de la Rose* (Romance of the Rose), begun by Guillaume de Lorris [ghee-OHM duh lor-EES] (d. ca. 1235) but largely written by Jean de Meung [zhun duh mun] (ca. 1240–ca. 1305). The book is the dream-vision of a 25-year-old narrator who finds himself, accompanied by Dame Oyouse, or Lady Idleness, before a walled garden full of roses and pleasure seekers (Fig. **12.18**). As he selects a rose for himself, the God of Love shoots him with several arrows, leaving him forever enamored of one particular flower. His efforts to obtain the Rose meet with little success. A stolen kiss alerts the guardians of the Rose, who then enclose it behind great fortifications. At the point where Guillaume de Lorris's poem breaks off, the narrator is

left lamenting his fate. Jean de Meung concludes the narrative with a bawdy account of the plucking of the Rose, achieved through deception, which is very unlike Guillaume's idealized conception of the love quest. The book

Fig. 12.18 **The Master of the Prayer Books.** *The Lover Being Shown the Entrance to the Garden by Lady Idleness, Roman de la Rose.* ca. 1500. British Library, Harley MS 4425, f. 14v. © British Library Board. All Rights Reserved/The Bridgeman Art Library. British Library, London. Inside the garden, a lady, the personification of pleasure, and her companions listen to a lute player beside the fountain of Narcissus.

also included the first translations of the letters of Héloïse and Abelard, originally written in about 1135–36 and rendered by Meung from Latin into the vernacular. They include Héloïse's arguments to Abelard against their marriage, and her declaration of loyalty to him after she became a nun (see **Reading 12.1**, page 427).

Meung's versions of the letters are highly poeticized and bowdlerized, that is, sexual references were deleted (*bowdlerized* originates from the 1807 expurgated edition of William Shakespeare's works, *The Family Shakespeare*, edited by Thomas Bowdler to make the plays suitable for women and children). Héloïse was a woman of considerable passion. Even during the celebration of Mass, she confesses, "lewd visions" of the pleasures she shared with Abelard "take such a hold upon my unhappy soul that my thoughts are on their wantonness instead of on prayers. I should be groaning over the sins I have committed, but I can only sigh for what I have lost." Though Meung praises Héloïse for her intelligence, he especially admires her unwillingness to marry, her dedication to Abelard, and her self-sacrifice. Later medieval commentators would regard the *Roman de la Rose* as a thoroughly misogynist poem (see Chapter 13).

The Education of Women Heloise's story reveals much about the education of women in the Middle Ages. Intellectually brilliant, she became Abelard's private student because women were not allowed to study at the university. There were some exceptions, particularly in Italy. At Bologna, Novella d'Andrea (1312–66) lectured on philosophy and law. At Salerno, in southern Italy, the chair of medicine was held by Trotula (d. 1097), one of the most famous physicians of her time, although some scholars debate whether she was actually a woman, and convincing evidence suggests that her works are actually compendiums of works by three different authors. Concerned chiefly with alleviating the suffering of women, the major work attributed to her is *On the Diseases of Women*, commonly known throughout the Middle Ages as the *Trotula*. As the author says at the beginning of the treatise:

> Because women are by nature weaker than men and because they are most frequently afflicted in childbirth, diseases very often abound in them. . . . Women, from the condition of their fragility, out of shame and embarrassment do not dare reveal their anguish over their diseases (which happen in such a private place) to a physician. Therefore, their misfortune, which ought to be pitied, and especially the influence of a certain woman stirring my heart, have impelled me to give a clear explanation regarding their diseases in caring for their health.

In 63 chapters, the book addresses issues surrounding menstruation, conception, pregnancy, and childbirth, along with general ailments and diseases. The book champions good diet, warns of the dangers of emotional stress, and prescribes the use of opiates during childbirth, a practice otherwise condemned for centuries to come. It even explains how an experienced woman might pretend to be a virgin. The standard reference work in gynecology and obstetrics for midwives and physicians throughout the Middle Ages, the *Trotula* was translated from Latin into almost all vernacular languages and was widely disseminated.

Thomas Aquinas and Scholasticism

In 1245, Thomas Aquinas [uh-KWY-nus] (1225–74), a 20-year-old Dominican monk from Italy, arrived at the University of Paris to study theology, walking into a theological debate that had been raging for nearly 100 years, ever since the conflict between Abelard and Bernard: How does the believer come to know God? With the heart? With the mind? Or with both? Do we come to know the truth intuitively or rationally? Aquinas took on these questions directly and soon became the most distinguished student and lecturer at the university.

Aquinas was accompanied to Paris by another Dominican, his teacher Albertus Magnus (ca. 1200–1280), a German who taught at both Paris and Cologne and who later produced a biological classification of plants based on Aristotle. The Dominicans had been founded in 1216 by the Spanish priest Dominic (ca. 1170–1221) as an order dedicated to the study of theology. Aquinas and Magnus, and others like them, increasingly trained by Dominicans, were soon labeled *scholastics*. Their brand of theological inquiry, which was based on Abelard's dialectical method, was called **Scholasticism**.

Most theologians understood that there was a seeming conflict between faith and reason, but, they argued, since both proceeded from God, this conflict must, by definition, be a misapprehension. In the universities, rational inquiry and Aristotle's objective descriptions of physical reality were all the rage (see Chapter 5), so much so that theologians worried that students were more enthralled with logical argumentation than right outcomes. Instead of studying heavenly truths and Scriptures, they were studying pagan philosophy, dating from the fourth century BCE. Scholasticism sought to reconcile the two. One of the greatest efforts in this direction is Aquinas's *Summa Theologica*, begun in 1265 when he was 40 years old. At Albertus Magnus's request, Aquinas set out to write a theology based entirely on the work of ancient philosophers, demonstrating the compatibility of classical philosophy and Christian religion. The *Summa Theologica* takes on virtually every theological issue of the age, from the place of women in society and the Church, to the cause of evil, the question of free choice, and whether it is lawful to sell a thing for more than it is worth. The medieval *summa* was an authoritative summary of all that was known on a traditional subject, and it was the ultimate aim of every highly educated man to produce one.

In a famous passage Aquinas takes on the largest issue of all—the summa of *summas*—attempting to prove the existence of God once and for all. Notice particularly the Aristotelian reliance on observation and logically drawn conclusions (**Reading 12.2**):

Is there a God?

REPLY: There are five ways in which one can prove there is a God.

The FIRST . . . is based on change. Some things . . . are certainly in the process of change: this we plainly see. Now anything in the process of change is being changed by something else. . . . Hence one is bound to arrive at some first cause of change not itself being changed by anything, and this is what everybody understands by God.

The SECOND is based on the nature of causation. In the observable world causes are found to be ordered in series. . . . Such a series must however stop somewhere. . . . One is therefore forced to suppose some first cause, to which everyone gives the name "God."

The THIRD way is based on what need not be and on what must be. . . . Some . . . things can be, but need not be for we find them springing up and dying away. . . . Now everything cannot be like this [for then we must conclude that] once upon a time there was nothing. But if that were true there would be nothing even now, because something that does not exist can only be brought into being by something already existing. . . . One is forced therefore to suppose something which must be . . . [and] is itself the cause that other things must be.

The FOURTH way is based on the gradation observed in things. Some things are found to be more good, more true, more noble. . . and other things less [so]. But such comparative terms describe varying degrees of approximation to a superlative . . . [something that is] the truest and best and most noble of things. . . . There is something, therefore, which causes in all other things their being, their goodness, and whatever other perfection they have. And this we call "God."

The FIFTH way is based on the guidedness of nature. An orderedness of actions to an end is observed in all bodies obeying natural laws . . .; they truly tend to a goal and do not merely hit it by accident. . . . Everything in nature, therefore, is directed to its goal by someone with intelligence, and this we call "God."

Such a rational demonstration of the existence of God is, for Aquinas, what he called a "preamble of faith." What he calls the "articles of faith" necessarily follow upon and build on such rational demonstrations. So, although Christians cannot rationally know the essence of God, they can, through faith, know its divinity. Faith, in sum, begins with what Christians can know through what God has revealed to them in the Bible and through Christian tradition. Aquinas maintains, however, that some objects of faith, including the Incarnation, lie entirely beyond our capacity to understand them rationally in this life. Still, since we arrive at truth by means of both faith and reason—and, crucially, since all truths are equally valid—there should be no conflict between those arrived at through either faith or reason.

Although conservative Christians never quite accepted Aquinas's writings, arguing, for instance, that reason can

never know God directly, his influence on Christian theology was profound and lasting. In the scope of its argument, the intellectual heights to which it soars, the *Summa Theologica* is at one with the Gothic cathedral. Like the cathedral, it is an architecture, built of logic rather than of stone, dedicated to the Christian God.

THE RADIANT STYLE AND THE COURT OF LOUIS IX

By the middle of the thirteenth century, the Gothic style in France had been elaborated into increasingly flamboyant patterns of repeated traceries and ornament that we have come to refer to as the *Rayonnant* [RAY-oh-nahnt] or **Radiant style**. Similarly elaborate styles developed in both England and Germany. Although only three feet high, the Three Towers Reliquary (Fig. **12.19**), from Aachen Cathedral in Germany, gives a fair impression of this new, more complex style. It might as well be a model for a small church. Its pinnacles and spires soar upward. Rather than presenting us with a veil of stone—compare the facade of

Fig. 12.19 Three Towers Reliquary. 1370–90. Chased and gilded silver, enamel, and gems, height 36 3/4". Cathedral Treasury, Aachen, Germany. This reliquary, probably of Flemish origin, has transparent containers just below the top of each spire, allowing light to pass over the sacred body parts contained within.

Amiens Cathedral (see Fig. 12.12), which, although highly decorated, is a solid mass—the reliquary seems more like a web of gossamer. It is as if the walls themselves should dissolve into air and light, as if the building—or reliquary—should float away in a halo of golden rays.

This style was associated closely with the court of Louis IX (r. 1226–70), in Paris. The Church especially valued Louis's dedication to its well-being. One of his most important contributions to the Church, and to the history of Gothic architecture, is the royal chapel of Sainte-Chapelle [sant-shah-PELL] (Fig. 12.20), constructed in the center of the royal palace on the Île de la Cité not far from Notre-Dame de Paris. Louis had the chapel designed so that the royal family could enter directly from the palace, at the level of the stained glass, thus symbolizing his own eminence, while others—court officials and the like—entered through a smaller, ground-level chapel below. He created for himself, in other words, a **palatine chapel**—a palace chapel—on the model of Charlemagne's at Aachen, thus connecting himself to his great predecessor.

The chapel was nothing short of a reliquary built large. While on Crusade, Louis purchased what was believed to be the crown of thorns that Christ wore at the Crucifixion, as well as other precious objects, from the emperor of Constantinople. These precious pieces were destined to be housed in Sainte-Chapelle. No other structure in the Gothic era so completely epitomized the Radiant style even as it embodied the original vision of the Abbot Suger:

> Thus, when—out of my delight in the beauty of the house of God—the loveliness of the many-colored gems [of stained glass] has called me away from external cares, and worthy meditation has induced me to reflect, transferring that which is material to that which is immaterial, on the diversity of the sacred virtues: then it seems to me that I see myself dwelling, as it were, in some strange region of the universe which neither exists entirely in the slime of the earth nor entirely in the purity of heaven; and that, by the grace of God, I can be transported from this interior to that higher world in an analogical manner.

Fig. 12.20 **Interior, upper chapel, Sainte-Chapelle, Paris. 1243–48.** Although the chapel was originally surrounded by the royal castle—today it is surrounded by the Ministry of Justice—it remains more or less intact, save for a nineteenth-century repainting. Its acoustics were originally among the best in Paris and remain so today.

Bathing the viewer in the light of its stained glass—light so bright, in fact, that the viewer can hardly distinguish the details of its biblical narrative—Sainte-Chapelle is designed to relieve the faithful of any external cares and transport them into a realm of heavenly beauty. It is spiritual space, the immateriality of its light comparable, in Suger's perspective, to the immateriality of the immortal soul. The ratio of glass to stone is higher than in any other Gothic structure, the windows separated by the slenderest of columns. The lower parts of the walls, beneath the windows, are richly decorated in red, blue, and gilt, so that stone and glass seem one and the same. Golden stars shine down from the deep blue of the delicately vaulted ceiling. Louis' greatest wish was to make Paris a New Jerusalem, a city as close to paradise as could be found on earth. For many visitors, he came as close as may be humanly possible in Sainte-Chapelle.

Louis was a born reformer, as much a man of the people as any medieval king could be. Under his rule the Scholastics and Aquinas argued theology openly in the streets of Paris, just across the river from the royal palace. Louis believed in a certain freedom of thought, but even more in the rule of law. He dispatched royal commissioners into all of the provinces to check up on the Crown's representatives and ensure that they were treating the people fairly. He abolished serfdom and made private wars—which many believe to have been the ultimate motivation for the First Crusade—illegal. He reformed the tax structure and gave his subjects the right to appeal decisions in court. He was, in short, something of a saint. Indeed, the Church later beatified him as Saint Louis.

The Gothic Style in the French Ducal Courts

In the fourteenth century, the authority of the French king, though never challenged, was rivaled by the power of the ducal courts outside of the Paris region. Among these dukes were the king's relatives, the dukes of Anjou, Berry, and Burgundy, who fashioned magnificent courts in their own capitals and employed vast numbers of artists charged with decorating them in a Gothic style directly indebted to the Radiant style of the century before.

The Burgundian dukes ruled from Dijon in eastern France, but they controlled as well the region of Flanders, encompassing present-day Holland, Belgium, and Luxemburg. When, in the early fifteenth century, they moved from Dijon to Flanders, their favorite destination was Bruges, which of all the Flemish towns, had been the first to build a town hall (Fig. **12.21**). Its lavish Gothic ornamentation—the tracery patterns in the upper windows to the ornamentation of the

roofs and towers—was designed to recall the palaces of the French and Burgundian nobility. Interestingly, Bruges's adaptation of this style for their civic government—a government at least theoretically independent of ducal authority—underscores not only its citizens' sense of self-worth, but also their growing independence from the very nobles they imitated.

Through the late Middle Ages, the population of Bruges ranged between 40,000 and 50,000, quite large by northern European standards. (Most cities averaged just 2,000 to 3,000 inhabitants, and across northern Europe, 70 percent of the population still lived in the countryside.) Wages in Bruges were the highest in northern Europe, especially for craftspeople, and the city took pride in providing one of the most extensive social-care networks anywhere—including 11 hospitals and hospices. The port in Bruges was the one of the leading trade depots in northern Europe, where fish from the Baltic, timber, grain, and furs from Poland and Russia, and silver from the mines of central Europe were exchanged for highly prized Flemish textiles and garments, and for commodities including spices, sugar, silk, and cotton. These arrived via the Venetian fleet, which, by the early fifteenth century, was dispatching 45 merchant galleys annually to Bruges and other nearby northern ports, each carrying over 250 tons of cargo.

The Miniature Tradition

It is perhaps no accident that a culture so concerned with material goods and material well-being should develop, in its art, a taste for detailed renderings of material reality. The northern European attention to detail in art derives, first of all, from the Gothic predilection for intricate traceries, the winding interplay of ornamental buds and leaves so often apparent in Gothic stone- and woodwork. As we have also seen, in the sculptural decoration of churches such as that at Reims (see Fig. 12.16), by the middle of the thirteenth century, there was a developing taste for naturalism in art. It is in the work of the medieval miniature painters of the fifteenth-century French and Burgundian courts that these two directions first merge.

A **miniature** is a very small painting associated with **illumination**, the painstakingly detailed, hand-painted decoration of manuscripts, usually in tempera on vellum. The most famous miniature painters were the Limbourg [LAM-boor] brothers (flourished 1380–1416), Paul, Jan, and Hermann, sons of a sculptor from the Netherlands. The brothers migrated to Paris in the late fourteenth century. There, they were sponsored by their uncle, the court painter to Philip the Bold, the Duke of Burgundy (r. 1363–1404). After Philip the Bold died, the Limbourgs

Fig. 12.21 Anonymous Flemish architects, Town Hall (at right) and Greffe (at left), Bruges, Belgium. Town Hall 1376–1402; Greffe, 1534–37. The Greffe is the office of civil clerks. The present-day sculptural decoration of the Town Hall dates from 1853. The original was destroyed during the French Revolution.

began working for his brother Jean [zhahn], Duke of Berry (r. 1360–1416). Jean was the wealthiest man in Europe at the dawn of the fifteenth century—not surprising, as his subjects paid the heaviest taxes in all of Europe. With those taxes, the duke funded ambitious projects designed to celebrate his status and interests. One of his most important commissions to the Limbourg brothers was the *Très Riches Heures du Duc de Berry* [tray reesh-zuhr dew dewk deh BEH-ree] (*The Very Sumptuous Hours of the Duke of Berry*), an illuminated **Book of Hours** begun in 1411. The brothers died five years later, most likely of the plague, and the work remained unfinished.

A Book of Hours typically begins with a calendar illustrated with images showing daily life or special events associated with each month of the year. It continues with short prayers to be recited during the eight designated times for prayer, or the canonical hours (see Chapter 12). Among the Limbourg brothers' illustrations, many depict the Duke of Berry's residences and those of the French royal family. The *Tres Riches Heures* thus provides us with a documentary record of their appearance, even though most of the buildings were destroyed long ago. Consider, for instance, their miniature painting of Mehun-sur-Yèvre [meh-UH ser YEV] (Fig. 12.22), built near Bourges in the late fourteenth century. This Gothic structure no longer stands, but at the time, many thought it was the most beautiful private home in the world. The Limbourg brothers used it to illustrate the story

of the devil's temptation of Christ. (Christ stands on the peak of a mountain at the top of the page, the devil flying beside him.) Christ refuses the riches of the world—represented by the Duc de Berry's very possessions—as if to remind the viewer, and the Duc himself, of the transience of worldly things. Nevertheless, the artistry of the Limbourgs captures every detail of the home's Gothic pinnacles and points, every rib and joint across the tracery of its facade, celebrating the Duc's riches even as it warns against putting too much faith in them.

THE GOTHIC IN ITALY

The Gothic in Italy manifested itself in ways quite different from the rest of Europe, in no small part because it consisted of a number of individual city-states independent of control by a king or the Holy Roman emperor. Even the papacy lacked real authority throughout most of the thirteenth century, since it had moved to France. Political power in these city-states—particularly in Florence and Siena—rested not with the landed aristocracy, who were often excluded from participation in civic affairs, but with the communities' leading merchant families. And these city-states competed with one another for the control of trade—and with it political influence and wealth.

This competitive atmosphere, and the civic pride associated with it, prompted civic leaders to commission new cathedrals and churches that would be, they hoped, the envy of their neighbors. Siena took the lead, commissioning a new facade for its magnificent cathedral in 1284 (Fig. 12.23). To the two-tone marble banding of the original Romanesque cathedral, the artist in charge, Giovanni Pisano, integrated

Fig. 12.22 Limbourg Brothers, ***The Temptation of Christ,*** **from** ***Les Très Riches Heures du Duc du Berry.*** **ca. 1415.** Illumination on parchment, 6 3/4″ × 4 1/2″. Musée Condé, Chantilly. Jean, Duke of Berry, was famous for the menagerie of exotic animals he kept, especially at Mehun-sur-Yèvre, including swans, bears, lions, and monkeys, as depicted in the foreground of this miniature.

Fig. 12.23 Giovanni Pisano, lower facade, Siena Cathedral, Siena, Italy. 1284–99. Pisano designed only the lower half of the facade. Except for the rose window, the upper half of the facade dates from the fourteenth century. The mosaics in the top gables date from the nineteenth century.

Fig. 12.24 Giovanni Pisano, *Mary, Sister of Moses.* 1284–99. Marble, height 74 $^3/_4$″. Museo dell'Opera del Duomo, Siena. This sculpture was once on the facade of the Siena Cathedral. The sculptures now in place on the facade are copies of the originals, which were removed to protect them from further deterioration.

features of the French Gothic style, such as the triple portal with its point gables over the tympanums, the soaring finials, the rose window, and an elaborate sculpture program.

Pisano's great innovation was, in fact, this sculpture program. It incorporated freestanding sculptures of prophets and saints on the pinnacles, arches, and gables of the facade. His *Mary, Sister of Moses* (Fig. **12.24**) is an example. She leans dramatically forward, as if turning to communicate with the other figures on the facade. But her pose also is the result of Giovanni's acute sense of his public. He realized that, when seen from street level, Mary's face would be hidden behind her dress and breasts if he did not arch her neck forward. The result is a figure that stands independently of the architecture and, like the other figures on

the facade, asserts its freedom in a manner comparable to the figures on the west portal of Reims Cathedral (see Fig. 12.16).

In 1294, Florence responded to Siena's initiative when it formed the Opera del Duomo, or Department of Works of the Duomo (*duomo* comes from *domus dei*, or "house of God"), a committee in charge of building a new cathedral of its own. Construction began in 1296, although the building would not be completed until the first half of the fifteenth century (see Chapter 14). The city claimed that the Duomo would be "the most beautiful and honorable church in Tuscany," an assertion that everyone understood to mean it would compete with Siena's cathedral.

The New Mendicant Orders Aside from cathedrals, civic leaders also engaged in building projects for the new urban religious orders: the Dominicans, founded by the Spanish monk Dominic de Guzman (ca. 1170–1221), whose most famous theologian was Thomas Aquinas; and the Franciscans, founded by Francis of Assisi (ca. 1181–1226). Unlike the traditional Benedictine monastic order, which functioned apart from the world, the Dominicans and the Franciscans were reformist orders, dedicated to active service in the cities, especially among the common people. Their growing popularity reflects the growing crisis facing the mainstream Church, as isolation and apparent disregard for laypeople plagued it well into the sixteenth century.

The mainstream Church held property and engaged in business—sources, many felt, of the Church's corruption. The Dominicans and Franciscans were both **mendicant orders**— that is, they neither held property nor engaged in business, relying for their support on contributions from their communities. The Dominicans and the Franciscans were rivals, and they often established themselves on opposite sides of a city. The Dominicans' priority was preaching. The Franciscans committed themselves to a severe regimen of prayer, meditation, fasting, and mortification of the flesh, based on Francis's conviction that one could come closer to God by rejecting worldly goods. But both orders borrowed freely from one another. The Franciscans adopted the more efficient organizing principles of the Dominicans as well as their love of learning and emphasis on preaching, while the Dominicans accepted the Franciscan repudiation of worldly goods.

Franciscan and Dominican Churches In Florence, the civic government and private citizens worked with the Franciscans to build the church of Santa Croce (Fig. **12.25**). Construction began in 1294 and continued even as the city began constructing its main

Fig. 12.25 Santa Croce, Florence, Italy. Begun 1294. Santa Croce was commissioned by the Franciscans with the support of the Florentine government and private citizens.

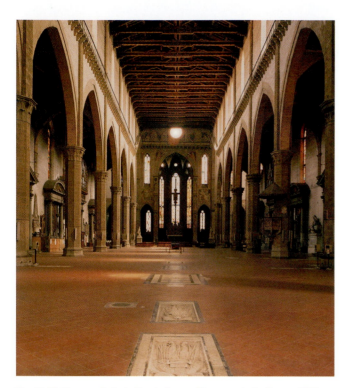

Fig. 12.26 Nave and choir, Santa Croce, Florence, Italy. Begun 1294. Santa Croce was commissioned by the Franciscans with the support of the Florentine government and private citizens.

cathedral. Compared to Gothic churches of the period, the mendicant churches are austere in their decoration. Nothing like the dramatic gables, finials, and sculpture program that decorate Giovanni Pisano's Siena Cathedral distinguishes

their plain facades, and their interiors are likewise unembellished. Gothic pointed arches together with vertical moldings designed to pull the eye upward decorate the nave arcade of Santa Croce (Fig. 12.26), but instead of continuing upward into the rising vaults of the Gothic interior, the nave and choir are topped by an open, wooden-trussed ceiling. There is no structural reason that the Franciscans should have chosen to cover the nave in this manner, but perhaps they simply wanted to emphasize the simplicity of their own practice by evoking the basilica tradition of early churches such as the original St. Paul's Outside the Walls in Rome (see Fig. 8.13).

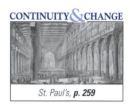

CONTINUITY&CHANGE

*St. Paul's, **p. 259***

Santa Croce was on the eastern side of the city, and the Dominican church of Santa Maria Novella (Fig. 12.27) was built on the western side, underscoring the rivalry between the two orders. (A Franciscan church and a Dominican church were also built in Siena.) At Santa Maria Novella, the marble striping that defines the rich surfaces of Siena's cathedral is used only on the facade, and, in fact, the facade was left unfinished above the Gothic row of niches with their Gothic portals (extended by walls both right and left) until the middle of the fifteenth century.

Families supported the construction of both Florentine mendicant churches by donating chapels, held as family property, and built on either side of the nave. Private family masses could be celebrated in these chapels, and, as opposed to the more public spaces in the churches, they were often richly decorated and their walls painted with frescoes. Thus, a rich family expected to guarantee its salvation by contributing to the church, and the order could accept the church and its chapels as a form of alms, consistent with its vow of poverty. This emphasis on painted decoration, instead of the stained glass that marks northern European Gothic architecture and which was also reflected in the decoration of Italian civic structures, contributed significantly to the rise of painting as an art in Italy in the thirteenth and fourteenth centuries.

The Appeal of Saint Francis Both the Dominican and Franciscan orders were sanctioned by Pope Innocent III (papacy 1198–1216). Innocent exercised papal authority as no pope had before him.

Fig. 12.27 Santa Maria Novella, Florence, Italy. Founded before 1246, nave begun after 1279. Santa Maria Novella was commissioned by the Dominicans and, like Santa Croce, its construction was supported by the Florentine government and private citizens.

He went so far as to claim that the pope was to the emperor as the sun was to the moon, a reference to the fact that the emperor received his "brilliance" (that is, his crown) from the hand of the pope. Innocent established the papacy as a self-sustaining financial and bureaucratic institution. He formalized the Church hierarchy, from pope to parish priest, and gave full sanction to the doctrine of *transubstantiation* (the belief that the bread and wine of sacrament become the true body and blood of Christ when consecrated by a priest), and made annual confession and Easter communion mandatory for all adult Christians.

Innocent was also a remarkably gifted preacher—his sermon *On the Misery of the Human Condition* was one of the most famous of its day (see Reading 10.5)—and the power of his words, if not the fierceness of his rhetoric, served as a model for both the Dominicans and the Franciscans. But, where Innocent appealed to the fear of death and damnation, mendicant orders appealed to the promise of life and salvation. Nevertheless, Innocent clearly understood the popular appeal of preaching and the influence that preaching gave to the new mendicant orders. He especially understood the attraction offered by the example of Francis of Assisi.

The son of a rich cloth merchant, Francis became disaffected with wealth and urged his followers to lead a life of poverty. Stories detailing the deeds and miracles of Francis's life embodied the reasons that he was to be revered. In his official biography of Francis, Bonaventure of Bagnoreggio (ca. 1217–74) tells how Francis created the first crèche (**Reading 12.3**):

There were so many such stories that Pope Gregory IX (papacy 1227–41) canonized Francis two years after his death, and ordered that the Upper Church of San Francesco be built in his honor at Assisi, Francis's hometown (Fig. **12.28**) Begun in 1228, it is one of the most

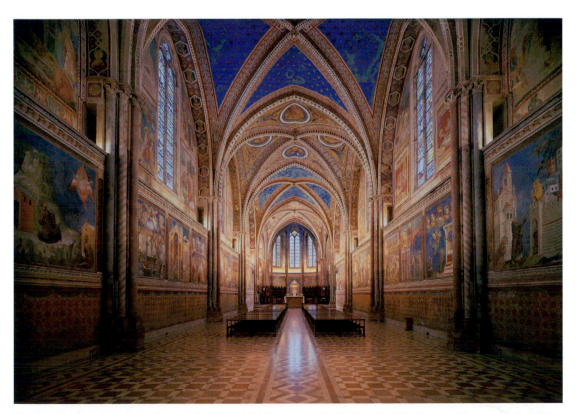

Fig. 12.28 Interior of the Upper Church, Basilica of San Francesco, Assisi, Umbria, Italy. Begun 1228; consecrated 1253.
Within a few years of its completion, the church became a popular pilgrimage site.

Fig. 12.29 Saint Francis Master, *Saint Francis Creates the First Christmas Crèche,* **fresco in Upper Church of San Francesco, Assisi, Umbria, Italy. ca. 1295–1305.** A severe earthquake gravely damaged the Assisi fresco cycle on September 26, 1997, when two sections of the church's roof collapsed.

beautiful of Italian Gothic churches. Although some of the finest stained-glass windows of the Italian thirteenth century decorate the interior, the primary decorative program are paintings of Old and New Testament scenes as well as a series of 28 frescoes narrating Francis's life as told by Bonaventure. The series has often been attributed to Giotto di Bondone, the first great Italian painter of the fourteenth century (discussed in Chapter 13). The Saint Francis paintings at Assisi are stylistically different enough from Giotto's other work, however, that many art historians believe them to be the work of an unknown Roman painter, often called the Saint Francis Master.

The faces and folds of cloth in the work of the Saint Francis Master are defined with broad lighter highlights applied over the darker background colors. Note the clothes of the two figures at the left of the scene depicting the saint creating the Christmas crèche as narrated by Bonaventure (Fig. 12.29). Giotto, as we will see, uses a gradual and continuous blending of dark colors to re-create the realistic appearance of shadows. Perhaps the most remarkable aspect of the painting is the artist's attempt to create an illusionistic space by means of one-point perspective (discussed more fully in Chapter 14). Here, the architectural forms recede into deep space but they do not do so in a uniform way throughout the composition.

Francis's love of the natural world was profound. In his mystical poem *Canticle of the Sun,* his language suggests an intimate bond with the universe. Addressing "brother sun" and "sister moon," "brother wind" and "sister water," this poem may be the first work of literature in the vernacular, or the language spoken by the people in everyday usage, as opposed to Latin (**Reading 12.4**):

READING 12.4

St. Francis of Assisi, *Canticle of the Sun*

Most high, all-powerful, all good, Lord!
All praise is yours, all glory, all honor
And all blessing.
To you alone, Most High, do they belong.
No mortal lips are worthy
To pronounce your name.
All praise be yours, my Lord, through all that you have made,
And first my lord Brother Sun,
Who brings the day; and light you give to us through him.
How beautiful is he, how radiant in all his splendor!
Of you, Most High, he bears the likeness.
All praise be yours, my Lord, through Sister Moon and Stars;
In the heavens you have made them, bright
And precious and fair.
All praise be yours, my Lord, through Brothers Wind and Air,
And fair and stormy, all the weather's moods,
By which you cherish all that you have made.
All praise be yours, my Lord, through Sister Water,
So useful, lowly, precious, and pure.
All praise be yours, my Lord, through Brother Fire,
Through whom you brighten up the night.
How beautiful he is; how cheerful and powerful and strong.
All praise be yours, my Lord, through Sister Earth, our mother,
Who feeds us in her sovereignty and produces
Various fruits and colored flowers and herbs.
All praise be yours, my Lord, through those who grant pardon
For love of you; through those who endure
Sickness and trial.
Happy those who endure in peace,
By you, Most High, they will be crowned.
All praise be yours, my Lord, through Sister Death,
From whose embrace no mortal can escape.
Woe to those who die in mortal sin!
Happy those She finds doing your will!
The second death can do no harm to them.
Praise and bless my Lord, and give him thanks,
And serve him with great humility.

The love of nature expressed here is fundamental to Franciscan theology. It sets out what amounts to a theology of incarnation—that is, a deep and abiding belief that God resides in the world, in his Creation, and can be understood by contemplation of that Creation.

Representing the Human

Among the surviving treasures of the Abbey Church of Saint-Denis is a sculpture of the Virgin and Child inscribed with the date 1339 and the name of Queen Jeanne d'Evreux [zhahn day-VRUH], wife of Charles IV of France (Fig. **12.30**). Just over two feet high, it embodies both the cult of the Virgin and the growing preference for naturalistic representation that is so evident in the jamb sculptures at Reims (see Fig. 12.16). The Virgin holds a scepter topped by a *fleur-de-lis* [flur-duh-lee], the heraldic symbol of the French monarchy, which served as a reliquary for what were said to be hairs from Mary's head. In this, she is a perfect medieval figure. But she also stands, her weight on one leg, in an exaggeration of the classical *contrapposto* pose into a pronounced S-curve, suggesting the Virgin's grace and elegance. Drapery falls around her, describing the body beneath as if it is actual flesh and bone. The softness of her face, the kindness of her expression, which the Christ child reaches out to touch, lend her a humanity that would become a characteristic of art made in the centuries to come. It is as if she is, in this sculpture, first a mother, then the mother of Christ.

Fig. 12.30 *Virgin and Child,* **from the Abbey Church of Saint-Denis, France. ca. 1339.**
Inv.: MR 342; MR 419. M. Beck-Coppola/Musée du Louvre/RMN Réunion des Musées Nationaux, France. Art Resource, New York. Silver gilt and enamel, height 27 ¹/₈″. Musée du Louvre, Paris.

Fig. 12.31 Duccio di Buoninsegna and Simone Martini, detail of *Virgin and Child with Saint Dominic and Saint Aurea.* **1310–20.**
Tempera on wood, 24 ¹/₄″ × 34 ¹/₄″. National Gallery, London.

EXPLORE MORE View a studio technique video about egg tempera painting at **www.myartslab.com**

Painted at almost the same time, in Italy, is a depiction of the Virgin and Child by the Sienese [see-uh-NEEZ] master Duccio [DOO-chee-oh] and his assistant Simone Martini (Fig. **12.31**). Here, too, the artists emphasize the human nature of the Virgin's expression, the feeling captured in the mother's facial expression—despite the obvious restraining influence of late Byzantine style on these masters. It may have been just this humanity that made the cult of the Virgin so attractive to so many. If most of the faithful found it impossible to identify with Jesus, who was, after all, a superhuman figure, they could identify with the completely human Mary. In both images, we see a hint of what would be the driving force of intellectual pursuit in the fourteenth and fifteenth centuries: the exploration not of the meaning of the Bible, but of what it means to be human. ■

What do we mean by Gothic style?

The architectural style that came to be known as Gothic originated at the Abbey Church of Saint-Denis just north of Paris, which was dedicated in 1144. It was the work of Saint-Denis's abbot, Suger, who dreamed of bringing prominence to the Île-de-France by creating an architecture surpassing all others in beauty and grandeur. How did stained glass fit into his ambitions? Chartres Cathedral, to the southwest, soon followed suit, after a fire destroyed the original structure in 1194, leaving only the west facade. The church was rebuilt into what many consider the most magnificent of all Gothic cathedrals, its stained glass unrivaled in Europe. Freed of load-bearing necessity by the innovative engineering that marks Gothic construction, the walls were thus also free to contain glass, which surrounds the entire cathedral.

As the Gothic style developed, important architectural innovations contributed to the goal of elevating the soul of worshipers to the spiritual realm. What makes the extremely high naves of Gothic cathedrals possible? During the thirteenth century, architects began to embellish the exteriors of their cathedrals with increasingly elaborate decoration, including ambitious sculptural programs. How do you account for the increasing naturalism of this sculptural decoration?

How did music develop in the Gothic cathedral?

With its vast spaces and stone walls, the Gothic cathedral could easily be as animated by its acoustics as it was by its light. At the School of Notre-Dame, in Paris, the first collection of music in two parts, the *Magnus Liber Organi* (*The Great Book of Polyphony*), chiefly the work of the composers Léonin and Pérotin, was widely distributed in manuscript by about 1160. Among their most significant innovations is their emphasis on counterpoint and the complex musical form of the motet. What role did the organ play in this new music?

How did cathedrals affect the development of learning?

In 1179, a papal decree ordered the cathedral schools to provide for the teaching of the laity (nonclerics), and the university as an institution was born. The quality of the teaching at the University of Paris distinguished it from the others. Peter Abelard, who taught by the dialectical method, was the school's most renowned lecturer. How would you describe the dialectical method? How does it differ from the Socratic method? His affair with a private female student, Héloïse, would cause them both great difficulty, and Héloïse's fate reveals much about the prospects for educated women in the Middle Ages. But probably the most important scholar at the University of Paris was Thomas Aquinas, who adopted Abelard's dialectical method to his own Scholasticism. What is Scholasticism and how does Aquinas's *Summa Theologica* reflect it?

What is the Radiant style?

By the middle of the thirteenth century, the Gothic style in France had been elaborated into increasingly flamboyant patterns of repeated traceries and ornament that we refer to as the Radiant style. How does the royal chapel of Sainte-Chapelle in Paris reflect this style?

How was the Gothic mood expressed in Italy?

Siena commissioned a new facade for its cathedral from Giovanni Pisano in 1284. Florence responded to Siena's initiative by beginning construction of its own new cathedral. Aside from cathedrals, civic leaders also engaged in building churches for the new urban religious mendicant orders: the Dominicans and the Franciscans. What decorative feature of these churches distinguishes them from Gothic architecture in the north?

PRACTICE MORE Get flashcards for images and terms and review chapter material with quizzes at **www.myartslab.com**

GLOSSARY

Book of Hours A type of prayer book that usually begins with an illustrated calendar followed by pages of short prayers to be recited at designated times.

buttress A pillar or other support typically built against an exterior wall to brace it and strengthen an interior vault.

counterpoint An opposing element.

crocket A leaflike form that curves outward, with edges curling up, that was often added to pinnacles, spires, and gables of cathedrals.

dialectical method A method that juxtaposes different points of view and seeks to reconcile them.

finial A knoblike architectural form; also found on furniture.

flying buttress A stone structure that extends from a wall and employs an arch to focus the strength of the buttress's support at the top of the wall.

Gothic A style of architecture and decoration prevalent in the twelfth through the fifteenth centuries in northern Europe, where, it was believed, classical traditions had been destroyed by Germanic invaders called Goths.

illumination The painstakingly detailed, hand-painted decoration of manuscripts, usually in tempera on vellum.

mendicant order A religious order whose members do not hold property or engage in business.

miniature A very small painting.

motet A polyphonic form consisting of three (and sometimes four) voices.

palatine chapel A palace chapel.

quadrivium In medieval universities, the mathematical arts, which included music, arithmetic, geometry, and astronomy.

Radiant style A development of the French Gothic style featuring increasingly flamboyant patterns of repeated traceries and ornament.

rose window A round window with mullions (framing elements) and traceries extending outward from its center in the manner of the petals of a rose.

Scholasticism A brand of theological inquiry based on the dialectical method.

summa An authoritative summary of all that is known on a traditional subject.

trivium In medieval universities, the language arts, which included grammar, rhetoric, and dialectic.

READINGS

READING 12.1

from Jean de Meun's *The Romance of the Rose*

The Romance of the Rose *is an allegorical dream vision about love, in which a young man endeavors to possess the rosebud with which he has become enamored. In Meung's hands, it becomes a satire on contemporary society. At the end of the poem, in an allegory of sexual intercourse, the lover finally penetrates the inner sanctum of the rose. The poem ends with the narrator awakening, fulfilled, at daybreak. The following represents the first publication of the letters of Héloïse and Abelard, included in the poem as part of a jealous husband's arguments against marriage.*

53

. . . Likewise did Héloïse entreat
(The abbess of the Paraclete)
Her lover Peter Abelard,
That he would utterly discard
All thought of marriage from his mind.
This lady, noble and refined,
Of genius bright and learning great,
Loving, and loved with passionate
Strong love, implored him not to wed,
And many a well-wrought reason sped   10
To him in letters, where she showed
That hard and troublous is the code

54

Of marriage, howsoever true
Are those who bind themselves thereto;
For not alone had she in books
Studied, but all the closest nooks
Of woman's heart explored, and she
Love's throes had suffered bitterly.
Therefore she begged they might atwain,[1]
Though dying each for each, remain,   20
Bound by no bonds but those of love,
Whose gentle ties are strong above
All marriage laws, yet frank and free
Leave lovers—in sweet amity—
To follow learning, and she said,
Moreover, that long absence bred
'Twixt lovers unexpressed delight,
Most poignant when they're lost to sight.

But Peter, as himself hath writ
In burning letters, so was smit[2]   30
With passion, that nought else would serve
Till Héloïse he drew to swerve
From her sage counsel, and thence fell
On him mischance most dire to tell;
For little more their course was run
Ere she at Argenteuil as nun

Was close immured,[3] while he was reft
Of manhood by his foes, who deft
As cruel were in his despite,
Seizing him as he lay one night   40
At Paris. After this mischance
Saint Denis, patron saint of France

55

Gave shelter to him as a monk;
And when this bitter cup he'd drunk,
Down to the dregs an abbey meet
He founded, hight[4] the Paraclete,
For Héloïse, and there with good
Success she ruled the sisterhood.
Her love-lorn story hath she told
In letters which she penned with bold   50
Unshamed assurance; therein she
Declares monk Abelard to be
Her lord and master; and some say
These far-famed letters but betray
Delirious love. When first the dress
She donned of abbess, her distress
Broke forth in these wild words: If he
Who rules Rome's Empire courteously
Deigned to demand that I, as wife,
To him would dedicate my life,   60
In proud estate, I should reply
Much rather would I live and die
Thy mistress, wrapped in shame profound,
Than empress of the world be crowned.

But never since that day till now
Hath such a woman lived, I trow.[5]

READING CRITICALLY

What does Jean de Meung value most in Héloïse's rejection of marriage, and why do you think a later medieval commentary, written by one of the leading female writers of the day, would reject it as misogynist?

---

[1]**atwain:** separate.   [2]**smit:** struck.

[3]**immured:** confined.   [4]**hight**: named.   [5]**trow**: believe

13

Siena and Florence in the Fourteenth Century
Toward a New Humanism

THINKING AHEAD

How do the Sienese and Florentine republics compare?

What came to replace the Byzantine style of painting in Italy?

Who was Dante?

What effects did the plague have on European consciousness?

The city halls of Florence and Siena, begun within two years of one another (1296 and 1298 respectively), and the broad plazas that fronted them, are eloquent symbols not only of the cities' many similarities but also the intensity of their rivalry in the fourteenth century (Figs. **13.1** and **13.2**). Both buildings are more or less rectangular, decorated with crenellations meant to evoke the security and safety of the medieval fortress, and capped by tall bell towers. They dominate their urban landscapes and are reminiscent of the medieval castle's keep. Florence's Palazzo Vecchio is heavy-looking, its massive stonework reflecting the solidity of the merchant class that erected it. In contrast, the light brickwork of the facade of Siena's Palazzo Pubblico, or "public palace," is interrupted by windows composed of thin marble columns supporting Gothic arches—as if to announce the artistic refinement of the city. Siena's bell tower purposefully dwarfs that of its Florentine rival. In front of both town halls are large public squares, places for the citizenry to gather to hear government decisions.

In both Siena and Florence, the fortunes of church and state were inextricably linked. Until the Palazzo Vecchio and the Palazzo Pubblico were built, both cities' governments met in churches. Afterward, the open squares in front of each building were used to host political events,

Fig. 13.2 Palazzo Pubblico, Siena. 1297–1310. The public palace faced the Campo, the large public square. Townspeople rushed back and forth, trading and bartering, and although the square was surrounded by the palaces of noble families, bankers, and merchants, the Campo was considered to be the property of all Sienese citizens. On the Campo, everyone was equal.

and public sermons supported by the government brought the church into the government's very sphere. The local governments also invested heavily in building projects for the church.

◀ **Fig. 13.1 Palazzo Vecchio, Florence. 1299–1310.** At the bottom right, before the main entrance, stands a replica of Michelangelo's famous sculpture of *David* (see Fig. 14.30). The original was put in place here in 1504. It was removed to protect it from damage in 1873. The replica seen here dates from 1910.

HEAR MORE Listen to an audio file of your chapter at **www.myartslab.com**

SIENA AND FLORENCE: CIVIC AND RELIGIOUS LIFE IN TUSCANY

The rival cities of Siena and Florence were located in Tuscany, the area of central Italy that lies between the Apennine Mountains, the central spine of the Italian peninsula, and a section of the Mediterranean known as the Tyrrhenian Sea (Map **13.1**). Siena lies in the mountainous southern region of Tuscany, at the center of a rich agricultural zone famous for its olive oil and wine. Florence is located in the Arno river valley, the region's richest agricultural district. Their rivalry dates back to the contest for supremacy between the pope and the Holy Roman Emperor during the time of Charlemagne (see Chapter 10). The Guelphs sided with the pope, while the Ghibellines sided with the emperor. Siena was generally considered a Ghibelline city, and Florence a Guelph stronghold, although factions of both parties competed for leadership within each city, especially in Florence. By the end of the thirteenth century, the pope retaliated against Siena for its Ghibelline leanings by revoking the city's papal banking privileges and conferring them instead on Florence. As a result, by the fourteenth century, Florence would become the principal economic and political power in Tuscany.

Siena: A Free Commune

But in the late Middle Ages, Siena was still one of the most powerful cities in Europe. Its sense of its past lent it a

Map 13.1 Central Italy in about 1494, showing the republics of Florence and Siena and the papal states.

Fig. 13.3 Ambrogio Lorenzetti, *Allegory of Good Government: The Effects of Good Government in the City and Country*, fresco in the Sala della Pace, Palazzo Pubblico, Siena. 1338–39. Across from this painting, Lorenzetti also painted an *Allegory of Bad Government*, in which there is no commerce, no dancing, only man killing man, destruction and darkness all around.

feeling of historical weight. According to legend, its founders were Senius [SEN-ee-oos] and Aschius [ASS-kee-oos], the sons of Remus, who with his brother, Romulus, founded Rome. Romulus had killed their father in a quarrel, and the boys, in retribution, stole Rome's she-wolf shrine and carried it back to Siena, protected by a white cloud by day and a black cloud by night. The facade of the Palazzo Pubblico celebrates their feat: Sculptures of Romulus and Remus suckled by the she-wolf decorate it, and a heraldic crest, the *balzana*, consisting of a white field atop a black one, appears under each arch.

Siena remained a small Etruscan village for 700 years, until the Roman emperor Augustus colonized it in 13 BCE. The town was dominated first by Rome and then by local nobles, Lombard and Frankish feudal counts, who arrived in successive invasions to rule in the name of their king. By the tenth century, large numbers of serfs had migrated from the surrounding countryside to three separate hilltop villages that soon merged into one. Feudal authorities were not altogether opposed to such migration. They had trained many of the serfs to manufacture the finished goods that they desired. It seemed practical to concentrate such production by chartering Siena and other towns. The charter stipulated that the townspeople would make manufactured goods, and in return, the feudal lord would protect them. Gradually, the towns gained more importance and power, and their citizens began to pay allegiance not to feudal lords or papal authority but to the wealthiest citizens of the community, whose power base was founded on

cooperation and the orderly conduct of affairs. When Siena established itself, in 1125, as a free **commune** (a collective of people gathered together for the common good), it achieved an immense advantage over its feudal neighbors. "Town air brings freedom" was a common saying in the late Middle Ages. As the prospect of such freedom attracted an increasing number of people to Siena, its prosperity was soon unrivaled.

Civic Life Crucial to the growing town's success was a new model of government, celebrated in 1338 by the painter Ambrogio Lorenzetti (active 1319–47) in a fresco called *Allegory of Good Government* (Fig. **13.3**), commissioned for the council chamber of Siena's Palazzo Pubblico. The fresco depicts Siena as it actually appeared. Richly dressed merchants dance in the street, one couple passing beneath the arching arms of another, followed by a chain of revelers dancing hand in hand. To the left, in an arched portico, three men play a board game. To their right is a shoe shop, behind that a schoolroom where a teacher expounds to a row of students, and beside the schoolroom, a wine shop. At the very top, masons construct a new building. Outside the city gate, to the right, the surrounding countryside is lush. Farmers bring livestock and produce to market, workers till the fields and labor in the vineyards. Above them all, floating in the sky, is the nearly nude figure of *Securitas* [she-koo-ree-TASS] ("Security"), carrying a gallows in one hand and a scroll in the other, to remind citizens that peace depends upon justice. At the horizon, the sky is ominously dark, suggesting perhaps that Siena's citizens thought of themselves as living in a uniquely enlightened place.

Watching over the city's well-being was the Virgin Mary, uniting civic and religious life. The city called itself "ancient city of the virgin," and by 1317, a *Maestà*, or *Virgin and Child in Majesty* (see Fig. 13.6), occupied the end wall of the council chamber of the Palazzo Pubblico. Painted by Simone Martini (active 1311–44), the *Maestà* depicts the Madonna and Christ Child surrounded by a heavenly court of saints and angels. Below, two kneeling angels offer up vessels of roses and lilies. The Virgin comments in verse, written on the platform below: "The angelic little flowers, roses and lilies, Which adorn the heavenly meadow, do not please me more than good counsel." Thus the Virgin exerts her moral influence over civic life.

The demands of daily life in Siena required divine intervention. The town had long divided itself into three distinct neighborhoods, corresponding to the three ridges of the hillside on which the city stands. With the advent of the commune, the city was ruled by three consuls, one for each neighborhood. There were other divisions as well. The wealthiest Sienese nobles, called the *grandi*, or "great ones," lorded over smaller neighborhoods, or wards, in a manner not unlike their feudal forebears. The clergy, headed by a bishop, were independent, and local

churches, convents, and other organizations devoted to deeds of charity were more or less self-governing. The common people organized themselves as military companies, which could unite to form a large Sienese army, but which also guaranteed local autonomy. And competing *arti*, or **guilds**, associations or groups of people with like-minded, often occupation-based interests, exercised power over their members.

The guilds became an increasingly powerful force in the commune. Leading the way was the merchants' guild, organized as early as 1192. The richest merchant families lent money (charging interest on their loans, despite a papal ban on the practice) and dealt in wax, pepper, and spices, as well as Flemish cloth, shoes, stockings, and belts. Other guilds, such as masons, carpenters, innkeepers, barbers, butchers, and millers, quickly established themselves, but none was as powerful as the merchants' guild. By 1280, its members controlled city government, excluding the nobility and declaring that only "good popular merchants" should be eligible to serve on the city council.

Other guilds resented the merchants' control over the city's government, and in 1355, the people gathered in the Campo before the Palazzo Pubblico and forced their resignation. From then on, anyone belonging to a guild was technically eligible to serve on the council, except

Map 13.2 Principal trade routes in medieval Europe.
As commerce grew among the regions of Europe, the cities on this map grew proportionately.

merchants and nobles. The exercise of power being what it is, however, control soon fell to the next great guilds below the merchants, the shopkeepers and notaries. By 1368, vying factions caused the disintegration of the government, as four revolutions rocked the city in as many months. The commune was a thing of the past.

Florence: Archrival of Siena

Like Siena, Florence was extremely wealthy, and that wealth was based on trade. By the twelfth century, Florence was the center of textile production in the Western world and played a central role in European trade markets (Map **13.2**). The Arno River provided ample water for washing and rinsing sorted wool and finished cloth. The city's dyeing techniques were unsurpassed—to this day, the formulas for the highly prized Florentine reds remain a mystery. Dyestuffs were imported from throughout the Mediterranean and even the Orient, and each year, Florentine merchants traveled to England, Portugal, Spain, and Flanders to purchase raw wool for their manufactories.

As in Siena, it was the city's bankers and moneylenders who made Florence a vital player in world trade. Florentine bankers invented checks, credit, even life insurance. Most important, in 1252, they introduced Europe's first single currency, the gold *florin*. By 1422, over 2 million florins were in circulation throughout Europe. This was a staggering number considering that a family could live comfortably on about 150 florins a year, and the finest palace cost about 1,000 florins. Florence was Europe's bank, and its bankers were Europe's true nobility.

The Guilds and Florentine Politics Only two other cities in all of Italy—Lucca and Venice—could boast that they were republics like Siena and Florence, and governing a republic was no easy task. As in Siena, in Florence the guilds controlled the commune. By the end of the twelfth century, there were 7 major guilds and 14 minor ones. The most prestigious was the lawyers' guild (the Arte dei Giudici), followed closely by the wool guild (the Arte della Lana) (Fig. **13.4**), the silk guild (the Arte di Seta), and the cloth merchants' guild (the Arte di Calimala). Also among the major guilds were the bankers, the doctors, and other merchant classes. Butchers, bakers, carpenters, and masons composed the bulk of the minor guilds.

As in Siena, the merchants, especially the Arte della Lana, controlled the government. They were known as the *Popolo Grasso* (literally, "the fat people"), as opposed to *Popolo Minuto*, the ordinary workers, who comprised probably 75 percent of the population and had no voice in government. Only guild members could serve in the government. Their names were written down, the writing was placed in leather bags (*borse*) in the Church of Santa Croce (see Chapter 12), and nine names were drawn every two months in a public ceremony. (The period of service was short to reduce the chance of corruption.) Those *signori* selected were known as the *Priori*, and their government was known as the *Signoria*—hence the name of the Piazza della Signoria, the plaza in front of the Palazzo Vecchio. Of the nine Priori—six from the major guilds, two from the minor guilds, and one standard-bearer.

The Florentine republic might have resembled a true democracy except for two details: First, the guilds were very close-knit so that, in general, selecting one or the other of their membership made little or no political difference; and second, the available names in the *borse* could be easily manipulated. However, conflict inevitably arose, and throughout the thirteenth century, other tensions made the problem worse, especially feuds between the Guelphs and Ghibellines. In Florence, the Guelphs were generally merchants and the Ghibellines were nobility. Thus, the battle lines between the two were drawn in class terms, often resulting in family feuds and street violence. In fact, the tower of the Palazzo Vecchio was built on the site of a pre-existing Ghibelline tower of the palace of the noble Uberti family, and the plaza in front was created by razing the remainder of the Uberti palace complex. Thus, both city hall and the public gathering place represented the triumph of Guelph over Ghibelline, the merchant class over the aristocracy.

Fig. 13.4 Andrea della Robbia, coat of arms of the Arte della Lana (Wool Guild of Florence). 1487. Glazed terracotta. Museo dell'Opera del Duomo, Florence. The guild chose for its coat of arms the Agnus Dei, the Lamb of God, carrying a banner inscribed with a red cross.

PAINTING: A GROWING NATURALISM

Even though Saint John the Baptist was the patron saint of Florence, the city, like Siena, relied on the Virgin Mary to protect it. Her image appeared frequently in the mendicant churches and elsewhere, and these images were said to perform miracles. Pilgrims from Tuscany and beyond flocked to Florence to receive the Madonna's good graces. As in Siena, whenever the city was threatened—by war, by flood, by plague—the Madonna's image was carried through the city in ceremonial procession. The two cities put themselves under the protection of the Virgin, and it was not long before they were competing to prove who could paint her the most magnificently. In the process, they began to represent her less in the stiff, abstracted manner of the Byzantine icon and more as a real person of flesh and blood.

Duccio and Simone Martini

After the Venetian rout of Constantinople in the Fourth Crusade in 1204 (see Chapter 10), Byzantine imagery flooded Europe. One of the first artists to break from the Byzantine tradition was the Sienese native Duccio di Buoninsegna (active 1278–1318). In 1308, the commune commissioned Duccio to paint a *Maestà*, or *Virgin and Child in Majesty* (Fig. **13.5**), to be set under the dome of Siena's cathedral. The finished work was greeted with a great celebration:

> "On the day that it was carried to the [cathedral]," a contemporary chronicler reports, "the shops were shut,

and the bishop conducted a great and devout company of priests and friars in solemn procession, accompanied by . . . all the officers of the commune, and all the people, and one after another the worthiest with lighted candles in their hands took places near the picture, and behind came the women and children with great devotion . . . making the procession around the Campo, as is the custom, all the bells ringing joyously, trumpets and bagpipes playing, out of reverence for so noble a picture as is this."

Duccio was well aware of the greatness of his achievement. Along the base of the Virgin's throne he wrote these words: "Holy Mother of God, give Siena peace and Duccio life because he painted Thee thus," announcing both the artist's piety and pride in his work and the growing prominence of artists in Italian society as a whole.

Duccio's *Maestà* begins to leave the conventions of the Byzantine icon behind and incorporates the Gothic tendency to naturalism. (Compare the Byzantine Fig. 8.31.) Duccio's Christ Child seems to be an actual baby, and a slightly chubby one at that. Similarly, beneath the Madonna's robes, we can sense a real body. Her knee especially asserts itself, and the

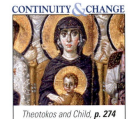

CONTINUITY & CHANGE

Theotokos and Child, **p. 274**

drapery falling from it drops in long, gentle curves, much more natural-looking than the rigid, angular drapery of earlier, Byzantine works. Four angels peer over the top of the Madonna's throne, gazing on the child like proud relations. The saints who kneel in the front row

Fig. 13.5 Duccio di Buoninsegna. *Maestà,* **main panel of** *Maestà Altarpiece,* **from Siena Cathedral. 1308–11.** Tempera and gold on wood, 7′ × 13′ 6¼″. Museo dell'Opera del Duomo, Siena. The Madonna's throne imitates the stone facade of the Siena cathedral.

Fig. 13.6 Simone Martini, *Maestà*, **Council Chamber, Palazzo Pubblico, Siena. ca. 1311–17, repaired 1321.** Fresco, 25′ × 31′9″. Martini's fresco covers the end wall of the Council Chamber, symbolically submitting that civic body's deliberations to the Madonna's watchful gaze and care.

appear to be individuals rather than types. Notice especially the aging and bearded cleric at the left. All are patron saints of the city, underscoring the fact that Duccio's painting is both an ecclesiastical and civic commission.

If Duccio's *Maestà* reflects the growing realism of Sienese art, the *Maestà* of Simone Martini, in the Hall of the Mappamondo in Siena's Palazzo Pubblico, is even more naturalistic (Fig. **13.6**). Simone had worked on the cathedral *Maestà* as Duccio's apprentice from 1308 to 1311, and he probably modeled his own work on it. Situated in a public building, overlooking the workings of civic administration, Simone's painting announces, even more dramatically than Duccio's, the blending of the sacred and secular in Tuscan culture.

One of the great innovations of Simone's fresco is the Virgin's crown, which signifies her status as Queen of Heaven. Surrounded by her celestial "court," she reveals the growing influence of French courtly poetry (see Chapter 10) in Italy. She becomes a model for human behavior, an emblem in the spiritual realm for the most noble types of secular love and devotion, including devotion to the right conduct of government. Highlighting the secular message, Jesus holds a parchment, adhered to the surface of the fresco, that reads, "Love Justice you who judge the earth." Like Duccio's painting, Simone's fresco carries a propagandistic message to the city fathers. As we have seen (see page 430), inscribed at the base of the throne are these words: "The angelic little flowers, roses and lilies, Which adorn the heavenly meadow, do not please me

more than good counsel." The painting suggests that the Virgin is as interested in worldly affairs as divine ones. Because of the realistic way Simone has represented her, she is as human as she is divine.

Stylistic differences separate the two works as well. As in the Byzantine icon from which she derives (see Fig. 8.31), Duccio's Madonna wears no crown, her brows turn without interruption down into the length of her nose, she is draped in blue, with an orange undergarment, and her rounded hood echoes the halo behind her head. She is much larger than those attending her, conforming to the hierarchies of Byzantine art. In Simone's version of the theme, the Virgin and surrounding figures are depicted almost in the same scale. As opposed to Duccio's painting, with its stacked receding space, Simone's Virgin sits in a deep space of the canopy with its delicate Gothic arches behind the throne. Both of the Virgin's knees are visible, with the Christ Child standing firmly on one of them. Her head and neck, rather than being shrouded behind an all-embracing hood, are rounded and full beneath the crown and its softly folded train, which is itself fully rounded in shadow behind her neck. Her robe, neglecting convention, is composed of rich, transparent silks, beneath which we can see her right arm. Above all, her porcelain-white skin, tinged with pink, gives her complexion a realistic tone. Blood flows through her body, rouging her cheeks, and her flesh breathes with life. She embodies, in fact, a standard of beauty absent in Western art since Classical times—the physical beauty of the flesh as opposed to the divine beauty of the spirit. In less formal pictures, Duccio, too, used a naturalistic style.

Cimabue and Giotto

Florence, too, had its master painters of the Virgin. At about the same time that Duccio was first becoming active in Siena, a painter known as Cimabue was painting a large-scale Virgin for the altarpiece of the Church of Santa Trinità in Florence (Fig. **13.7**). Cimabue's *Madonna Enthroned with Angels and Prophets* solidified his position as the leading painter in Florence. Although its Byzantine roots are clear—following closely, for instance, a Byzantine hierarchy of figures, with the Madonna larger than the figures that surround her—the painting is remarkable on several fronts. First, it is enormous. Standing over 12 feet high, it seems to have begun a tradition of large-scale altarpieces, helping to affirm the altar as the focal point of the church. But most important are Cimabue's concern for spatial volume and his treatment of human figures with naturalistic expressions. The throne is especially interesting, creating as it does a spatial setting for the scene, and the angels seem to be standing on the architectural frame; the front two clearly are. If the Virgin and Child are stock Byzantine figures, the four prophets at the base of the throne are surprisingly individualized, suggesting the increasing prominence of the individual personality in the era, an especially important characteristic, as we will see later in the chapter, of the literature of the period. These remarkably individual likenesses also tell us that Italian artists were becoming more skillful in painting with **tempera**, which allowed them to portray the world in ever-increasing detail (see *Materials & Techniques*, page 440). Perhaps most interesting of all is the position of the Virgin's feet, the right one propped upon the throne in an almost casual position.

According to an old story, one day Cimabue discovered a talented shepherd boy by the name of Giotto di Bondone and tutored him in the art of painting. The pupil soon surpassed the teacher. The sixteenth-century

Fig. 13.7 Cimabue, *Madonna Enthroned with Angels and Prophets*, from high altar of Santa Trinità, Florence. ca. 1285. Tempera and gold on wood, 11′ 7 ½″ × 7′ 4″. Galleria degli Uffizi, Florence. The later Renaissance historian Giorgio Vasari would claim that Cimabue had been apprenticed to a Greek painter from whom he learned the fundamentals of Byzantine icon painting.

historian Giorgio Vasari would later say that Giotto set "art upon the path that may be called the true one, learned to draw accurately from life and thus put an end to the crude Greek [i.e., Byzantine] manner."

Giotto's 1310 *Madonna Enthroned with Angel and Saints* (Fig. **13.8**), painted just a quarter century after Cimabue's, is as remarkable a shift toward naturalism as Simone's *Maestà* is over Duccio's. While it retains a Byzantine hierarchy of figures—the Christ Child is almost as big as the angels and the Virgin three or four times their size—it is spatially convincing in a way that Cimabue's painting is not. Giotto apparently learned to draw accurately from life, and his figures reveal his skill. Light plays across their forms—note the folds and pleats of the angels' gowns in the foreground—and substantial bodies seem to press outward from beneath the material. Unlike the paintings in the Upper Church of San Francesco in Assisi (see Fig. 12.29), often attributed to him, Giotto's colors gradually and continuously blend from light to dark around the contours of his figures and their draperies, re-creating the realistic appearance of shadows.

Giotto was also a master of the human face, capable of revealing a wide range of emotion and character. The total effect is to humanize Christ, the Virgin, and the saints, to portray them as real people. This skill is particularly evident in the frescoes of the Arena Chapel (see *Closer Look*, pages 438–439). (The chapel is also known as the Scrovegni Chapel, after the family that commissioned it in Padua.) The paintings in the Chapel were done in **buon fresco**. In this technique, the artist applies pigments onto wet rather than dry plaster. (See *Materials & Techniques*,

Fig. 13.8 Giotto di Bondone, *Madonna Enthroned with Angels and Saints*, from Church of the Ognissanti, Florence. ca. 1310. Tempera and gold on wood, 10'8" × 6'8 ¼". Galleria degli Uffizi, Florence. Giotto's contemporary, the writer Boccaccio, discussed later in this chapter, said that he "brought back to light that art which had for many ages lain buried beneath the blunders of those who painted rather to delight the eyes of the ignorant than to satisfy the intelligence of the wise."

CLOSER LOOK

Giotto's greatest paintings are surely those in the Arena Chapel in Padua, painted around 1305. Giotto covered virtually every space of the barrel-vaulted family chapel of the Scrovegni family with *buon fresco* (see *Materials & Techniques*, page 441), the technique of painting on wet plaster. The top of the vault is a starry blue sky, painted with lapis lazuli. Lapis lazuli does not properly combine with wet plaster, so it was applied on a dry wall. As a result, the blues of the ceiling and other blues in the frescoes have faded far more than the other colors, most of which still look fresh. On the side walls are scenes from the life of the Virgin and the life of Christ.

The Arena Chapel, Padua. The Life of Christ and the Virgin frescoes by Giotto. 1305–1306. A view of the Arena (Scrovegni) Chapel. In the bottom layer of images, closest to the floor, figures of the Virtues and Vices appear as painted, black-and-white simulations of sculpture, a technique known as *grisaille*. On the back wall above the door is a Last Judgment, figured as the final episode in the life of Christ.

Even the angels are wracked with grief.

The blue void at the center of the painting is a metaphor for the emptiness felt by the mourners.

The direction of the Virgin Mary's grief-stricken gaze continues down the diagonal line created by the barren ridge, reinforcing its emptiness.

Giotto was the first artist since antiquity to depict figures from behind, contributing to the sense that we are viewing a real drama.

John the Evangelist flings his arms back in a gesture that echoes that of the angels, almost as if his arms were wings.

The single leafless tree is a traditional symbol of death. It sits on a barren ridge that plunges in a stark diagonal toward the dead Christ.

Mary Magdalene, recognizable by her long hair, is traditionally represented at the Crucifixion kissing Christ's feet. Here, the Crucifixion over, she holds his feet in her hands, in an act of consummate tenderness and affection.

Giotto, *The Lamentation*, Arena Chapel, Padua. 1305–1306. Fresco, 78 $\frac{1}{2}$″ × 73″. Among the most moving scenes in the chapel is Giotto's depiction of human suffering. The painter focused on the real pain felt by Jesus's followers upon his death, rather than the promise of salvation that it symbolized.

Giotto's Arena Chapel

Halley's Comet made one of its regular appearances in 1301, just a few years before this painting was made. (We saw it depicted in the *Bayeux Tapestry* of 1066 [see Chapter 10, *Closer Look*, page 336]). Giotto apparently modeled the star that guides the Magi on that phenomenon.

The boy looks up at the Magi's camels in astonishment. This expression of emotion is typical of Giotto's frescos. Giotto had probably never seen a camel: These have blue eyes and cows' feet.

Note Giotto's attempt to render the wooden shed in perspective. If he does not quite "get it," he is coming close.

Giotto has abandoned the Byzantine hierarchy of figures. The angels, the Magi, the Virgin, and the Child are all drawn to the same scale. (For a comparison, see Duccio's *Maestà Altarpiece*, Fig. 13.5.)

The king, Caspar, has removed his crown and placed it at the foot of the angel receiving gifts. The gesture signifies his understanding that Christ is the "King of Kings."

The blue of Mary's skirt has almost completely flaked off. Lapis lazuli, the stone used to make blue pigment, does not combine with wet plaster, so the blue had to be painted on after the plaster had dried, leaving it far more susceptible to heat and humidity, which eventually cause flaking.

Giotto, *Adoration of the Magi*, Arena Chapel, Padua. 1305–1306. Fresco, 78 $\frac{1}{2}$" × 73". Boccaccio, author of the extraordinarily realistic story-cycle the *Decameron*, admired Giotto's painterly realism: "There is nothing in the whole creation he cannot depict," Boccaccio wrote.

Above the door is a depiction of the Last Judgment, in which the patron, Enrico Scrovegni, offers a model of the chapel to the Virgin. The purpose of the chapel seems clear: It was meant as penance on Enrico's part for his own and his father's sins—notably their flagrant usury.

The paintings depicting the life of Christ and the Virgin deliberately abandon the balance and symmetry that distinguish Byzantine painting (and, for that matter, the *Maestàs* of the period) in order to create a heightened sense of reality. In *The Lamentation*, for instance, Giotto places Christ in the lower left-hand corner of the work, at the bottom of a stark diagonal. Throughout the cycle, the action takes place on a narrow platform at the front of the painting. The architecture in the paintings is small in comparison to the figures, as in *The Adoration of the Magi*. Giotto may have been influenced by the stage sets made for the contemporary revival in Padua of Roman theater. Whatever the case, the drama of Giotto's paintings is undeniable. They possess a psychological intensity and emotional immediacy that involve the viewer directly in the scene.

Something to Think About . . .

If Giotto's paintings do, in fact, possess an intensity and immediacy that serve to involve the viewer directly in the scene, how might his paintings be compared to the role of music in the liturgy?

SEE MORE For a Closer Look at Giotto's Arena Chapel, go to **www.myartslab.com**

page 441.) Giotto's contemporaries were profoundly moved by the newfound realism of his work. In fact, the poet Dante Alighieri, whose *Divine Comedy* we will discuss in the next section of this chapter, would write in that poem: "Cimabue thought to hold the field in painting, but now Giotto has the cry, so that the other's fame, grown dim, must yield."

THE SPREAD OF VERNACULAR LITERATURE IN EUROPE

Until the early twelfth century, the language of almost all educated circles in Europe, and certainly in literature, was Latin. Gradually, however, writers began to address their works to a wider lay audience and to write in the **vernacular**, the language spoken in the streets. The French led the way, in twelfth-century works such as the *Song of Roland* (see Chapter 10) and Chrétien de Troyes's *Lancelot* (see Chapter 10), but early in the fourteenth century, vernacular works began to appear throughout Italy as well, spreading to the rest of Europe.

Dante's *Divine Comedy*

One of the greatest medieval Italian writers working in the vernacular was the poet Dante Alighieri (1265–1321). In Florence, in about 1308, he began one of the greatest works of the literary imagination, the *Divine Comedy* (Fig. **13.9**). This poem records the travels of the Christian soul from Hell to Purgatory and finally to Salvation in three books—the *Inferno*, *Purgatorio*,

and *Paradiso*. It is by no means an easy journey. Dante, who is the leading character in his own poem, is led by the Roman poet Virgil, author of the *Aeneid* (see Chapter 6). (Virgil, too, visits the underworld in the sixth book of his poem.)

Virgil cannot lead Dante into Heaven in the *Paradiso*, since he is a pagan who is barred from salvation. He is thus condemned to Limbo, the first level of Hell, a place of sorrow without torment, populated by virtuous pagans, the great philosophers and authors, unbaptized children, and

Fig. 13.9 Domenico di Michelino, ***Dante and His Poem.*** **1465.** Fresco, 10'6" × 9'7". Florence Cathedral, Italy. To Dante's right is the Inferno, and behind him the seven-stepped hill of Purgatory. To his left is Paradise, imaged as Florence Cathedral, here topped by Brunelleschi's dome (discussed in Chapter 14). Dante himself would never live to see or even imagine the dome.

Materials & Techniques

Buon Fresco

Buon fresco (literally, "true fresh") is a type of wall painting that the Italians learned from Byzantine artists. Although it had been used in earlier cultures, from the Minoans to the Romans, it was perfected in Italy during the fourteenth and fifteenth centuries. Pigments are applied to a wet wall, which made the finished work far less likely to fade or flake than paintings made with the **fresco secco** ("dry" fresco) method. The buon fresco technique permanently bonds the pigment to the wall.

In *buon fresco*, a rough, thick undercoat of plaster is applied to a wall. When the wall has dried, the artist's assistants transfer a full-size drawing of the work—called a **cartoon**—to the wall. Typically, small holes were pricked in the paper cartoon, through which a dotted image of the drawing was transferred through the holes onto the plaster. The resulting drawing on the wall, often elegantly filled out and perfected in charcoal, is known as a **sinopia**.

Assistants next applied a fresh, thin coat of plaster over a section of the sinopia, and pigments, mixed with water, were painted on just before this coat set. Since the paint had to be applied on a wet wall, only sections small enough to be completed in a single day—before the plaster dried—could be worked. The boundaries of these sections, known as **giornata**, literally a "day's work" in Italian, often conform to the contours of major figures and objects. If the area to be painted was complex—a face, for instance—the *giornata* might be no larger. Detailed work was added later, in the *fresco secco* method, as were those pigments that did not generate the chemical reaction necessary to bond the pigment to the wall. Blue was a notable example; it was made from lapis lazuli, which does not chemically combine with wet plaster.

---

others unfit to enter the kingdom of heaven. Among those who inhabit the realm with Virgil are Caesar, Homer, Socrates, and Aristotle. There is no punishment here, and the atmosphere is peaceful, yet sad. Virgil is, in fact, the model of human rationality, and in the *Inferno*, he and Dante study the varieties of human sin. Many of the characters who inhabit Dante's Hell are his contemporaries—the lovers Paolo and Francesca from Ravenna and Rimini, the usurer Reginaldo Scrovegni (patron of the chapel painted by Giotto; see *Closer Look*, pages 338–339), and so on. Dante also makes much of the Guelph/Ghibelline rivalries in his native Florence. He was himself a Guelph, but so divided were the Guelphs among themselves—into factions called the Blacks and the Whites, papal versus imperial bankers—that his efforts to heal their schism as one of the *Priori*, one of the nine leaders of the Florentine commune, resulted in a two-year exile beginning in 1302. Embittered, he never returned to Florence.

Dante's *Inferno* is composed of nine descending rings of sinners undergoing punishment, each more gruesome than the one before it (Fig. **13.10**). In the poem's first canto, the poet is lost in a Dark Wood of Error, where Virgil comes to his rescue, promising to lead him "forth to an eternal place" (see **Reading 13.1**, pages 454). In Hell, the two first encounter sinners whose passion has condemned them to Hell—Paolo and Francesca, whose illicit love was motivated, they tell Dante, by reading Chrétien de Troyes's *Lancelot*. The lovers are forever condemned to unreconciled love, to touch each other but never consummate their feelings. In the next ring are the gluttonous, condemned to wallow like pigs in their own excrement. Sinners, in other words, are punished not *for* their sins but *by* their sins. Dante finds intellectual dishonesty more sinful than any sin of passion, and thus flatterers,

hypocrites, and liars occupy the next lower rings of hell. The violent are further down, immersed for eternity in boiling blood. And finally, at the very bottom of the pit, imprisoned

Fig. 13.10 Plan of Dante's Inferno.

in ice "like straws in glass," are the traitors. Among the lowest of the low are Guelphs and Ghibellines from all over Tuscany who betrayed their cities' well-being. Finally, in Canto 34, Dante once again integrates the pagan and Christian worlds as Satan himself chews on the worst of all traitors—Judas (thought to have betrayed Jesus) and Brutus and Cassius (assassins of Julius Caesar) (Reading 13.2):

READING 13.2

from Dante, *Inferno*, Canto 34

. . .With what a sense of awe I saw his head
towering above me! for it had three faces:[1]
one was in front, and it was fiery red;

the other two, as weirdly wonderful,
merged with it from the middle of each shoulder
to the point where all converged at the top of the skull;

the right was something between white and bile;
the left was about the color one observes
on those who live along the banks of the Nile.

Under each head two wings rose terribly,
their span proportioned to so gross a bird:
I never saw such sails upon the sea.

They were not feathers—their texture and their form
were like a bat's wings—and he beat them so
that three winds blew from him in one great storm:

it is these winds that freeze all Cocytus.
He wept from his six eyes, and down three chins
the tears ran mixed with bloody froth and pus.[2]

In every mouth he worked a broken sinner
between his rake-like teeth. Thus he kept three
in eternal pain at his eternal dinner.

For the one in front the biting seemed to play
no part at all compared to the ripping: at times
the whole skin of his back was flayed away.

"That soul that suffers most," explained my Guide,
"is Judas[3] Iscariot, he who kicks his legs
on the fiery chin and has his head inside.

Of the other two, who have their heads thrust forward,
the one who dangles down from the black face
is Brutus: note how he writhes without a word.

And there, with the huge and sinewy arms,[4] is the soul
of Cassius. But the night is coming on
and we must go, for we have seen the whole.". . .

[1]**three faces:** Numerous interpretations of these three faces exist. What is essential to all explanation is that they be seen as perversions of the qualities of the Trinity.

[2]**bloody froth and pus:** The gore of the sinners he chews which is mixed with his slaver (saliva).

[3]**Judas:** Note how closely his punishment is patterned on that of the Simoniacs (Canto XIX).

[4]**huge and sinewy arms:** The Cassius who betrayed Caesar was more generally described in terms of Shakespeare's "lean and hungry look." Another Cassius is described by Cicero (*Catiline* III) as huge and sinewy. Dante probably confused the two.

The rhyme scheme of the *Divine Comedy* is **terza rima**—an interlocking three-line pattern invented by Dante that goes a/b/a, b/c/b, c/d/c, and so on. (The translator here has chosen to sacrifice the melodic harmonies of Dante's original in the interest of readability and accuracy and has foregone the interlocking rhyme, rhyming only the first and third lines of each stanza.) Just as Satan has three heads, just as there are three consummate sinners in his jaws, the three-line stanza is part of a numerological pattern in the poem. Each of the three books is composed of 33 cantos, to which Dante has added an introductory canto, for a total of 100—a number signifying perfection. There are nine circles of Hell (three squared), nine circles of penitents in Purgatory, and nine spheres of Heaven.

In the universe of the *Divine Comedy* (Fig. **13.11**), Virgil, as the embodiment of rationality, can take Dante no further than Hell and Purgatory, since in order to enter Paradise, faith must triumph over reason, something impossible for the pagan Roman. Dante's guide through Paradise is Beatrice, the love of his life. Beatrice was the daughter of the Florentine nobleman Folco Portinari, and Dante first saw her when she was nine years old and he was eight. He describes meeting her in his first major work, *La Vita Nuova*: "love ruled my soul . . . and began to hold such sway over me . . . that it was necessary for me to do completely all his pleasure. He commanded me often that I should

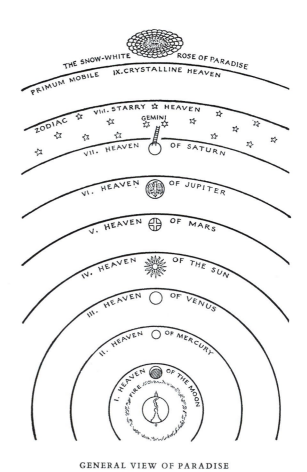

GENERAL VIEW OF PARADISE

Fig. 13.11 Plan of Dante's Universe.

endeavor to see this youthful angel, and I saw her in such noble and praiseworthy deportment that truly of her might be said these words of the poet Homer—*She appeared to be born not of mortal man but of God.*"

Dante wrote these words in 1293. Ten years earlier, when she was 18, Beatrice had entered into a marriage, arranged when she was eight, with Simone di Bardi. It lasted only seven years, ending in her death at age 25. Dante's love for her was, then, the classic love of the courtier for his lady, marked by an unconsummated physical desire necessarily transformed into a spiritual longing, a longing he finally imagines, at the end of the *Paradiso*, as a perfect circle (**Reading 13.3**):

READING 13.3

from Dante, *Paradiso*, Canto 33

. . . But oh how much my words miss my conception,
which is itself so far from what I saw
that to call it feeble would be rank deceptional
O Light Eternal fixed in Itself alone,
by Itself alone understood, which from Itself
loves and glows, self-knowing and self-known;
that second aureole which shone forth in Thee,
conceived as a reflection of the first—
or which appeared so to my scrutiny—
seemed in Itself of Its own coloration
to be painted with man's image. I fixed my eyes
on that alone in rapturous contemplation.

Like a geometer wholly dedicated
to squaring the circle, but who cannot find,
think as he may, the principle indicated—

so did I study the supernal face.
I yearned to know just how our image merges
into that circle, and how it there finds place;

but mine were not the wings for such a flight.
Yet, as I wished, the truth I wished for came
cleaving my mind in a great flash of light.

Here my powers rest from their high fantasy,
but already I could feel my being turned—
instinct and intellect balanced equally

as in a wheel whose motion nothing jars—
by the Love that moves the Sun and the other stars.

Dante's physical desire has been transformed into a spiritual longing that has led him to a comprehension of God's love. So ends the *Divine Comedy*, in a vision of humankind woven into the very substance and coloration of God, a vision so powerful that Dante can barely find words to express it.

THE BLACK DEATH AND ITS AFTERMATH

In 1316 and 1317, not long before Dante's death, crop failures across Europe resulted in the greatest famine the continent had ever known. For two summers, the sun rarely shone (no one knew that huge volcanic eruptions thousands of miles away in Indonesia had sent vast clouds of ash into the atmosphere). Furthermore, between 1000 and 1300, the continent's population had doubled to a point where it probably exceeded its ability to feed itself even in the best of times. In these dark years, which were followed by a century-long cooling period marked by too much rain to allow for good grain harvests, common people were lucky to eat, let alone eat well. Then, in December 1347, rats infested with fleas carrying bubonic plague arrived on the island of Sicily. They were carried on four Genoese ships that had set sail from Kaffa, a Genoese trading center on the Black Sea.

Since 1346, Kaffa had been under siege by Huns intent on taking control of east–west trade routes. But the Huns had fallen victim to the plague themselves, infected by traders from China, where beginning in 1334 as many as 5 million people had died. The Hun siege collapsed under the plague's scourge, but the Huns catapulted the diseased corpses of their dead into Kaffa. The four Genoese ships escaped, believing they were free of infection. Unfortunately, this was not true, and soon after the ships arrived in Sicily, the contagion spread through the port cities of Venice, Genoa, and Pisa. An already severely weakened population was almost pitifully vulnerable. Within months, the disease spread northward, through the ports of Venice, Genoa, and Pisa, across Italy, southern France, and eastern Spain.

The disease began in the lymph glands of the groin or armpits, which slowly filled with pus and turned black. The inflammations were called *buboes*—hence the name *bubonic plague*—and their black color lent the plague its other name, the *Black Death*. Since it was carried by rodents, which were commonplace even in wealthy homes, hardly anyone was spared. It was an egalitarian disease—archbishops, dukes, lords of the manor, merchants, laborers, and peasants fell equally before it. For those who survived the pandemic, life seemed little more than an ongoing burial service. In many towns, traditional funeral services were abandoned, and the dead were buried in mass graves. By 1350, all of Europe, with the exception of a few territories far from traditional trade routes, was devastated by the disease (Map **13.3**, on page 444). In Tuscany, the death rate in the cities was near 60 percent. In Florence, on June 24, 1348, the feast day of the city's patron saint, John the Baptist, 1,800 people reportedly died, and another 1,800 the next day—about 4 percent of the city's population in two days' time. Severe outbreaks of the plague erupted again in 1363, 1388–90, and 1400.

The impact of the Black Death on the popular imagination cannot be overstated. Among the most extreme reactions was that of the **flagellants**, penitents who marched from town to town beating themselves, in the belief that such behavior might atone for the human sins they were sure had caused the plague. But the social disruption that the flagellants created paled beside the outbreak of violent anti-Semitism across Europe. On October 30, 1348, officials at the village of Chatel, in the

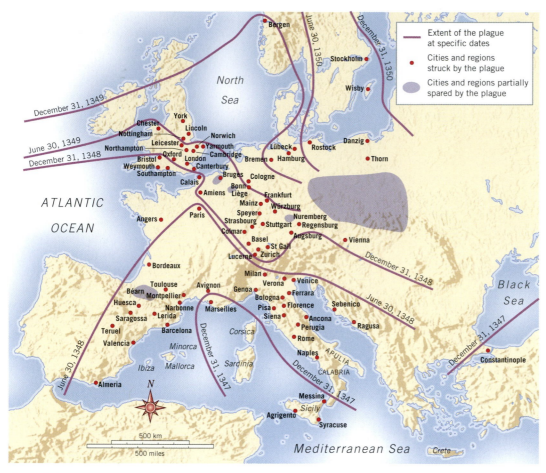

Map 13.3 Spread of the Black Death. 1347–50. Between 1347 and 1350, 30 to 50 percent of Europe's population—about 25 million people—died of the bubonic plague.

French Alps near Geneva, arrested and tortured a Jew named Agimet [ah-zhee-MEH], forcing a false confession that he had been sent by the local rabbi to poison the drinking water of Venice, Calabria, Apulia, and Toulouse. Soon, in Spain, France, and particularly Switzerland and Germany, the citizenry began to murder their Jewish neighbors. In early January 1349, in Basel, a number of Jews were burned. A few weeks later, on Saint Valentine's Day, in Strasbourg, 900 of the town's 1,884 Jews were burned, the rest banned from the city. In Speyer, Augsburg, Stuttgart, Regensburg, Bonn, Mainz, and town after town, the persecutions continued. In July, in Frankfurt, the Jews set their own houses on fire when they were attacked, causing much of the city to burn. The need to find a scapegoat for the plague spurred on the general population, but it seems likely that officials and city leaders, well aware that the Jews were being blamed for something they had nothing to do with, allowed these **pogroms** (massacres of Jews) to occur as a way to eliminate their own personal debts and capture Jewish wealth for themselves, much as Count Emicho of Leiningen had done during the First Crusade (see Chapter 10).

More subtle than this wave of violence were the lasting psychological effects of the epidemic, including the doubt cast upon the Church's belief in divine justice. Even more pronounced was a growing social obsession with death. A good example is a Book of Hours commissioned by Bonne of Luxembourg, wife of the Dauphin of France, from her court illuminator, Jean Le Noir, at some point probably not long before her own death from the plague in 1348 (Fig. **13.12**). On the left page, three horsemen contemplate three cadavers in increasing states of decay on the right page. One horseman brings a handkerchief to his nose to fight off the stench. The cadavers address the horsemen: "What you are we were and what we are you will be!" The artist's depiction of the human body in decay is astonishingly realistic—especially in light of the Church ban on performing autopsies. It is as if, in making us confront death, the artist is determined to bring us face-to-face with the ultimate truth of things.

Literature after the Black Death: Boccaccio's *Decameron*

The frank treatment of reality found in the visual arts carried over into literature, where the direct language of the vernacular proved an especially appropriate vehicle for rendering truth. The *Decameron*, or "Work of Ten Days," is a collection of framed prose tales in the manner of *The Thousand and One*

Fig. 13.12 Jean Le Noir, pages with *The Three Living* (left) and *The Three Dead* (right), from the *Psalter and Book of Hours of Bonne of Luxembourg*. Before 1349. Grisaille, color, gilt, and brown ink on vellum, 5″ × 3½″. The Metropolitan Museum of Art, The Cloisters Collection. 1969 (69.86). Image copyright © The Metropolitan Museum of Art/Art Resource, NY. Note the naturalism of the birds that decorate the margins of the manuscript.

Nights and Nezami's *Haft Paykar* (see Chapter 9). The Florentine writer Giovanni Boccaccio (1313–75), who lived through the plague, sets the stage for the 100 prose stories of the collection with a startlingly direct description of Florence in the ravages of the disease (**Reading 13.4a**):

READING 13.4a

from Boccaccio, *Decameron*

The virulence of the plague was all the greater in that it was communicated by the sick to the well by contact, not unlike fire when dry or fatty things are brought near it. But the evil was still worse. Not only did conversation and familiarity with the diseased spread the malady and even cause death, but the mere touch of the clothes or any other object the sick had touched or used, seemed to spread the pestilence. . . .

Because of such happenings and many others of a like sort, various fears and superstitions arose among the survivors, almost all of which tended toward one end—to flee from the sick and whatever had belonged to them. In this way each man thought to be safeguarding his own health. Some among them were of the opinion that by living temperately and guarding against excess of all kinds, they could do much toward avoiding the danger; and forming a band they lived away from the rest of the world. Gathering in those houses where no one had been ill and living was more comfortable, they shut themselves in. They ate moderately of the best that could be had and drank excellent wines, avoiding all luxuriousness. With music and whatever other delights they could have, they lived together in this fashion, allowing no one to speak to them and avoiding news either of death or sickness from the outer world.

Others, arriving at a contrary conclusion, held that plenty of drinking and enjoyment, singing and free living and the gratification of the appetite in every possible way, letting the devil take the hindmost, was the best preventative of such a malady; and as far as they could, they suited the action to the word. Day and night they went from one tavern to another drinking and carousing unrestrainedly. . . .

Meanwhile, in the midst of the affliction and misery that had befallen the city, even the reverend authority of divine and human law had almost crumbled and fallen into decay, for its ministers and executors, like other men, had either died or sickened, or had been left so entirely without assistants that they were unable to attend to their duties. As a result everyone had leave to do as he saw fit. . . .

It used to be common, as it is still, for women, friends and neighbors of a dead man, to gather in his house and mourn there with his people. . . . Now, as the plague gained in violence, these customs were either modified or laid aside altogether. . . . It was a rare occasion for a corpse to be followed to church by more than ten or twelve mourners—not the usual respectable citizens, but a class of vulgar grave-diggers who called themselves "sextons" and did these services for a price. . . .

More wretched still were the circumstances of the common people and, for a great part, of the middle class, for, confined to their homes either by hope of safety or by poverty, and restricted to their own sections, they fell sick daily by thousands. There, devoid of help or care, they died almost without redemption. A great many breathed their last in the public streets, day and night; a large number perished in their homes, and it was only by the stench of their decaying bodies that they proclaimed their death to their neighbors. Everywhere the city was teeming with corpses. A general course was now adopted by the people, more out of fear of contagion than of any charity they felt toward the dead. Alone, or with the assistance of whatever bearers they could muster, they would drag the corpses out of their homes and pile them in front of the doors, where often, of a morning, countless bodies might be seen. Biers were sent for. When none was to be had, the dead were laid upon ordinary boards, two or three at once. It was not infrequent to see a single bier carrying husband and wife, two or three brothers, father and son, and others besides. . . .

So many bodies were brought to the churches every day that the consecrated ground did not suffice to hold them, particularly according to the ancient custom of giving each corpse its individual place. Huge trenches were dug in the crowded churchyards and the new dead were piled in them, layer upon layer, like merchandise in the hold of a ship. . . .

Boccaccio describes a world in virtual collapse. The social breakdown caused by the plague is especially evident in the widespread death of the ruling class and the rise of the class of men who called themselves "sextons," technically guardians of the church edifice, treasures, and vestments, but now a vile band of mercenary gravediggers. All tradition has been abandoned.

Nevertheless, a good deal of the power of Boccaccio's book is that in this atmosphere of dark matter-of-factness, he inaugurates something entirely different, suggesting that society might be ready to be reborn:

[O]n a Tuesday morning after Divine Service the venerable church of Santa Maria Novella [see Fig. 12.27] was almost deserted save for the presence of seven young ladies habited sadly[1] in keeping with the season. All were connected either by blood or at least as friends or neighbors; and fair and of good understanding were they all, as also of noble birth, gentle manners, and a modest sprightliness. In age none exceeded twenty-eight, or fell short of eighteen years. . . .

[1] **habited sadly:** dressed in mourning

One of the citizens, Pampinea [pam-pee-NEH-ee-ah], observing the dire nature of their plight, makes this suggestion:

I should deem it most wise in us, our case being what it is, if, as many others have done before us, and are still doing, we were to quit this place, and, shunning like death the evil example of others, betake ourselves to the country, and there live as honorable women on one of the estates, of which none of us has any lack, with all cheer of festal gathering and other delights, so long as in no particular we overstep the bounds of reason. There we shall hear the chant of birds, have sight of verdant hills and plains, of cornfields undulating like the sea, of trees of a thousand sorts; there also we shall have a larger view of the heavens, which, however harsh toward us, yet deny not their eternal beauty; things far fairer for eyes to rest on than the desolate walls of our city. Moreover, we shall there breathe a fresher air, find ampler store of things meet [fitting] for such as live in these times, have fewer causes of annoy[ance].

Three young men, all of whom the women know, happen to enter the church, and it is determined that they should be invited to join them, even though, as one of the young women mentions, it is well known "that they love some of us here. . . [and] if we take them with us, we may thereby give occasion for scandal and censure. . . ."

Thus, the entire enterprise takes place in an atmosphere of potential scandal—certainly an atmosphere outside the bounds of normal social behavior. They enter a new moral space, evidenced by the difference between the Florence they have left behind and their new surroundings:

The estate lay upon a little hill some distance from the nearest highway, and, embowered in shrubberies of divers hues, and other greenery, afforded the eye a pleasant prospect. On the summit of the hill was a palace with galleries, halls and chambers, disposed around a fair and spacious court, each very fair in itself, and the goodlier to see for the gladsome pictures with which it was adorned; the whole set amidst meads and gardens laid out with marvelous art, wells of the coolest water, and vaults of the finest wines, things more suited to dainty drinkers than to sober and honorable women.

The reader is aware that this idyllic island is surrounded by the terror of the Black Death, and that the sensual atmosphere of the setting offers—as arguably some of the best fiction always does—a refuge from the realities of everyday life.

The group determines that each day it will gather together and each will tell a story to entertain the others. As one of the young men, Dioneo [dee-OH-nay-oh], puts it, "I pray you, either address yourselves to make merry, to laugh and sing with me (so far, I mean, as may consist with your dignity), or give me leave to hie me back [return] to the stricken city." Of course, no sooner do they gather together on their first day than Dioneo challenges the ladies' dignity with a tale about a young monk from a monastery "once more saintly . . . than it now is" who one day spies a beautiful young woman gathering herbs in a field (see **Reading 13.5**, pages 455–457, for the tale in its entirety):

> The moment he saw her, he was passionately attacked by carnal desire. He went up to her and began a conversation. One subject led to another, and finally, they came to an understanding; he took the girl to his cell.

Dioneo's stories evoke "some qualms of shame in the minds of the ladies, as was apparent by the modest blush that tinged their faces." But the ladies are also "scarcely able to refrain their mirth." Dioneo is the embodiment of freedom, and his stories represent Boccaccio's own license to exceed the bounds of acceptable literary decorum. Not all of the other 99 tales are as ribald—that is, vulgar and indecent—as this one, but although all ten of the storytellers are aristocrats, a great many of their tales involve people of the lower, especially middle classes, and their characters, in their shrewdness and wit, ingenuity, and resourcefulness, unscrupulous behavior and bawdy desires, introduce into Western literature a kind of social realism previously unexplored. Perhaps reflecting the reality of death that surrounds them, the stories depict daily life as it is truly lived. Boccaccio's stories express the realities of life in a way that the classic tales of medieval chivalry could only intimate. His world is of flesh and blood, not knights in shining armor. If the world of the *Decameron* is a fictitious one, in its penetrating revelation of workings of human psychology, it also represents an unprecedented brand of literary realism.

Petrarch's Sonnets

One of Boccaccio's best friends was the itinerant scholar and poet Francesco Petrarca (1304–74), known as Petrarch (Fig. **13.13**). Raised near Avignon, in France, where the papacy had established itself in 1309 and where it remained through most of Petrarch's lifetime, Petrarch studied at Montpellier and Bologna and traveled throughout northern France, Germany, and Italy. He was always in search of manuscripts that preserved the priceless literary works of antiquity—copying those he could not pry loose from monastic libraries. As he wrote to a friend in 1351, these manuscripts, in a classical Latin and hard for monks to decipher, were in danger of being lost forever:

> It is a state of affairs that has resulted in an incredible loss to scholarship. Books that by their nature are a little hard to understand are no longer multiplied [i.e., copied and distributed], and have ceased to be generally intelligible, and so have sunk into utter neglect, and in the end have perished. This age of ours consequently has let fall, bit by bit, some of the richest and sweetest fruits that the tree of knowledge has yielded; has thrown away the results of the vigils and labors of the most illustrious men of genius, things of more value, I am almost tempted to say, than anything else in the whole world.

It was Petrarch who rediscovered the forgotten works of the Roman orator and statesman Cicero, and his own private library consisted of over 200 classical texts. He persuaded Boccaccio to bring the Greek scholar Leo Pilatus to Venice to teach them to read Greek. Boccaccio learned the language, but, put off by Pilatus's bad manners, Petrarch did not. Both, however, benefited from Pilatus's translation of Homer into Latin prose, as well as from his genealogy of the Greek gods.

Perhaps Petrarch's greatest work was his book of over 300 poems, the *Canzoniere* (*Songbook*), inspired by his love for a woman named Laura, whom he first met in 1327 in Avignon, where he was working for an influential cardinal. She is generally believed to have been the 19-year-old wife of Hugues de Sade. Whether Petrarch ever revealed his love to Laura, or simply poured it into his verses, remains a matter of speculation.

The majority of Petrarch's verses to Laura take the form of the **Italian sonnet**, known also as the **Petrarchan sonnet** because he perfected the form. Petrarch had been deeply influenced by the poetry of the troubadours, written in sonnet form (see Chapter 10). The Petrarchan sonnet is composed of 14 lines divided into two parts: an *octave* of

Fig. 13.13 Andrea Del Castagno, *Francesco Petrarca*. ca. 1450. Fresco transferred to wood, 97 ¼" × 60 ¼". Galleria degli Uffizi, Florence. So great was Petrarch's zeal for the classics that he would become known as the Father of Humanism, the revival of Greco-Roman culture that would come to define the Renaissance in the two centuries to follow.

Troubadour poetry, *p. 346*

eight lines that presents a problem, and a *sestet* of six lines that either attempts to solve the problem or accepts it as unsolvable. The octave is further divided into two four-line *quatrains*. The first presents the problem and the second develops the idea. Many of Petrarch's verses to Laura were composed after her death from the bubonic plague in 1348, and it seems likely that her death motivated Petrarch to circulate them. His devastation is clear in these three lines from Sonnet 338:

> Earth, air, and sea should weep together,
> for the human lineage, once she's gone, becomes
> a meadow stripped of flowers, a gemless ring.

More influential, however, were the pure love poems. One of the most famous of these is Sonnet 134, in which Petrarch explores the complexities of his feelings—all the ambivalence, contradiction, and paradox—in the face of his love for Laura (**Reading 13.6**):

READING 13.6

Petrarch, Sonnet 134

I find no peace, and yet I am not warlike;
I fear and hope, I burn and turn to ice;
I fly beyond the sky, stretch out on earth;
my hands are empty, yet I hold the world.

One holds me prisoner, not locked up, not free;
won't keep me for her own but won't release me;
Love does not kill me, does not loose my chains,
he'd like me dead, he'd like me still ensnared.

I see without my eyes, cry with no tongue,
I want to die and yet I call for help,
hating myself but loving someone else.

I feed on pain, I laugh while shedding tears,
both death and life displease me equally;
and this state, Lady, is because of you.

Such poems would have a lasting influence, especially in the poetry of the English Elizabethan Age, because they seemed to capture all the emotional turbulence of love (see Chapter 19).

Chaucer's Canterbury Tales

The first Englishman to translate Petrarch was Geoffrey Chaucer (ca. 1342–1400). Well-educated, able to read both Ovid and Virgil in the original Latin, Chaucer was a middle-class civil servant and diplomat. In 1368, both he and Petrarch were guests at a wedding in Milan Cathedral, and four years later, he was in Florence, where he probably met Boccaccio. Chaucer's masterwork, *The Canterbury Tales*, is modeled roughly on Boccaccio's *Decameron*, but it is written in verse, not prose, and is composed in **heroic couplets**. Like the *Decameron*, it is a framed collection of stories, this time told by a group of pilgrims traveling from London to the shrine of Saint Thomas à Becket, Archbishop of Canterbury. In 1170, Becket had been murdered in Canterbury Cathedral by followers of King Henry II in a dispute over the rights and privileges of the Church.

Chaucer had planned to write 120 tales. Before his death, he completed only 22 tales and fragments of two others, but they are extraordinary in the range of characters and social types that they portray. Not only are the characters in the stories fully developed, but so are their narrators, and as a result the stories reflect perhaps the most fully developed realism of the era. Consider Chaucer's description of the Wife of Bath (Fig. **13.14**) from the Prologue to the work (**Reading 13.7**):

READING 13.7

from Chaucer, *The Canterbury Tales*, Prologue

A worthy woman there was from near the city
Of Bath, but somewhat deaf, and more's the pity.
For weaving she possessed so great a bent
She outdid the people of Ypres and Ghent.[1]
No other woman dreamed of such a thing
As to precede her at the offering.
Or if any did, she fell in such a wrath
She dried up all the charity in Bath.
She wore fine kerchiefs of old-fashioned air,
And on a Sunday morning, I could swear,
She had ten pounds of linen on her head.
Her stockings were the finest scarlet-red,
Laced tightly, and her shoes were soft and new.
Bold was her face, and fair, and red in hue.
She had been an excellent woman all of her life.
Five men in turn had taken her to wife,
Not counting other youthful company—
But let that pass for now! Over the sea
She'd traveled freely; many a distant stream
She crossed, and visited Jerusalem
Three times. She had been at Rome and at Boulogne,
At Compostella's shrine, and at Cologne.
She'd wandered by the way through many a scene.
Her teeth were set with little gaps between.[2]
Easily on her ambling horse she sat.
She was well wimpled, and she wore a hat
As wide in circuit as a shield or targe,[3]
A skirt swathed up her hips, and they were large.
Upon her feet she wore sharp-roweled spurs.
She was a good fellow; a ready tongue was hers.
All remedies of love she knew by name,
For she had all the tricks of that old game.

[1] **Ypres and Ghent:** Centers of the weaving industry in Flanders.
[2] **teeth . . . gaps between:** For a woman to be gap-toothed was considered a sign of being highly sexed.
[3] **targe:** A type of shield.

Chaucer accomplishes what few writers before him had—he creates character and personality through vivid detail and description. This elaborately dressed, gap-toothed, large-hipped, easy-riding survivor of five husbands comes off as a real person. The tales themselves

Fig. 13.14 Wife of Bath, from Geoffrey Chaucer's *Canterbury Tales* ("The Ellesmere Chaucer"). ca. 1400–05. The Art Archive/Victoria and Albert Museum London/Eileen Tweedy. Illumination on vellum. Victoria & Albert Museum, London. This image is from the earliest complete surviving text of Chaucer's work, which contains 23 portraits of the storytellers.

sometimes rival Boccaccio's in their bawdy realism, but the variety of the pilgrims and the range of their moral characters creates at least as profound a moral world as Boccaccio's, one whose scope even rivals that of Dante. The integrity of the Knight plays against the depravity of the Pardoner, just as the sanctity of the Parson plays against the questionable morals of the Wife of Bath. Chaucer's characters come from all three **estates**, or social ranks—the nobility, the clergy, and the common people—a fact that has led some to refer to his work as an "estates satire," a critique of social relations in his day.

Evolving English Chaucer wrote *The Canterbury Tales* in the English of his day, a language we now call Middle English. After the Norman invasion in 1066, the common people spoke one language—Anglo-Saxon (or Old English)—and the nobility in another, French. The language of the learned continued to be Latin. In Chaucer's time, a new spoken vernacular, Middle English, had supplanted Anglo-Saxon among the common people. It combined elements of French, Anglo-Saxon, and the Scandinavian languages. Chaucer himself spoke French, and that he chose to write *The Canterbury Tales* in the Middle English of his day (actually a London dialect, one of about five dialects used across Britain at the time) is a significant development in the history of the English language.

Before 1385, roughly the time that Chaucer began the *Tales*, English had replaced French as the language of instruction for children. By 1362, the Chief Justice opened Parliament with a speech in English. That same year, Parliament enacted the Statute of Pleading, providing that "All pleas which shall be pleaded in his [the King's] courts whatsoever, before any of his justices whatsoever . . . shall be pleaded, shewed, defended, answered, debated, and judged in the English tongue." Still, the records of the pleas were kept in Latin. By mid-century, then, even the nobility, though raised speaking French, also spoke English. Chaucer's London dialect became the dominant one thanks largely to William Caxton, the London printer of Chaucer's works, who used the London dialect—the English of Britain's intellectual, political, and commercial center—in all his publications, thus making it the standard.

To provide an idea of the history of the language, here are the opening lines of the General Prologue of *The Canterbury Tales* in Middle English, as Chaucer wrote them, followed by a modern rendition.

> *Whan that Aprill with his shoures soot*
>   When April with its sweet-smelling showers
> *The droghte of March hath perced to the roote,*
>   Has pierced the drought of March to the root,
> *And bathed every veyne in swich licour*
>   And bathed every vein (of the plants) in such liquid
> *Of which vertu engendred is the flour;*
>   By the power of which the flower is created;
> *Whan Zephirus eek with his sweete breeth*
>   When the West Wind also with its sweet breath,
> *Inspired hath in every holt and heeth*
>   In every wood and field has breathed life into
> *The tendre croppes, and the yonge sonne*
>   The tender new leaves, and the young sun
> *Hath in the Ram his half cours yronne,*
>   Has run half its course in Aries,
> *And smale foweles maken melodye,*
>   And small fowls make melody,
> *That slepen al the nyght with open ye*
>   Those that sleep all the night with open eyes
> *(So priketh hem Nature in hir corages),*
>   (So Nature incites them in their hearts),
> *Thanne longen folk to goon on pilgrimages. . . .*
>   Then folk long to go on pilgrimages. . . .

Chaucer understood the power of this new vernacular English to evoke the reality of fourteenth-century English life, and his keen ear for the cadences and phrasings of actual speech underscores the reality of his characters and the tales they tell.

Women in Late Medieval Society

The seven women in Boccaccio's *Decameron* and characters like Chaucer's Wife of Bath represent the increasing social prominence of women in medieval society. This is no doubt at least in part a reflection of the growing role of the Virgin in medieval religious life, and her prominence helped raise the dignity of women in general. By the thirteenth century, women were active in all trades, especially the food and clothing industries; they belonged to guilds, and increasingly had the opportunity to go to school and learn to read, at least in their vernacular languages. They were, however, still generally excluded from the learned professions of medicine and law, and they performed the same work as men for wages on the average 25 percent lower.

Women in Boccaccio and Chaucer Neither Boccaccio nor Chaucer could ever be called a feminist—in fact, both depict misogynist characters—but both do recognize these new women as real forces in contemporary social life. Chaucer's women leave prevalent and prescriptive views of women's proper roles far behind. Boccaccio's story of Filippa, told by Filostrata [fee-loh-STRAY-tah] on the sixth day, is another case in point. It recounts how Filippa is charged by her husband with the crime of adultery, punishable by death in the town of Prato where they live, a crime to which she freely admits. But in court she argues that the law represents a double standard, one for men, quite another for women, and that, further, laws should be made by the consent of the people, and no woman ever consented to the death penalty for giving "pleasure to many more people than men ever could." If, she argues, she has always satisfied her husband's every desire,

> what was I to do with what was left over? Indeed, what am I to do with it? Throw it to the dogs? Isn't it far better to give enjoyment to some gentleman who loves me more than his life, than to let it go to waste or ruin?

The court agrees, the law is overturned, and Filippa is victorious (See Reading **13.8**, page 457 for the tale).

Boccaccio did, in fact, write a book explicitly "for the ladies," his *De Claris Mulieribus* [deh KLA-rees moo-lee-YEH-ree-bus] (*Concerning Famous Women*), a work of Latin prose published in 1362. The first collection of biographies in Western literature dedicated solely to women, it consists of 106 entries beginning with "Eve Our First Mother." It then moves on to both exemplary and notorious figures from history and mythology as well as from among Boccaccio's own contemporaries. The book was immensely popular across Europe and survives in over 100 manuscripts—an unusually high number. It was nevertheless an extremely misogynist text that assumes women's inferiority to men from the outset.

Christine de Pizan: An Early Feminist Women began to play an increasingly active role in the courts of Europe. In 1404, Philip the Bold, Duke of Burgundy, commissioned Christine de Pizan (1364–ca. 1430) to write a biography of his deceased brother, titled *The Book of the Deeds and Good Manners of the Wise King Charles V*. Christine had been educated at the French court, apparently against her mother's wishes, by her father, a prominent Venetian physician, who had been appointed court astrologer to King Charles V. Her husband, secretary and notary to the king, further promoted her education. But when her father and husband died, she needed to support three children, a niece, and her mother. To do so she became the first female professional writer in European history.

As she gradually established her reputation as a writer, she worked as a copyist and illustrator, and her first successes were books of poems and ballads. In 1402, she made her reputation by attacking as misogynistic and demeaning to women the popular thirteenth-century poem the *Roman de la Rose* ("Romance of the Rose") (see Chapter 10). Two years later, in her *Book of the City of Ladies*, she again attacked male misogyny by recounting the accomplishments of women throughout the ages in an allegorical debate between herself and Lady Reason, Lady Rectitude, and Lady Justice (Fig. **13.15**). Her most immediate source was Boccaccio's *Concerning Famous Women*, but her treatment is completely different, treating only good women and freely mixing pagan and Christian examples. Her city's queen is the Virgin Mary herself, a figure whose importance confirms the centrality of women to Christianity. Thus, she opens the book by wondering why men are so inclined to demean women (**Reading 13.9**):

READING 13.9

from Christine de Pizan, *Book of the City of Ladies*

[I wondered] how it happened that so many different men—and learned men among them—have been and are so inclined to express both in speaking and in their treatises and writings so many wicked insults about women and their behavior. Not only one or two . . . but, more generally, from the treatises of all philosophers and poets and from all the orators—it would take too long to mention their names—it seems that they all speak from one and the same mouth. Thinking deeply about these matters, I began to examine my character and conduct as a natural woman and, similarly, I considered other women whose company I frequently kept, princesses, great ladies, women of the middle and lower classes, who had graciously told me of their most private and intimate thoughts, hoping that I could judge impartially and in good conscience whether the testimony of so many notable men could be true. To the best of my knowledge, no matter how long I confronted or dissected the problem, I could not see or realize how their claims could be true when compared to the natural behavior and character of women.

She then turns to God for guidance and is granted a dream vision in which the three allegorical ladies encourage her to build an Ideal City, peopled with a variety of women, from Sappho to her own name-saint, all of whom help her to redefine what it means to be female.

Christine de Pizan Glorifies Joan of Arc De Pizan was writing in the context of the so-called Hundred Years' War between England and France, generally dated at 1337 to 1429. The origins of the war went all the way back to 1216, when the English Normans (who had invaded England from France in 1066) finally lost control of all their possessions on the continent. In the early fourteenth century, the French throne was increasingly contested, and the English king proclaimed himself as the rightful heir. Thus the stage was set for war, driven

Fig. 13.15 Anonymous, *La Cité des Dames de Christine de Pizan*. ca. 1410. Illumination on parchment, page size 4 3/4″ × 7″. Bibliothèque Nationale, Paris. On the left stands Christine de Pizan, engaged in composition while receiving the visit of Reason, Honesty, and Justice. On the right, Christine and one of the royal ladies build the Ideal City.

largely by the English Normans' desire to recapture their homeland in Normandy. The war was fought entirely on French soil, and although the English were usually outnumbered by as much as three to one, they were generally victorious because of two technological innovations. First, the longbow's six-foot length allowed the English infantry to pierce the chain-mail armor of the French. Second, the introduction of gunpowder and cannon made armor altogether irrelevant. Suddenly the model of heroic hand-to-hand combat, the basis of the chivalric ideal, was obsolete, and with it, the codes of loyalty, honor, and courage upon which the entire French literary tradition since the *Song of Roland* had been based.

Even more damaging to this masculine tradition was the fact that it was a woman, Joan of Arc, who saved the French. A 17-year-old peasant girl, she approached the French king and begged him to allow her to obey the voices of the saints who ordered her to drive the English out of France. Christine de Pizan, who had retired to an abbey in 1418, after the arrival of the Burgundian troops in Paris had forced her and many others to seek protection outside the city, was overjoyed. The year before her death, de Pizan wrote a 61-stanza poem that glorified Joan's achievements (rendered in prose in **Reading 13.10**):

READING 13.10

Christine de Pizan, *Tale of Joan of Arc*

I, Christine, who have wept for eleven years in a walled abbey . . . begin to laugh heartily for joy . . .

Oh! What honour for the female sex! It is perfectly obvious that God has special regard for it when all these wretched people who destroyed the whole Kingdom—now recovered and made safe by a woman, something that 5000 men could not have done—and the traitors [have been] exterminated. Before the event they would scarcely have believed this possible.

A little girl of sixteen (isn't this something quite supernatural?) who does not even notice the weight of the arms she bears—indeed her whole upbringing seems to have prepared her for this, so strong and resolute is she! And her enemies go fleeing before her, not one of them can stand up to her. She does all this in full view of everyone, and drives her enemies out of France, recapturing castles and towns. Never did anyone see greater strength, even in hundreds or thousands of men!

For Christine, Joan's achievement was as much a victory for women as for France. Christine, though, would not live to see her captured by the English, betrayed, probably by Burgundian French, then tried and executed as a heretic in March 1431. Joan's mysticism, like that of Hildegard of Bingen before her (see Chapter 10), undermined the authority and (male) hierarchy of the Church. But the chief charge against her was cross-dressing! She dared challenge, in other words, the human-constructed gender roles that the Church fathers assumed to be the will of God. Still, probably no other figure better sums up the growing self-assurance of women in late medieval society and the sense of personal worth—both male and female—that would increasingly inform European society as the fifteenth century unfolded.

The Dance of Death

We do not know who, in 1424, painted a series of pictures representing a Dance of Death along the walls backing the **charnel houses**—houses where the bones of the dead were stored—that ran the length of the Cemetery of the Holy Innocents in Paris on the Rue de la Ferronnerie. These paintings were undoubtedly inspired by a clergy bent on encouraging Christian feeling and sentiment in their parishioners and on reminding them of their Christian duties in the face of certain death. Every rank and order of human society was represented in this procession, the pope and emperor at its head (Fig. **13.16**), a fool and an author pulling up the rear. Verses attributed to the Chancellor of the University of Paris, Jean de Charlier de Gerson, accompany the paintings:

Fig. 13.16 *Dance of Death*. ca. 1490. Woodcut. Library of Congress, Washington, D.C. Lessing J. Rosenwald Collection. This print is one of a series copying the images on the charnel house walls of the Cemetery of the Holy Innocents.

> By divine sentence
> No matter what your estate
> Whether good or evil, you will be
> Eaten by worms. Alas, look at us,
> Dead, stinking, and rotten.
> You will be like this, too.

The toll the Black Death wreaked on the arts was indeed devastating. In Siena, Giovanni Pisano and Ambrogio Lorenzetti were among the many victims of the Black Death. In Florence, almost all of Giotto's best students succumbed. But since the plague destroyed people and not possessions, the enormous decrease in population resulted in a corresponding increase in per capita wealth, and those who survived invested in religious art—chapels and hospitals, altarpieces and votive statues—in gratitude for being spared or in the hope of preventing future infection. Painters and sculptors turned their attention to the representation of the sufferings of Christ, the sorrows rather than the joys of the Virgin, and the miracles of the saints. The Art of Dying Well and the Triumph of Death became important themes in art and literature. The new humanism, or belief in the value of individuals and their human potential, so evident in the realist art of Giotto and in the writings of Petrarch, Boccaccio, and Chaucer, suggests that the plague stimulated the Western imagination perhaps more than it defeated it.

Nevertheless, the specter of death, which the Black Death so thoroughly embedded in the popular imagination, haunted Western society for at least 400 years. The Cemetery of the Holy Innocents, which was the size of a large city block and occupied the area of Paris today known as Les Halles, accommodated many of the dead, but by the middle of the eighteenth century, the cemetery was almost literally exploding with corpses. Many people, who now possessed at least a rudimentary understanding of infection, argued that this cemetery was a breeding ground of disease. On December 1, 1780, a cellar wall on the Rue de la Ferronnerie burst, releasing noxious gases and fluids into the streets, and the cemetery was permanently closed. The charnel houses were demolished—along with the Dance of Death images that covered their walls. As for the dead, they were reburied in catacombs dug from ancient quarries beneath the city streets, today a tourist site.

This vast removal of the dead amounted to a banishment of the specter of death from the daily life of the city, culminating finally, in 1804, with the Emperor Napoleon's Imperial Decree on Burials. Henceforth, burial was banned within the city. Each corpse would have an individual plot, permanent if space allowed, in one of four garden environments outside the city proper—among them, the bucolic Père Lachaise Cemetery, which even today attracts Parisians to its hills and paths. All were designed to aid in absorbing what the Ministry of Interior called "cadaverous miasmata." It was envisioned that in these new Elysian Fields, children would periodically scatter flowers over the tombs. Thus, the idea of the cemetery as a kind of landscape garden, as we know it today, was born. ■

How do the Sienese and Florentine republics compare?

Tuscany was dominated by two competing city-states, Siena and Florence. Both were republics, and central to their success was a new form of government in which church and state were closely aligned. Siena established itself in 1125 as a free commune. What is a commune? By the twelfth century, Florence was the center of textile production in the Western world and played a central role in European trade markets. As in Siena, it was the city's bankers and money lenders who made Florence such a vital player in world trade. Also as in Siena, in Florence, the guilds controlled the commune. How would you define a guild?

What came to replace the Byzantine style of painting in Italy?

In both Siena and Florence, artists began to break from the Byzantine style. One of the first was Duccio, who began to incorporate the Gothic tendency to naturalism into his *Maestà*, painted for Siena's cathedral. Even more naturalistic is Simone Martini's *Maestà*, painted for the city hall. How would you compare them? Florence, too, had its master painters of the Virgin, Cimabue and Giotto. In what did the latter exceed the others in terms of the naturalism of his art?

Who was Dante?

In the early twelfth century, writers across Europe began to address their works to a wider lay audience and to write in the vernacular. How would you define the vernacular? What does it imply about this new literature's audience? One of the greatest medieval Italian vernacular writers was the poet Dante Alighieri, whose *Divine Comedy* records the travels of the Christian soul from Hell to Purgatory and finally to Salvation in three books—the *Inferno*, *Purgatorio*, and *Paradiso*. How does Dante's poem reflect the epic tradition? Consider its relation to, for instance, the *Odyssey* and the *Aeneid*.

What effects did the plague have on European consciousness?

In December 1347, bubonic plague arrived in Sicily. Within months, the disease spread northward, through Europe. In Tuscany, the death rate in the cities ran somewhere near 60 percent. Many blamed the Jews, who were widely persecuted. One of the most remarkable accounts of the plague opens Boccaccio's *Decameron*, a collection of stories told by young noblemen and women who escaped Florence for the countryside. Perhaps reflecting the reality of death that surrounds them, the stories are themselves imbued with a realistic representation of life as it is truly lived. After the Black Death, the realistic treatment of life continued in vernacular literature. The sonnets of Petrarch, composed in memory of the poet's beloved Laura, inaugurate one of the most important poetic forms in Western literature. Chaucer's *Canterbury Tales*, modeled on Boccaccio's *Decameron*, approach life in the Middle Ages with a realism even more profound than Boccaccio's. Many of both Boccaccio's and Chaucer's characters are women. How do their women and Christine de Pizan's help to establish new roles for women?

PRACTICE MORE Get flashcards for images and terms and review chapter material with quizzes at **www.myartslab.com**

GLOSSARY

buon fresco A type of painting applied to a wet plastered wall.

cartoon A full-size preparatory drawing for a final artwork, especially a fresco or painting.

charnel house A building in which bones or bodies of the dead were stored.

commune A collective of people gathered together for the common good.

estate A social rank, namely, the nobility, the clergy, and the common people.

flagellant A penitent who beats himself or herself to atone for sin.

fresco secco A type of fresco painting applied to a dry wall.

gesso A thick medium made of glue, gypsum, and/or chalk that creates a smooth, sealed ground for painting.

giornata The boundaries of the small sections of fresco that could be completed in a single day; often conformed to the contours of major figures and objects.

guild An association or group of people with like-minded interests or skills.

heroic couplet A rhyming pair of iambic pentameter lines.

Italian sonnet A Petrarchan sonnet.

Petrarchan sonnet A sonnet composed of 14 lines divided into two parts: an *octave* of eight lines that presents a problem, and a *sestet* of six lines that either attempts to solve the problem or accepts it as unsolvable.

pogrom A massacre of Jews.

sinopia A preliminary drawing for a fresco that is often elegantly filled out and perfected in charcoal.

stylus A hard-pointed, pen-shaped instrument.

tempera A type of painting process using a water-soluble material, such as egg yolks, instead of oil paint.

terza rima An interlocking three-line pattern invented by Dante that uses the pattern a/b/a, b/c/b, c/d/c, and so on.

vernacular The language spoken in the streets.

READINGS

from Dante, *Inferno*, Canto I

Dante wrote the Divine Comedy *between 1308 and 1321, completing the* Inferno *by about 1312. The whole recounts the journey of Dante (the character, as opposed to the author) into the afterlife in three books—the* Inferno, Purgatorio, *and* Paradiso—*accompanied, at least as far as he can go, by the Roman poet Virgil. In the* Inferno, *Dante visits Hell. Each book is composed of 33 cantos, with the addition of one extra canto, the first, presented in full below, which serves as a prelude to the entire work. These numbers are symbolic. The number 3 is especially important. The poem is written in tercets, three-line stanzas. There are 9 (3 × 3) circles or spheres in each realm. And the number reflects, as well, the divine Trinity.*

Midway in our life's journey, I went astray
   from the straight road and woke to find myself
   alone in a dark wood. How shall I say   3
what wood that was! I never saw so drear,
   so rank, so arduous a wilderness!
   Its very memory gives a shape to fear.   6
Death could scarce be more bitter than that place!
   But since it came to good, I will recount
   all that I found revealed there by God's grace.   9
How I came to it I cannot rightly say,
   so drugged and loose with sleep had I become
   when I first wandered there from the True Way.   12
But at the far end of that valley of evil
   whose maze had sapped my very heart with fear
   I found myself before a little hill   15
and lifted up my eyes. Its shoulders glowed
   already with the sweet rays of that planet
   whose virtue leads men straight on every road,   18
and the shining strengthened me against the fright
   whose agony had wracked the lake of my heart
   through all the terrors of that piteous night.   21
Just as a swimmer, who with his last breath
   flounders ashore from perilous seas, might turn
   to memorize the wide water of his death—   24
so did I turn, my soul still fugitive
   from death's surviving image, to stare down
   that pass that none had ever left alive.   27
And there I lay to rest from my heart's race
   till calm and breath returned to me. Then rose
   and pushed up that dead slope at such a pace   30
each footfall rose above the last. And lo!
   almost at the beginning of the rise
   I faced a spotted Leopard, all tremor and flow   33
and gaudy pelt. And it would not pass, but stood
   so blocking my every turn that time and again
   I was on the verge of turning back to the wood.   36
This fell at the first widening of the dawn
   as the sun was climbing Aries with those stars
   that rode with him to light the new creation.   39
Thus the holy hour and the sweet season
   of commemoration did much to arm my fear
   of that bright murderous beast with their good omen.   42
Yet not so much but what I shook with dread
   at sight of a great Lion that broke upon me
   raging with hunger, its enormous head   45

held high as if to strike a mortal terror
   into the very air. And down his track,
   a She-Wolf drove upon me, a starved horror   48
ravening and wasted beyond all belief.
   She seemed a rack for avarice, gaunt and craving
   Oh many the souls she has brought to endless grief!   51
She brought such heaviness upon my spirit
   at sight of her savagery and desperation,
   I died from every hope of that high summit.   54
And like a miser—eager in acquisition
   but desperate in self-reproach when Fortune's wheel
   turns to the hour of his loss—all tears and attrition   57
I wavered back; and still the beast pursued,
   forcing herself against me bit by bit
   till I slid back into the sunless wood.   60
And as I fell to my soul's ruin, a presence
   gathered before me on the discolored air,
   the figure of one who seemed hoarse from long silence.   63
At sight of him in that friendless waste I cried:
   "Have pity on me, whatever thing you are,
   whether shade or living man." And it replied: 66
"Not man, though man I once was, and my blood
   was Lombard, both my parents Mantuan.
   I was born, though late, *sub Julio*, and bred   69
in Rome under Augustus in the noon
   of the false and lying gods. I was a poet
   and sang of old Anchises' noble son   72
who came to Rome after the burning of Troy.
   But you—why do *you* return to these distresses
   instead of climbing that shining Mount of Joy   75
which is the seat and first cause of man's bliss?"
   "And are you then that Virgil and that fountain
   of purest speech?" My voice grew tremulous: 78
"Glory and light of poets! now may that zeal
   and love's apprenticeship that I poured out
   on your heroic verses serve me well!   81
For you are my true master and first author,
   the sole maker from whom I drew the breath
   of that sweet style whose measures have brought me honor.   84
See there, immortal sage, the beast I flee.
   For my soul's salvation, I beg you, guard me from her,
   for she has struck a mortal tremor through me."   87
And he replied, seeing my soul in tears:
   "He must go by another way who would escape
   this wilderness, for that mad beast that fleers   90

before you there, suffers no man to pass.

　　She tracks down all, kills all, and knows no glut,
　　　but, feeding, she grows hungrier than she was.　　93

She mates with any beast, and will mate with more
　　　before the Greyhound comes to hunt her down.

He will not feed on lands nor loot, but honor　　96
and love and wisdom will make straight his way.

　　He will rise between Feltro and Feltro, and in him
　　　shall be the resurrection and new day　　99

of that sad Italy for which Nisus died,
　　and Turnus, and Euryalus, and the maid Camilla.

He shall hunt her through every nation of sick pride　　102
till she is driven back forever to Hell
　　whence Envy first released her on the world.

　　Therefore, for your own good, I think it well　　105
you follow me and I will be your guide
　　and lead you forth through an eternal place.

　　There you shall see the ancient spirits tried　　108
in endless pain, and hear their lamentation
　　as each bemoans the second death of souls.

　　Next you shall see upon a burning mountain　　111
souls in fire and yet content in fire,
　　knowing that whensoever it may be
　　they yet will mount into the blessed choir.　　114

To which, if it is still your wish to climb,
　　a worthier spirit shall be sent to guide you.

　　With her shall I leave you, for the King of Time,　　117
who reigns on high, forbids me to come there
　　since, living, I rebelled against his law.

　　He rules the waters and the land and air　　120
and there holds court, his city and his throne.
　　Oh blessed are they he chooses!" And I to him:

　　"Poet, by that God to you unknown,　　123
lead me this way. Beyond this present ill
　　and worse to dread, lead me to Peter's gate
　　and be my guide through the sad halls of Hell."　　126

And he then: "Follow." And he moved ahead
in silence, and I followed where he led.

---

1. **midway in our life's journey:** The Biblical life span is three-score years and ten. The action opens in Dante's thirty-fifth year, i.e., 1300 CE.

17. **that planet:** The sun. Ptolemaic astronomers considered it a planet. It is also symbolic of God as He who lights man's way.

31. **each footfall rose above the last:** The literal rendering would be: "So that the fixed foot was ever the lower." "Fixed" has often been translated "right" and an ingenious reasoning can support that reading, but a simpler explanation offers itself and seems more competent: Dante is saying that he climbed with such zeal and haste that every footfall carried him above the last despite the steepness of the climb. At a slow pace, on the other hand, the rear foot might be brought up only as

far as the forward foot. This device of selecting a minute but exactly centered detail to convey the whole of a larger action is one of the central characteristics of Dante's style.

The Three Beasts: These three beasts undoubtedly are taken from *Jeremiah* 5:6. Many additional and incidental interpretations have been advanced for them, but the central interpretation must remain as noted. They foreshadow the three divisions of Hell (incontinence, violence, and fraud) which Virgil explains at length in Canto XI, 16–111.

38–9. **Aries . . . that rode with him to light the new creation:** The medieval tradition had it that the sun was in Aries at the time of the Creation. The significance of the astronomical and religious conjunction is an important part of Dante's intended allegory. It is just before dawn of Good Friday 1300 CE when he awakens in the Dark Wood. Thus his new life begins under Aries, the sign of creation, at dawn (rebirth), and in the Easter season (resurrection). Moreover the moon is full and the sun is in the equinox, conditions that did not fall together on any Friday of 1300. Dante is obviously constructing poetically the perfect Easter as a symbol of his new awakening.

69. **sub Julio:** In the reign of Julius Caesar.

95. **The Greyhound . . . Feltro and Feltro:** Almost certainly refers to Can Grande della Scala (1290–1329), great Italian leader born in Verona, which lies between the towns of Feltre and Montefeltro.

100–101. **Nisus, Turnus, Euryalus, Camilla:** All were killed in the war between the Trojans and the Latians when, according to legend, Aeneas led the survivors of Troy into Italy. Nisus and Euryalus (*Aeneid* IX) were Trojan comrades-in-arms who died together. Camilla (*Aeneid* XI) was the daughter of the Latian king and one of the warrior women. She was killed in a horse charge against the Trojans after displaying great gallantry. Turnus (*Aeneid* XII) was killed by Aeneas in a duel.

110. **the second death:** Damnation. "This is the second death, even the lake of fire." (*Revelation* 20:14)

118. **forbids me to come there since, living, etc.:** Salvation is only through Christ in Dante's theology. Virgil lived and died before the establishment of Christ's teachings in Rome, and cannot therefore enter Heaven.

125. **Peter's gate:** The gate of Purgatory. (See *Purgatorio* IX, 76 ff.) The gate is guarded by an angel with a gleaming sword. The angel is Peter's vicar (Peter, the first pope, symbolized all popes: i.e., Christ's vicar on earth) and is entrusted with the two great keys.

Some commentators argue that this is the gate of Paradise, but Dante mentions no gate beyond this one in his ascent to Heaven. It should be remembered, too, that those who pass the gate of Purgatory have effectively entered Heaven.

The three great gates that figure in the entire journey are: the gate of Hell (Canto III, 1–11), the gate of Dis (Canto VIII, 79–113, and Canto IX, 86–87), and the gate of Purgatory, as above.

READING CRITICALLY

This canto serves as the prelude to the whole of the *Divine Comedy*. It introduces both Dante and his guide, Virgil. How does it also introduce Dante as the reader's guide on the same journey that he and Virgil are about to undertake?

READING 13.5

from Boccaccio, *Decameron*, Dioneo's Tale

Boccaccio completed the Decameron *in 1353. It is a transitional work, looking backward in many of its stories to the values and mores of medieval chivalry and mainstream Christianity even as it anticipates the individualism and ingenuity that the coming age, the Renaissance, will celebrate. A single example of its 100 tales, such as Dioneo's ribald classic below, does not do justice to the variety of subject matter and tone, the wide spectrum of human characters, and the scope of narrative structure that Boccaccio employs. But Dioneo's tale encapsulates the worldliness of the* Decameron, *a newfound frankness perhaps made possible only in the context of the Black Death, which has precipitated the book's storytellers to escape Florence and entertain one another in the countryside.*

Loving ladies, if I have well understood the intention of you all, we are here to afford entertainment to one another by story-telling; wherefore, provided only nought is done that is repugnant to this end, I deem it lawful for each (and so said our queen a little while ago) to tell whatever story seems to him most likely to be amusing. . . . I hope to escape your censure in narrating a brief story of a monk, who by his address delivered his body from imminent peril of most severe chastisement.

In the not very remote district of Lunigiana there flourished formerly a community of monks more numerous and holy than is [10] there to be found to-day, among whom was a young brother, whose vigour and lustihood neither the fasts nor the vigils availed to subdue. One afternoon, while the rest of the confraternity slept, our young monk took a stroll around the church, which lay in a very sequestered spot, and chanced to espy a young and very beautiful girl, a daughter, perhaps, of one of the husbandmen[1] of those parts, going through the fields and gathering herbs as she went. No sooner had he seen her than he was sharply assailed by carnal concupiscence,[2] insomuch that he made up to and accosted her; and (she hearkening) little by little they came [20] to an understanding, and unobserved by any entered his cell together. Now it so chanced that, while they fooled it within somewhat recklessly, he being overwrought with passion, the abbot awoke and passing slowly by the young monk's cell, heard the noise which they made within, and the better to distinguish the voices, came softly up to the door of the cell, and listening discovered that beyond all doubt there was a woman within. His first thought was to force the door open; but, changing his mind, he returned to his chamber and waited until the monk should come out. [30]

Delightsome beyond measure though the monk found his intercourse with the girl, yet was he not altogether without anxiety. He had heard, as he thought, the sound of footsteps in the dormitory, and having applied his eye to a convenient aperture[3] had had a good view of the abbot as he stood by the door listening. He was thus fully aware that the abbot might have detected the presence of a woman in the cell. Whereat he was exceedingly distressed, knowing that he had a severe punishment to expect; but he concealed his vexation from the girl while he busily cast about in his mind for some way of escape [40] from his embarrassment. He thus hit on a novel stratagem which was exactly suited to his purpose. With the air of one who had had enough of the girl's company he said to her: "I shall now leave you in order that I may arrange for your departure hence unobserved. Stay here quietly until I return." So out he went, locking the door of the cell, and withdrawing the key, which he carried straight to the abbot's chamber and handed to him, as was the custom when a monk was going out, saying with a composed air: "Sir, I was not able this morning to bring in all the faggots[4] which I had made ready, so with your leave I [50] will go to the wood and bring them in." The abbot, desiring to have better cognisance of the monk's offence, and not dreaming that the monk knew that he had been detected, was pleased with the turn matters had taken, and received the key gladly, at the same time giving the monk the desired leave. So the monk withdrew, and the abbot began to consider what course it were best for him to take, whether to assemble the brotherhood and open the door in their presence, that, being witnesses of the delinquency, they might have no cause to murmur against him when he proceeded to punish the delinquent, [60] or whether it were not better first to learn from the girl's own lips how it had come about. And reflecting that she might be the wife or daughter of some man who would take it ill that she should be shamed by being exposed to the gaze of all the monks, he determined first of all to find out who she was, and then to make up his mind. So he went softly to the cell, opened the door, and, having entered, closed it behind him. The girl, seeing that her visitor was none other than the abbot, quite lost her presence of mind, and quaking with shame began to weep. Master abbot surveyed her from head to foot, and seeing that [70] she was fresh and comely,[5] fell a prey, old though he was, to fleshly cravings no less poignant and sudden than those which the young monk had experienced, and began thus to commune with himself: "Alas! why take I not my pleasure when I may, seeing that I never need lack for occasions of trouble and vexation of spirit? Here is a fair wench, and no one in the world to know. If I can bring her to pleasure me, I know not why I should not do so. Who will know? No one will ever know; and sin that is hidden is half forgiven; this chance may never come again; so, methinks, it were the part of wisdom to take the boon [80] which God bestows." So musing, with an altogether different purpose from that with which he had come, he drew near the girl, and softly bade her to be comforted, and besought her not to weep; and so little by little he came at last to show her what he would be at. The girl, being made neither of iron nor of adamant,[6] was readily induced to gratify the abbot, who after bestowing upon her many an embrace and kiss, got upon the monk's bed, where, being sensible, perhaps, of the disparity between his reverend portliness and her tender youth, and fearing to injure her by his excessive weight, he refrained from lying [90] upon her, but laid her upon him, and in that manner disported himself with her for a long time. The monk, who had only pretended to go to the wood, and had concealed himself in the dormitory, no sooner saw the abbot enter his cell than he was overjoyed to think that his plan would succeed; and when he saw that he had locked the door, he was well assured thereof. So he stole out of his hiding-place, and set his eye to an aperture through which he saw and heard all that the abbot did and said. At length the abbot, having had enough of dalliance with the girl, locked her in the cell and returned to his chamber. [100] Catching sight of the monk soon afterwards, and supposing him to have returned from the wood, he determined to give him a sharp reprimand and have him imprisoned, that he might thus secure the prey for himself alone. He therefore caused him to be summoned, chid him very severely and with a stern countenance, and ordered him to be put in prison. The monk replied trippingly: "Sir, I have not been so long in the order of St. Benedict as to have every particular of the rule by heart; nor did you teach me before to-day in what posture it behooves the monk to have intercourse with women, but limited your instruction to [110] such matters as fasts and vigils. As, however, you have now given me my lesson, I promise you, if you also pardon my offence, that I will never repeat it, but will always follow the example which you have set me."

---

[1] **husbandmen:** farmers.
[2] **carnal concupiscence:** sexual desire.
[3] **aperture:** opening.

[4] **faggots:** firewood.
[5] **comely:** beautiful.
[6] **adamant:** diamond (i.e., a hard substance).

The abbot, who was a shrewd man, saw at once that the monk was not only more knowing than he, but had actually seen what he had done; nor, conscience-stricken himself, could he for shame mete out to the monk a measure which he himself merited. So pardon given, with an injunction to bury what had been seen in silence, they decently conveyed the young girl out of the monastery, whither, it is to be believed, they now and again caused her to return. 120

READING CRITICALLY

The circulation of stories such as this certainly contributed to the growing crisis of trust faced by the Church throughout the Middle Ages and into the Renaissance. How does it raise broader issues than just the question of clerical celibacy?

READING 13.8

from Boccaccio, *Decameron*, Filippa's Tale

Filippa's tale is the seventh story told on the sixth day of the Decameron. *The story is particularly notable for its heroine's independence from received notions of proper behavior, and her astute critique of the justice system in her native Prato.*

Once upon a time, in the town of Prato, there used to be a law in force—as pernicious, indeed, as it was cruel—to the effect that any woman caught by her husband in the act of adultery with a lover, was to be burned alive, like any vulgar harlot who sold herself for money.

While this statute prevailed, a beautiful lady called Filippa, a devout worshiper of Cupid, was surprised in her bedroom one night by her usband, Rinaldo de' Pugliesi, in the arms of Lazzarino de' Guazzagliotri, a high-born Adonis of a youth of that city, whome she loved as the apple of her eye. 10

Burning with rage at the discovery, Rinaldo could scarcely forbear running upon them, and slayin them on the spot. Were it not for the misgivings he had for his own safety, if he gave vent to his wrath, he would have follwed his impulse. However, he controlled his evil intenet, but could not abandon his desire to demand of the town's statute, what it was unlawful for him to bring about—in other words, the death of his wife.

As he had no lack of evidence to prove Filippa's guilt, he brought charges against her, early in the morning, at daybreak, and without further deliberation, had her summoned before the court. 20

Now Filippa was a high-spirited woman, as all women are who truly love, and though many of her friends and relatives advised her against going, she resolved to appear before the magistrate preferring a courageous death, by confessing the truth, to a shameful life of exile, by a cowardly flight that would have proved her unworthy o the lover in whose arms she had lain that night.

Accordingly, she presented herself before the provost, with a large following of men and women who urged her to deny the charges. She asked him firmly and without moveing a muscle what he desired of her. The provost, seeing her so beautiful, 30 courteous and so brave—as her words demonstrated—felt a certain pity stirring in his heart at the thought that she might confess a crime for which he would be obliged to sentence her to death to save his honor. But then, seeing he could not avoid cross-questioning her on the charge proffered against her, he said:

"Madame, here as you see, is Rinaldo, your husband, who is suing you on the grounds of finding you in the act of adultery with another man, and who therefore demands that I sentence you to death for it, as the law, which is in force, requires. I cannot pass sentence if you do not confess your guilt with your 40 own lips. Be careful of our answers, then, and tell me if what your husband charges you with is true."

Filippa, not at all daunted, replied in a very agreeable voice: "Your honor, it is true that Rinaldo is my husband, and that last night he found me in the arms of Lazzarino, where I had lain many another time, out of the great and true love I bear him. Far be it from me ever to deny it.

"As you are doubtless aware, laws should be equal for all, and should be made with the consent of those whom they may affect. Such is not the case with this particular statute, which is 50 stringent only with us poor women, who, after all, have it in our power to give pleasure to many more people than men ever could. Moreover, when this law was drawn up, not a single woman gave her consent or was so much as invited to give it. For all these reasons, it surely deserves to be considered reprehensible. If you insist upon enforcing it, not at the risk of my body, but of your immortal soul, you are at liberty to do so; but before you proceed to pass judgment, I beg you to grant me a small request. Simply ask my husband whether I have ever failed to yield myself to him entirely, whenever he chose, and as often as he pleased." 60

Without waiting for the magistrate to question him, Rinaldo immediately answered that there was no doubt Filippa had always granted him the joy of her body, at each and every request of his.

"That beging the case, your honor," she went on directly, "I'd like to ask him, since he has always had all he wanted of me and to his heart's content, what was I to do with all that was left over? Indeed, what am I to do with it? Throw it to the dogs? Isn't it far better to let it give enjoyment to some gentleman who loves me more than his life, than to let it go to waste or ruin?" 70

As it happened the whole town had turned out to attend the sensational trial that involved a lady of such beauty and fame, and when the people heard her roguish question, they burst into a roar of laughter, shouting to a man that she was right and had spoken well.

That day before court was adjourned, that harsh statute was modified at the magistrate's suggestion to hold only such women as made cuckolds of their husbands for love of money.

As for Rinaldo, he went away crest-fallen at his mad venture, while Filippa returned home victorious, feeling in her joy that 80 she had, in a sense, been delivered from the flames.

READING CRITICALLY

When Filippa declares that "laws should be equal for all, and should be made with the consent of those whom they may affect," she anticipates arguments that will be used to justify, for instance, the American Revolution in 1776. What is surprising about finding such arguments in a story written in 1351?

INDEX

PHOTO CREDITS

Chapter 8

PO Scala/Art Resource, NY; **8-01** © Hanan Isachar/JAI/Corbis All Rights Reserved; **8-2** Erich Lessing/Art Resource, NY; **8-04** Scala/Art Resource, NY; **8-06** Alinari/Art Resource, NY; **8-7** Araldo de Luca Archives \ Index Ricerca Iconografica; **8-8** © IKONA Photo/FOTO VASARI ROMA; **8-9** Alessandro Vasari/IKONA; **8-10** Canali Photobank, Milan Italy.; **8-11** Jacopo Grimaldi, "Interior of Old St. Peter's, Rome". 1619. Drawing, Ms.: Barbarini Lat. 2733 fols. 104v-105r. Vatican Library, Rome.; **8-13** Interior of the Basilica of San Paulo Fuori le Mura, Rome, from 'Le Antichita Romane de G.B. Piranesi (1756)', published in Paris, 1835 (engraving), Piranesi, Giovanni Battista (1720-78) (after)/Bibliotheque des Arts Decoratifs, Paris, France/Archives Charmet/The Bridgeman Art Library; **8-14** Scala/Art Resource, NY; **8-16** C. M. Dixon/The Ancient Art & Architecture Collection Ltd.; **8-17** Bildarchiv Preussischer Kulturbesitz/Art Resource, NY; **8-18** Image copyright © The Metropolitan Museum of Art/Art Resource, NY; **8-19** © Achim Bednorz, Koln; **8-20** Walter B. Denny; **8-22** Sonia Halliday Photographs; **8-23** Studio Kontos Photostock; **8-24** Scala/Art Resource, NY; **8-25** Scala/Art Resource, NY; **8-26** Canali Photobank; **8-28** Canali Photobank, Milan, Italy; **8-29** Canali Photobank, Milan, Italy; **8-30** Firenze, Biblioteca Medicea Laurenziana ms. Laur. Plut. 29.1, c. 1v. Su Concessione del Ministero per i Beni e le Attivita Culturali. E'vietata ogni ulteriore riproduzione con qualsiasi mezzo. Photo: Donato Pineider.; **8-31** Studio Kontos Photostock; **8-32** The State Historical Museum; **8-33** Studio Kontos Photostock; **8-34** Sonia Halliday Photographs; **8-35** © Guenter Rossenbach/Corbis; pages 252-253, Fabbrica di San Pietro/IKONA.

Chapter 9

9-1 John Vernor-Miles, Executor for A.F. Kersting; **9-2** Peter Sanders/The Image Works; **9-3** © Edinburgh University Library; **9-4** © The British Library Board: Add. 22406, f.1v; **9-5** © Blom Aerofilms Ltd; **9-7** MS ARABE 5847, fol. 125, Bibliotheque Nationale de France; **9-8** Christopher Rennie/Robert Harding World Imagery; **9-9** RAPHO/CICCIONE; **9-10** © The British Library Board: I.O. Islamic 1129, f.29; **9-11** © Peter Langer - Associated Media Group - All rights reserved.; **9-12** (top) Catalan Atlas: Detail of North Africa and Europe, by Abraham and Jafunda Cresques, 1375, /Bibliotheque Nationale, Paris, France/Index/The Bridgeman Art Library; **9-12** (bottom) HIP/Art Resource, NY; **9-13** © Achim Bednorz, Koln; **9-14** Erich Lessing/Art Resource, NY; **9-15** © Achim Bednorz, Koln; **9-16** ©Linda Whitwam/Dorling Kindersley; **9-17** Calouste Gulbenkian Foundation Museum, LA161-FI.066v; **9-18** Bodleian Library, University of Oxford; **9-19** Erich Lessing/Art Resource, NY; **9-20** Sacred Destinations Images; **9-21** Scala/Art Resource NY; page 290 (top), Huseyin Zulfikar Usta; page 290 (bottom), Cincinnati Art Museum, Fanny Bryce Lehmer Fund. Acc. #1977.65; page 291 (right), © 1982 The Metropolitan Museum of Art/Art Resource, NY.

Chapter 10

10-1 Eirik Irgens Johnsen/©Museum of Cultural History - University of Oslo, Norway; **10-2** © The Trustees of the British Museum/Art Resource, NY ;**10-3** The Art Archive/British Library; **10-4** (top) © The British Library Board: Add.42130, f.163v; **10-4** (middle) © The British Library Board: Add. 42130, f.166v; **10-4** (bottom) © The British Library Board: Add. 42130, f.193v; **10-5** Courtesy of Sheffield Galleries & Museums Trust; **10-06** © The British Library Board: Cotton Nero D., f.94v; **10-7** Chi Rho page, from the "Book of Kells". c. 800 AD. 13″ × 9 1/2″ (33 × 24.1 cm). Trinity College Lirary, Dublin. MS58 fol. 34r; **10-8** © The British Library Board: Cotton Vespasian A. I, f.30v; **10-9** Erich Lessing/Art Resource, NY; **10-10** University Library, Utrecht, the Netherlands; **10-11** © The British Library Board: Harley 603, f.57v; **10-13** Fotowerkstatte/Embassy of the Federal Republic of Germany; **10-14** Erich Lessing/Art Resource, NY; **10-15** Rheinisches Bildarchiv, Museen Der Stadt Koln; **10-16** ©Stephen Biesty/Dorling Kindersley; **10-17** Erich Lessing/Art Resource, NY; **10-18** Erich Lessing/Art Resource, NY;**10-19** Scala/Art Resource, NY;**10-21** Scala/Art Resource, NY; **10-23** © Vanni Archive/CORBIS; **10-24** © Vanni Archive/CORBIS; **10-25** © Stephen Conlin/Dorling Kindersley; **10-26** Capital depicting the Third Key of Plainsong with a lute player, c.1095 (stone), French School, (11th century)/Musee du Farinier, Ancienne Abbaye, Cluny, France /The Bridgeman Art Library; **10-27** Michael Jenner/Robert Harding World Imagery; **10-28** Dorling Kindersley Media Library, Joanna Cameron © Dorling Kindersley; **10-29** © The Trustees of The British Museum/Art Resource, NY; **10-30** The Pierpont Morgan Library/Art Resource, NY;

10-31 © Achim Bednorz, Koln; **10-32** © Angelo Hornak/CORBIS; page 336 (top), King Edward the Confessor (c.1003-66) giving his instructions to Earl Harold, detail from the Bayeux Tapestry (wool embroidery on linen), French School, (11th century)/Musee de la Tapisserie, Bayeux, France/With special authorisation of the city of Bayeux/The Bridgeman Art Library; page 336 (bottom) Harold Swears an Oath that he will Accept William as King of England, from The Bayeux Tapestry (embroidery on linen) (detail of 115615), French School, (11th century))/Musee de la Tapisserie, Bayeux, France/With special authorisation of the city of Bayeux/The Bridgeman Art Library; page 337 (top left), Here Duke William of Normandy (c.128-87) crosses the sea, detail from the Bayeux Tapestry, before 1082 (wool embroidery on linen) (detail of 183132), French School, (11th century))/Musee de la Tapisserie, Bayeux, France/With special authorisation of the city of Bayeux/Giraudon/The Bridgeman Art Library; page 337 (top right), Halley's Comet and Harold Receiving Bad News, detail from the Bayeux Tapestry (wool embroidery on linen), French School, (11th century))/Musee de la Tapisserie, Bayeux, France/With special authorisation of the city of Bayeux/The Bridgeman Art Library; page 337 (bottom), Erich Lessing/Art Resource, NY.

Chapter 11

11-1 © Ian Griffiths/Robert Harding World Imagery/Corbis; **11-2** © Wolfgang Kaehler/CORBIS; **11-4** Culture Relics Publishing House; **11-5** Cheng Sixiao, Ink Orchids, Yuan dynasty, 1306. Ink on poaper, 10 1/8 × 16 3/4 in. Municipal Museum of Fine Art, Osaka, Japan.Photo: Galileo Picture Services LLC, NY; **11-6** Rossi & Rossi; **11-7** © Keren Su/Corbis All Rights Reserved; **11-8** © Neil Grant/Alamy; **11-10** Andrew Gunners/Digital Vision/Getty Images; **11-11** Philip Baird/Anthroarcheart.org; **11-12** "Shiva Nataraja, Lord of the Dance". South India. Chola period, 11th Century. Bronze. 111.5 × 101.65 cm. © The Cleveland Museum of Art, Purchase from the J.H. Wade Fund 1930.331.; **11-13** © Sakamoto Photo Research Laboratory/CORBIS S All Rights Reserved; **11-14** Courtesy of Japanese Art/Laurence King Publishing Ltd.; **11-15** The Tokugawa Reimeikai Foundation; **11-16** Asanuma Photo Studios, Kyoto, Japan; **11-17** Detail of Night Attack on the Sanjo Palace. Kamakura period, late 13th century CE. Handscroll, ink and colors on paper. 16 1/4″ × 275 1/2″ (41.3 × 699.7 cm). Museum of Fine Arts, Boston. Fenollosa-Weld Collection (11.4000). Courtesy, Museum of Fine Arts, Boston. Reproduced with permission. ©2006 Museum of Fine Arts, Boston. All Rights Reserved.; **11-18** Dirk Bakker, Museum of Ife Antiquities, Nigeria; **11-19** © The Trustees of the British Museum/Art Resource, NY; **11-20** Laurence King Publishing Limited; **11-21** Image copyright © The Metropolitan Museum of Art/Art Resource, NY; **11-22** © Kazuyoshi Nomachi/HAGA/ The Image Works; **11-23** Werner Forman/Art Resource, NY; **11-24** Great Zimbabwe Site Museum, Zimbabwe; **11-25** Werner Forman/Art Resource, NY; **11-26** Scala/Art Resource, NY; **11-27** Elizabeth Barrows Rogers/Mexican Government Tourism Office; **11-28** © Francesca Yorke/Dorling Kindersley; **11-29** Mandatory adjacent credit: Museo de América, Madrid.; **11-30** The Museum of Modern Art/Art Resource, NY.; **11-31** The Art Archive/Gianni Dagli Orti; **11-32** Moche Lord with a Feline, from Moche Valley, Peru. Moche culture, c. 100 BCE-500 CE. Painted cramic. H: 7 1/2″ (19 cm). Buckingham Fund. 1955-2281. Photograph ©2006, The Art Institute of Chicago. All Rights Reserved.; **11-33** The Art Archive/Gianni Dagli Orti;**11-34** Dumbarton Oaks Research Library and Collections, Washington, D.C. Photograph by Justin Kerr.; **11-35** © Barry D. Kass@ImagesofAnthropology.com; **11-36** The Art Archive/ Gianni Dagli Orti; page 366 (top), Art Resource, N.Y.; page 366 (bottom), Art Resource, N.Y.; page 367, Art Resource, N.Y.

Chapter 12

12-1 Courtesy of Bernard Beaujard; **12-2** © Achim Bednorz, Koln; **12-4** © Achim Bednorz, Koln; **12-5** © Achim Bednorz, Koln; **12-6** Photo Josse; **12-7** Jean Bernard Photographe/Bordas Publication; **12-8** © Achim Bednorz, Koln; **12-9** © Achim Bednorz, Koln; **12-10** John Bryson/ Photo Researchers, Inc.; **12-12** Patric Muller/CMN Centre des Monuments Nationaux; **12-13** Angelo Hornak Photo Library; **12-14** © Achim Bednorz, Koln; **12-15** © Achim Bednorz, Koln; **12-16** Scala/Art Resource, NY; **12-17** Group of Students from Bologna (marble), Masegne, Jacobello & Pier Paolo dalle (fl.1383-1409)/Museo Civico, Bologna, Italy/Giraudon/The Bridgeman Art Library; **12-18** Harl 4425 f.12v Garden scene, the lover and dame Oyseuse (Idleness) outside the garden walls, from the 'Roman de la Rose', Bruges, c.1490-1500 (vellum), Netherlandish School/ British Library, London, UK/© British Library Board. All Rights Reserved/The Bridgeman Art Library;

12-19 Erich Lessing/Art Resource, NY; 12-20 Giraudon/Art Resource, NY; 12-21 © Achim Bednorz, Koln; 12-22 Réunion des Musées Nationaux/Art Resource, NY; 12-23 © Achim Bednorz, Koln; 12-24 Scala/Art Resource, NY; 12-25 View of the church Santa Croce and its surroundings (photo)/Florence, Tuscany, Italy/© Sylvie Allouche/The Bridgeman Art Library; 12-26 Scala/Art Resource, NY; 12-27 Alinari/Art Resource, NY; 12-28 Scala/Art Resource, NY; 12-29 "St. Francis of Assisi Preparing the Christmas Crib at Grecchio, 1296-97 (fresco) by Giotto di Bondone (c.1266-1337)San Francesco, Upper Church, Assisi, Italy/Giraudon/The Bridgeman Art Library International"; 12-30 Réunion des Musées Nationaux/Art Resource, NY; 12-31 © National Gallery, London/Art Resource, NY; page 408 (left), Sonia Halliday Photographs; pages 408-409, Vanni/Art Resource, NY; page 409, © Dorling Kindersley.

Chapter 13

13-1 © Atlantide Phototravel/Corbis; 13-2 © Hideo Kurihara/Alamy; 13-3 Effects of Good Government in the Countryside, 1388-40 (fresco), Lorenzetti, Ambrogio (1285-c.1348)/Palazzo Pubblico, Siena, Italy/Alinari/The Bridgeman Art Library; 13-4 © Alinari/Art Resource, NY"; 13-5 Canali Photobank, Milan, Italy; 13-6 Scala/Art Resource, NY; 13-7 Cimabue (Cenni di Pepi)/Index Ricerca Iconografica; 13-8 Galleria degli Uffizi, Florence.; 13-9 The Art Archive/Duomo Florence/Alfredo Dagli Orti; 13-10 G. W. Scott-Giles;13-11 G. W. Scott-Giles; 13-12 Image copyright © The Metropolitan Museum of Art/Art Resource, NY; 13-13 Erich Lessing/Art Resource, NY; 13-14 The Art Archive/Victoria and Albert Museum London/Eileen Tweedy; 13-15 Snark/Art Resource, NY; 13-16 Courtesy of the Library of Congress; page 438 (top), Alinari/Art Resource, NY; page 438 (bottom), Canali Photobank, Milan, Italy; page 439, Scala/Art Resource, NY.

TEXT CREDITS

Chapter 8

Reading 8.2, page 248: From the Bible, Romans 5:1–11 from the NEW REVISED STANDARD VERSION OF THE BIBLE, copyright © 1989 by the National Council of the Churches of Christ in the U.S.A. Used by permission. All rights reserved. **Reading 8.3,** page 250: From the Bible, Matthew:6:25–33 from the NEW REVISED STANDARD VERSION OF THE BIBLE, copyright © 1989 by the National Council of the Churches of Christ in the U.S.A. Used by permission. All rights reserved. **Reading 8.5,** page 281: From Augustine: Confessions and Enchiridion, tr. and ed. by Albert C. Outler, copyright © 1955 SCM Press. Reproduced by permission of Westminster John Knox and Hymns Ancient & Modern Ltd. rights@hymnsam.co.uk. **Reading 8.5a,** page 262: From Augustine: Confessions and Enchiridion, tr. and ed. by Albert C. Outler, copyright © 1955 SCM Press. Reproduced by permission of Westminster John Knox and Hymns Ancient & Modern Ltd. rights@hymnsam.co.uk. **Reading 8.6,** page 282: From Augustine's City of God Reprinted by permission of the publishers and the Trustees of the Loeb Classical Library from AUGUSTINE, Vol. IV, Loeb Classical Library vol. 414, trans. by Philip Levine, Cambridge, Mass: Harvard University Press. Copyright © 1966 by the President and Fellows of Harvard College. Loeb Classical Library® is a registered trademark of the President and Fellows of Harvard College. **Reading 8.6a,** page 263: From Augustine The city of God. Reprinted by permission of the publishers and the Trustees of the Loeb Classical Library from AUGUSTINE, Vol. IV, Loeb Classical Library vol. 414, trans. by Philip Levine, Cambridge, Mass: Harvard University Press. Copyright © 1966 by the President and Fellows of Harvard College. Loeb Classical Library® is a registered trademark of the President and Fellows of Harvard College.

Chapter 9

Reading 9.1, page 311: From Surah 47 from HOLY QUR'AN trans. by M.H. Shakir (1982). Reprinted by permission of Tahrike Tarsile Qur'an, Inc. **Reading 9.1a,** page 288: From Surah 76 from HOLY QUR'AN trans. by M.H. Shakir (1982). Reprinted by permission of Tahrike Tarsile Qur'an, Inc. **Reading 9.1b,** page 289: From Surah 5 from HOLY QUR'AN trans. by M.H. Shakir (1982). Reprinted by permission of Tahrike Tarsile Qur'an, Inc. **Reading 9.4,** page 302: "My Heart is in the East" by Judah Halevi, trans. by Willis Barnstone from LITERATURES OF THE MIDDLE EAST (Pearson Education 2003) is reprinted by permission of Willis Barnstone. **Reading 9.5,** pages 305-306: From HAFT PAYKAR: A MEDIEVAL PERSIAN ROMANCE, trans. by Julie Scott Meisami (1995) 28 lines from "The Tale of the Black Princess." by permission of Oxford University Press. **Reading 9.6,** pages 311-313: "The Tale of the Fisherman and the Genie" adapted text reprinted by permission of Emma Varesio. **Reading 9.8,** page 313: "Love's Body" and "Caring for My Lover" by Rumi, trans. by Tony Barnstone, Willis Barnstone, and Reza Baraheni from LITERATURES OF THE MIDDLE EAST (Pearson 2003). Reprinted by permission of Tony Barnstone and Willis Barnstone. "The Clear Bead at the Center" by Rumi from OPEN SECRET: VERSIONS OF RUMI, trans. by John Moyne and Coleman Barks (1984) is reprinted by permission of Coleman Barks.

Chapter 10

Reading 10.1 a-d, pages 319-320:From BEOWULF, trans. by Seamus Heaney. Copyright © 2000 by Seamus Heaney. Used by permission of W.W. Norton & Company, Inc. and Faber and Faber Ltd. **Reading 10.2,** page 321: "Caedmon's Hymn" trans. by John C. Pope. Copyright © 1993, 1986, 1979, 1974, 1968, 1962 by W.W. Norton & Company, Inc. from THE NORTON ANTHOLOGY OF ENGLISH LITERATURE, 6th ed., Vol. 1, ed. by M.H. Abrams. Used by permission of W.W. Norton & Company, Inc. **Reading 10.3,** page 326: From SONG OF ROLAND, trans. by Patricia Terry, 2nd ed., © 1992. Reprinted by permission of Pearson Education, Inc., Upper Saddle, River, NJ. **Reading 10.4,** pages 353-354: Excerpts from HILDEGARD OF BINGEN: SCIVIAS, trans. by Columba Hart and Jane Bishop. Copyright © 1990 by the Abbey of Regina Laudis: Benedictine Congregation Regina Laudis of the Strict Observance, Inc. Paulist Press, Inc., New York/Mahwah, NJ. Reprinted by permission of Paulist Press, Inc. www.paulistpress.com. **Reading 10.7,** page 347: Bernard de Ventadour, from "The Skylark," trans. by W.D. Snodgrass from LARK IN THE MORNING: THE VERSES OF THE TROUBADOURS, ed. by Robert Kehew. Translations by Ezra Pound, W.D. Snodgrass, & Robert Kehew. Chicago: University of Chicago Press, 2005. Reprinted by permission of Kathleen Snodgrass. **Reading 10.8,** page 347: Comtessa de Dia's "Cruel are the Pains I've Suffered", tr. by Robert Kehew, from LARK IN THE MORNING: THE VERSES OF THE TROUBADORS, ed. by Robert Kehew, trans. by Ezra Pound, W.D. Snodgrass, and Robert Kehew. Copyright © 2005 by The University of Chicago. Reprinted by permission of the publisher. **Reading 10.9,** pages 355-357: "Bisclavret (The Werewolf)" from The Lais of Marie de France, trans. by Robert Hanning and Joan Ferrante is published by Baker Academic, a division of Baker Publishing Group, 1990. Used by permission.

Chapter 11

Reading 11.1, page 397: "Drinking Alone by Moonlight" by Li Bai, trans. by Willis Barnstone, Tony Barnstone, and Chou Ping and "Dreaming of Li Bai" by Du Fu, trans. by Tony Barnstone and Chou Ping from LITERATURES OF ASIA, ed. by Tony Barnstone. Reprinted by permission of Willis Barnstone and Tony Barnstone. **Reading 11.1a,** pages 362-363: "Summer Day in the Mountains" by Li Bai, trans. by Willis Barnstone, Tony Barnstone, and Chou Ping and "Broken Lines" by Du Fu, trans. by Tony Barnstone and Chou Ping from LITERATURES OF ASIA, ed. by Tony Barnstone (Pearson 2003). Reprinted by permission of Willis Barnstone and Tony Barnstone. **Reading 11.3,** page 375: From DIARIES OF COURT LADIES OF OLD JAPAN, trans. by Annie Shepley Omori and Koch Doi (Houghton Mifflin 1920). **Reading 11.4,** page 375: "This Perfectly Still" by Ki no Tomonori from ANTHOLOGY OF JAPANESE LITERATURE, comp. and ed. by Donald Keene, copyright © 1955 by Grove Press, Inc. Used by permission of Grove/Atlantic, Inc. **Reading 11.5,** page 398: From "Hateful Things" from THE PILLOW BOOK OF SEI SHONAGON, tr. Ivan Morris. Copyright © 1991 by Columbia Univ. Press. Reprinted by permission of Columbia University Press and Oxford University Press (UK). Electronic rights for THE PILLOW BOOK OF SEI SHONAGON, tr. and ed. by Ivan Morris by permission of Georges Borchardt, Inc., on behalf of the Estate of Ivan Morris. **Reading 11.5a,** page 375: "Elegant Things" from THE PILLOW BOOK OF SEI SHONAGON, tr. Ivan Morris. Copyright © 1991 by Columbia Univ. Press. Reprinted by permission of Columbia University Press and Oxford University Press (UK). Electronic rights for THE PILLOW BOOK OF SEI SHONAGON, tr. and ed. by Ivan Morris by permission of Georges Borchardt, Inc., on behalf of the Estate of Ivan Morris. **Reading 11.7,** page 391: Excerpt from POPUL VUH, trans. by Ralph Nelson. Copyright © 1974, 1976 by Ralph Nelson. Reprinted by permission of Houghton Mifflin Harcourt Publishing Company. All rights reserved.

Chapter 13